MASTERS OF THE WORD

Also by William J. Bernstein

The Intelligent Asset Allocator
The Four Pillars of Investing
The Birth of Plenty
A Splendid Exchange
The Investor's Manifesto

MASTERS OF THE WORD

*How Media Shaped History
from the Alphabet to the Internet*

WILLIAM J. BERNSTEIN

ATLANTIC BOOKS
London

First published in the United States in 2013 by Grove Press an imprint of Grove/Atlantic, Inc.

First published in Great Britain in 2013 by Atlantic Books, an imprint of Atlantic Books Ltd.

10 9 8 7 6 5 4 3 2 1

A CIP catalogue record for this book is available from the British Library.

Hardback ISBN: 9781782390008
Ebook ISBN: 9781782390022
Export/Airside Trade Paperback ISBN: 9781782390015
Trade Paperback ISBN: 9781782390039

Printed in Great Britain by TJ International Ltd, Padstow, Cornwall.

Atlantic Books
An Imprint of Atlantic Books Ltd
Ormond House
26–27 Boswell Street
London
WC1N 3JZ
www.atlantic-books.co.uk

To Jane

CONTENTS

INTRODUCTION

The morning, like all mornings, began poorly for Winston Smith. Awakened by the screeching alarm of the omnipresent telescreen, Winston, the hero of George Orwell's *Nineteen Eighty-Four,* hurled his cold, naked, arthritic body out of bed for the mandatory calisthenics. "Thirty to forty group! Thirty to forty group! Take your places, please. Thirties to forties!" screamed the personal trainer from hell.

Winston—or, more accurately, 6079 Smith W—struggled gamely against his infirmities, but his efforts did not satisfy his tormentor, whose exhortations to bend lower yielded only waves of searing spinal pain.[1]

From the moment of the book's appearance in 1948, both casual readers and critics argued about its meaning. Was it a specific indictment of socialism, as conservative readers supposed? Or was it a more generalized warning about the totalitarian tendencies inherent not only in communism and fascism, but also in liberal democracies? (Orwell eventually made clear that he meant the latter.)[2]

The debate over *Nineteen Eighty-Four*'s political meaning obscured a much larger point: by the middle of the twentieth century, advances in telecommunications had decisively tipped the balance of power between the ruler and the ruled toward the former, and the book's miserable characters could not hope to escape the malevolent new electronic media technologies. Almost a decade before the book's publication, Orwell wrote:

> The Inquisition failed, but then the Inquisition had not the resources of the modern state. The radio, press censorship, standardized education, and the secret police have altered everything. Mass-suggestion is a science of the last twenty years, and we do not yet know how successful it will be.[3]

Orwell certainly had in mind Hitler's fascist state and the security apparatus of Stalin, the likely model for Big Brother. Yet no state organ, before or since, has ever exceeded the relentless efficiency of the *Ministerium für Staatssicherheit* of the German Democratic Republic—the feared Stasi. At its height, its ranks comprised nearly 100,000 East Germans, one of every 160 in the population.

Walter Ulbricht and Erich Honecker commanded a larger security apparatus in their small corner of the Teutonic world than Adolf Hitler had in all of greater Germany. The Stasi employed more resources, and about as many personnel, as East Germany did for health care. East Germans even coined a word that described a life permeated by listening devices and informers: *flächendeckend*—nothing left uncovered. Three thousand operatives tapped telecommunications, a remarkable number considering the scarcity of private phone service; the wait for a new line could be twenty years, and quicker installation generally meant that the applicant had been targeted for surveillance. The Stasi could place a hidden camera in a room in any large hotel on two hours' notice.

East German surveillance was not all high-tech. In a police state, the avoidance of microphones, wiretaps, and cameras becomes second nature, and the Stasi increasingly relied on older methods, particularly informers. Overall, about 2 percent of East Germans regularly snitched on their friends, neighbors, and colleagues. In many professions and locales, the Stasi penetrated even more deeply. For example, it responded to high defection rates among physicians with intense recruitment of informers; one doctor in twenty spied on his or her colleagues.

After the regime fell, citizens rummaging through Stasi facilities came across rooms filled with numbered, sealed glass jars containing bits of cloth. In time, their purpose was discovered: each specimen was impregnated with sweat, obtained from men's armpits and between the thighs of women, so dogs could track them, if necessary, at some future date.[4]

Counting the newborn People's Republic of China, at the time of *Nineteen Eighty-Four*'s publication, nearly a third of the planet's population lived in Orwellian states.[5] But something happened on the road from *Nineteen Eighty-Four* to 1984, or at least 1989, the year East Germans threw out Big Brother. After the Berlin Wall fell, the portion of the world's population suffering under the heel of technologically empowered totalitarian regimes plummeted. By the turn of the twenty-first century, the number of such smothering, omniscient regimes could be counted on the fingers of one hand: Myanmar (Burma), North Korea, and perhaps Cuba and Vietnam. Data from Freedom House, an organization that systematically tracks human rights, confirm that political freedom is breaking out all around the world: between 1975 and 2010, it estimates that the portion of "free" and "partially free" nations has increased from 54 percent to 78 percent.[6]

Longer-run data confirm this trend. Many researchers have compiled measures of global democracy over the past two centuries, but their data tell a curious story: increasing democratic development over the course of the nineteenth century suffered a "setback," characterized by a stagnation in the percent of nations considered democratic, which lasted from about 1920 to 1980, followed by a rapid upswing in the past few decades.[7]

Even more dramatically, between 1920 and 1980—the decades of the primacy of radio and television—the world saw a sharp upward spike in the number of nations considered despotic. (Figures I-1 and I-2 are not symmetrical, because they do not include a third category of nations: those with indeterminate governmental systems.) Note how the early- and mid-twentieth century increase in the percent of despotic states coincides with Orwell's literary career; the downswing after about 1980 would certainly have surprised the author.

Obviously, correlation is not causation, but this turn of events would certainly have astounded Orwell, since the technology available to today's totalitarian state would have overwhelmed even his fertile imagination: cameras capable of reading license plates from space, Internet-based "data mining" technology with an analytic capacity of millions of messages per minute, and microphones able to record the sonarman's "gnat's fart at fifty thousand yards." Given, then, the ever-advancing nature of surveillance technology, how did the state lose the battle for control of the individual?

Simply put, in a free market economy, communications and surveillance technologies rapidly become cheaper and more accessible to and—more important—controlled by the general population. Any device that increases the speed and volume of communication enhances the ability of its user to influence events; and, after all, such influence is the very essence of political power. With the passage of time, the same communications technologies that empowered the state in due course empowered the individual even more; the same technologies that allowed governments

Percent of Nations Considered Democracies

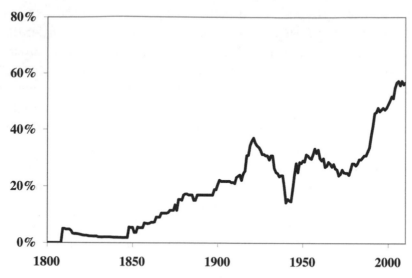

Figure I-1. Percent of Nations Considered Democracies

Percent of Nations Considered Despotic

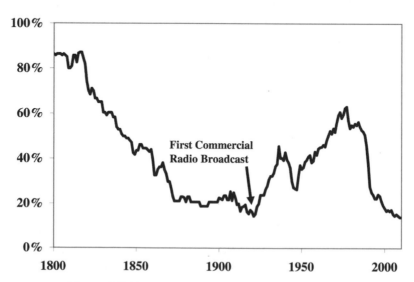

Figure I-2. Percent of Nations Considered Despotic

to spy on citizens allowed citizens to evade surveillance, and indeed to monitor governments themselves.[8]

After the development of the telegraph by Morse, Cooke, and Wheatstone in the 1830s and 1840s, the first commercial services were so expensive as to prohibit their deployment in everyday life, and their use was largely restricted to the transmission of essential financial, government, and military data. Later, radio and television stations were, similarly, so costly that they and their enormous propaganda potential were either directly run, or at least closely regulated, by the state. Even the lowly printing press, then entering its fifth century, still lay beyond the control of most private citizens.

When Orwell wrote *Nineteen Eighty-Four* in the mid-twentieth century, he could not have imagined that mere individuals would ever command such complex and expensive technologies. Orwell died in 1950, so he never lived to see the spread of modern communications devices into everyday personal use—the photocopying and fax machines, the cassette tape, the personal computer, the Internet, and the camera-equipped cell phones that helped save the world from the end he so feared.

The spread of these new technologies occurred with stunning speed. By 1960, only armies, governments, and very large corporations operated computers; by 1970, even small organizations had acquired them. By 1980, hobbyists happily assembled kits; by 1990, inexpensive personal computers had entered the home; by 2000, most citizens of the developed world had access to the Internet; and by 2004, residential broadband penetration in the United States, by no means in the vanguard of high-speed access, exceeded 50 percent. In the second half of the twentieth century, the easy availability of such communication technologies helped dismantle the totalitarian regimes that had originally used them to oppress citizens.

This cycle, in which cutting-edge communications technologies are first acquired by the state and employed to oppress the population, and then are embraced and controlled by the general population, thus enabling the people to take back power, is nothing new.

Further back in history, the growing availability of more basic technologies drastically altered the political, religious, and even cultural balance of power. In eighteenth- and nineteenth-century England, the so-called "corn laws" oppressed the urban poor by placing onerous tariffs on imported grain. (For centuries the word "corn" simply referred to grain in general, particularly wheat.) Simple economics mandates that tariffs on imported goods benefit the domestic producers by shielding their goods from competition. In this way, the corn laws increased the price of imported grain to consumers and so, too, raised the price of domestic grain, with which it competed. Consequently, the corn laws greatly profited the landowning aristocracy and simultaneously savaged the pocketbooks of the urban and rural poor, and occasionally precipitated outright mass starvation.

By the early nineteenth century, a titanic battle raged between the ruling aristocracy, who favored the laws, and two groups that supported repeal: urban slum dwellers and the factory owners who employed them. The ground for repeal had been laid by the Reform Act of 1832, which expanded the voting franchise; by the spread of the railroad; and by the establishment of the penny post, which greatly lowered the cost of sending letters. In the end, poor wheat harvests and the Irish potato famine in 1845–1846 provided the final impetus for repeal.

What did the railroad and the passage of the penny post have to do with repealing the corn law? Everything. Cheap rail travel enabled the leaders of the Anti–Corn Law League to crisscross the country to give speeches and organize their supporters, and cheap postage allowed the League to send out millions of pamphlets, newspapers, and magazines. When the penny post cleared the House of Lords, Richard Cobden, the charismatic leader of the League, shouted, "There go the Corn Laws!"[9]

If we go back another four hundred years, to around AD 1500, we find that industrially produced paper and the printing press amplified the burgeoning literacy revolution, and with it, the power of ordinary people to spread their opinions and influence. By the time Martin Luther arrived at the University of Wittenberg, its library shelves already groaned with the fruit of the Gutenberg revolution. It was not Luther the theologian who effected the Reformation, but rather Luther the publisher.

Throughout history, novel communications technologies have fascinated the public. Well before Luther's time, lay readers had became so entranced with vernacular Bibles, lurid accounts of papal corruption, and the new heresies that the Roman Catholic Church found it difficult to sell its own texts. Moreover, the new presses became, as coffeehouses would become two centuries later, meeting places where the most philosophically and technologically advanced practitioners of the age exchanged ideas and fomented change.

The relationship between the accessibility of communications technology and individual liberty, in fact, extends all the way back to the dawn of human history. Five thousand years ago in Sumer and Egypt, literate elites exploited the new—and highly complex, and thus inaccessible—cuneiform and hieroglyphic scripts to exert power over increasingly large populations and geographic areas. It is no coincidence that the rise of the world's first large-scale empires in Mesopotamia and Egypt followed fast on the heels of dramatic improvements in cuneiform and hieroglyphic writing, respectively. Although very different in outward form, Mesopotamian cuneiform and Egyptian hieroglyphic had quite similar inner structures: in each written language, individual symbols stood for syllables and entire words. In both Mesopotamia and Egypt, writing consisted of several hundred to a thousand such symbols, and the mastery of literacy could take decades; the scholar and scribe did not so much read a text as decipher it.

Not only was reading conceptually difficult in remote antiquity; so, too, was the mechanical act of writing. Merely obtaining writing materials could constitute an insurmountable hurdle; a single sheet of papyrus, the medium of everyday correspondence in Egypt, cost the equivalent of at least several hours of a skilled craftsman's time. Outside the Nile Valley, even less appealing materials were available: stone and animal skins. Until papermaking technology spread from China to the Muslim world and Europe in the late first millennium after Christ, the production of a single folio might consume an entire herd of sheep. Only in Mesopotamia, with its abundant moist clay—cheap, durable, and relatively easy to write on—was this problem less acute.

Small wonder, then, that before about 1000 BC, rulers deployed these complex and powerful writing systems to gradually increase their power over individuals and to assemble ever-larger nation-states. The scribe became the ancient equivalent of a high-tech entrepreneur, whose command of the era's cutting-edge technology—literacy—gave him an unbeatable edge on the road to wealth and power. Said one Egyptian father to his son:

> Put writing in your heart that you may protect yourself from hard labor of any kind. . . . I have seen the metal-worker at his task at the mouth of the furnace with fingers like a crocodile's. He stank worse than fish spawn. . . . The weaver in a workshop is worse off than a woman; he squats with his knees to his belly and he does not taste fresh air.[10]

In any age, illiteracy disempowers, and the formidable physical and cognitive barriers to reading and writing in Mesopotamia and Egypt served to exclude almost everyone except the aristocrats and their scribes from meaningful political influence. In societies where only a tiny minority can read and write, the illiterate are in awe of literacy and of the literate, and the ruling classes exploit this awe to the hilt. That was especially true in the ancient world, where religion provided ruling elites with their most potent source of political power. In Egypt the god Thoth, "The Lord of the Divine World," was, in the words of philologist Harold Innis,

> the unknown and mysterious, the lord of scribes and of all knowledge, since the setting down of words in script suggested the possession of mysterious and potent knowledge in the scribe who "brought into being what was not."[11]

In preliterate societies, that magic is yet more powerful, evoking a special wonder, even among native elites. Anthropologists have long observed the divine properties assigned by preliterate cultures to written material. Historians and paleographers (specialists in ancient documents and scripts) even have a term—the adjective *numinous*—that is used as shorthand to describe the nearly magical power exuded by the potency of the word in ancient societies.

The British social anthropologist Jack Goody, for example, noted that Africans used books as magic totems. A book "is a powerful object, and too close an acquaintance with it can drive a man to madness."[12] The experience of Cyprian Equiano, a Nigerian slave brought to England in the eighteenth century, illustrates this awe: taken to church, he waited for others to leave before placing the Bible to his ear to hear its words.[13] America's most famous escaped slave, Frederick Douglass, well understood both the magical and the repressive power of literacy: "Once you learn to read, you will be forever free."[14]

On the other hand, the French ethnographer Claude Lévi-Strauss enunciated perhaps the best-known, and certainly the darkest, assessment of the power, magic, and omnipotence of writing. He began by noting that none of mankind's greatest early technological achievements—the domestication of animals, the development of settled agriculture, the invention

of the wheel, and the mastery of fire—required this satanic art. He then
went on to equate literacy with subjugation:

> The only phenomenon with which writing has always been concomi-
> tant is the creation of cities and empires, that is, the integration of
> large numbers of individuals into a political system and their grading
> into castes or classes. . . . It seems to have favored the exploitation
> of human beings rather than their enlightenment. . . . The primary
> function of written communication is to facilitate slavery. The use
> of writing for disinterested purposes, and as a source of intellectual
> and aesthetic pleasure, is a secondary result.[15]

In a world where only the thin upper crust can master the written word,
this rings more or less true. Sometime around 1500 BC, however, the first
cracks in this ancient monopoly of the scribal class appeared. During that
period, somewhere in the southern Levant, possibly at a turquoise mine near
Serabit el-Khadim in the western Sinai Peninsula, the worlds of literacy and
politics turned on their respective axes. At this dusty location, surely one
of history's least likely fulcrums, a small number of Egyptian overseers
directed a workforce of foreigners, most likely from Palestine or Syria.
These Semitic laborers felt the magic and power of Egyptian writing, and
they extracted from it the key to mass literacy: about two dozen individual
phonemes—elemental sounds, each represented by its own symbol, that is,
a letter—that could be combined to yield any known word. That an entire
language could be encoded with so few symbols, and thus easily used by
the general population, had probably not escaped the Egyptians, but their
empire's scribal class was unlikely to simplify its meal ticket out of existence;
outsiders were far more inclined to start the literacy revolution.

Biblical scholar Martin Sprengling speculated about how the complex Egyptian system might have become transmuted to an alphabetic
one: The Egyptians frequently honored the Semitic foremen at their
mines by naming individual shafts after the men who oversaw them.
These foremen would probably have been in contact with the low-level
Egyptian scribes, who generally wrote in hieratic script, a simplified
cursive form of hieroglyphics. (Egyptians used hieratic for everyday
writing, and reserved the more complex and pictographic-appearing
hieroglyphic forms for stone monuments.) The foremen, in order to

memorialize themselves, would naturally have implored the scribes to teach them hieratic, and the scribes would have responded by showing the foremen—brush, ink, and papyrus in hand—the simplest characters, which the foremen would later inscribe into stone.[16] This so-called proto-Semitic system was a vast improvement over the Egyptian and Sumerian syllabic scripts; in due course it evolved into the Phoenician, Hebrew, and Arabic alphabets. To this day, modern Western alphabets consist of essentially the same few dozen phonemes.

The Hebrew alphabet may have produced the first faint stirrings of mass literacy in the kingdom of Judea just before Babylonian exile in the sixth century BC, and the later prophets probably used the new medium to reach the masses. Historian William H. McNeill suggests:

> Prophesies and protests, criticisms of prevailing customs, and radical assertion of new standards of righteousness could create only tempo-rary and local disturbances so long as their impact was confined to the range of a man's voice and the memory of the immediate hear-ers. . . . Had writing remained the monopoly of a privileged clique, the angry words of prophets who so freely attacked established practices would never have been written down. Hence the democratization of learning implicit in simplified scripts must be counted as one of the major turning points in the history of civilization.[17]

The Phoenicians, indefatigable traders, spread their alphabet far and wide throughout the Mediterranean. Sometime in the eighth century BC, they, and their writing, arrived in Greece. Several of the Phoenician consonants en-coded sounds not used in Greek, and at some point an unknown genius took a momentous step: he or she converted these unneeded letters into vowels. The new Greek vowels eliminated nearly all the ambiguity of a consonant-only script and thus enabled mastery of the alphabet by children as young as five or six.[18] By the fourth century BC, literacy in Athens probably ap-proached a third to half of male citizens; for the first time in history, writ-ten language, civilization's primary method of control, was shared widely among the population. The banishment of an Athenian required that six thousand citizens write the victim's name on pottery fragments, ostraca (in Greek, *ostraka*, from which the word "ostracism" derives). That democracy developed in Greece, rather than Egypt or Mesopotamia, was no accident.

*   *   *

For the past fifteen years, I have been writing about finance and history. I laced my first two books, which focused on finance, with a liberal amount of market and economic history. Just as the most successful military officers, lawyers, and political practitioners possess a keen sense of history, so, too, can the best investors detect not merely the echoes of the past but entire symphonies of it in current market events. This ability yields both intellectual and material benefits.

No work of history has influenced me more than Daniel Yergin's 1991 book, *The Prize.* Ostensibly the story of the petroleum industry, it was nothing less than a *tour d'horizon* of the modern world as seen through the murky and turbulent prism of oil. When I wrote *The Birth of Plenty,* the story of the nineteenth-century acceleration of world economic growth, I used Yergin's magisterial volume as my model. My book laid the epic of modern economic growth over the fabric of modern history, and this in turn led to my next effort, *A Splendid Exchange,* which followed global trade from its beginnings in prehistory to the 1999 World Trade Organization riots in Seattle.

While researching *A Splendid Exchange,* I was riveted by the repeal of the corn laws, a major event in the ideological history of world trade. Since AD 1066, a tiny minority of aristocrats had dominated England's rich agricultural endowment; drawing on this wealth, and the influence it produced, they dominated its politics as well, using the corn laws to impose high grain prices on both peasants and the urban poor. As recounted earlier in this introduction, the deft use of the printing press, the penny post, and inexpensive rail travel by Richard Cobden and his associates broke that stranglehold. The inescapable conclusion: in a world where only the powerful and wealthy can communicate over long distances, everyone else is disenfranchised.

Once we are aware of the connection between political power and access to communication technology, it becomes obvious throughout all of human history. These technologies are not in and of themselves oppressive or liberating. Rather, it is relative access to them that determines political reality. Hitler and Stalin, who inspired *Nineteen Eighty-Four,* had complete control of the era's leading-edge communications and surveillance technologies. That their hapless populations did not have access to these devices resulted as much from their expense and the expertise required to operate them as from their illegality.

When ordinary people eventually gain access to and control of leading-edge communication technologies, they can more effectively oppose the power of the state. In the democratic Greek city-states, the alphabet proved mightier than the sword; in the medieval era, the printing press was mightier than the Roman Catholic Church; and in the modern world, the cell phone camera is mightier than the surveillance camera.

Viewed through the widest possible lens, four great communications technologies have engulfed the human race: first, language itself; second, writing; third, the mechanization of writing, that is, printing with movable type; and fourth, the electronic encoding of information. In the mid-twentieth century, George Orwell, and numerous other observers, viewed the electronic technologies of the era with dread; as the twenty-first dawns, our view of these technologies has executed a complete *volte face*. Neither view is correct. It is not enough to ask, "What do these machines do?" We must also ask, "How many control them?"

The persistence of a form of black slavery long after the end of the Civil War highlights how poor access to even the simplest of communications technologies can yield gross injustice. For generations after the Emancipation Proclamation and Reconstruction, hundreds of thousands of black men found themselves victims of a new form of slavery: arbitrary arrest for minor crimes—vagrancy and loitering would do—followed by sentencing to privately owned factories, farms, and mines.[19]

These facilities often featured working conditions and mortality rates worse than those on the slave plantations of the antebellum South. In 1906 the U.S. Department of Labor sent a team of researchers under the direction of the pioneering black sociologist W. E. B. Du Bois to investigate the condition of African Americans in Lowndes County, Alabama, which had become a hotbed of the new slavery.

Du Bois submitted his report to the government later that year, and waited—and waited—for its publication. A year later, the government finally informed Du Bois that it had found his report too hot to handle, and destroyed the single handwritten copy he had submitted. For want of a mid-twentieth-century commonplace—a copying machine—his report was lost forever, and this clandestine form of black slavery continued well into the twentieth century.[20]

I have not attempted to write an encyclopedic history of communications technology and politics. It is simply not possible to conduct a rigorously chronological survey of the topic within a single volume of moderate size, nor will it be possible to cover in great detail all of the significant technologies. Radio more clearly demonstrates the nature of the communications/power nexus than does television, particularly in totalitarian states, and so the former will receive much more attention than the latter; for similar reasons, more time will be spent on copying machines, and, in particular, carbon paper, than on the telephone and fax machine. Rather, the book's structure will be thematic; I have selected the most compelling illustrative anecdotes available to me and woven them into a historical narrative. This thread winds through Mesopotamia, Serabit el-Khadim, ancient Athens, Strasbourg, and ultimately the media complexes and research labs of the modern West.

Mere edification and amusement, while worthy enough goals in and of themselves, should not satisfy the nonfiction reader. If an author has truly succeeded, he or she also provides a conceptual framework within which to grasp the present and glimpse the future. In the process of writing this book, I have become convinced that precisely how technologies disseminate constitutes their most important aspect.

At this point in history it seems plausible that the affordability and widespread availability of both older analog and newer digital communications technologies have tipped the balance of power toward the individual and away from the state. In 2010–2011, amateur video clips of the self-immolation and subsequent funeral of a Tunisian vegetable seller, Mohammed Bouazizi, triggered the fall of Tunisia's brutal and corrupt regime. This uprising was followed shortly thereafter by similar events, some successful and some not, but all fed by personal communications technologies, all across the Arab world.

Alas, the invention of the telegraph, radio, and television also raised hopes that they would, by bridging the communications gap among peoples and among nations, usher in the New Jerusalem. But, as John Adams famously pointed out, political wisdom has not improved over the ages; even as technology has advanced, mankind steps on the same rakes, and the new inventions often magnify the damage.

Historian Daniel Boorstin referred to the nonprogressivity of human nature and politics as "Adams' law," but Boorstin was far too modest, for he appended several of his own astute observations to it, among which was that technology, far from fulfilling needs and solving problems, creates needs and spreads problems. "Boorstin's law," then, could be formulated thus in the modern world: beware of optimism about the social and political benefits of the Internet and social media, for while technology progresses, human nature and politics do not.[21]

It is quite fair to ask if technologies alone can determine politics, independent of their social and political context. The cynic can easily argue that who uses these technologies, and where they are used, rather than their nature, determines their political fallout. This is usually followed by the scornful hurling of the epithet "determinism" at anyone foolish enough to suggest that technologies can be inherently democratic or despotic.[22]

Yet, when viewed over the ages, technologies *do* matter: a writing system that is simple to master is inherently more democratic than one that is difficult; a printing press capable of inexpensively turning out thousands or millions of tracts is inherently more democratic than limiting book production to a few Church-controlled *scriptoria,* and two-way cell phone and Internet communications are inherently more democratic than mass-market one-way radio and television. The history of the past two centuries, I believe, confirms this view; over the course of the twentieth and twenty-first centuries, an ever greater portion of the human race lives under democratic rule, and it is not difficult to credit this happy result to recent advances in two-way communications technologies.

In the future science may yet provide governments with complex, powerful, and expensive new tools with which to observe and control citizens. Optimists would do well to expand their definition of "information technology." Over the past decade, the cost of sequencing the human genome has fallen even faster than the cost of computing; within the next decade, this technology could become available in pharmacies and bathrooms. While these advances will likely bestow upon humankind untold medical bounties, they may also give dictators new tools with which to oppress their citizens.

This book's rationale is deceptively simple: at the most basic level, the words "politics" and "communication" are nearly synonymous; all politics, after all, is nothing more and nothing less than communication applied in the service of power. Only by understanding the relative access to and control over information and communications technology, which has grown ever more complex over the centuries, can we understand the ebb and flow of politics, of culture, and of the human condition itself.

1

ORIGINS

Speech, the universal way by which humans communicate and transmit experience, fades instantly: before a word is fully pronounced it has already vanished forever. Writing, the first technology to make the spoken word permanent, changed the human condition. —Denise Schmandt-Besserat[1]

The Greek historian Herodotus tells us that Oroetes, the Persian satrap of Sardis, could reckon with men and arms, but not with the might of the written word.

First appointed to the post around 530 BC by Cyrus the Great, Oroetes had ruled his satrapy (near present-day Izmir in western Turkey) for decades, through the reigns not only of Cyrus but of his successors, Cambyses II and then Darius I. The last transition had been particularly turbulent, and during it Oroetes grew increasingly independent of the empire's capital in faraway Susa, in what is now southern Iran.

With this independence came increasingly erratic behavior. When Mitrobates, the governor of a neighboring province, taunted him for not dealing decisively with Polycrates, the Greek tyrant of Samos, Oroetes first killed Polycrates, then the complaining governor, and finally the governor's son. Later, Oroetes' apparent neutrality in the revolt of the Greek Ionians against the empire further displeased Darius. The last straw came when the satrap began murdering the king's couriers when their messages displeased him. Not for Darius the subtlety of "Who will rid me of this troublesome priest?" Oroetes "has made away with Mitrobates and his son, and now he kills my messengers whom I send to summon him," Herodotus records Darius as saying. "This is a defiance of authority which is not to be tolerated. Before he can do us further harm he must be stopped—and the way to stop him is by death."[2]

Dealing with the irritating graybeard, however, would prove problematic. The widespread revolts during and following Darius's accession had sapped the imperial army of its vigor. Moreover, Sardis lay 1,500 miles of mountainous terrain northwest of Susa—a formidable distance even today, let alone 2,500 years ago, in spite of the road built by Darius. In addition, Oroetes commanded a thousand crack Persian troops. Nonetheless, each of Darius's courtiers clamored so loudly for command of this seemingly suicidal mission that the king resolved the matter by lot. The "winner," Bagaeus, realized that brains would have to succeed where brawn could not. He had the royal scribes prepare several papyrus scrolls on various subjects, closed them with the king's seal, and set off for Sardis.

When he arrived, he handed the scrolls to Oroetes' scribe in a carefully choreographed order. The first few scrolls pertained to innocuous topics, but when Bagaeus observed the respectful hearing given those first missives by the satrap's guards, he gathered up his courage and handed the scribe a scroll instructing the guards to refuse further service to Oroetes. Upon hearing this imperial command, they threw their spears down at Bagaeus's feet. The final scroll read: "King Darius commands the Persians in Sardis to kill Oroetes." Problem solved.[3]

In all likelihood, Darius, Bagaeus, and Oroetes could not read or write fluently, if at all—certainly Oroetes could not, since had he been literate he would have read the scrolls himself, interpreted them more favorably, and survived. In fact, the only truly literate participants in the tale likely were the scribes at either end of this 1,500-mile information chain. Such was the magic and power of the written word that Herodotus, who was not shy about expressing his skepticism of many of the tales he related in *The Histories,* took this particular one at face value.

Archaeologists and paleographers pinpoint the birth of that magic and power to a small area in southern Mesopotamia about five millennia ago. Their discoveries make one paramount fact nearly certain: the first writing arose not from the desire to record history or produce literature, but rather to measure grain, count livestock, and organize and control the labor of the human animal. Accounting, not prose, invented writing.

About a hundred thousand years ago, probably in northeast Africa, humans rapidly evolved the repertoire of behaviors that define our species. These included the desire to cooperate, the ability to conceive abstractions of the physical world, and, critically, the first major communications technology: language. The second major communications technology, writing, is simply the *recording* of those abstractions.

Humans abstract and record information in five major ways: with writing, mathematical notation, painting/photography/videography, maps, and clocks—that is, we can abstract and record verbal, numerical, visual, spatial, and temporal information. (Scholars might argue about whether to include additional classes, such as musical notation.) Since interpreting a painting, map, or clock requires little training, this book will focus almost exclusively on writing, and to a much lesser extent, numbering.[4]

As measured by standardized testing, human intelligence seems to be increasing at a rapid clip, on the order of several IQ points per decade. This phenomenon, known as the "Flynn effect," cannot possibly be real, since extrapolating the process backward implies that the average IQ would have been approximately zero in Newton's time, and about negative 1,000 in Aristotle's.

To resolve this conundrum, it helps to think about the format of the modern IQ test. A typical question runs something like this: Which item does not belong in the following list—gun, arrow, chisel, and deer? The overwhelming majority of modern people would not hesitate to answer "deer," since the other three are inanimate objects. People from preliterate societies, on the other hand, usually give the "wrong" answer to this question: chisel.

Why? Because guns and arrows are used to kill deer, but chisels are not. Simply put, separating the living deer from the other three inanimate objects requires a significant degree of abstraction. Human intelligence has almost certainly not been increasing all that rapidly, if at all, over the past few centuries—but the level of abstraction demanded by modern civilization certainly has.[5]

Among the multitude of abstractions ultimately mastered by humans, arguably the first and most important is counting. Well into modern times, not all societies have emphasized this basic skill; many aboriginal languages contain only three numbers: "one," "two," and "many." (To be sure, all peoples can tell the difference between five and six things, but not all languages have words denoting these quantities.) If writing is nothing more and nothing less than the notation of abstractions, then the first, and easiest, place to look for the development of abstract ability is counting.

Archaeologists have found complex carved notches in bones from as early as one hundred thousand years ago in southern France at sites inhabited by Neanderthal man. By 28,000 BC, more complex notched specimens turn up at sites in Lebanon and Israel, and one particularly complex bone sample, dating to approximately 15,000–12,000 BC, contains scores of elaborately arranged V- and X-shaped incisions.[6]

Precisely what these incised bones represent is anybody's guess. The best-accepted theory—that they compute lunar cycles—remains highly controversial.[7] But *something* was being counted, and so these specimens are probably the earliest known examples of the physical recording of abstract information for later use. Archaeologists and paleographers have postulated that Paleolithic peoples almost certainly employed other counting devices—knots in string, carvings in wood, and carefully arranged twigs—but only more durable bone and stone have survived through the millennia. Further, the archaeological flashlight shines brightest in dry climates: because moisture destroys, the researcher is far more likely to find interpretable specimens of any type and from any era in the Middle East than in England or Cambodia.

The significance of this escape from the chains of memory is impossible to overestimate. The new recorded abstractions changed the very way that humans thought, behaved, and probably evolved. They made armies more effective and societies more prosperous. Those cultures that understood the value of record keeping would advance, while those that did not would sooner or later succumb to their more abstractly endowed competitors.

After 10,000 BC a new counting technology, based on small tokens, took hold in the Fertile Crescent. Strangely, until very recently these tokens remained largely ignored by paleographers, anthropologists, and archaeologists.

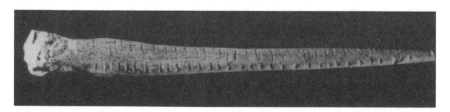

Figure 1-1. The first long-lasting notation systems were likely notched bones, like this specimen from the Ksar Akil site in Lebanon, ca. 15,000–12,000 BC.

That would change in 1968, when Denise Schmandt-Besserat, a recent graduate of the École du Louvre, headed off to Middle Eastern museums to examine pots, figurines, and fragments of ovens. She also began to notice smaller clay tokens that were frequently scattered around them.[8] For generations before, archaeologists had puzzled over these disks, cones, cylinders, and other, more complex shapes. As noted by one archaeologist, "From Levels 11 and 12 come five mysterious unbaked conical clay objects, looking like nothing in the world but suppositories. What they were used for is anyone's guess."[9]

Over the ensuing decades, Schmandt-Besserat solved this arcane mystery. The earliest tokens, dating to about 7500 BC, were unadorned spheres, cylinders, cones, tetrahedrons, and disks, almost all a centimeter or two in size, and were usually found in association with grain storage sites. That they appeared in the same place, time, and precise locations as storage facilities was no coincidence. Schmandt-Besserat found no evidence of the tokens in the deepest—that is, oldest—levels of excavation, associated with hunter-gatherers; she took particular note that archaeologists found tokens only in levels containing evidence of settled agriculture.

With the spread of farming after 7500 BC, the geographical extent of token finds also expanded; by 6000 BC, their use had spread to many sites in the Fertile Crescent. With the passage of time, their shapes became more complex, and they began to carry incised markings.

The development of settled agriculture and, four thousand years later, of cities, and with them civilization itself, meant increasing specialization of labor. While most people farmed, other groups that did not produce their own food—slaves, industrial workers, soldiers, priests, and bureaucrats—became prominent. An accounting system for transferring food from producers to these groups, or to the state, became necessary. Gradually, Schmandt-Besserat concluded that the tokens served this purpose. One of the most common tokens, the cone, probably represented about a liter of grain, whereas a small sphere signified approximately a bushel, and a large sphere stood for some larger amount. Similarly, a small and a large incised ovoid might have represented small and large jars of oil. A certain quantity of grain might be represented by five small spheres, and a certain quantity of oil by five small ovoids.[10] Note that at this stage, the tokens' users had yet to abstract the actual numbers. The system employed no tokens symbolizing quantities themselves; entirely different tokens stood for a given quantity of grain or of oil. The abstraction of the detached number five, which could be applied to any object, remained millennia in the future.

Around 3300 BC, with the appearance of large administrative municipal centers, the Sumerians began to seal groups of tokens within spherical clay containers, or "envelopes," upon which was incised a symbolic representation of the contents. One of the first such envelopes found contained three cones and three spheres, representing three small and three large measures of grain.[11] Archaeologists have found a surprising number of sealed, intact envelopes, suggesting that they perhaps served as a sort of legal document, which might be opened in the event of a dispute.[12] In the most likely scenario, the contents of the envelopes referred to debt.

Sometime around 3250 BC, the tokens began to disappear, and the envelopes rapidly evolved into flat tablets upon which only the token symbols were written. Because the "backup information" of the contents was lacking, the clarity of the symbols impressed upon the tablets became critical. Did an impressed design represent a disk or a sphere, a triangle or a tetrahedron? At this point, the need for a more clear and definitive system of notation arose. Schmandt-Besserat contends that the first writing

Figure 1-2. Simple tokens, representing measures of grain.

Figure 1-3. An ancient legal contract? Envelope containing one large cone, three small cones, and three disks; note the impressions of each on the face of the envelope.

system—the familiar Sumerian cuneiform script—evolved in this way directly from the token system.[13]

Precisely how, or even if, the Sumerians extended their accounting notation to written language will probably never be known. Schmandt-Besserat's work caused a stir mainly because it seemed to contradict the "pictographic theory," that writing evolved directly from pictures—a theory that is still taught to schoolchildren. Her "token hypothesis" was so bold and so different from the pictographic theory that it could not help but evoke controversy.[14] In reality, there's no real contradiction between the token and pictographic hypotheses; after all, Schmandt-Besserat's tokens are nothing if not "three-dimensional pictographs."

The token hypothesis need not be accepted to understand the importance of the cuneiform script that appeared around 3150 BC. Both tokens and early scripts had three pivotal effects: First, they freed humans from the limitations of memory. Second, they almost certainly imparted to those who mastered them enormous advantages over those who did not;

it is not difficult to imagine the token users as the administrative elite of preliterate Sumerian society who dealt out life and death according to how much food each member contributed and how much each received. Third, these tokens probably served a central role in the formation of history's first city-states around 3300 BC. The Sumerian economy was based on the temple, and its priests collected and accounted for "gifts to the gods," particularly the monthly festivals.

The older pictographic theory still has some virtues. First proposed by William Warburton, an Anglican cleric who eventually became bishop of Gloucester and who wrote in the 1730s, it was, and probably remains, the most commonly accepted theory about the origins of writing. Warburton, who appears never to have traveled outside Europe, propounded his theory in *The Divine Legation of Moses Demonstrated.* He proposed that written language passed through three stages of development: a "Mexican" painting stage, based on Spanish reports of Aztec storytelling with the use of pictures painted on cloth; a "hieroglyphic" stage, in which pictures were gradually abstracted and simplified; and a final, "Chinese" phase, in which the actual images were discarded in favor of more abstract symbols that increased dramatically in number to the tens of thousands over the subsequent millennia. In Warburton's scheme a hieroglyphic eye represented God's omniscience, while a serpent in a circle stood for the universe.[15]

To the modern eye, and certainly to Warburton's, Egyptian hieroglyphics *look* pictographic. What he could not know was that the "eye of god" and the "serpent" actually conveyed a meaning that was simultaneously far more banal, but ultimately far more powerful, than the mystical, abstract meanings he ascribed to them.

Egyptian writing went undeciphered until Napoleon invaded Egypt in 1798, when, in the process of fortifying the port of Rosetta on the Nile Delta, French engineers came upon a stone inscribed in three different scripts: Greek, hieroglyphic, and demotic (the cursive form of hieroglyphic used in the first millennium BC for everyday writing). After the British ejected the French from Egypt, the stone found its way to London, where both British and French scholars struggled with the three texts. Paleographers generally give credit for its ultimate decipherment to Jean-François Champollion, whose knowledge of the later Egyptian Coptic alphabet enabled him to translate the stone's demotic passage, since the two scripts share several characters. As demotic is simply a different rendition of hieroglyphic, Champollion soon deciphered it as well.

At the time that Warburton wrote *Divine Legation,* Europeans had a relatively high awareness of Egypt. They had, however, almost no knowledge of Mesopotamian civilization. True, fragmentary Greek and biblical sources made frequent reference to the Assyrians and Babylonians. As early as the twelfth century, travelers had returned from the Land Between the Rivers with stories of ancient cities buried under mounds scattered across the region's hot, dusty plains. But the Greeks, Romans, and medieval Europeans were utterly unaware of the earlier Sumerian civilization buried under many of those mounds. The Egyptians and the later Mesopotamians often built with durable stone. The early Mesopotamian cities, in contrast, arose in an alluvial environment that offered scant access to stone, and so the inhabitants built their cities and temples from mud brick that the forces of nature leveled into near-invisibility over the ages. In 1849, archaeologist Austen Henry Layard remarked that from the walls of the northern Iraqi city of Tel Afar, "The ruins of ancient towns and villages rose on all sides; and, as the sun went down, I counted above one hundred mounds, throwing their dark and long thinning shadows across the plain. These were the remains of Assyrian civilisation and prosperity."[16]

Not until the late nineteenth century did British, French, German, and American adventurers penetrate the mounds' treasures, and not until the 1920s did the painstaking, systematic layer-by-layer excavation that is the hallmark of modern archaeology begin to slowly expose the spectacular secrets of these long-lost civilizations.

In the 1920s and 1930s, near Ur, in modern-day southern Iraq, Sir Leonard Woolley first opened royal tombs dating to approximately 2500 BC. The most lurid and spectacular, dubbed the "Great Death Pit," contained dazzling hoards of lapis lazuli, gold, and silver—as well as the remains of over seventy retainers, almost all female, who had been sacrificed and buried with their ruler.[17]

The mounds' contents dazzled archaeologists, yet in the end their intellectual treasures far outshone the bones and baubles. For centuries, Westerners had been dimly aware of an angular script—now known as cuneiform—found on ancient ruins and pottery in Mesopotamia. Easily the most spectacular specimen of this mysterious ancient writing was inscribed, not on the clay tablets inside a mound, but rather on a faraway cliff that rose nearly two thousand feet above the tiny town of Bisitun, in what is now northwest Iran. Constructed between 520 BC and 518 BC by the Persian emperor Darius I, it depicted a warrior with a bow in one hand towering over his enemies, his foot on the neck of one of them. This forbidding image was surrounded by several panels of engraved inscriptions in different languages, all in cuneiform-like scripts.

To prevent vandalism, Darius ordered all of the monument's lower paths quarried away and the cliff's footholds removed. The destruction of these approaches succeeded in preserving the monument over the next two millennia, but at a price: the lack of access prevented travelers on the ancient road from Ecbatana in Persia to Babylon in Mesopotamia, along the Zagros Mountains, from getting close enough to actually *read* the inscriptions.

In the 1820s, an Englishman, Robert Kerr Porter, made some sketches of the reliefs and intuited the significance of the inscriptions; were they ever deciphered, he mused, "what a treasure-house of historical knowledge would be unfolded here."[18] Alas, like all previous visitors to Bisitun, he had neither the time nor the climbing ability to get close enough to the inscriptions to copy them. The task required a unique combination of athleticism, intellectual drive, and linguistic talent; these three factors finally came together in the person of a young British subaltern, Henry Rawlinson, who had been assigned by the East India Company (EIC) as military adviser to the shah's brother, the local governor.[19]

When Rawlinson left England in 1827, the seventeen-year-old soldier knew nearly nothing about ancient Mesopotamian languages beyond the fact that travelers occasionally came across seemingly impenetrable wedge-shaped inscriptions. As was usually the case in that era with English military missions abroad, Rawlinson's employer was not the British army, but rather the EIC, in whose service he remained for nearly three decades. In the EIC's employ he acquired a thirst for Oriental languages, and he mastered, among others, Persian, Sanskrit, Hebrew, and Arabic.

When he first came to Bisitun, Rawlinson did not know that in the late eighteenth century and the early nineteenth two Germans—the explorer Carsten Niebuhr and the classicist Georg Friedrich Grotefend—had met with limited success deciphering some short cuneiform inscriptions from the ruins of Persepolis, Darius's palace. Decoding any cipher or script, however, usually requires a large amount of it, and the relatively brief passages at Persepolis simply did not provide enough cryptographic fuel.

At Bisitun, Rawlinson struck linguistic paydirt: over a thousand lines of text in three different cuneiform-based scripts: Babylonian, Elamite, and Old Persian. Over the next decade, the young, athletic Rawlinson scaled the slippery face of the cliff—at first, without rope, ladder, or assistant. In the words of his brother George, his efforts "were made at some risk to life and limb—happily, however, he was a good cragsman."[20]

Because of the monument's layout, each language group in the inscription required a different climbing approach. As we'll soon learn, the characters of scripts can represent letters, syllables, whole words, or some combination of these. Rawlinson deduced that Old Persian constituted an alphabetic, and not a logographic or syllabic, script, since it contained only thirty-six different symbols. Since this would make the Old Persian inscriptions relatively easy to decipher, he attacked them first, making as many as four perilous ascents per day using nothing more than boots, notepad, and pen. He noticed that three groups of characters frequently repeated in the same order, and reasoned that they must be the names of three successive emperors. He quickly noted that the phonetic sequence of Hystaspes, Darius, and Xerxes (the pronunciation of which was known from Herodotus) perfectly fitted the pattern of the symbols in each group. This allowed him to deduce the phonetic values of twelve symbols; he was soon able to identify six more.

The decipherment of the Bisitun inscriptions underscores how peculiar skill sets often underlie many intellectual discoveries; it is doubtful, for example, that anyone without Rawlinson's climbing ability could have turned the trick. Over the ensuing years, other climbers found it nearly impossible to repeat his ascents up the sheer cliff face, yet Rawlinson remarked little on making several sorties per day for weeks at a time.[21]

In 1838, the untutored Rawlinson communicated his findings to the Royal Asiatic Society in London, where they created a sensation; the Society almost immediately accorded him membership, an unheard-of honor for an inexperienced outsider. He would soon be acclaimed by Assyriologists across Europe, and in collaboration with his new colleagues, he would decode the rest of the Old Persian alphabet.

The EIC, whose interests extended well beyond paleography, later posted Rawlinson all over Asia, but he regularly returned to Mesopotamia, where he collected more inscriptions and helped excavate the Assyrian capital of Nineveh. In spite of his far-flung postings, he visited Bisitun repeatedly, ultimately recording all its inscriptions. Rawlinson instinctively understood that the cliff's inscriptions were the "Mesopotamian Rosetta stone," containing identical passages in three extinct languages and scripts, one of which he and others had already decrypted. Ultimately, he deciphered 246 Babylonian cuneiform characters and laid the foundation for the translation of that language by those who followed, and of the much earlier texts uncovered by subsequent generations of Assyriologists.[22]

This work at least partly confirmed Warburton's pictographic hypothesis: the earliest Egyptian and Mesopotamian systems contained many pictograms (literally, "word pictures," words whose appearance clearly conveyed their meaning) and logograms (words conveying a more abstract meaning not obvious from their appearance) that perhaps evolved from earlier pictograms. Far more important, however, the efforts of Champollion and Rawlinson demonstrated that the heart of both systems was largely *syllabic,* with the most commonly used symbols—even those that superficially appeared to be pictographic—representing a distinct syllable.

Champollion and Rawlinson supplied the essential linguistic tools to later generations of archaeologists who plumbed the origins of writing in southern Mesopotamia and in Egypt. Working at the site of the Sumerian city of Uruk, researchers dated its first evidence of urban civilization in deep strata to about 3500 BC; this evidence was defined by particular building, utensil, and pottery styles.

Archaeologists do not know whether the appearance of these artifacts around 3500 BC signified the conquest of one ethnic group by another, or simply the slow evolution of a culture. One thing is certain: in more superficial strata, dating to around 3100 BC, archaeologists have unearthed approximately five thousand clay tablets containing symbols that probably constituted the first writing. Paleographers can distinguish the symbols found in the deepest, and thus oldest, Uruk IV layer, from those found in the slightly more superficial Uruk III layer. Further, while archaeologists have found Uruk III–type specimens outside the city of Uruk, Uruk IV–type specimens appeared only in this city and its immediate environs, suggesting that the birth of writing occurred in Uruk just before 3100 BC.[23]

The probable origin of writing in Uruk was no accident. Archaeologists estimate that during the late fourth millennium, its city walls

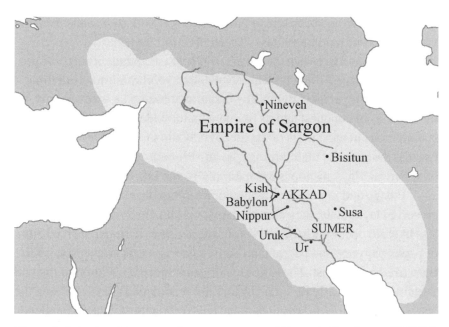

Figure 1-4. Ancient Mesopotamia; greatest extent of Sargonic Empire, ca. 2300 BC.

encompassed an area of over two square miles, with much of the city apparently lying outside those walls. This made Uruk the largest city not only of its age but for the next three thousand years. The Athens of Pericles occupied only one square mile; the Jerusalem of Christ and Herod, less than one-half square mile. Even first-century Rome, the capital of a vast empire, encompassed only five square miles.[24]

Mesopotamia has favored historians with rare fortune—what Assyriologist Marc Van De Mieroop calls "the accident of recovery": a combination of climate, soil composition, and not a little luck that yielded an enormous volume of revealing artifacts.[25] In the rest of the world, the ravages of time despoil inscriptions on papyrus, cloth, parchment, and wood within a few millennia. Even in the hot, dry climate of Egypt, only a few words not carved in stone survive more than about two and a half millennia. (One of the oldest papyrus records ever discovered, the Prisse Papyrus, dates to approximately the XII Dynasty of the Middle Kingdom—around 2000 BC, or four thousand years ago. Papyrus is produced from the pith of the papyrus plant, which grows best in swampy areas such as the Nile Delta; parchment, which would not be invented until about 200 BC, is manufactured from sheepskin or goatskin, while vellum is made from the youngest, or stillborn, animals, who are free of blemishes.)

In the Land Between the Rivers, by contrast, abundant soft clay provided the primary writing medium. Not only does clay harden with time; it can be rendered yet more durable by intentional baking or, inadvertently, by the vagaries of conquest and its frequent handmaiden, conflagration. Clay is ubiquitous in most parts of the globe; why did only the Mesopotamians use it as the basis for their writing system? Probably because the initial use of spherical clay envelopes led naturally to the use of flat clay tablets.[26]

Pillage and fire are the archaeologist's friends: not only do they help preserve clay tablets; they also render wood into charcoal, which is much less likely to decay with time. By contrast, because of the perishable nature of paper, papyrus, and parchment, entire historical eras and episodes have been irretrievably lost. These lost histories include the creation of the Old Testament, all of early Egyptian history not recorded in stone, and even the last several centuries of Mesopotamian civilization itself, which abandoned clay for parchment and papyrus. The likely evanescence of our own era's historical corpus—recorded on pitifully short-lived paper, magnetic media, and optical media—is profoundly humbling and worrisome.

Alone among historians of the ancient world, Assyriologists are blessed with access to hundreds of thousands of documents in the form of Sumerian, Akkadian, Babylonian, and Assyrian tablets that have been unearthed in the past century and a half; one excavation alone, of a royal palace at Tell Mardikh in modern Syria, yielded seventeen thousand documents.[27] Undoubtedly, hundreds of thousands more, and possibly millions, still lie buried. The large number of tablets, dating from the inception of cuneiform in approximately 3150 BC near or around the city of Uruk, provide a fairly detailed picture of the development of what may be mankind's first written records.

The tablets come in all sizes and shapes. Some are the size of postage stamps and bear only a few characters; others are a yard across and bear thousands. Some are square, some oblong, and some oval. Thousands bear the unmistakable mark of the school tablet, with expertly executed symbols of the teacher on one side, and the same symbols in the awkward scrawl of the student on the reverse. Scribes in Susa—in modern-day Iran—turned out mass-produced priestly curses imprinted onto tablets with cylinders, arguably the first printing press. Others inscribed bricks for temples and palaces with stamps containing changeable inserts to vary the inscription—the first movable type.

Less frequently, scribes produced tablets in stone or even metal, presumably for high-priority, archival documents. Scribes and students also wrote on more perishable media, such as waxed wooden practice boards that could be "erased" and reused, and thin, expensive hardwood sheets that could be carried around in "books."[28]

The earliest tablets indeed depict scripts that are highly pictographic, with little or no abstraction. The early Sumerian pictogram for woman clearly depicts the female genitalia, and the symbol for man just as obviously resembles a penis. Similarly, the logogram for mountains is also highly pictographic. The same is true for the symbol for the human head, the human mouth, and water.

Over the ensuing centuries, most of these symbols rotated ninety degrees counterclockwise, probably for ease of composition by right-handed writers. A degree of abstraction then appeared, as pictograms evolved into ideograms—for example, the symbol originally used to depict a star came to stand for "heavens" or "spirit."

Initially, scribes used a pointed reed stylus, but they soon found that clay's propensity to crumble and for pieces of it to break away made it difficult to produce curved figures. Gradually, they adopted a triangular stylus, which was depressed deep into the clay, then withdrawn as the straight stroke progressed, yielding cuneiform's characteristic wedge-shaped appearance. ("Cuneiform" derives from the Latin *cuneus*, or

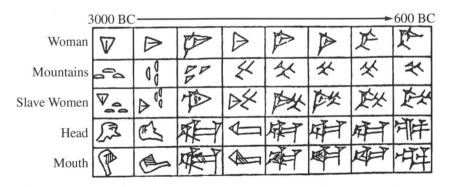

Figure 1-5. The evolution of cuneiform symbols from 3000 BC (left) to 600 BC (right). See text for detailed description.

wedge.) The use of multiple straight strokes for each character, in turn, encouraged abstraction. At the same time, symbols could be combined; for example, "mouth" and "water" could be juxtaposed to signify "drink," and "woman" and "mountain" to signify "female slave," since slaves came from the less civilized mountainous regions beyond the Euphrates and Tigris valleys.

Early on, scribes used a circular stylus for the notation of numbers; this tool yielded its own peculiar script, which over time was replaced with cuneiform. [29]

At some point relatively early in the third millennium, the Sumerians took the next step with what we now call the "rebus": the phoneticization of words too abstract to depict with pictograms or ideograms. In English we might use the sole of a foot to symbolize "soul." Remnants of rebuses persist to this day in heraldic coats of arms: the bear in Berlin's, an ox fording a stream in Oxford's, and so forth.[30]

Even more important, both the Sumerians and the Egyptians transformed their initially pictographic symbols into phonemes—the most basic units of sound—according to the so-called acrophonic principle, in which

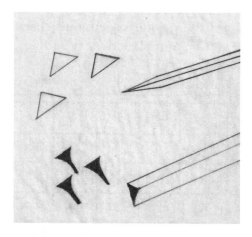

Figure 1-6. The top row shows an early pointed stylus, and the sharp, narrow stroke it left in clay, which was prone to cracking. The Sumerians accordingly developed a wedge-shaped one.

a pictogram comes to represent not just a word, but the *first phoneme* of that word. The most celebrated example of the acrophonic principle is the rippling hieroglyphic symbol for water, which Egyptian scribes centuries later transformed into the consonant for *n*, the first phoneme, or sound, of the Egyptian word for water, *nu*.[31]

Later, the Semitic letter *mem*—the first phoneme in the word for "water" in Semitic languages—evolved in the same way. While the acrophonic principle is controversial, most paleographers today believe that it played a critical role in the development of the increasingly abstract scripts throughout the ancient world.

A writing system that relies solely on individual symbols for each word, be they pictograms, logograms, or ideograms, presents the student with a steep learning curve. As an example, the second edition of the *Oxford English Dictionary* contains 171,476 words, while the vocabulary of the average American high school graduate contains approximately 12,000 words.

Both the Sumerians and the Egyptians attacked this problem by assigning individual symbols to syllables, reducing the number of characters to the few thousand syllables possible in most languages.[32]

Both civilizations further reduced the number of required symbols by allowing for ambiguity, the Sumerians by not specifying the consonants in each syllable symbol, and the Egyptians by doing away with vowels altogether, a characteristic that has survived down to modern Arabic and Hebrew.

This process of simplification through ambiguity developed slowly over the ages. In the very deepest—that is, oldest—strata in which full-fledged Sumerian writing is found, archaeologists and paleographers counted about 2,000 different symbols. But by the middle of the third millennium, cuneiform had been scaled down to about 100 to 150 commonly used syllables, with another 800 less commonly used individual words.

Hieroglyphic symbols represented their consonants singly, in pairs, or in triads—about 180 in all. Like Sumerian writing, Egyptian writing also contained several hundred logograms signifying words, with many symbols doing double duty as both logograms (words) and syllables.

The final simplification—a compact alphabet—grew out of the fact that the Egyptian script contained approximately twenty-five symbols that coded for only one consonant—essentially, letters. The Egyptians attached no particular significance to these "monoconsonantals." While some scribes may have realized that monoconsonantals could provide the basis for a much simpler writing system, they may also have known that the resultant wider literacy would devalue their own status and income. Only much later would the Egyptian monoconsonantals evolve into the modern Western alphabets.

By the late fourth millennium BC, Egypt and Sumer almost certainly conducted trade with each other, so it's not surprising that the Egyptians adopted writing shortly after the Sumerians did—around 3100 BC. Further, although hieroglyphic and cuneiform differ radically in superficial appearance, their underlying syllabic structures are remarkably similar, as is the size of the vocabulary: approximately a few hundred syllables and several hundred logograms each. Again, this could hardly have been a coincidence; for this reason, most paleographers now believe that the "idea of writing" must have spread along with commerce, most likely from Sumer to Egypt.[33]

Since almost everything known about ancient Egypt flows from archaeological sources, which in turn rely on the most durable materials, the modern world has focused on the pictorial-appearing hieroglyphic script,

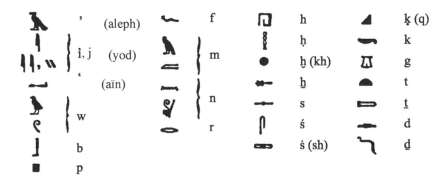

Figure 1-7. Egyptian single-phoneme (monoconsonantal) symbols. These would eventually give rise to the first Western alphabets.

which was used in stone monuments. For everyday religious, administrative, and business purposes, Egyptian scribes invented simpler, and thus even more abstract, cursive scripts: hieratic and, later, demotic. (The word "hieratic" probably derives from the Greek word for "priestly"; much later, hieratic script was supplanted by the more widely used demotic script—one of the three on the Rosetta Stone—whose name derives from the Greek word for "popular.") Since these far less elaborate cursive scripts were written largely on papyrus, relatively few specimens survive from before the first millennium BC.

Ancient Egyptian, like all languages, was rich with vowels. But they were not explicitly expressed in any of the three scripts and had to be determined from context. Modern languages, too—particularly English—fairly burst at the seams with inconsistencies and ambiguities that the reader decodes from context and experience. Consider George Bernard Shaw's famous spelling of "fish" as "ghoti"—the first two letters pronounced as the last two in "tough," the middle letter as in "women," and the last two as in "nation."

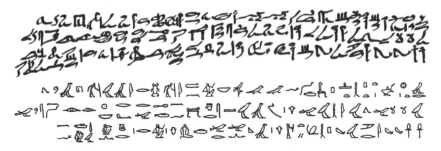

Figure 1-8. Early hieratic top, corresponding hieroglyphic below. (Ca. 1900 BC)

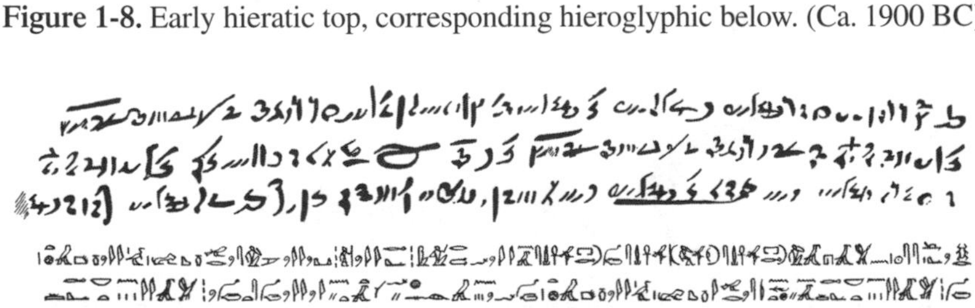

Figure 1-9. Demotic above, corresponding hieroglyphic below. (Ca. 200 BC)

Next, consider the biconsonantal ![mn symbol], which stood for *mn*. Was it pronounced *man*, *mun*, *manu*, or in dozens of other possible ways? We simply don't know. So, just like cuneiform, the three Egyptian scripts were syllabic, with the reader extracting the silent vowels from context.[34]

Sound is a far more abstract concept than image. Pictures, after all, can be captured, and moving pictures can be slowed down or even frozen completely in time. Not so with sound. Slow it down and it becomes unintelligible; stop it, and it disappears entirely. Therefore the invention of syllabic writing, which allowed the encoding not just of ideas or objects, but of the human voice itself, arguably constitutes one of mankind's greatest accomplishments.

In ancient Sumer and Egypt, only those with time, leisure, and intellect could master this complex new technology. Worse, whereas the older ideographic writing systems easily crossed linguistic borders—both an Egyptian and a Sumerian easily understood what the image of an ox head meant—the newer syllabic systems did not. During the third millennium, the Sumerians, who were of uncertain racial origin, were gradually conquered by the Semitic Akkadians, who adapted Sumerian cuneiform to their

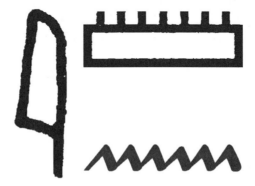

Figure 1-10. These three symbols sound out the Egyptian word "Jmn," the god Amun. The left symbol stood for the uniconsonantal "j"; the top right symbol, the biconsonantal "mn"; and the bottom right symbol, the uniconsonantal "n."

own different-sounding language. Akkadians and Sumerians employed a common script, but an Akkadian could not understand a Sumerian cuneiform tablet unless he also *spoke* Sumerian; in the same way, Westerners today recognize each other's Latin-based scripts without necessarily understanding their written or spoken languages.

Five millennia ago, Mesopotamia and Egypt saw the emergence of this powerful and highly complex new communications technology—writing. Because of its complexity, it was accessible only to a tiny elite, and that narrowness of access played out in two closely related ways: by creating a much more unequal, highly stratified social structure, and by making possible ever larger political entities and, eventually, empires.

In exploring this process, we shall focus on Mesopotamia for two reasons: first, because of its abundance of surviving clay-based historical material; and second, because Mesopotamia's profusion of city-states in the third and second millennia clearly demonstrates how an efficient writing system allows towns to grow into cities, and cities to grow into empires.

Anthropologists have found modern-day preliterate hunter gatherer societies to be relatively egalitarian. Interestingly, so, too, are pirate organizations, and for much the same reason: both are relatively small. Humans can maintain only so many functioning relationships; when group size exceeds about 150 members, it becomes impossible to remember not only their individual preferences and peculiarities, but also the complexities of the group's internal dynamics. Thus, with group sizes larger than 150, direct, face-to-face interaction no longer produces adequate social control, and members tend to drift off and form new tribes. Among behavioral scientists, the 150-person limit is known as "Dunbar's number," after the anthropologist/evolutionary psychologist who first proposed it.[35] Larger groups—city-states, nation-states, and empires—require more advanced communication techniques: writing, tokens, seals, and other counting devices.

The deployment of power in civil society—politics—is nothing more and nothing less than an exercise in communication. In the words of Assyriologist Jean-Jacques Glassner,

> [A king] has to show even more ability and willingness than others
> to be generous. He has to create around himself increasingly large
> circles of relatives, friends, and allies. In short, he must know better
> than anyone else how to put another person in a position of debt to

himself. He also has to know how to receive, and how to delay in
returning the favor [and] how to receive without giving back, as he
does when commandeering the labor of young people, of waifs, or
uprooted people.[36]

Dunbar's number severely constrains the illiterate, scribe-less king, who
is wholly reliant on word of mouth. Perhaps he can orally control 150
retainers, each of whom can in turn control 150 citizens—a medium-size
ancient city at best. The ruler with a corps of scribes and messengers, by
contrast, can command "circles of relatives, friends, and allies" that are
orders of magnitude larger, and, at times, whole empires.

   The most extreme form of social stratification, slavery, is encountered
almost exclusively in settled, highly organized societies and is infrequently
seen among hunter-gatherers. The rarity of slavery among nomadic peoples
has less to do with literacy than with the fact that a nomadic existence
severely limits the amount of personal possessions that can be transported
easily, including slaves. Slavery becomes possible only in sedentary, agricultural communities, where the usual source of chattel is captured soldiers
and defeated cities. By contrast, hunter-gatherers may or may not absorb
the small children and young women from defeated neighbors; all others
are dispatched on the spot.[37]

   Along the same lines, like most primitive societies, preliterate Sumer
was likely a fairly egalitarian place. Assyriologist Thorkild Jacobsen
plumbed Sumerian myth and legend and noted that most important state
decisions were made by two types of citizen councils: an assembly consisting of all the city's free males, and a smaller group of prominent senior
community members. The latter group usually determined kingship, which
during prehistory was probably not a hereditary institution. Jacobsen also
observed the same social structure in the prehistoric Teutonic tribes that
conquered northern and central Europe and featured two different ruling
councils: the *folkmoot,* which consisted of all the tribe's arms-bearing
members, for minor matters; and a council of elders, which decided major
issues, including leadership.

   The *Epic of Gilgamesh,* Jacobsen thought, demonstrated the relative powerlessness of prehistoric kings. Gilgamesh was the ruler of Uruk
around the dawn of literacy. When that city's archrival, the neighboring

city of Kish, attacked Uruk, Gilgamesh, supposedly the "greatest king on Earth," first had to seek approval from the council of elders to mount Uruk's defense.

Gilgamesh was no mythic king; he actually reigned sometime around 2700 BC.[38] The precise dating of his rule becomes important to us, because the cuneiform script was still evolving rapidly during this period; before about 2600 BC, it was capable of enumerating lists of nouns and some verbs and transmitting simple commands. It had not, however, developed syntactically to the point that scribes could communicate a sophisticated narrative or allow rulers to transmit highly detailed commands. In other words, the reason why Gilgamesh needed the assent of his elders to defend his city was probably that he did not have at his disposal the writing tools necessary to command absolute political control over large numbers of citizens. By the same token, Uruk's literate, scribal elite was not yet able to disempower its illiterate masses.

In 2700 BC, early cuneiform was simply not up to the task of concentrating power in the hands of a single king, not even the greatest king; likewise, it was not capable of transmitting the quality and quantity of data necessary to organize large empires. During the first half of the third millennium BC, Sumer consisted of dozens of medium-size and hundreds of smaller city-states, which were almost constantly at war with each other.

By around 2600 BC, a new ethnic force from the west began to make itself felt in Mesopotamia—the Akkadians, who, as already mentioned, adopted cuneiform to their own language. Interestingly, although Sumerian fell into disuse as a spoken tongue beginning in the middle of the third millennium, the Akkadians retained it as a written, administrative, and liturgical language.

During this period, the written language—Sumerian, whether in the hands of Sumerians or Akkadians—developed greatly in syntactical complexity, adding suffixes, prefixes, and subject/verb conventions that are the hallmarks of everyday speech. Once cuneiform could transmit this degree of semantic detail, it became the first script capable of administering vast empires.

Simultaneously with cuneiform's increasing syntactical and grammatical sophistication, or perhaps even because of it, the Akkadians gained the upper hand in the Land Between the Rivers. Sometime around 2300

BC, Sargon, an Akkadian member of the royal household of Kish, over-threw that city's king and went on to conquer a large swath of territory extending from the Persian Gulf to the Mediterranean Sea.

In short, during the mid-third century BC, advances in cuneiform script allowed Sargon and his successors to assemble and rule the world's first great empire. Not only did this new tool enhance the political and administrative reach of the leader; it also enabled him to deploy, for the first time, a nationwide propaganda campaign driven by the magical effect of the tablet on an illiterate population.[39] After 2300 BC, the Fertile Crescent had no place for a king without an army of scribes—better yet if the king himself could read and write, and was thus more able to control his literate minions. Most of the time, the messenger delivered the message to his audience orally and used the written tablet simply as a memory aid.[40] But even so, tablet and messenger served as a virtual propaganda howitzer that could amplify whatever message the ruler wished to communicate to his subjects.

Sargon himself did not use the propaganda potential of writing to elevate his royal status. Probably because of his humble origins, of which he seemed proud, Sargon simply assumed the role of *nam-lugal*: loosely, "the Great Man." Traditionally, the *nam-lugal* ruled over a major city-state that most of the other city-states recognized as the region's cultural center and arbiter of high-level disputes. Before Sargon, the king of Nippur—a holy city in the Sumerian religion, but never an imperial capital—served as *nam-lugal*. Sargon's two sons, both of whom succeeded him, followed their father's low-key style of suzerainty, eschewed divine status, and allowed the new empire's cities autonomy in day-to-day affairs.

That would change under Sargon's grandson, Naram-Sin, who became the first Mesopotamian ruler to assume divine status and proclaimed himself "king of the four corners of the world." He succeeded in no small part because of the skill of his scribes, who helped bring Naram-Sin's empire to the apogee of power in remote antiquity. One historian noted that administrative records from his reign reflected a sense of permanence and eternality similar to those of Augustus Caesar, Louis XIV, or Queen Victoria, with "undiminished success as far back as human memory and as far in all directions as human knowledge."[41]

The empire of Akkad lasted about a century and a half before finally falling prey to what would become the scourge of Asian and European civilizations for the next three and a half millennia: fierce nomadic tribes who usually invaded from the north to feast on the wealth of their sedentary, luxury-loving southern neighbors. The invaders broke the empire up into the usual tangle of small warring states; archaeologists have yet to find Agade, its capital city.

The barbarians who destroyed Akkad—the Gutians—were in their turn deposed by the ruler of Uruk, the birthplace of writing. This leader, named Utu-hegal, was in turn deposed by Ur-Nammu, who revived Naram-Sin's divine status and founded the so-called Ur-III Empire, which was to last approximately 100 to 150 years.

By this point, Sumerian had become all but extinct as a spoken tongue, but, as in Akkad, it remained the written language of the Ur III Empire, paradoxically connecting power and literacy in a dead language—a hurdle leaped by only a favored, privileged few. In much the same way, three millennia later, Latin remained the language of liturgy and scholarship until the early modern period. And just as Latin marked its medieval possessors as scholars, so, too, did the mastery of Sumerian by an Akkadian connect power and literacy to mark him as a member of the elite.[42]

By the beginning of the second millennium BC, written language had evolved to the point that it could transmit the command-and-control data necessary for military operations, the building and maintenance of empires, and large-scale civil projects. Just as important, it was now up to the highly abstract task of codifying and recording laws, which the ruler had inscribed on tablets in cities throughout his realm.

In ancient societies, the law functioned as a two-edged sword; while standardizing procedure and bringing it out into the open, the law also concentrated power in those few who could read and write. Whatever its effect on the society's balance of power, it became as essential to empire as the sword and the shield. The first legal tablets appeared during the reign of Ur-Nammu, more than three centuries before the better-known Code of Hammurabi. No detail of conduct escaped their ambit: "If a man proceeded by force and deflowered the virgin slavewoman of another man, that man must pay five shekels of silver."[43]

Mesopotamian cities identified closely with their deities, and their temples functioned as the main social and economic engines. The king served as the intermediary between the city and its deity, and his palace operated side by side with the temple. Both palace and temple commanded the key function in any society: the production and distribution of food.

Small, free farmers did produce grain and other foodstuffs for their own consumption and for sale elsewhere, but in southern Mesopotamia's hot, dry, alluvial landscape, successful agriculture usually required large-scale irrigation, which, in turn, required control by the temple and palace.

The most obvious locus of state and temple control was the huge canal and irrigation projects that characterized many Mesopotamian city-states. Less obvious, but just as important, were the threshing rooms scattered throughout all but the smallest of urban settlements. Whether the male workers on the canal and irrigation projects and the female workers on the threshing room floor were slaves or free cannot, in most cases, be determined. The rich historical record left in the cuneiform-clay makes clear that both state and temple controlled and fed a vast workforce. The threshing rooms served at least two critical purposes in Mesopotamian society: redistributing agricultural output from farmers to urban workers, and as a sort of collection office where tenant farmers satisfied their landlords with that fraction of grain due as rent.

Both the written record and archaeological excavations reveal a complex system of distribution among the working populace. The authorities gave sixty liters of grain per month to men, and thirty to women. Bread and beer were supplied as well, and larger cities usually maintained silos that held enough grain to feed their populations for up to six months.[44]

The tablets make clear that large-scale enterprises in remote antiquity managed two main items: labor output and input of grain to feed workers. For example, one typical tablet precisely records the amount of labor performed by thirty-seven women over a period of one year—13,320 working days—on a threshing room floor. A foreman who failed to deliver the required labor could bring down on himself the direst of consequences, and if he died without providing for his surviving relatives, they were liable to be conscripted to make up the missing work.[45]

Another set of tablets documents a vast works project, probably performed by about 3,600 war prisoners in "Sabum," most likely in the mountains of western Iran. The work was not precisely described but may have been a quarry, as it involved numerous copper hammers and had a relatively small physical volume of output.[46]

The organization of the canal projects, threshing rooms, grain silos, and large public works and military projects required precise record keeping, and the scribe, as the master record keeper, stood at the very center of such vast works. The scribe was no mere linguistic technician, but rather the sole possessor of the skill set that made civilization hum, a sort of investment banker, engineer, and diplomat all rolled up into one. Or, in the words of the linguist Ignaz Gelb, "Writing exists only in a civilization, and a civilization cannot exist without writing."[47]

Scribal training thus paved the road to power and wealth, and was open only to a lucky few, most often the sons of scribes. The scribes themselves were known in Sumerian as *dub-sar,* "tablet writers"; a scribal schoolhouse was an *é-dub-ba,* "tablet house"; and a student was a *dumu-é-dub-ba,* "son of the tablet house." In the 1940s the Sumerologist named Samuel Noah Kramer uncovered a "schoolboy's story" that described the educational process in engaging and realistic detail.

The tale itself was probably written by a teacher, and proved so popular in its day that many copies were made. The abundance of source material allowed Kramer, a master of archaeological detective work, to painstakingly reassemble from fragments in archives around the world nearly the complete narrative.

The story begins with the narrator asking the student to describe what he does in school: a session of tablet writing followed by lunch, which was followed by more tablet writing. He goes home, reads his work to his father, and the next morning departs for school with some lunch rolls made by his mother. He arrives late and is lucky to get off with a mere verbal rebuke. Later, he is not so fortunate and receives multiple beatings and canings for sloppy cuneiform-manship. When he returns home, the boy suggests to his father that it might not be a bad idea to invite the teacher over. The pupil's father does so and sits the teacher at the head of the table, where he is wined, dined, flattered outrageously, thanked for imparting to his son the secrets of scribal technique, and, last, showered with gifts. The teacher, in turn, praises the student and opines that he has a most promising future.[48]

This story, as well as other records, makes clear the central importance of scribal education, as well as its grim, repetitive nature, liberally laced with corporal punishment. Students began by copying simple written symbols and then progressed to more complex words; long lists of occupations, places, animals, and plant varieties; and finally, narrative sagas. They also studied the sophisticated sexagesimal (base-sixty) Sumerian system of mathematics/bookkeeping, astronomy, and the arts of divination. One of the most common Mesopotamian schoolhouse artifacts was the *bà*, a clay model of a sheep's liver, which served as a training device for the all-important science of hepatoscopy (the foretelling of the future by the examination of the freshly removed organ).

Had George Orwell and Claude Lévi-Strauss been born in ancient Mesopotamia or Egypt, they surely would have despaired of the future of human freedom. Here, after all, were the tools—the complex and nearly magical cuneiform and hieroglyphic writing systems—that enabled the few to subjugate the awed, illiterate multitudes.

In the middle of the second millennium BC, in the wastes of the Sinai desert, an obscure group of Semitic miners would appropriate for themselves that magic and power, transmute it into a form that could be learned with relative ease by ordinary people, and forever change the calculus of power between the rulers and the ruled.

2

THE ABCS OF DEMOCRACY

Now the Phoenicians . . . introduced into Greece upon their arrival a great variety of arts, among the rest that of writing, whereof the Greeks till then had, as I think, been ignorant.—Herodotus

They don't make archaeologists like Flinders Petrie any more.

Petrie's background was characteristic of eccentric British inventors, adventurers, and academics of his era: Scottish clergy and distinguished empire-serving forebears scattered around the globe, all leavened with moderate, but not excessive, financial comfort.

Typical of his family was his maternal grandfather, Matthew Flinders, who surveyed Australia (particularly the Great Barrier Reef and Gulf of Carpentaria), wrote treatises on magnetism, and invented the Flinders Bar, which is used to this day to compensate for the compass error caused by the iron in ships' hulls. His name is well known to Australian schoolchildren, and the country is thick with cities, streets, and even an island, a river, and a mountain range named after him; each year large numbers of Aussies make the pilgrimage to his birthplace, Donnington, in Lincolnshire.[1]

Matthew raised an accomplished French-speaking daughter, Anne, who was courted by William Petrie, an unsuccessful inventor who had tinkered with electrical and magnetic inventions. Before they could marry and raise a family, William would need to land a paying job, which he finally did at a chemical factory in 1851. On June 3, 1853, William Matthew Flinders Petrie was born.

Young Willie, as he was called, quickly demonstrated a thirst for knowledge; by age nine, he had digested his father's thousand-page chemistry text. Nothing, however, fascinated him as much as old objects, particularly his mother's collection of minerals and fossils.

After Willie had a disastrous experience with an overly strict governess/tutor, his physician recommended that he be kept out of school, so he never obtained a formal education. He soon fell under the influence of a self-educated polymath, N. T. Riley, the proprietor of a local antique shop. Petrie thrived amid Riley's collection of tripods, sextants, and coins, and under his tutelage became an expert surveyor and numismatist.

In Riley's shop, Petrie acquired a talent for authenticating rare coins. This, in turn, attracted the attention of a customer of Riley's, the Coins and Medals curator at the British Museum. By age twenty-one Petrie was awarded a coveted reader's ticket at the museum, which became his university. In addition, Petrie's surveying skills turned him into a meticulous archaeologist. When he discovered that the museum's Map Room contained no accurate surveys of England's most prominent ancient stone circles, he plotted numerous sites, including Stonehenge, over the next several years.

Petrie developed a fascination with the Egyptian pyramids, both from his work at the museum and, curiously, from Piazzi Smyth, the author of a crackpot volume, *Our Inheritance in the Great Pyramid*. Smyth posited that, since according to the strict interpretation of scripture, the world was created in 4004 BC, the Egyptians could not possibly have mustered the expertise to have built the pyramids by the third or second millennium BC. Reasoning that the pyramids could only have been divine creations, Smyth scavenged all manner of evidence in support of this idea, most prominently the 3.14 ratio of their circumference to their height—the approximate value of pi. Petrie began corresponding with Smyth and publishing pamphlets in support of Smyth's theories, but the two soon fell out regarding theological matters.

Petrie resolved to learn the truth about the pyramids, and in 1880 he sailed to Alexandria and so began a six-decade career as one of England's greatest Egyptologists. He accomplished seminal surveys of the pyramids, along with hundreds of other sites in the Levant.[2]

In February, 1905, after exploring the Middle East for more than two decades, Petrie and his wife arrived at an old turquoise formation in the western Sinai at Serabit el-Khadim, which had been mined as recently as fifty years before by a retired English major and his family. There, although he and others did not realize it for years, Petrie made the most important discovery of his career.

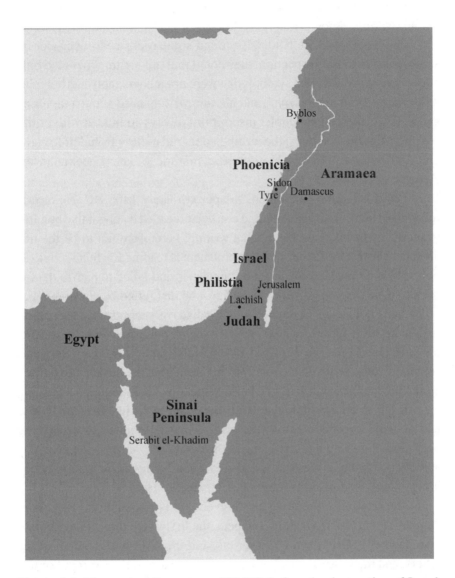

Figure 2-1. The ancient Levant, ca. 800 BC, before the destruction of Israel, Judah, and the Aramaean states.

At the mine the Petries came upon a large collection of statues and inscriptions. Most were expertly carved and bore standard hieroglyphic or hieratic writing, almost certainly produced by the mine's Egyptian overseers.[3]

His observant wife Hilda also found some rocks bearing cruder inscriptions. On closer inspection, they noted that this writing included only about thirty or so different symbols that were not recognizably hieroglyphic or hieratic—both hieroglyphic and hieratic writing used about a thousand symbols. Further, these simpler inscriptions always coincided with primitive, non-Egyptian statues; the writing appeared to flow from left to right, also unlike the well-known hieroglyphic, hieratic, or later Phoenician and Hebrew alphabets.

Petrie dated the inscriptions to approximately 1400 BC. He clearly recognized them as an alphabet, and one that preceded by about five hundred years the earliest known Phoenician writing, heretofore felt to be the first alphabet.[4] Ironically, Petrie, although proficient at reading Egyptian script, did not possess a broader knowledge of linguistics and failed to realize the full import of his discovery. Although he knew he had found an alphabet much older than Phoenician, he did not think his discovery represented the earliest one. In his book *The Formation of the Alphabet*, published seven years after his Sinai discoveries, he theorized that the inhabitants of northern Syria had somehow gathered diverse symbols from throughout the Levant into the first workable alphabet; amazingly, he failed to mention his discoveries at Serabit.[5]

It fell to an Egyptologist, Alan Gardiner, to realize that the Petries had actually stumbled across the origin of the alphabet, or something very close to it. Linguists had long known that Latin script—the everyday alphabet of today's Western world—evolved from Greek letters, which had themselves derived from Phoenician, as did Hebrew.[6]

The relationship among all these scripts is ironclad: the very word "alphabet" derives from alpha and beta, the first two letters of the Phoenician, Hebrew, Greek, and Latin scripts, and the sounds and names of the letters, and their alphabetical order as well, are also quite similar. For this reason it is in many cases possible to approximate the sound of a long-lost language if it was written in an alphabetic script.[7]

All of these alphabets, consisting of between twenty-two and thirty letters, represented nearly identical phonemes—the basic sound units of human speech. Gardiner was the first to realize that the letters found by the

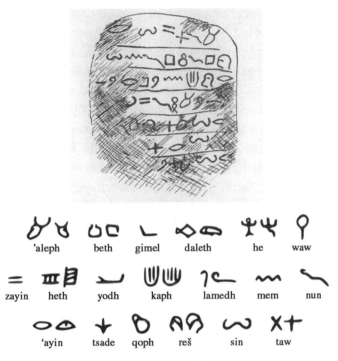

Figure 2-2. Early proto-Semitic letters, ca. 1400 BC. *Top:* Serabit Tablet. *Bottom:* Proto-Semitic Alphabet.

Petries at Serabit, or close relatives of these letters, most likely comprised the original alphabetic script. He named the symbols the "proto-Semitic alphabet."[8]

The last chapter of Petrie's life befitted his eclectic roots and eccentric personality. During his final hospitalization for malaria in Jerusalem in 1942, he requested that his head be donated to the Royal College of Surgeons in London as a specimen of a typical Englishman. His physicians, understanding the extraordinary nature of his accomplishments and hopeful that the study of his brain might provide medical science insight into the nature of genius, complied. Wartime conditions, however, delayed shipment of Petrie's pickled cranium back to Britain until after 1945, and when it finally arrived at the Royal College, it was absentmindedly stored away. It was not rediscovered until the 1970s, by which time the examination of great men's brains had fallen out of favor.[9]

Over the millennium following the alphabet's invention around 1500 BC, the simple phonemic lettering system Petrie discovered made possible the first stirrings of mass literacy that would unleash much of the subsequent political and social ferment of human history.

On the basis of archaeological and linguistic evidence, most authorities believe that the proto-Semitic inscriptions the Petries first found at Serabit derived from Egyptian hieratic or hieroglyphic writing. While the precise origin of the proto-Semitic alphabet will never be known, the Serabit inscriptions suggest that it was probably invented somewhere in the Sinai or Canaan by non-Egyptian Semites who had come there from somewhere in the Levant to work as miners for the Egyptians.

Did the first simplified alphabetic script really originate in the mines at Serabit? After Flinders' excavations there, archaeologists uncovered, at several other sites in Palestine, more primitive inscriptions that look alphabetic and possibly predate the Serabit inscriptions by as much as a century or two. More recently, an American research team has uncovered proto-Semitic inscriptions at Wadi el-Hol, several hundred miles south of Serabit el-Khadim, on the Nile; they suggest that the Egyptians may have in fact invented the script to better communicate with their Semitic workers/slaves.[10]

Another intriguing candidate for "inventor of the alphabet" is the Midianites, a Sinai people who mined copper and who could have derived it from the writing of their Egyptian overseers in the same way as did the miners of Serabit. The Bible has Moses marrying Zipporah, the daughter of the Midianite high priest Jethro, who himself was probably literate. Did Moses's father-in-law teach him how to read and write?[11] Whatever the ultimate truth of the matter, it seems probable that the Serabit script or one of its close and never-to-be-discovered relatives gave rise to all of the modern Western alphabets.

The Jewish people's supposed escape from slavery in Egypt—the Exodus—happened at approximately the same time as the creation of the Serabit inscriptions. Unfortunately, biblical scholars have great difficulty pinpointing the time of the Exodus. Many, in fact, go further, and suggest that it never occurred, but rather that the ancient Israelites evolved from the native Canaanite communities. Nor, for that matter, has the historical existence of Moses been substantiated with archaeological data or independent written sources.[12]

If the Exodus did take place, it must have happened sometime between the rise of the Iron Age empires of the Nile around 1550 BC and the first Egyptian mention of the people of Israel around 1200 BC. Coincidentally, roughly halfway between these two dates, Pharaoh Amenhotep IV (Akhenaten) convulsed Egyptian society by establishing a "monotheistic" belief system centering on the sun-disk deity Aten; some have speculated that Moses was influenced by Atenism, or was perhaps even a believer. Thus, in the middle of the second millennium, the Egypt/Sinai area saw the advent of Western monotheism, starting with the first short-lived Egyptian dalliance, followed by the more permanent Hebrew variety, the putative Exodus, and the invention of the alphabet.

The temporal and geographic connection between the alphabet and monotheism in Egypt-Palestine during the middle of the second millennium may be more than coincidence. What might tie them together? The notion of a disembodied, formless, all-seeing, and ever-present supreme being requires a far more abstract frame of mind than that needed for the older plethora of anthropomorphized beings who oversaw the heavenly bodies, the crops, fertility, and the seas. Alphabetic writing requires the same high degree of abstraction and may have provided a literate priestly caste with the intellectual tools necessary to imagine a belief system overseen by a single disembodied deity. Whatever the reason, Judaism and the West acquired their God and their Book.

From the modern perspective, it seems inevitable that the complex cuneiform writing system described in Chapter 1 would succumb to the simpler, more nimble alphabetic system, as indeed in the end it did. Yet cuneiform survived longer than any other system—over three millennia—before it finally fell into disuse sometime around the first century after Christ.

The demise of cuneiform was largely the work of an obscure Semitic tribe living on the western fringes of the great Mesopotamian empires. Modern people dimly remember that Jesus spoke Aramaic, but few, even among contemporary practicing Jews, recall that so did the majority of his fellow Jews.[13] Fewer still realize that the modern "Hebrew alphabet" is actually Aramaic. The silent tragedy of the Aramaeans is that they created a language and alphabet that long outlived their culture and civilization.

Like the Hebrews, the Aramaeans began as desert and semidesert nomads. During the second millennium BC, they gradually settled in the northern Levant and in the far northwest of Mesopotamia. By 1200 BC they had founded what eventually became one of their capitals, Damascus. As with the classical period Greeks, there was no single Aramaean state, but rather a host of small city-states and tribal confederations. While the Aramaeans gradually assimilated the cultures of the Canaanites and Amorites who surrounded them, they kept their distinctive language and—far more important—their own easy-to-learn version of the proto-Semitic script discovered by the Petries.

At the same time that the Aramaeans adapted the alphabet to their own use, they also benefited from the domestication of the camel and the development of the North Arabian saddle. The combination allowed them to mount in excess of five hundred pounds of cargo on the average animal, and about half a ton on the strongest beasts; a single camel driver, conducting a train of three to six animals, could move a ton or two of cargo between twenty and sixty miles a day. This was one of history's great transportation revolutions, and it made the Aramaeans the terrestrial equivalent of the Phoenicians: a trading people who spread far and wide a powerful alphabet.[14]

History intertwined the fates of Hebrews and Aramaeans. When Abraham sought a wife for his son Isaac, he sent a messenger east to the Aramaean city of Harrān, in what is now eastern Syria, to fetch Rebekah; Jacob's wives Leah and Rachel probably hailed from Aramaea as well. Abraham's migration from northwestern Mesopotamia to Canaan was part of a larger westward movement of Aramaean peoples sometime in the second millennium BC. The conclusion seems inescapable: Abraham himself may have been Aramaean, and wished his son's seed mingled with the women of his own tribe, and not with the local Canaanite women.[15]

Generally, the relationship between the Jews and Aramaeans was hostile. Between roughly 1000 BC and 750 BC, dominance seesawed between the two peoples; David briefly occupied Damascus, and a century and a half later the Aramaeans nearly sacked Jerusalem. Less frequently, the Jews and Aramaeans were allied, particularly against the increasingly powerful Assyrians to the east, who, in 853 BC, led by their emperor Shalmaneser III, were held off by a complex coalition of Jews, Aramaeans, and Phoenicians.

In 732 BC, the Aramaeans' luck ran out. The Assyrians under Tiglath-pileser III took Damascus, pillaged it, and deported its inhabitants to the Euphrates. Ten of the original twelve tribes of Israel disappeared into history with them, lost when the northern Jewish kingdom of Israel, which had fatefully allied itself with the Aramaeans, also fell victim to the Assyrian hordes.

The Assyrians spared the southern Jewish state of Judah and its capital at Jerusalem for reasons that remain controversial to this day. The traditional view, supported mainly by biblical evidence, is that Judah's wily King Ahaz resisted alliance with the Aramaeans and the northern kingdom of Israel. Instead, he made his kingdom a vassal state of Assyria, which, in exchange for an annual tribute of silver, and perhaps some military assistance as well, would have allowed the Jews nearly complete autonomy. Another view has the southern kingdom surviving because of disease among the Assyrian armies; still another is that the Assyrians wished to maintain Judah as an independent buffer state against Assyria's major rival to the west, Egypt.

Whatever the reason, Judah would outlive the northern kingdom of Israel. Ahaz' son Hezekiah was less favorably disposed toward the Assyrians, and after he succeeded his father around 715 BC, it was only a matter of time before hostilities erupted. In 704 BC, after the mighty Assyrian emperor Sargon II was killed in a military campaign, Hezekiah decided to test the new emperor, Sennacherib, by stopping tribute payments. This was a near-fatal misstep; it prompted a devastating siege of Jerusalem in 701 BC that brought starvation, but not conquest, to the Jews.

The Assyrians usually made an example of such outright rebellion; around the same time as Sennacherib's siege of Jerusalem, Babylon also revolted, and Sennacherib was said to have spilled so much blood into the Euphrates that the Persian Gulf ran red, informing all on its shores of the costs of opposing him. Yet in the end, Sennacherib spared Jerusalem.

After the fall of the kingdom of Israel, Judah survived for nearly another century and a half until its final, horrifying conquest in the high summer of 587 BC by Nebuchadnezzar's Babylonians (the conquerors of the overextended Assyrians), which brought the burning of Jerusalem and the deportation of the Jews to the banks of the Euphrates. The Assyrians' earlier decision to spare the southern kingdom proved one of history's fulcrums, for at least two reasons. First, it allowed the Jews, and their cultural contribution to the West, to survive. Second, the sparing of the southern state resulted in a socioeconomic transformation that probably produced mankind's first small step toward mass literacy. While mass literacy requires both a simplified alphabet and readily available writing implements, they are not in and of themselves sufficient. Literacy is also spurred by two other conditions: prosperity, which gives people the leisure to pursue it; and urbanization, which provides the critical mass of human contact to propagate it.

In the wake of Israel's fall, Judah received large numbers of northern refugees who possessed in abundance all four of the requirements for literacy. The proximity of the northern state to Phoenicia gave it access to both that culture's alphabet and, critically, to supplies of papyrus shipped from Egypt. In addition, Judah's flat terrain (at least compared with that of the more hilly Israel) made for a more urban, sophisticated, and thus literate society.

The flood of transplanted northerners transformed the agrarian and less sophisticated south and probably produced a significant increase of literacy among its inhabitants. After 700 BC, the Judeans probably consumed ever-increasing supplies of papyrus, but the ravages of time have allowed for the recovery of only one fragmentary specimen from this period. The papyrus may have perished, but the inscribed seals used to close the letters and documents survived, and the period's intellectual awakening is reflected in the appearance of large numbers of these round, durable artifacts in the southern kingdom after 700 BC. Many of these seals are crudely crafted and misspelled, suggesting that they were the work of ordinary citizens.

In the Old Testament, the Book of Jeremiah's famous Chapter 36 supplies another clue to the extent of Judean literacy in this period. The passage begins with the Lord informing the erstwhile prophet of His displeasure at the idolatry, blasphemy, and immorality of his chosen people. Jeremiah calls on the scribe Baruch to take some dictation.

The year is approximately 605 BC, and the Babylonians loom menacingly on the eastern horizon. Jeremiah warns the Judean king, Jehoiakim, and his people to repent lest the Lord, through the Babylonians, his chosen agents of destruction, annihilate Judah:

> Then read Baruch in the book the words of Jeremiah in the house of the LORD, in the chamber of Gemariah the son of Shaphan the scribe, in the higher court, at the entry of the new gate of the LORD's house, in the ears of all the people.[16]

By and by, Jehoiakim's minions take the scroll and bring it to the king. Not surprisingly, the king is displeased; as his scribes read the document, he cuts off successive parts of it, throws them into the fire, and orders the arrest of Jeremiah and Baruch, whom the Lord conveniently hides. In the chapter's final verse, Jeremiah dictates yet another scroll to Baruch.

By Jeremiah's time—very roughly, 600 BC—the Hebrews had employed their alphabet for centuries, yet the average Judean remained largely illiterate. There is not even the absolute certainty that Jeremiah could read. Further, the entirety of the Old Testament, written mainly during the first millennium BC, shows the classic signs of having its origins in a largely illiterate, oral tradition: the use of meter, formulaic exposition, repetition, and, most characteristically, epithets. For example, of the twenty-three mentions of Baruch in Jeremiah, eight are "Baruch son of Neriah."[17]

Just as clearly, the written word had the power to sway the people; while ultimately this prophecy did not save Judah from itself or from the Babylonians' wrath, Jeremiah would probably not have commanded the people's attention without the magic and amplifying power of the scroll.

Around 588 BC, as Nebuchadnezzar was systematically reducing Judah to rubble, either as Yaweh's agent of divine retribution or on his own account, he besieged the fortress of Lachish, about thirty miles southwest of Jerusalem. Archaeologists excavating the site have found numerous ostraca—inscribed pottery shards—written during the chaos of the fort's final days. The most famous is the so-called Lachish Letter 3, or "Letter of a Literate Soldier," an apparently complete text of about one hundred fifty words written by Hoshayahu, most probably a junior officer, to his commander, Yaush. Apparently Yaush had suggested that the soldier employ a scribe, at which the latter took great offense: "As God lives, never has any man read a letter to me." The entire letter actually consists of the soldier's anger at such an offensive slur: "And also every letter that comes to me, surely I read it and, moreover, I can repeat it completely!"[18]

Hoshayahu's letter contains slang, and this was almost certainly the proximate cause of the commander's recommendation that his underling hire a scribe. Nonetheless, this letter provides one of the first indications of the spread of literacy down to at least mid-level officers and, further, that a stigma was becoming attached to illiteracy.

Many have used such vignettes, particularly biblical passages, to overestimate the extent of literacy in Judah. In the first place, we must define what is meant by "literacy." In the full modern sense of the word—reasonable fluency and accuracy with both reading and writing—certainly not more than a few percent of the population qualified. Because papyrus was expensive, many more people could read than write. Also, there was little to read: only scattered stone inscriptions and a relatively small number of papyrus scrolls secreted away in temples, palaces, and the homes of the very wealthy. Scribes wrote and stored records, but literature and the arts of storytelling and poetry remained almost exclusively oral activities.

Other barriers kept a lid on the literacy rate as well: the likely absence of organized schooling in Judah and the fact that before the medieval period, scribal practices paid little attention to evenness of script, line breaks, or sometimes even word breaks. Reading was a laborious process that was meant to be performed aloud—even in the modern world accounts are "audited." The practice of silent reading would not become common until almost the modern period, and some linguists argue that while most modern Western languages are easy to read silently, the ancient Semitic languages, particularly vowel-less Hebrew, could not be read silently, a contention that most bar and bat mitzvah boys and girls would surely agree with.[19]

In the words of biblical scholar David Carr,

> When you list those people who are depicted as writing in ancient Israel, it quickly becomes evident that virtually all are some sort of official. Aside from God, who is one of the Bible's most prolific writers, virtually all writers and readers in the Bible are officials of some kind: scribes, kings, priests, and other bureaucrats.[20]

Baruch's scrolls may have had only limited effect, and Hoshaya-hu's letter may have been of only modest quality. Both, however, were symptomatic of the first feeble efforts by ordinary people at wresting the lever of literacy from the hands of the state.

Forty years after Nebuchadnezzar burned Jerusalem and deported the Judeans, the Babylonians in their turn fell to the Persians under Cyrus, who allowed the Jews to return home.[21] Because the Judean exile was only fifty years old when Cyrus vanquished the Babylonians, the Judeans who made the fearsome trek across the Syrian Desert back to their ancient homeland easily retained their cultural heritage, which survives to the present day. But this was not true of the northern kingdom's population, who by that point had been in exile for nearly two centuries, long enough to erase their religious and ethnic identity; Israel's ten tribes would remain forever "lost."[22]

By 600 BC, Aramaic became the dominant language and script of the Land Between the Rivers, and it bound together the Babylonians and the subject peoples they had sent into exile there. It became the lingua franca first of the Mesopotamian empires and then of the Persian Empire, and it would later battle Greek and Latin for linguistic dominance in the Middle East.[23]

Why was Aramaic so successful? The French physician turned historian Georges Roux ascribed the dominance of the language of the Aramaeans

> partly to the sheer weight of their number and partly to the fact that they adopted, instead of the cumbersome cuneiform writing, the Phoenician alphabet slightly modified, and carried everywhere with them the simple, practical script of the future. As early as the eighth century BC Aramaic language and writing competed with the Akkadian language and script in Assyria, and thereafter gradually spread throughout the Orient.[24]

The Aramaeans also, for the first time in the ancient world, began to separate their words, not only with small spaces, but also by inventing a "final" form for letters when they were used at the end of a word, which also denoted a word space.[25]

Sometime toward the end of the second millennium BC, the Aramaeans evolved into a trading people who occupied the corridor between the Phoenicians in the west and the Mesopotamians in the east. The utility of their new script became immediately apparent to the Assyrians, Babylonians, and Persians, and to their subject peoples. A famous biblical passage attests to the use of Aramaic as the diplomatic language of the Middle East as early as the end of the eighth century BC, when Jerusalem was besieged by the Assyrian king. His cupbearer Rab-shakeh approaches the city to demand surrender. Hezekiah's representatives beg Rab-shakeh to speak to them in Aramaic, the diplomatic language of the day, so Judah's citizens will not understand their desperate situation. The cupbearer, however, springs a surprise: speaking in Hebrew, he urges Jerusalem's citizens to capitulate and reveals to the city's population how dire the situation has become.[26]

At first, Assyrians and Babylonians wrote summaries of their cuneiform tablets in the compact Aramaic script along their thicker outside edges, like the spines of modern books, so that their contents could be ascertained while the tablets were stacked. Gradually, Aramaic script spread to the inside of the tablets, which over time evolved into an all-Aramaic format.[27]

Another reason for the spread of the script may simply have been the commercial vitality of the Aramaeans, who were to the deserts of the northern Levantine region what the Phoenicians were to the sea, trading

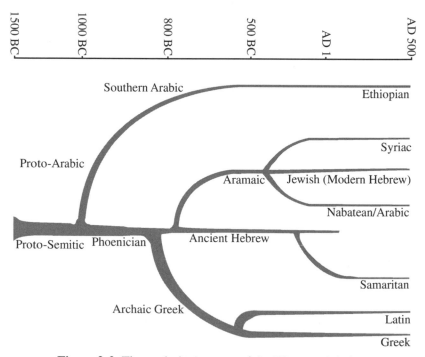

Figure 2-3. The evolutionary tree of the Western alphabets.

particularly in copper, ivory, incense, and textiles of all descriptions. Whatever the reason, with each change of political dominance, from Assyrian to Babylonian, and from Babylonian to Persian, Aramaic only became more prominent.

Sometime around 525 BC, the Persians began to experiment with an alphabetic form of cuneiform, the "old Persian" script decoded by Rawlinson. This innovation was short-lived; Darius I, the second successor to Cyrus and author of the Bisitun inscriptions, ultimately discarded it in favor of Aramaic as the language of his empire. Aramaic remained the lingua franca in the Middle East until it was eclipsed, first by Greek in the wake of Alexander's conquests, and then by Arabic in the seventh century after Christ, following Islam's initial conquests.

The Jews did not migrate back to Palestine all at once upon their emancipation by Cyrus in 539 BC. Among the most important later returnees was a group led by the prophet Ezra, who was also a scribe and who probably came to Jerusalem about 450 BC. He bore the now familiar square Aramaic alphabet, which he spread along with his influence in Palestine. It rapidly supplanted the original Hebrew alphabet, and within a few centuries spoken Hebrew largely disappeared along with it, living on only, as Sumerian before it and Latin after it, in liturgy.[28]

As influential as the Aramaic script became, it would be the simplicity and elegance of Greek letters that would change the very nature of human politics. The first literate people to occupy Greece, the Mycenaeans, settled the region around 1600 BC, and, like the Egyptians and Mesopotamians, they employed a syllabic script, so-called Linear B (derived from the Minoan Linear A). As in Mesopotamia and Egypt, this writing served only administrative and record-keeping purposes, and it vanished when this civilization mysteriously disappeared around 1100 BC. The region remained illiterate throughout the subsequent Greek "Dark Age," which would end with the arrival of Phoenicians on the Aegean scene.

The Phoenicians were one of the world's first peoples to engage in direct, long-distance commerce; the Bible records that their vessels returned from India with large amounts of gold around 950 BC, and Herodotus relates an astonishing Phoenician circumnavigation of Africa around 600 BC.[29] Sometime after 800 BC, one of their vessels traveled from Phoenicia to Greece with an even more precious cargo: the Phoenician script, derived from the proto-Semitic.

Only the precise timing and geography of this transfer stir debate among specialists, who have long noted that the first Greek inscriptions, which date to roughly the eighth century BC, strongly resemble the Phoenician script of the same era. Phoenician traders, the only people at that time capable of routinely braving the entirety of the Great Sea, must have effected this fateful transfer of information technology.[30]

The Greeks, however, made one critical change to the Phoenician system: they converted several unneeded consonant symbols into vowels, thus eliminating nearly all the phonemic ambiguity of all of the older alphabetic systems. As discussed in the Introduction and Chapter 1, syllabic systems, with their hundreds of symbols, took upwards of a decade to master; consonant-only Semitic systems needed perhaps five years, as evidenced by the use of vowel markings in modern Israeli education until students are about age ten, by which point the vowel markings are abandoned. (Not a few Israelis regret that everyday Hebrew script lacks vowels, which the father of novelist Amos Oz piquantly called "the traffic police of reading.")[31] The average Western child, by contrast, can achieve functional literacy in the unambiguous consonantal/vowel environment of Latin, Greek, or Cyrillic script within a year or two; so, presumably, could the average child in ancient Greece.

Around the same time that the Phoenicians imparted their alphabet to the Greeks, the Egyptian pharaoh granted the Greeks the trading city of Naucratis in the Nile Delta. The Greeks' main interest in Egypt was grain for feeding the burgeoning Greek population; but along with grain, traders carried another treasure across the sea: papyrus on which to write their new alphabet.[32]

This combination of papyrus and a vowel-and-consonant alphabet allowed, for the first time in human history, the potential for mass literacy. Imagine a world in which the storage of information is primarily oral. Think first about the parlor game "Whisper Down the Alley," in which a simple sentence becomes hopelessly garbled by the time it is passed to the third or fourth person. Modern historians estimate that preliterate societies can accurately retain historical information for no more than three generations—not much more than the living memory of a single long-surviving individual.[33] Given the extreme fragility of memory for normal conversational speech, how, in the absence of writing, are a family's, a tribe's, or even a nation's essential narratives and skills preserved over the generations and centuries?

By the use of the mnemonics implicit in poetic structure: meter, rhyme, repetition, and the incessant use of stereotyped adjectives. In short, with poetry. Ulysses sailed, not over mere waters, but over the wine-dark sea; the handsome hero of the Trojan War was not just Achilles, but swift-footed Achilles. Further, the storytellers seemed uninterested in character development, at least by means of dialogue; in many instances, the speeches of major characters in the Homeric epics are nearly interchangeable.[34] Technical expertise in storytelling also factors in strongly: in preliterate societies, the art of the oral narrative becomes a skilled and valued craft, a feat of memory and performance requiring years of training for the aspiring storyteller.

In the early twentieth century, Harvard classicist Milman Parry noted with great interest the repetition and stylized epithets that saturated the Homeric epics. He further noted that each epithet appeared in the same part of each hexameter line, and if the character had to be mentioned in a different part of the line, a different epithet was used. He realized that Homer—if Homer existed at all—was almost certainly not an "author" in the modern sense, especially since the epics originated in Greece's preliterate Dark Age. Rather, "Homer" was one storyteller or more than one—perhaps many—who used poetic/narrative devices to keep the story lines of the *Iliad* and the *Odyssey* more or less intact throughout the ages until these epics finally reached the safe harbor of ink and papyrus around the seventh century BC.

A relative of Odysseus who wished to contact him had only one choice: since the *Odyssey* took place in an illiterate age, a letter could not be sent to or received from the peripatetic hero; rather, the relative would have to get on a ship, sail the wine-dark seas, and find him. In the words of classicist Jennifer Wise, "With little exaggeration, it could be said that the entirety of the Odyssey ultimately boils down to one simple technological problem: the epic hero's inability to write home."[35]

Milman Parry's mentor at the Sorbonne, the linguist Antoine Meillet, suggested that Parry travel to the Balkans, an area of widespread illiteracy, and also home to the last traditional folk storytellers in Europe, to observe how they learned their craft. Tragically, Parry died of an accidental gunshot wound soon after he returned from Yugoslavia, but his assistant Alfred Lord carried on his work. Eventually, Lord produced the celebrated *The Singer of Tales,* a detailed description of the years of apprenticeship served by aspiring Yugoslav storytellers, a process likely similar to that undergone by the original tellers of the *Iliad* and the *Odyssey.*[36]

Oral societies, which must of necessity embed information in a complex matrix of meter, rhyme, repetition, and epithet, differ fundamentally from literate societies, in which information can be quickly encoded with a few strokes of the pen or keyboard and then just as rapidly forgotten. Ethnographers and anthropologists almost universally remark on the extraordinary retentive powers of storytellers in oral societies. When the Tahitians alphabetized their language in 1805, some of the first of them to master literacy were said to easily memorize entire books of the New Testament. Even today, the ability of many in Islamic and Indian societies to retain word for word large swaths of literature, particularly traditional and religious texts, amazes Westerners.[37]

In ancient Greece, the change from oral to written transmission was by no means immediate; the writings of Solon, who laid down some of the first democratic Athenian reforms around 600 BC, are largely in verse. After that time, in the words of the French paleographer Henri-Jean Martin, "All subsequent works among the Greeks and Latins had an author and a birth certificate as soon as they were written."[38] By the time of Plato, in the early to middle fourth century BC, prose had become well established.

Certainly, among the Greeks, and perhaps earlier among the Phoenicians, Hebrews, and Aramaic speakers, something profound had occurred: writing had ceased being the exclusive realm of a professional class—in this case, the scribes. Almost by definition, the term "profession" implies the scarcity of a skill; in the ancient world, the scribe was someone in possession of a rare ability. In the future, other rare communication skills and abilities—particularly the production of books and of print and broadcast journalism—would become more available to the general public, and this would provoke an often fierce backlash by professional castes now shorn of their long-standing privilege and status.

Yet in the fifth century BC, the Greeks themselves commented little on the literacy revolution taking place in their midst, either as to its nature or as to its consequences. The modern historian searches Plato and Aristotle in vain for any expression of pride in, or at least any awareness of, the growing literacy and the political changes it must have wrought. Instead, when the Greeks comment on education in their city-states, we find only lengthy descriptions of military training or of the societal importance of music and gymnastics. The most authoritative modern expert on literacy in ancient Greece, William Harris, notes that while the later Hellenistic Greeks and the Romans occasionally mentioned the literacy of individuals, the classical Greeks almost never did.[39]

The new literacy evoked recorded commentary in only one area of Greek life: theater. Scores of plays, both comic and tragic, mention all modes of writing, from scrolls to inscriptions to waxed tablets. The new communications technology seems to have obsessed the playwrights. Sophocles, Aristophanes, and Euripides all had actors mime letter shapes with their bodies. One of Callas's plays, known only from a few surviving fragments, featured the alphabet itself in the starring role, with members of the chorus, like Village People, miming letters with their bodies, both singly and in syllabic pairs: "Beta alpha, ba; beta epsilon, be; beta eta, bē . . ." and so forth.[40] This production is flippantly known as the "ABC show" among classicists, who have speculated that the actors mimed and danced the letters of the new alphabet with pornographic effect.[41]

The impact of literacy in Greek theater ran in both directions. From the audience's perspective, the playwrights crammed so many literary allusions into their productions that Aristophanes joked that those attending the performances, presumably drawn from the Athenian upper classes, came well prepared: "Each a book of the words is holding; never a single point they'll miss."[42]

At the same time, from the performers' perspectives, literacy itself transformed and expanded their very art. As late as the sixth century BC, public renditions of the orally derived classics, prime among which were the Homeric epics, were "staged" in the traditional fashion: by a solo performer who simply recounted the narrative in formulaic verse.

Sometime in the late sixth century, a resident of Icaria (just north of Athens) named Thespis invented a radically new mode of performance. First, he applied his dramatic talent to the actual *creation* of new plots and characters, not merely using those from previous oral traditions. And were that not innovation enough, instead of merely narrating a story, he then *pretended that he was those characters*. This concept of converting storyteller into character must have proved so daunting that the recruitment of additional actors into the performance far exceeded the imagination of even this great innovator. (Thespis's plays are thought to have consisted of dialogues between one main character and a chorus.)

In order to assume his roles, Thespis initially applied a white lead paste to his face. Too clumsy, too slow. Next, he hid his face with flowers: too flimsy, not realistic enough. Finally, he settled on individual linen masks, which his successors, particularly the playwright and actor Aeschylus, often dyed and painted in vivid colors, to terrifying effect.[43] Further, with a permanent written script, his characters could speak in prosaic, everyday language. In short, Thespis became the first playwright and the first actor, and his very name became synonymous in most Western tongues with both actors and acting.

Needless to say, given the vagaries of human memory, without the ability to permanently record words, there can be no soliloquy and no dialogue; indeed, there can be no playwright. Furthermore, without soliloquy and dialogue, there can be little character development.

The written script thus broadened the complexity of character development and dialogue, and this broadening in turn greatly increased the logistic demands of the performance, particularly of the relatively large choruses of Greek dramas and comedies. By the fifth century BC, two of the major Athenian festivals—the Lenaia and City Dionysia—revolved around dramatic competitions. These festivals consumed such a large part of the city-state's budget that the Festival Fund evolved into one of the most powerful Athenian political institutions, and its commissioners were chosen by direct popular ballot—not by random lot, as were most lesser officials.[44] (The only other major officials elected by popular ballot in Athens were the ten *strategoi*, or generals; and the chief magistrates, that is, the archons.)

Even so, these productions required additional private money from well-endowed benefactors. Just as Athens' wealthy citizens, known as "trierarchs," funded and often commanded the massive and expensive hundred-oared trireme warships, so, too, did other rich citizens—*choregoi*—fund and direct the theatrical choruses.

Alas, history dealt Thespis the short straw: none of his plays survived; only his techniques remain. The intensity of the dramatic competitions in

Athens attested to the output of its greatest dramatists: Sophocles is said to have written 123 plays; Aeschylus, about 80; and Euripides, about 95; respectively, only 7, 7, and 17 have survived. Euripides' relatively good historical fortune resulted from the discovery of a single intact medieval volume, presumably one of several, containing all the plays with titles beginning with the Greek letters eta through kappa.

It is humbling to realize that such a prodigious output arose from, and was aimed at, such a small population base. At its height in the middle of the fifth century BC, Athens had only about a quarter million residents, and fewer still in its urban center. Even among this small audience, only a minority possessed what we would today call literacy: the ability both to read and write fluently. The scarcity of objective data on the topic—much of which derives from the hints in Greek drama discussed above—has led to estimates of Athenian literacy ranging from a few percent to "near-universal." The consensus falls in the range of 5 to 10 percent for the entire population of Attica, but this estimate implies a much higher rate among male citizens, perhaps around 25 to 50 percent. Only among the Athenian elite was literacy near-universal.[45]

This should not surprise us. Although the Greeks had solved many of the abstract hindrances to literacy that plagued their ancient predecessors, they had not overcome all of them. One in particular that persisted was *scriptura continua*—a nearly total lack of punctuation, and even of word, sentence, and paragraph breaks. Further, the Greeks had made no progress in overcoming the mechanical hindrances to literacy: the difficulty of working in stone, the expense of papyrus, the absence of the printing press, and the lack of universal education. In the early fifth century BC, a roll of papyrus, consisting of about twenty sheets, cost between one and three drachmas—that is, one to three days' wages for a semiskilled worker.

Of all the world's peoples, the Greeks may have written on the widest range of materials: not only on papyrus, but also on gold, silver, bronze, pots and pot fragments, wood, wax, and even thin sheets of lead, which, since they could be easily folded and placed in coffins, were used to transmit curses to the underworld.[46]

In the predominantly oral societies of the ancient world, the reader declaimed aloud to the group; not until the early modern period, centuries *after* the invention of the printing press, would large numbers of people acquire the modern habit of rapid silent reading. Still, by the standards of the ancient world, the Greeks had wrought a revolution in communication; the new literacy brought with it new philosophical and logical constructs, and a new concept of theatrical performance to boot.

The advance of literacy in Greece was accompanied by a revolution in politics. Sometime around the middle of the seventh century BC, Athens began its long, gradual, and occasionally stuttering march toward ever-greater diffusion of political power among its population. By around 650 BC, the leading families of Athens had amalgamated the city and surrounding countryside, collectively known as Attica, into a cohesive city-state. Initially, each year these aristocrats elected a single chief magistrate—the archon. Next, the archonship was divided into three offices—one each for political, military, and religious affairs. Not long after, the Athenians added six more archons to record the law for all citizens to read; thus it is likely that all archons had to be literate. (Confusingly, classicists commonly refer to the "political," or chief, archon as *the* archon; henceforth in this text, the singular form of this word refers to this particular official.)

As these nine aristocrats rotated out of office each year, they joined the real locus of power in early Athens, the Areopagus (roughly, the high court), for life. Although all free citizens could participate in the Assembly, it held little power. In actuality, only a few families controlled the political process, largely through the Areopagus, and this leadership exerted power in no small part through one preferred instrument: expulsion, or the threat of expulsion, from the city.

Upon being expelled, the losing party took up exile in a neighboring city and immediately began to plot, with both domestic and foreign allies, his return. Thereupon followed a never-ending cycle in which the expelled replaced the expellers. By the late seventh century BC, Athenians began to weary of this instability, and they invested the archon Draco with the authority to devise a written legal code to mitigate the turmoil. His extraordinarily strict system of laws (hence the word "draconian"), alas, did not stop the expulsions.[47]

In the early sixth century BC, Athens gave another archon, Solon, much the same mandate. His laws also failed to stop the expulsions, but by means of these written laws, for the first time accessible to an increasing number of literate citizens, Athens got its first real democratic reforms.

Solon's reforms gave citizens the right to prosecute on behalf of the public good—the *graphē*. Needless to say, while any citizen could exercise this privilege, it required an understanding of the written law—the very term *graphē,* which derives from the Greek verb "to write," embodies the link between widespread literacy and political empowerment.

In preliterate societies, the magistrate himself embodied the law, and in subsequent ancient societies in which a small elite could read and interpret the written code, the balance of power still heavily favored the person in the chamber able to decode the tablets. When Athenian litigants began to wield the power of their simple alphabet, the rights of ordinary citizens expanded greatly.

In the seventh and sixth centuries BC, then, Athens slowly acquired institutions that allowed "ordinary" citizens the tools with which to wield political power. Nonetheless, the expulsions continued, and power remained highly concentrated among a continually shifting, unstable mix of rival elites. After a long series of coups, expulsions, and exile-driven countercoups, one family, the Alcmaeonids, wound up in control around 508 BC.[48] This aristocratic family, an ancient version of the Kennedys, produced generations of politicians and soldiers, most famously Pericles. They wisely allied themselves with the middle classes and enacted a series of laws, known as the "Cleisthenic reforms" after the Alcmaeonid, Cleisthenes, who devised them. These changes produced the commonly recognized features of the famous Athenian democracy, and they did so by, for the first time, codifying and institutionalizing exile into two separate procedures: ostracism and expulsion.

The first process, ostracism, required no well defined offending act. Loosely speaking, its most common rationale seemed to involve the target's "growing too big for his britches," and ostracism may even have been considered, at least in some quarters, an honor. Each winter, the Assembly held a vote that determined *if* an ostracism would be held. If that vote passed, then the Assembly decided two months later *who* would be ostracized. If, and only if, a quorum of six thousand was present for the second vote, the "winner" was expelled for ten years, following which he came back with full privileges; in the interim, his property was held in trust.[49]

The Athenians tended to ostracize only their best and brightest. For example, when the Athenian Hyperbolus was ostracized in 415 BC, contemporary observers scoffed that he was not worthy of the honor, since he did not belong to the landed class.[50] Citizens *wrote* the names of candidates for ostracism on the ostraca described in the Introduction;

consequently, archaeologists have acquired a compendium of those considered for the process, and the list reads like a Who's Who of Athenian politics.

Among those actually ostracized were Thucydides, for falling short during command of a naval campaign during the Peloponnesian War; and Aristides, who was cast out around 482 BC after valiantly serving the city in multiple capacities, most notably at Marathon. According to Plutarch, the following occurred at Aristides's ostracism:

> As the voters were inscribing their *ostraca,* it is said that an unlettered and utterly boorish fellow handed his *ostracon* to Aristides, whom he took to be one of the ordinary crowd, and asked him to write *Aristides* on it. He, astonished, asked the man what possible harm Aristides had done him. "None whatever," was the answer, "I do not even know the fellow, but I am tired of hearing him everywhere called 'the just.'"[51]

By requiring six thousand ballots—a fair percentage of citizens—the ostracism process depended upon widespread, if rudimentary, literacy among at least a substantial minority of citizens. Were all, or even a majority, of this quorum able to read and write at a basic level? The thousands of ostraca in the archaeological record do cast some doubt on the notion of widespread Athenian literacy. One archaeologist found 191 ostraca inscribed with Themistocles' name and concluded that they had been written by just fifteen people, the clear implication being that they had been premanufactured.[52]

Were ostraca premanufactured because illiterate citizens required them for "ballot-stuffing" campaigns, or merely because even literate citizens appreciated the convenience of instant ballots? All things considered, it seems unlikely that this institution could have functioned as smoothly as it did in a society in which only a few literate citizens were able to make informed decisions about whom to cast out, and consequently would have been easily manipulated by the wealthy and powerful.

Archaeologist Eugene Vanderpool imagined the technical process surrounding an ostracism vote as follows:

> The party heelers assigned the job of collecting sherds very sensibly decided to go to the source—the potter's shop—and get them from his dump of broken or discarded pots. . . . Other heelers were summoned, were shown the pile of sherds and were told to sit down and write the

name of Themistocles on as many pieces as they could. On Ostracism
Day each took as many sherds as he could conveniently carry, went
down to the Agora and circulated among the crowds, handing out his
ready-made *ostraca* to any who wanted one.[53]

Such finds demonstrate the telltale signs of widespread but imperfect
literacy, such as nearly constant variations in and errors of spelling and
even in the direction of writing. In addition, ostraca writers frequently
added extraneous comments, such as the reasons for the vote or merely
some variation of "Out with him!"

Well-defined high crimes—corruption and treason—could be answered with permanent expulsion, confiscation of property, and execution,
but this, too, required formal judicial criminal proceedings. Athenian juries
consisted of several hundred citizens each, thus preventing the elite from
meting out arbitrary punishment.

Aristotle describes in some detail the voting procedure for civil and
criminal cases: Officials assigned each juror a colored staff so that he
could find his way to the proper court. Officials limited the pleadings "by
the clock," that is, a water clock. In a civil case involving more than five
thousand drachmas, each side was allowed two speeches: ten gallons of
water for the first, and three for the last; the less money involved, the less
water allotted.

At the conclusion of each case, the jurors' staffs were exchanged for
two bronze disks: one pierced with a hollow stem, signifying a vote for
the plaintiff, the other pierced with a solid stem, signifying a vote for the
defendant. Carefully keeping his hand closed to ensure secrecy, the juror
then placed the "active" vote in a brass urn and the "discarded" vote in a
wooden urn. In addition, each urn was carefully crafted so that only one
disk could be inserted at a time. After the juror had disposed of his two
disks, he received in return a brass disk on which the number three was
inscribed, his voucher for the three obol (one-half drachma) jury fee.[54]

Aristophanes' *Wasps*, a comedy focused largely on the Athenian
jury system, makes clear the centrality of literacy in that system. Of the
enthusiastic juror Philocleon, his slave complains, "He is a merciless judge,
never failing to draw the convicting line and return home with his nails
full of wax [from writing on wax-covered tablets] like a bumble-bee."[55]
(The Michael Moore of his day, Aristophanes satirized the ease with which

the jury and assembly could be influenced by demagogues, his favorite target being the lowborn, real-world demagogue Cleon: hence the name of *Wasps'* protagonist, Philocleon.)

Unsurprisingly, playwrights often found themselves legal targets; Cleon took Aristophanes to court, just as two generations before Aeschylus was prosecuted for supposedly revealing religious secrets onstage. In both cases, the playwrights' literary skills secured their successful defense.[56]

Ostracism and expulsion, both democracy-based and literacy-dependent processes, became rule-bound, legitimate, and infrequent; the overwhelming majority of ostracisms occurred in the half century following the Cleisthenic reforms, and almost none in the last century of Athens' independent existence. Today we realize that one bedrock principle of democracy is the limitation of official power; the mere presence of formalized writing-based institutions in Athens meant that the rich and powerful could no longer embroil the city in an endless cycle of mass expulsion and civil war.

The Cleisthenic reforms, besides taming the scourge of indiscriminate expulsion, started Athens down a road of increasing democratization that did not cease until the conquests of Alexander two centuries later. These reforms increased the number of "tribes" from four to ten, each of which elected fifty members of the Council (Boule). The four original tribes may have possessed a kinship/hereditary character, but the Cleisthenic reforms almost certainly intended the ten new ones to function only as civic units,

Figure 2-4. Bronze jury ballots; the hollow stemmed ballot on the far left signifies a vote for the plaintiff; the solid stemmed ones, a vote for the defendant.

much like modern political wards. The Boule prepared the issues to be addressed in the Assembly, which ultimately decided the important military, legal, and economic business of the state. Finally, in the middle fifth century BC, the Areopagus, which was dominated by the aristocracy, was stripped of all but its ceremonial power. The Assembly and Boule were at least theoretically open to all citizens, and increasing literacy translated into more public participation and democratization.

The tribes also elected by ballot archons, *strategoi,* and the festival commissioners, all of whom needed highly specific skill sets for their critical posts. The elected position of *strategos* carried with it political as well as military power, since, unlike other officials, the most successful commanders could serve numerous terms. Consequently, the ranks of the *strategoi* include the most famous names in Greek history: Aristides, Themistocles, Thucydides, Pericles, and Demosthenes. For all practical purposes, "civilian leadership" in the modern sense did not exist in Athens; after the Cleisthenic reforms, virtually all of its great politicians served multiple terms as *strategoi.* Such prominence, in turn, almost inevitably made them targets for punishment at the hands of an increasingly literate public.

Every year the tribes also selected six thousand citizens by lot for jury duty. The juries were then broken into panels of several hundred. Lots were also drawn to assign ordinary citizens to serve in the mundane, technocratic machinery of government. Each year the ten tribes randomly chose one of their members to serve on the Commission for Public Contracts, which, among its other tasks, kept track of taxes, executed court-ordered confiscations of property, and leased out public mines.[57]

Athens also chose by lot "the Eleven," who oversaw the arrest of prisoners and—when these sentences were ordered by the courts—their jailing and execution. State slaves, who during the fifth and fourth centuries BC mainly consisted of around three hundred Scythian archers, performed the actual dirty work under the Eleven's orders.

Each tribe also selected, in rotation and by lot, a city commissioner whose duty was

to see that female flute- and harp- and lute-players are not hired at more than two drachmas, and if more than one person is anxious to hire the same girl, they cast lots and hire her out to the person to whom the lot falls. They also provide that no collector of sewage shall shoot any of his sewage within ten stradia of the walls. They prevent people from blocking up the streets by building, or stretching barriers across them, or making drain-pipes in mid-air with a discharge into the street, or having doors which open outwards. They also remove the corpses of those who die in the streets, for which purpose they have a body of state slaves assigned to them.[58]

The all-inclusive Assembly, which met about forty days per year, decided the key policy and military issues. Someone with the oratorical skill to sway opinion—a *rhētōr*, literally, "talker"—wielded the greatest power. (Contrariwise, the Athenians expressed their disdain for someone who remained silent in the Assembly through the name used to describe him: *idiōtēs*.) Debate, and particularly procedural maneuvering, carried real risks; any Assembly member who violated these rules could be indicted for the lapse, the most common of which was known as a *graphē paranomōm*, the making of an illegal proposal.

A term as a *strategos* or an archon provided the vital debating and parliamentary skills necessary to wield influence in the Assembly. Obviously, while no literacy requirement is known for any position, the ability to read and interpret laws, to understand accounts, and to follow agendas would prove essential to a citizen to wield influence in such a meritocratic environment.[59]

The epic life of one of the greatest of Greek heroes, the *strategos* Themistocles, provides a lens through which to understand the nexus of citizenship, democratic politics, and literacy in ancient Athens.

Probably born to upper-class parents around 524 BC, Themistocles was a clever, impetuous youth who forsook the musical instruments and idleness of his peers to burnish his rhetorical skills. When taunted by his more aristocratic classmates about his lack of musical ability, he replied that he would rather use his hands to make a small city great than to tune a lyre or handle a harp.[60] Which is exactly what he did.

Recall the story of Oroetes, Polycrates, and Darius. Along with the capture of Sardis by Cyrus in the sixth century BC, the Persians had subjugated the Greek city-states on the mainland of Asia Minor (western Turkey) and on the islands lying off it. The Ionians, a linguistically and culturally homogeneous group of Greeks who inhabited many of these Persian-occupied city-states, revolted around 499 BC. Athens, also founded by Ionians, aided and abetted its brethren's ultimately unsuccessful cause, and thereby provoked the massive Persian invasion of mainland Greece several years later. This titanic clash of civilizations—the Persian Wars—engulfed the entire Greek world.

After the Ionian Revolt finally collapsed in 494 BC, the Persians sent emissaries to the Greek city-states demanding gifts of earth and water, signifying submission. The Athenians buried the Persian messengers alive in a pit—the punishment for common criminals. The Spartans went one better and took their Persians to a well, told them that this was the best place to find earth and water, and then tossed them into it.[61] Not long after, in 493–492 BC, Themistocles ascended to the high office of archon, just after he attained the age of thirty—the qualifying age for the post. Foreseeing the approaching Persian hurricane, he moved the main port of Athens from Phaleron Bay to more easily protected Piraeus.

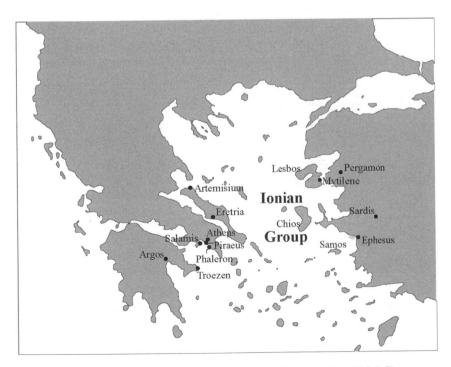

Figure 2-5. Ancient Greece in the classical period (ca. 500 BC).

The Persians invaded the mainland in 490 BC and made fast work of the city-state of Eretria, which, like Athens, had sent warships and troops in support of the Ionian Revolt. Darius burned its temples, carried its populace off into slavery, and then set his sights on Athens, choosing the plain of Marathon—which as every modern running enthusiast knows, is about twenty-six miles east of the city—as his beachhead for its conquest.

Miltiades, the Athenian commander at Marathon, executed a brilliant tactical retreat in the center of his battle line, which allowed his forces to encircle and defeat the Persians. Themistocles, who had participated in the battle in a subordinate position, returned to Athens restless and uneasy. He was restless because he had achieved too little glory at Marathon. According to Plutarch, "the generalship of Miltiades was in everybody's mouth," but subsequent events demonstrated the fickleness of Athenian politics. Soon after Marathon, Miltiades led an unsuccessful mission against Paros, an island city-state which had supported the Persians by sending them a warship. For this failure, he was brought up on charges of "deceiving the people" and fined fifty talents—about three thousand pounds—of silver.

Themistocles was uneasy because he also understood, as many of his countrymen did not, that the Battle of Marathon had not ended the Persian Wars—not by a long shot. So distraught was Themistocles that he refused even to drink and carouse with friends.

In 480 BC, the Persians returned, as Themistocles had known they would. The Greeks could do little against the Persians' massive onslaught save for a few delaying actions: the disastrous slaughter of the cream of Sparta's troops at Thermopylae, and an equally fruitless stand by the Athenian fleet, now under the command of Themistocles, at nearby Artemisium. The Greeks repaired south, leaving their homeland defenseless before the victorious barbarians from the east.

What Athens did next is vividly described by a marble inscription recently found in a coffeehouse in the city of Troezen, in the northeast Peloponnese, across the Saronic Gulf from the city:

> This decree was passed by the [Council] and by the [Asscmbly]; Themistocles, the son of Neocles, of Phrearrhioi, proposed it; The city is to be entrusted to [the gods]. . . . Children and women are to be taken to Troezen. . . . Old men and [slaves] are to be taken to Salamis; treasurers and priestesses are to remain on the Acropolis watching

over the things of the gods; all other Athenians and foreigners of military age are to embark on two hundred ships, which have been made ready, and ward off the foreign enemy for the sake of freedom, both their own and that of the other Greeks.[62]

Themistocles realized that the Greeks had only one chance in the face of nearly certain doom: avoid a land battle with the vastly superior army of Persia and instead draw its fleet into the narrow waters between the Attic mainland and the island of Salamis, where the heavier but less maneuverable Greek ships held the advantage. Indeed, Themistocles triumphed in just this way: he persuaded Athens' reluctant allies to join him, tricked the Persians into fighting at Salamis, and prevailed in a naval battle that gave maximum advantage to the ponderous but lethal Greek triremes.

He returned to Athens with the glory that had eluded him at Marathon, and he was lionized even more in Sparta than in his native city. After Salamis, the Spartans awarded Themistocles olive branches, and they also bestowed upon him a chariot, "the finest in Sparta." He was then escorted back to the Athenian frontier by three hundred handpicked hoplites—this number being symbolic of their number fallen at Thermopylae—"the only person we know of who ever received the honor of an escort from the Spartans," according to Herodotus.[63]

In the afterglow of Salamis, Themistocles went on to hold many important Athenian offices, which enabled him to complete the fortification of both Athens and Piraeus. He intentionally concealed these works from the Spartans, thus angering them. An even more potent hindrance to his career was the perverse logic of Athenian politics, which dictated that his triumph only made his countrymen fearful of his growing power and influence. In the end, it would be this growing Spartan animosity, combined with the Athenian mistrust of successful politicians, that ended his political career at Athens.

Around this time, Pausanias, a traitorous Spartan general, and Themistocles spoke or at least wrote to each other. The Spartans used the communication between the two generals to impugn Themistocles' loyalty to the Greek cause, but no evidence ever surfaced that the two had actually conspired against their homelands. Sometime around 471 BC, nearly a decade after the naval battle at Salamis, domestic opponents of Themistocles seized upon these Spartan fabrications to have him ostracized.

Our slandered hero chose nearby Argos as his place of refuge. At this point Pausanias supposedly asked Themistocles to join him in his collusion with the Persians: Themistocles refused, but kept the episode secret. After the death of Pausanias, the Spartans came across letters between the two generals and demanded that Themistocles be tried for treason, a capital offense that by Greek custom would be adjudicated by a congress of several city-states.

Themistocles understood that he could not obtain a fair trial in such circumstances, and so embarked on an odyssey that took him across the length and breadth of Greece. Finding no refuge there, he eventually obtained shelter in the service of Xerxes's successor, his son Artaxerxes I. Themistocles' flight to Susa was certainly a calculated risk; initially, given his role at Salamis, the Persians did not exactly greet him with open arms. His political and intellectual skills, nonetheless, enabled him to learn Persian late in life and gain such influence at court that Artaxerxes made him governor of several satraps in Asia Minor; subsequently, upon being ordered to attack the Greek mainland, he supposedly committed suicide with a draught of bull's blood.[64]

It is remarkable that the Athenians cast out, on what seems to be the flimsiest of evidence, the man who had saved Athens, and, arguably, Western civilization as well, to say nothing of other heroes, such as Miltiades, the victor at Marathon. Amazingly, Athens ostracized, or at least attempted to ostracize, nearly *all* its greatest leaders.

Ostracism puzzles and at times outrages Western readers; much of the wariness of the American founding fathers of direct participatory democracy originates from this ancient institution. John Adams, for example, wrote of ostracism:

> History nowhere furnishes so frank a confession of the people themselves, of their own infirmities and unfitness for managing the executive branch of government, or an unbalanced share of the legislature, as this institution [ostracism]. . . . What more melancholy spectacle can be conceived even in imagination, than that inconstancy which erects statues to a patriot or a hero one year, banishes him the next, and the third erects fresh statues to his memory?[65]

Adams' disdain aside, the above history demonstrates how the Athenian combination of ostracism, literacy, and unique participatory system of government lay at the heart of its democracy.

Modern readers might well wonder why anyone of ability and ambition bothered with Athenian politics, given the punishments meted out for even the smallest of errors—actual, perceived, or simply manufactured by opponents. During the fourth century BC alone, Athens prosecuted twenty-seven *strategoi* for malfeasance; four were executed, five fled under sentence of death, and others were expelled or heavily fined.[66] Even riskier than generalship was leading a criminal prosecution, a role, open to any citizen, that painted a virtual legal bull's-eye on one's back.

Athenians participated in the process for one simple reason: *timē* (honor). Athenian citizenship, generally open only to those who could claim it from both parents, constituted one of the most sought-after commodities in the ancient world. Athenians measured each other's status not so much in terms of silver or land, but rather according to their performance in the Assembly and on the battlefield; that a citizen risked life and treasure in the process mattered less than the esteem of the polis. The citizen of any Greek city-state best expressed *timē*, of course, by falling in battle for his polis.

Thus, for almost two hundred years, two features, both of which required widespread literacy, lay at the center of Athenian democracy: widespread citizen officeholding that would be impossible in a modern nation-state and the peculiar institutions of ostracism and expulsion. These latter processes served as safety valves that prevented the undue accumulation of power by removing from the city-state those who might threaten its democracy. It is difficult to imagine officeholders randomly drawn from a largely illiterate populace maintaining a more or less orderly city-state for the better part of two centuries, and it is equally difficult to imagine the processes of ostracism and judicial expulsion functioning smoothly in an illiterate environment.

Although America's founding fathers did not think much of Athenian "radical democracy," and thought particularly ill of ostracism, even cursory consideration of the city-state's history shows that its politics grew ever more stable and inclusive between the Cleisthenic reforms of the late sixth century BC and the city's conquest by the Macedonians in the late fourth.[67] True, in 411 BC, and again in 404 BC, tyrannical Athenian regimes captured power, the reign of 404 BC proving particularly murderous. Both episodes, however, occurred during the extreme geopolitical stress of the Peloponnesian War. Both oligarchic interludes proved remarkably brief, and the democratic institutions of Athens, and its respect for the rule of law, seemed to grow continuously stronger right up to the moment that Macedonia's army overpowered the city and overturned its constitution.

To its very end, Athenian democracy remained robust, destroyed not from within but by foreign military force. Ostracism, rather than being a blot on the political life of Athens, prevented the undue accumulation of power in a few hands and constituted the cement that held its democracy together even as it paradoxically fell into disuse because of its own success—a cement whose primary ingredient was widespread literacy.

Likewise, without a critical mass of literate citizens, chosen at random to perform key legislative, judicial, and especially executive duties, it is hard to imagine Athens surviving for very long, let alone rising to the pinnacle of the ancient Greek world. Similarly, those who wished to exert influence in the Assembly and on the battlefield had, of necessity, to acquire literacy and deploy it with skill.

By contrast, in oligarchic Sparta, few read or wrote, as evidenced not only by the frequent observations of Spartan illiteracy by the admittedly chauvinistic Athenians, but also by the scarcity of inscriptions in the southern Peloponnese. Greek tradition suggests that the Spartans forbade the writing down of their laws, and that only the elite—their two kings, five ephors (judges), diplomats, and high military commanders—possessed the literacy demanded by their roles.

Sparta's social structure probably contributed in no small part to this distrust of the written word. Sparta, the largest city-state in Greece, attained its size and prominence through the conquest of the Messenians, who inhabited most of the southern Peloponnesian peninsula. The Spartans enslaved this unfortunate people, who evolved into a vast underclass of so-called helots. Since they greatly outnumbered the relatively small number of Spartan citizens—by some estimates, the ratio was in excess of ten to one—the helots had to be brutally suppressed by means of the *krypteia*. This term had two meanings: the first, a secret police charged with keeping the helots in line; and the second, an annual rite of passage in which young Spartans went out and slaughtered them.

Fear of helot rebellion held the city-state's constant attention, and so the Spartans restricted literacy, lest the power and knowledge it conferred wind up in the wrong hands. The Spartan distrust of literacy entailed denying it not only to the helots, but to the citizen rank and file as well; thus did democracy fail to flourish in the Peloponnese.[68]

Curiously, though official Athens looked with favor upon individual literacy, it seemed indifferent to detailed written records, and this, paradoxically, may have contributed to the city-state's robust democratic institutions. Not until the middle fifth century BC did the city-state establish a central records repository, the Metroon, which served mainly to store laws, treaties, and decisions of the Assembly, and other public documents. Athens largely ignored private data. For example, citizens did not publicly record land sales or surveys, but rather demarcated their property boundaries with simply inscribed stone monuments.

And therein lies the last piece of the puzzle of ancient Greek democratic exceptionalism: unlike the despotic empires of Mesopotamia and Egypt, the "Athenian empire" did not maintain an army of scribes and bureaucrats to deploy the awesome power of the written record to organize and control empires and millions. Instead, the Athenians staffed their offices and ministries with an ever-changing retinue of farmers, merchants, and artisans, most of whom had to be literate. Further, ordinary Athenians could not be cowed by the "magic of the written word" characteristic of illiterate societies.

What was lost in technical efficiency with this less than optimal bureaucratic manpower was more than offset by the freedom from tyranny it afforded ordinary citizens and the avoidance of the institutional sclerosis and corruption characteristic of both ancient and modern scribal elites.

The apparent unwillingness of the classic-era Greek city-states to deploy the full power of the written record ended with Alexander's conquests in 334–323 BC, which resulted in several large successor states following his death: the Seleucid Empire in the Middle East and the Pergamon, Macedonian, and Ptolemaic kingdoms in Asia Minor, Greece, and Egypt, respectively.

The Greek/Egyptian kingdom founded by Alexander's lieutenant Ptolemy provides historians with the world's richest source of papyrus records for at least four reasons. First, Egypt produced nearly all of the world's papyrus. Second, because of the country's dry climate, its papyrus records were preserved better than those from any other ancient civilization. Third, his heirs, the Ptolemies, reigned less than two-and-a-half millennia ago, well within the survivability of papyrus records under optimal conditions. Fourth, the Ptolemies, like their Egyptian and Mesopotamian predecessors, fully grasped the value of written records for command and control.

A simple business transaction in 248 BC provides a flavor of the Ptolemaic penchant for record keeping: in that year, a pig keeper named Petosiris paid to another named Heracleides seventeen piglets in return for a year's rent of ten sows. The fifty-seven-word recorded receipt of this loan survives to this day.[69]

And so it went, all the way up the pyramid of power. Around the same time, Apollonius, Ptolemy II's finance minister, received 434 papyrus rolls in just over a month. To a certain extent, the Greek Ptolemies may have simply inherited the bureaucratic habits of the pharaohs, but the Ptolemies certainly expanded the role of written records in everyday life.

The Ptolemies, like their Greek cousins in Asia Minor and Mesopotamia, ruled with the magic and power of the written document over vast illiterate native populations, a despotism magnified by Egypt's abundant supplies of papyrus. Petosiris was an ethnic Egyptian, and almost certainly could neither read nor write, whereas Heracleides was an ethnic Greek, the agent of a wealthy man named Zeno, and both he and his employer almost certainly could.

No aspect of Ptolemaic literacy captures the modern Western imagination as does the "library" of Alexandria. Its modern narrative goes something like this: After the breakup of Alexander's empire following his death in 323 BC, Athens found itself a virtual satrap under the rule of Demetrius of Phaleron, who had been appointed by the Macedonian king, Cassander. After Cassander's death, Demetrius fled to Alexandria, the grandest of the cities founded by the great conqueror.

Demetrius supposedly built a library of half a million scrolls for the greater glory of the first two Ptolemies, with pride of place given to the works of Aristotle and his students, the Peripatetics (so called because the great philosopher lectured while walking). The library was said to contain the literature and intellectual capital of all nations, diligently translated by its scribes into Greek. Amid this Noah's Ark of knowledge is the Septuagint, the Greek version of the Old Testament, so named because seventy-two Jewish scholars—six from each of the twelve tribes—took seventy-two days to accomplish the task. According to another delightful piece of library mythology, the Ptolemies ordered the seizure of all scrolls from arriving ships, and then had royal scribes repay the theft with hastily written replacement copies.

Alas, the library was destroyed: the villain, depending upon which version of the fable is believed, was Julius Caesar, who set fire to it while under siege in the adjoining royal palace; the Roman emperor Aurelian, who burned it in the course of suppressing a local revolt in the late third century after Christ; the Coptic Pope Theophilus; or the Muslim general Amr—the last two of whom were supposed to have burned the library and/ or its scrolls in the fourth and seventh centuries, respectively, because the writings contained pagan blasphemy.

Needless to say, none of the above has any substantive factual basis. In the first place, the library, to the extent that it existed at all, was not a physical building—no reputable ancient scholar described such a structure. As best historians and classicists can tell, the "library" consisted of a collection of scrolls residing on shelves in the *Musaeum* (the house of the Muses, hence "museum"), itself possibly housed in one of the royal palaces. Second, the library cannot possibly have contained anywhere near half a million scrolls; even if one generously multiplies all of the ancient world's known and reported manuscripts by a factor of ten, the number of possible documents runs perhaps into the tens of thousands, not the hundreds of thousands. Last, none of the primary stories of its destruction check out; for example, the eastern Roman geographer Strabo, to whom we owe the best, if somewhat vague, ancient description of the collection, visited it about a century after Caesar's Egyptian sojourn.

Almost certainly, the library's contents simply fell prey to time's ravages. Alexandria, unlike Egypt's dry interior, is no friend of papyrus, which does not last more than several centuries in its moist coastal climate. In addition, handling papyrus drastically shortens its survival; thus, the more important a document, the more ephemeral its existence.[70]

The grandest version of the library's mythology concludes with Europe plunged into the Dark Ages in the wake of the catastrophic loss of its manuscripts, a canard perpetuated even by eminent scholars. This is unlikely for at least two reasons. In the first place, by late antiquity, the collection at Alexandria had been surpassed by those at Ephesus and Pergamon in Asia Minor. Further, this notion reverses cause and effect; in the words of classicist Roger Bagnall,

It is not that the disappearance of a library led to a dark age, nor
that its survival would have improved those ages. Rather, the dark
ages . . . show their darkness by the fact that the authorities both east
and west lacked the will and the means to maintain a great library.
An unburned building full of decaying books would not have made
a particle's worth of difference.[71]

Certainly, the library little benefited the ordinary Greek citizen of
Alexandria, let alone the vast ethnic Egyptian underclass of Ptolemaic
society. The collection was located deep within the royal palace, and only
a small cadre of scholars, who were, in the words of one ancient observer,
"a breed of bookish scribblers who spend their whole lives pecking away
in the cage of the Muses," had access to it. This tiny elite enjoyed the rich
royal patronage that afforded them free access to its scrolls, along with
a generous living, complimentary meals, and freedom from taxation.[72]

What did these scholars provide in return? Alexander saw himself
as the conqueror not only of men and territory, but also of knowledge;
he planned a huge library in Nineveh, the old Assyrian capital, to house
Greek translations of all of that civilization's major and minor works.[73] The
"scribblers," then, produced the munitions in the great intellectual arms
race of the Hellenistic world, in which Alexander's successors strove to
outshine each other as the rightful heirs of Plato, Demosthenes, and, of
course, Alexander's tutor Aristotle. When the Library of Pergamon in Asia
Minor announced that it had found one of Demosthenes' lost Philippics
(as his speeches against Philip II of Macedon were known), supposedly
delivered a few months before Athens lost its independence at the Battle
of Chaeronea in 338 BC, the Alexandrian scholars swung into full defen-
sive mode: they scoured the library's shelves and gleefully proclaimed
the Pergamon scroll a forgery, clearly plagiarized from a previous minor
work in their possession.[74]

In the end, the rulers of Pergamon had the last laugh. In the middle
second century BC, the rival Ptolemies, in an attempt to cripple the Pergamon library, forbade the export of papyrus. Pergamon's king, Eumenes
II, proved equal to the challenge; about this time, parchment had been
invented at Pergamon, possibly under the direction of Eumenes, who established a large slave-staffed parchment factory to supply the library.
Parchment is far more durable than papyrus, so it seems likely that the

lion's share of the Greek texts that survived into the modern era originated from Pergamon's long-lived parchment volumes, and not from Alexandria's papyrus ones.[75]

Parchment came far more dearly, though, than paper; most precious of all was vellum. So prized were parchment and vellum that older, seldom-used texts were scraped down so that newer texts could be inscribed over them. Yet the faint image of the older text—the palimpsest—often remained, allowing modern scholars a look at some of the earliest known writings.[76]

The successor Hellenist states of Alexander's empire, then, restricted and judiciously meted out their documents as tools of control and awe. By contrast, the earlier rise of Athenian democracy resulted from a happy coincidence in the way it approached literacy and the duties of citizenship; not only did Athens benefit from widespread citizen literacy, but it also avoided the pitfalls of an overbearing, literacy-wielding bureaucracy.

In the middle of the first millennium BC, literacy-fueled institutions such as widespread officcholding and ostracism enabled ordinary Athenian citizens to wield the lever of literacy-derived political power in a way never before imagined. The decline of widespread literacy in the post-Alexandrian empires and, later, in the Roman Empire rang the death knell of democracy in Europe for centuries. This blessing would not return until the elimination of *scriptura continua,* the advent of relatively inexpensive paper, and the printing press—in that order—once again restored this lever, ever so slowly, to the general European populace.

3

TWELVE TABLETS, SEVEN HILLS, AND A FEW EARLY CHRISTIANS

Written procedures assist in control from above; yet they can give those who are underneath a means of asserting their rights. But it is only rather rarely in Rome that the latter possibility comes to the fore.—William V. Harris[1]

During the contentious deliberations of the Constitutional Convention in Philadelphia in 1787, a certain Mrs. Powel asked Benjamin Franklin, "What have we got, a republic or a monarchy?" His famous reply: "A republic—if you can keep it."[2] The disintegration of an earlier republic, Rome, weighed heavily on Dr. Franklin's mind, to say nothing of the chaotic five centuries of tyranny that followed it. While the causes of the Roman Republic's fall were complex and to this day are controversial, one undeniable factor involved the bizarre and lopsided distribution of literacy in the Republic.

A curious Roman "literacy triangle" centered on three groups: the legions, easily the most literate mass institution in the late Republic; the Christians; and most bizarrely, the slaves—particularly Greek slaves— who did much of Rome's writing, and even its reading. The literacy of the legionaries and slaves contributed mightily to the destruction of the ancient world's largest, longest-running, and most successful democratic society, the Roman Republic, while a few centuries later the literacy of the Christians enabled them to triumph over Roman paganism.

In many ways, Rome's democracy resembled the earlier Athenian one in its fundamental aspects; in both, assemblies of soldier-citizens managed civil and military affairs and governed both city-states. Literacy played an important role in the two democracies, particularly in the later Roman Republic, where voting was by secret written ballots. Tragically, the extraordinary degree of literacy in the army, Rome's burgeoning geographic expansion, and the much lower degree of literacy in the newly conquered areas combined to make the literate army the only institution capable of binding the vast new empire together, and so doomed the Republic.

The origins of Roman democracy hark back to the sixth century BC, when legend has it that Rome sent a legation to Athens to learn about Solon's legal reforms, which loosened the noose of debt around the neck of that city-state's poor. Then, as now, debt was a hot-button issue. Until very recently, all societies operated near the subsistence level, with little surplus of cash and goods left after the most basic needs for food and shelter had been satisfied. Spare capital, whether in the form of coins, silver ingots, cattle, or grain, constituted a scarce commodity, and the very few "rich" farmers, merchants, and traders who had some could extract a high price for it.

This scarcity of capital drove its price—that is, its interest rate—sky high. In the earliest agricultural societies, interest rates stood at around 100 percent per year—a calf or a bushel of seed corn was repaid twice over at birthing or harvest time. As societies became wealthier and capital became more abundant, interest rates fell: at the height of the Athenian Empire, rates for the best creditors hovered around 10 percent, and later, during the Pax Romana, around 4 percent.[3]

In Solon's time, capitalists in both Rome and Athens probably charged farmers and city dwellers well in excess of the 18 percent rate quoted for that period by modern scholars, similar to that levied on today's credit card holders. Back then, as now, these high rates drove large numbers of ordinary citizens into a downward spiral of rapidly compounding debt.[4]

Creditors exacted far higher penalties from defaulters two millennia ago; these included seizure of property, and the enslavement of both the creditor and his family. The resultant financial and social imbalances ignited the era's main political flash point: debt reform.

Solon's laws, discussed in Chapter 2, abolished many of those debts and provided the poor of Athens with modest relief from future creditors; most important, they outlawed debtor enslavement. The Roman legation to Athens would have brought home the same message, and Rome did subsequently appoint two successive panels of ten men each—*decemvirs*—that enacted the famous Twelve Tablets. These statutes precisely spelled out the meager due process and grace periods for indebted Romans.[5] The *decemvirs* probably wrote the original Twelve Tablets on wood in the first primitive Latin alphabet, which owed much to Greek influence. The tablets perished by fire a few centuries later.

In early antiquity, the Greeks were the most powerful and influential of Mediterranean peoples, and Rome was not much more than a political, and certainly cultural, backwater; the Romans imported from the Greeks not only their legal system, but also, indirectly, their alphabet. During this period, both trade and colonization connected Greece and the Italian peninsula. Around 750 BC, colonists from Chalcis, near Athens, established the city of Cumae near modern Naples; there, the Greeks both warred and traded with the native Etruscans over the next two centuries.

Around 535 BC, another Greek city-state in Asia Minor, Phocaea, responded to its impending conquest by the Persian armies under Cyrus with what modern historians have called the "Phocaean option": to sail away and replicate their city, along with its political and cultural structures, at multiple sites on foreign shores. The most famous of these later became Marseille; another was Alalia on the island of Corsica, where the Greeks again came into both commercial and hostile contact with the Etruscans.

At some point, Greeks from either Alalia or Cumae imparted their alphabet to the Etruscans, who adapted it to their language. The Romans, in their turn, adapted the Etruscan script to Latin and created the lettering that is today the dominant alphabet of the modern West.[6]

At the time that the *decemvirs* wrote the Twelve Tablets in the fifth century BC, literacy rates in Rome must have been very low, at most a few percent. It seems unlikely, then, that the Twelve Tablets represented any sort of triumph for the common man; rather, the patricians presumably formulated them in order to perpetuate the status quo. Like the Greeks, the Romans recognized several classes of citizen, the primary cleavage being between the plebeians (*plebs*) and patricians (*patricii*), the latter of whom descended from the senators who advised the first Roman kings and enacted laws.

The repressive nature of the Twelve Tablets is clearly revealed in their prohibition against intermarriage between patricians and plebeians, and particularly in the harsh punishment of debtors, which, despite the lessons of Solon's reforms, involved being sold into slavery abroad or even executed. Admittedly, these provisions probably mirrored the unwritten common law, but their codification did nothing to loosen the grip of the patricians on Roman society. As had the written law in Mesopotamia and Egypt, the Twelve Tablets deployed the numinous power of the word in an illiterate society to enhance aristocratic power, not to share it.[7]

The rapid spread of Greek literacy in the fifth and fourth centuries BC coincided with the first written histories of Herodotus and Thucydides, who recorded, respectively, the electrifying events of the Persian and Peloponnesian conflicts. In Rome, literacy seems to have advanced in the third century BC, when the first known Roman historians, most notably Quintus Fabius Pictor, wrote about the First and Second Punic Wars.[8]

Paradoxically, in Rome, unlike Greece, the nexus of power and literacy was intertwined with slavery. While educated Greeks wrote reasonably well in their own hand, the few surviving writing samples of Roman intellectuals and aristocrats often resemble a child's scrawl, for in ancient Rome, anyone who was anyone employed at least one slave scribe.[9]

How did Roman slaves acquire literacy? The answer is that they weren't Romans at all, but rather Greeks. Since time immemorial, vanquished nations fed the slave trade of the victors; those men defeated on the battlefield, as well as their women and children, fortunate enough to escape the sword often wound up packed off to the victor's homeland as war booty.

As Rome expanded, it acquired huge swaths of prime agricultural real estate in the Italian peninsula and in Sicily that fell under the rubric of *ager publicus*—public land. From these areas, and then overseas, the Republic likewise acquired large numbers of slaves. The term *ager publicus* was largely a fiction; these lands were in actuality latifundia: vast tracts privately owned by aristocrats and worked by the slaves acquired abroad. These industrial-scale farms tended to become ever larger as their wealthy owners accrued smaller plots from surrounding farmers who left to seek better prospects in the legions, and who sold their land outright or whose wives and children lost it to debt.[10]

The latifundia lasted for centuries, but the initial slave captives died off rather more quickly. Rome thus required a continuous flow of slaves to work most of its farmland, and slave traders who supplied the ongoing needs of this agricultural workforce followed its conquering legions. Nowhere is this process better described, and more relevant to the story of literacy, than in the Aegean region.

After Rome conquered the Italian peninsula in the third century BC, it set its sights on Greece, and the Republic began its first forays there around 220 BC. When the largest and most powerful western Greek state, Epirus, just across from Italy's heel, fell in 167 BC, the Romans took 150,000 *capita humana,* who were presumably fed into the slave markets.[11] By the middle of the second century BC, all of Greece lay under Roman suzerainty. Some Greek states, most notably Athens, allied themselves with the conquerors and consequently were well treated, but Rome made harsh examples of those who resisted, such as Corinth, which was sacked, rendered uninhabitable, and its people slaughtered and enslaved in 146 BC, the same year as Carthage's destruction.

The slave traders sailed in the legions' wakes. The Aegean island of Delos served as their primary entrepôt. Said the geographer Strabo, the island "could both admit and send away ten thousand slaves on the same day; whence arose the proverb, 'merchant, sail in, unload your ship, everything has been sold.'"[12]

Thousands of Romans entrepreneurs and colonists emigrated to Asia Minor and the Aegean islands to seek their fortunes, and the stereotypical wealthy, swaggering "ugly Roman" soon became an object of Greek hatred. Oppressive Roman taxation forced many Asian and Greek peoples into a downward whirl of debt that led to slavery, while the slave trade itself attracted pirates who raided local sea traffic for human treasure. It did not help that centuries before Rome conquered Greece and Asia Minor, the Persians had outlawed slavery in their conquered territories, and its reimposition by the Romans deepened Greek antagonism in Asia Minor and the eastern Aegean.

This Greek animosity found its focus in the legendary king of Hellenic Pontus, Mithridates VI, a preternaturally skilled military commander. This charismatic leader cleverly portrayed himself as the savior of the Greek peoples. He organized history's most complex and widespread act of coordinated mass terrorism: the surprise slaughter on a single day in 88 BC and in more than a dozen cities hundreds of miles apart, of approximately one hundred thousand men, women, and children—e.g., most of the Roman population of Asia Minor and the Aegean islands.[13] He then proceeded to plague Roman forces around the Aegean and repeatedly eluded capture over the next quarter century until he was finally cornered into suicide by Pompey in 63 BC. Local anti-Roman anger was directed primarily at the Republic's economic behavior, as symbolically and grue-somely manifested by the execution meted out to the commander Aquillius, down whose throat Greek captors poured molten gold, history's signature punishment for greed.[14]

Historians are unable to even approximate the number of captives sent to Rome, but it must have run into the millions.[15] So massive was the trade in slaves that many were simply fed into the gladiatorial maw, and occasionally even to wild animals, in the amphitheaters of the Republic and then the Empire, a fate most likely to befall captives from Syria, Judea, and the untamed wilds of Thrace. Those from Gaul and Spain, on the other hand, because of their equestrian skills, more often found their way into the stables of the wealthy.[16]

Luckiest, in a relative sense, were literate Greek slaves, whom their Roman masters treasured. As many of a certain age will recall, prolonged handwriting can be a tedious and even painful process. For such "scri-bophobes" the advent of the typewriter, and later the microprocessor and home printer, constituted nothing less than deliverance. No doubt, in pre-vious eras, with much cruder writing implements and materials, many similarly detested handwriting, and when, beginning in the late third cen-tury BC, Rome found itself home to thousands of literate slaves, the local aristocracies must have looked upon these relatively inexpensive human writing machines with the same delight as today's boomers did their first word processor.[17]

So strong was the connection between literacy in Rome and its Greek inhabitants that most of peninsula's earliest historians wrote in Greek, and of the four best-known "Roman" historians—Dionysius of Halicarnassus, Polybius, Plutarch, and Livy—all but the last were Greeks.[18] (Halicarnassus—modern Bodrum in western Turkey—produced not only Dionysius but Herodotus as well.)

Slaves relieved the well-to-do Romans of the effort not only of writ-ing, but frequently of reading as well. As the historian Suetonius relates in his biography of Augustus, "If he could not again fall asleep, as some-times happened, he called for someone to read or tell stories to him."[19] Pliny the Younger records that his famous uncle, Pliny the Elder, was a compulsive *listener* of books, being read to constantly, whether walking, eating, bathing, enjoying a massage, or simply relaxing, and also kept at his side a "shorthand writer" to take notes when necessary.[20] His uncle, of course, was no layabout; he was the author of, among many other works, the thirty-seven-volume *Historia Naturalis* and later died from toxic fumes while commanding the rescue fleet at Mount Vesuvius's eruption.

Because of their fondness for giving dictation to slaves, the Romans probably invented shorthand. Tradition has it that Marcus Tullius Tiro, Cicero's highly accomplished slave scribe-editor, pioneered the technique, although documentation of this oft-repeated chestnut is lacking.[21] Modern historians have also asserted that by means of dictation to groups of slave scribes, hundreds or even thousands of books could be produced as cheaply as with the first Gutenberg-type presses, though this, too, must be taken with a grain of salt. One thing, however, can be said with certainty: when the Empire reached the limits of conquest and the supply of slaves ran out, the price of books rose dramatically. By the time of Diocletian in the late third century after Christ, books that could be purchased relatively cheaply in the time of Augustus had become nearly unaffordable to all but the very wealthy.[22]

That the Romans founded both public and private libraries around 220 BC, at almost exactly the same time as their first forays into Greece, can hardly be a coincidence. Modern historians have discovered evidence of about a dozen "public" repositories (that in fact belonged to the emperor), and their organization tells us much about the relationship between slavery and literacy. Roman librarians generally organized their collections into separate Latin and Greek sections. In those cases where historians can identify their workforces, most of the lower-level workers were either slaves or freedmen (manumitted slaves).

The Romans recognized two classes of library workers: at the lowest level were *villici*, who filed new volumes, repaired old ones, and controlled or assisted patrons; and slaves *a bybliothece*, who repaired and copied sections of manuscripts. In addition, the wealthiest private households, such as Cicero's, employed large numbers of a third class of slaves and freedmen—*librarii*—essentially, human copying machines who reproduced whole volumes from other collections or manufactured duplicates from those of their masters as "backups" or gifts.[23]

The craft of the *librarius* was painstaking; he first wrote out the manuscript on separate sheets of papyrus, similar to the leaves of a modern book. Next, he oiled the pages for protection against vermin and the elements. Then he assembled them into a scroll by gluing the pages end to end, smoothing the first and last pages and attaching the top of the former and the bottom of the latter to painted sticks, each end of which might be capped with carved ivory. Finally, he appended an elegantly inscribed title page and constructed a colored envelope for the scroll, usually from parchment. The final product, which held the text of a small modern volume, was precious indeed.[24] It goes without saying that *villici, bybliothece,* and *librarii* all required a high degree of literacy.

Over time, scribal slavery broke free of its Greek moorings. Non-Greek foreign captives might be literate or be trained in Latin and Greek after capture.[25] A literate Roman citizen might default on debt and become an enslaved scribe. *Expositio*—the abandonment, usually in well-known public places, of infants by the poor—also seems to have provided wealthy Romans with large numbers of young educable slaves, and it was not unknown for successful foundlings to be reclaimed by their mothers. (Most victims of this practice, unfortunately, were female, and thus not eligible for education; a well-known saying in both ancient Greece and Rome ran, "If it is a boy, rear it; if it is a girl, throw it out.") A majority of survivors of *expositio* became slaves, but adoptive parents occasionally raised these children to be free men and women.[26]

Aristocratic slaveholders often viewed their chattel as worthy of educational investment, as illustrated by a scene from Petronius's play *Satyricon.* Trimalchio, an uncouth nouveau riche social climber, conducts a wild, drunken banquet during which he plants a long, affectionate kiss on the mouth of his handsome slave boy. When his wife Fortunata, herself a recently freed slave chorus girl, protests, Trimalchio evenly observes, "I gave this model slave a kiss not because he's handsome, but because he applies himself so well. He knows his tens-times table. He can read at sight."[27]

The wise master thus had a keen eye for human capital, and the wealthiest Romans picked out the brightest slave boys for special schools, *paedagogia,* where they received educations that could be the equal of those given the master's own sons. If a literate slave performed well in later life, he might be manumitted and retained as a secretary, bookkeeper, or chamberlain; presumably, the prospect of manumission also served as an incentive to the slave workforce.

Slaveholders sought and cultivated particular talents, such as those of the *comoedi,* who entertained guests with comic and dramatic readings.

According to Seneca, Roman slave owners prized those with the deftest tongues, who were kept "under a teacher to sharpen their skill in impudence, so that they may become expert in casting studied insults."[28]

In addition to slaves, another group of ordinary Romans stood out for their literacy—the several hundred thousand men serving in the legions. Starting in the late Republic, the increasingly bureaucratic legions forced upon legionaries at least rudimentary reading and writing skills, and the ability to read and write must have increased the chances of promotion. The military historian Publius Flavius Vegetius Renatus wrote a compact "field manual" of army procedures, *Epitoma rei militaris*, in which he described how each eighty-man "century" mustered ten soldiers each night for watch duty, and upon relief, their names were entered on a list, so that "no one is overburdened or unjustly exempted." For the same reason, legionaries made lists of those granted leave. Vegetius also recommended that military recruiters

> should test for tall stature, physical strength, and alertness in everyone indeed, but in some the knowledge of shorthand writing and calculation and reckoning is selected. For the administration of the entire legion, including special services, military services, and money, is recorded daily in the Acts with one might say greater exactitude than records of military and civil taxation are noted down in the official files.[29]

The legionaries constituted the cream of Rome's manpower. Often, they were the educated sons of independent farmers who saw the twenty-five-year term of military service as the road to advancement, and on retirement they received a grant of land and a comfortable pension. Classical historian William V. Harris noted that he was able to document the illiteracy of only one legionary, in spite of the fact that he is generally skeptical about the degree of literacy in ancient Greece and Rome.[30]

The auxiliaries, a second type of Roman military unit, drew their manpower from the fringes of the empire and ranged from cultured and often literate Greeks to "barbarians"—Thracians, Germans, and Gauls. Yet even here, the incentive of promotion drove up literacy rates. For example, among Egyptian cavalry auxiliaries, all officers and approximately one-third of ordinary enlisted men could read and write.

As with other records and artifacts, philologists and classicists are most likely to uncover the papyrus and parchment documents that bear on the extent and role of military literacy in hot, dry climates such as that of the Middle East. Easily the largest of such finds—approximately two-thirds of extant Roman military papyrus records—was the spectacular collection of records uncovered at a Roman fort at Dura-Europos on the upper Euphrates in modern Syria in the 1920s.[31]

In the eighteenth and nineteenth centuries, England became the modern hotbed of classical research, but the last place Britons could reasonably expect to find a collection of Roman military records would be on their cold, soggy home turf. Not that they didn't fantasize about it; the historian Harold Idris Bell's obituary noted that he hoped that "one day he would find a letter on papyrus written by a soldier on Roman service in Britain."[32] Bell died in 1967; just six years later archaeologist Robin Birley realized Bell's holy grail at a fort the Romans called Vindolanda near the midpoint of Hadrian's Wall, just south of the modern Scottish border.

Birley's archaeologist father had purchased the Vindolanda site in 1929 and begun its excavation, and Robin and his brother followed in their father's footsteps. Over the decades, the site yielded an increasing treasure trove of artifacts, but nothing in Robin's training and experience prepared him for the day in 1973 when he found himself deep in a muddy trench, face-to-face with two thin pieces of wood:

> I . . . passed one fragment up to my assistant on the surface for his opinion. He examined the wood and passed it back to me, observing that it seemed to have some peculiar markings on it. I had another look at it and thought I must have been dreaming, for the marks appeared to be ink writing.[33]

Indeed, Birley had uncovered the first of over a thousand documents, written mainly in ink on approximately postcard-size thin wooden tablets, dating to around AD 100, just before the construction of Hadrian's Wall. A smaller number were "stylus tablets" of inscribed wax on a wood bed. The wax was long gone, but the messages could occasionally be read by the faint markings left in the wood. How had the fragile ink-stained strips of wood survived nearly two thousand years in the cold, sodden soil? Apparently, the high concentration of decayed organic matter surrounding them and the very low oxygen concentration at the site combined to preserve the local birch, alder, and oak used as writing material.[34]

The Vindolanda Tablets provided historians with a remarkable window on Roman rule, particularly how a few scattered literate legions could co-opt and control a vastly larger native population. These records minutely detailed unit rosters, supply purchases, construction of weapons and buildings, and communications with other units and with the central command in newly founded Londinium (London), hundreds of miles to the south. Over the decades since their initial discovery, scholars have applied handwriting analysis to identify literally hundreds of different authors among the Vindolanda Tablets. Considering that only about eight hundred men were stationed at the fort, this suggests that the legions possessed a degree of literacy that had never before been experienced in the ancient world, and which would not be realized again until the modern era.

Perhaps the most famous, and certainly the most charming, of the tablets is an invitation to a birthday party extended from one officer's wife, Claudia Severa, to another, Sulpicia Lepidina:

Claudia Severa to her Lepidina, greetings.

On the third day before the Ides of September, sister, for the day of celebration of my birthday, I give you a warm invitation to make sure that you come to us, to make the day more enjoyable to me by your arrival. . . . Give my greetings to your [husband] Cerialis. My [husband] Aelius and my little son send him their greetings. I shall expect you, sister. Farewell, sister, my dearest soul, as I hope to prosper and hail.[35]

Like most Roman correspondence, this invitation was written in multiple hands. Typically, the author dictated the letter to an assistant or slave, then added his or her own handwritten salutation or addendum. As in Italy, slaves penned many of the Vindolanda letters, and correspondence among Vindolanda's slaves was not uncommon.[36]

This body of documents makes clear the advantages that the Romans possessed over the illiterate native population. On hardly more than a moment's notice, commanders could fashion precise written orders, unencumbered by the shackles of human memory, to organize and coalesce forces in a way that their local opponents could not.[37] In short, the Romans

conquered most of their known world as much with the deeply institution-
alized pen as with the sword, shield, and catapult.

The names of the soldiers, officers, and their families at Vindolanda
reveal that many came either from Tungria—roughly, the modern Franco-
Belgium border area—or Batavia, just to the north of that, approximately
the area around Nijmegen, in today's Netherlands; Julius Caesar had pacified both areas around 58 BC. Such was the pattern employed by the Romans during their centuries of conquest: first, recruit the ablest soldiers
from recently pacified local populations overawed by the legionaries' size,
military prowess, technology, and literacy; second, teach the new troops
not only to fight but also to read and write Latin (or, in the East, Greek);
and last, employ these intellectually and physically impressive specimens
to conquer, pacify, overawe, and recruit adjoining peoples. The Romans
first invaded England in force in AD 43, and by AD 100 Britons themselves
served as legionaries on the European mainland.

Beyond the confines of the army, the aristocracy, and their slaves,
not much more than a few percent of Rome's peoples could read or write;
outside the capital, the literacy rate was even lower. Here, then, in perhaps
its most distilled form, was the despotic literacy of the Egyptians and
Mesopotamians: a relentlessly efficient engine of oppression borne of stylus and ink and concentrated in Rome's organ of subjugation, the legions.

We can now give voice to Benjamin Franklin's famous worry that the new
American republic might suffer the same fate as the Roman one. While
historians have variously blamed the fall of the Roman Republic on the
formation of the First Triumvirate of Julius Caesar, Pompey, and Crassus
in 60 BC; Julius Caesar's crossing of the Rubicon in 49 BC; his assas-
sination in 44 BC; or the accession as emperor of his grand-nephew (and
adopted son) Augustus in 27 BC, the roots of the Republic's demise, in
fact, lay more than two centuries before those occurrences. No one captured
its essence better than Montesquieu, who in 1753 intuited that Rome had
simply gotten too large to be governed effectively: "The unbounded extent
of the Roman Empire proved the ruin of the Republic."[38] More recently,
historians have confirmed and built upon Montesquieu's incisive thesis.

Before exploring this new history of the Republic's collapse, it
helps to recap one of the key lessons of Chapter 1: the relationship among

Figure 3-1. The growth of the Republic, 400 BC–218 BC.

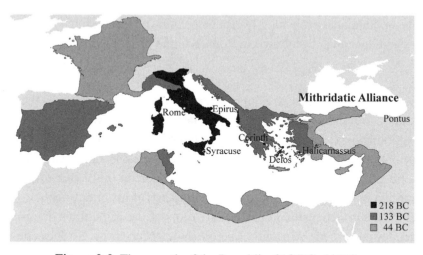

Figure 3-2. The growth of the Republic, 218 BC–44 BC.

group size, political structure, and literacy. Recall "Dunbar's number," the maximum number of human beings who can maintain a stable governing relationship through direct contact, generally felt to be approximately 150. When everyone in a small group has direct face-to-face access to every other member, its structure tends to be relatively democratic, as is seen in most hunter-gatherer tribes, small farming settlements, and pirate ships. Literacy, especially when limited to a small elite, allows command-and-control down through multiple levels of authority, and thus over exponentially larger numbers of subjects, and so encourages despotism.

As populations grow beyond Dunbar's number, face-to-face contact no longer suffices to maintain political control. At this point, writing supplies the best mechanism for communicating among large numbers of people, and power naturally accrues to the literate. Consequently, societies with high rates of literacy, such as Athens, tend to have more smoothly running republics than those with low rates, such as the late Roman one.

Distance also enters into the political calculation. However hard it is to maintain control over a tightly confined city of ten thousand, it is far more difficult to govern ten thousand inhabitants dispersed over tens or hundreds of miles; the greater the distance, the more important the distribution of literacy. Again, recall that history's first large empire—that of the Mesopotamian ruler Sargon around 2300 BC—became possible only after cuneiform script evolved to the point that it could convey grammatically complex commands and records.

In many respects, the early Roman Republic was at least as democratic as Athens. Its major features were two assemblies, in which any Roman citizen could participate: the *comitia tributa*, so called because it elected tribunes, the protectors of plebeian citizen rights; and the *comitia centuriata*, which elected the highest magistrates. The relationships between the *comitia tributa* and the *comitia centuriata* and among the officers they elected (who included not only the tribunes and the magistrates, but also, indirectly, the senators) gave rise to a delicate system of checks and balances; a grasp of this complex institutional anatomy is necessary to comprehend the Republic's rise, long survival, and ultimate demise.

In the *comitia tributa*, voting was representative; as in Athens, all citizens were members of geographically defined "tribes," each of which carried one vote in that assembly, with a majority of attending citizens from each tribe determining its vote, roughly similar to the operation of the U.S.

House of Representatives.[39] Because each citizen wielded a more or less equal vote in the *comitia tributa*, it was dominated by the plebeians; its major function was to elect about ten tribunes per year (hence its name), whose job was to safeguard the liberties of the plebeians.

The *comitia centuriata*, on the other hand, was stratified into five classes depending upon wealth; the higher a citizen's class, the more his vote counted. Further, the voting proceeded from the highest class to the lowest; when a majority had been reached, voting ceased. Thus, while the *comitia centuriata* was theoretically open to all citizens, the lowest classes found themselves disenfranchised in all but the closest votes in this body.[40]

The senior magistrates elected by the *comitia centuriata* served for a year, then more often than not ran for the next highest office: from censor to praetor, and praetor to consul. After serving their twelve-month term, consuls generally joined the senate. The patricians therefore dominated not only the *comitia centuriata*, but also the senate, which was composed largely of consuls it had previously elected.

It bears repeating that in the ancient world, the civil and the military were inextricably intertwined. In general, a Roman could not run for elective office until he had served in three campaigns on horse or six on foot.[41] Magistrates of all ranks frequently left Rome with their legions; in the later Republic, the *comitia centuriata* often elected magistrate-commanders in absentia.

The *comitia tributa* and the *comitia centuriata* not only effectively represented separate social classes, but also convened separately. The former assembled in the Forum, just west of the later site of the Colosseum. The latter, because of its military duties, consisted of armed soldiers who assembled outside the city's walls in the Campus Martius (the modern Campo Marzio, just across the Tiber from today's Vatican).[42]

As time passed, the plebeians grew more powerful; in 367 BC they were permitted to hold the highest magistrate positions, including the consulship. Over time, the *comitia tributa* effectively excluded patricians, becoming known as the *comitia plebis*.[43]

A meeting of the *comitia tributa* must have been a sight to behold; the Forum could contain seventy thousand citizens, who made a point of standing for the duration of the assembly, both to impress visitors with Roman vigor and as a contrast to the effete Athenians, who sat. A priest would offer a prayer; then speakers orated for and against proposed legislation.

In the early Republic, each citizen had to approach an official tabulator, who recorded the citizen's oral vote with a point on a clay tablet. This process allowed much chicanery, and after about 150 BC, the plebeian leadership of the *comitia tributa* changed the oral procedure to a written secret ballot in which voters inscribed their choices on clay tokens or wax tablets that were then deposited in ballot boxes.

Contemporary commentators did not much remark upon this reform, but surely the introduction of the secret ballot must have tied in with the increasing literacy of Roman citizens, since it required writing down simple words or candidates' names. It must also have been a blow to patricians, who had been better able to influence the older oral procedure through bribery and intimidation. Alas, the literacy skills of urban citizenry were far higher than in the far reaches of Italy, let alone in transalpine Rome, with grave consequences for the rapidly expanding Republic.[44]

A set of rules—an unwritten "constitution of Rome"—that delicately balanced the interests of the patricians and plebeians evolved, but it was one in which the latter increasingly dominated. The *comitia tributa* elected the lower magistrates (aediles and quaestors), and the *comitia centuriata* elected the higher magistrates (consuls, praetors, and censors). The patrician-dominated senate, populated by ex-consuls, functioned as the Republic's policy-making arm, and issued instructions to the magistrates. Any magistrate's decision could be overruled by a higher-ranked magistrate, and the plebeian-elected tribunes could veto any act of any magistrate, including a consul, the *comitia centuriata*, or the senate (which could only propose, but not pass, legislation). Of the two consuls elected every year by the patrician-dominated *comitia centuriata*, it was understood that one would be a plebeian. Not only were the plebeian tribunes immune from prosecution, but their persons were physically sacrosanct; an assault on a tribune constituted an attack on the state itself. As a final check, although legislation passed by the plebeian-dominated *comitia tributa* applied to all Romans, it was also understood that the tribunes would not introduce legislation without at least the tacit approval of the senate.[45]

One of the most sacred of the Republic's unwritten rules forbade military weapons within the confines of the city. Rome's founders understood the centrality of this prohibition for maintaining order, and its flouting in the second century BC contributed greatly to the Republic's downward spiral, a fact with no small relevance to today's Second Amendment controversy.

A sense of how Romans viewed their place in the Republic can be gained from the funeral processions of magistrates, which featured actors representing the deceased and all of his ancestors who had held magistrate-rank offices. The actors wore wax masks and the robes of their rank. The procession marched to the Forum, the site of the *comitia tributa*, where the "ancestors" sat on ivory chairs, also appropriate to their rank, and listened to the funeral orations. In time, the term *nobilis*, roughly equivalent to the modern term "elite," came to refer to any patrician or plebeian family that could boast a magistrate ancestor to "parade" in a wax funerary mask.[46]

Unlike Athenian citizenship, Roman citizenship was liberally granted to all male landowners and to the offspring of any male citizen, no matter who the mother was; early on it was even opened to newly manumitted slaves. Manifestly, republican Rome was the ancient world's most inclusive representative democracy. The ambitious Roman politician spent much of his working career conducting *ambitus*—literally, walking around the Forum, slapping backs and pressing the flesh.[47]

The Republic's delicate system of checks and balances operated, as in all democratic societies based on the rule of law, on the Tinkerbell Principle: it functioned only so long as its participants believed in it.[48] As long as Rome remained a small republic where a significant minority of citizens lived close to the city walls and where most of the rest could walk to the Forum and Campus Martius in a few days to interact face-to-face, the Tinkerbell Principle held.

As late as 264 BC, the Roman Republic extended no farther than the central and southern Italian peninsula. The transition from a relatively small and easily governed Roman city-state into a geographical monstrosity that covered most of western Europe, combined with the fact that anyone could show up in the Forum and vote, meant that no one knew for certain how many of the Republic's new far-flung citizens, nearly all illiterate and unfamiliar with the traditional rules of the game, would trek to Rome for a given assembly. This uncertainty effectively shifted control to the one group that had the literacy skills and the mobility to communicate over such vast distances: the legions.

The first real cracks in the democratic system appeared in 134 BC with the election of Tiberius Gracchus as a plebeian tribune. He hailed from a well-connected family, and, like virtually all Roman politician-officers, had begun his career in the legions, distinguishing himself in the Third Punic War at Carthage, where he was reputedly the first man over its wall.[49]

Gracchus's army service impressed upon him how unfairly Rome treated its rank-and-file legionaries, who frequently returned home to find their meager plots seized from their wives and children by wealthy neighboring landlords. This was not only unjust, but strategically unsound as well, since it stripped their sons of land ownership, the essential prerequisite for enlistment. Nor was this all: the new latifundia consumed vast amounts of slave labor, which bred slave revolts. If Rome was to maintain societal stability and supply its legions with manpower, the *comitia tributa* needed to redistribute land from the patricians to the plebeians.

Roman law of the period forbade private ownership of more than about three hundred acres, but this limit had been ignored since the Second Punic War in 201 BC, when Rome distributed to its aristocrats huge tracts of land seized from Italian cities that had sided with Hannibal. Following his election as tribune in 133 BC, Tiberius Gracchus proposed a commission to survey the excess land and redistribute it to veterans and other citizens.

But by this time, these generous awards had been held for up to three generations by private landowners, who had improved the land with their own money, subdivided it among their sons, or distributed it as dowry to their new sons-in-law. Because of this, Gracchus's proposal met with a firestorm of opposition. In spite of this, he managed to ram the requisite legislation through the *comitia tributa*.

At this point, the fragile, complex fabric of tacit rules that held the Republic together began to unravel. Since tribunes and magistrates were immune from prosecution during their tenure, it was generally understood that they could not run for consecutive terms, lest they become permanently immune. Gracchus broke decisively with this tradition; in order to follow through on his reform, he ran for reelection.

Hotheads in the patrician senate, alarmed at what they saw as a naked grab for power, organized a mob of senators and other aristocrats who clubbed Gracchus to death. He was no easy target, for his routine escort comprised three thousand to four thousand men, hundreds of whom died along with him.[50] The shock at Gracchus's murder must have been enormous. For over three centuries following the Republic's founding around 500 BC, tribunes and other magistrates had been physically untouchable; it was as if the United States Senate had organized the murder

of a Supreme Court justice. The demons of civil strife had been let loose
in the Republic, and they would not rest until it met its final end in 27 BC
with the accession of Augustus.

Gracchus's supporters rallied behind his cause and won the day; over
the next four years, the land commission he organized broke up many large
estates. In 123 BC the slain leader's younger brother, Gaius Gracchus, was
elected tribune; he ran again the next year and, unlike his brother, survived
long enough to serve his second term.

Gaius Gracchus took as his cause the extension of citizenship to
Rome's allies on the Italian peninsula. In 121 BC a relatively minor conflict in the Campus Martius caused his supporters to flee south to the
Aventine Hill in fear of a repeat of the events of a decade before. They
had every right to be afraid; the patrician consul Optimus (literally, "the
best," a name adopted by many patricians) led his forces up the hill and
slaughtered thousands; Gaius Gracchus escaped but was quickly cornered
and committed suicide. Ominously for the fate of the Republic, Optimus
had called in foreign troops, including specially trained Cretan archers.
Optimus likely knew that Gaius had been planning to extend citizenship,
and this knowledge allowed Optimus to ensnare Gaius's panicky plebeian
supporters in the Forum.[51]

By this point, Rome was ruled, no longer by laws, but rather by force
of arms, particularly at public meetings. By the first century after Christ,
many politicians, most famously Publius Clodius Pulcher, specialized in
legislation effected by thugs and murderers. Wealthy Romans often counted
gladiators among their armies of slaves, for whom training schools were
set up, and who "performed" in both private and public contests. The
gladiators proved useful to ambitious politicians, whose retinues included
large numbers of these skilled killers.

These undisciplined private armies often got out of hand, as happened
at a gladiatorial school in Capua, just north of modern Naples, which
spawned the famous slave revolt led by Spartacus between 73 BC and 71
BC. Pompey finally put down the slaves, who were bent on escape from
Italy, not insurrection, and who saw six thousand of their numbers nailed
to crosses on the Via Appia between Capua and Rome.[52]

If the mob proved mightier the ambit of the law, then what better than
an entire legion? Magistrates were both political and military leaders who
frequently absented themselves from Rome to lead campaigns. By 200 BC

or so, Rome had become a plunder state whose wealth derived from the fruits of conquest; the profits that flowed from military command became a self-sustaining machine in which war booty would buy the loyalty of troops to the commander, who could then use the threat of arms against the state to pry from the Republic further scope for command, which led to yet more conquest and riches. Again, Montesquieu:

> But after the legions had passed the Alps and crossed the sea, the soldiers, who the Romans had obliged to leave during several campaigns in the countries they were subduing, left insensibly that genius and turn of mind which characterized a Roman citizen, and the generals, having armies and kingdoms at their disposal, were sensible of their own strength and could no longer obey. The soldiers therefore began to acknowledge no superior but their general; to found their hopes on him only. . . . They were no longer citizens of the Republic, but of Sylla, of Marius, of Pompey, and of Caesar.[53]

In an era when civilian and military leaders can command officers and troops, and even remotely pilot aircraft from half a world away, we can only wonder at the temptations available to an ancient commander who knew he might remain incommunicado for months or even years at a time, and we can be even more amazed that the Republic and, later, the Empire were able to bring such huge swaths of territory under nominal control with such limited communication.

The political independence and literacy skills of geographically isolated commanders came to full fruition with the conflict between Gaius Marius and Lucius Cornelius Sulla, two capable military men who began as colleagues. Sulla started his career as Marius's lieutenant and ended it as his mortal enemy. Both had successfully climbed the magistrate office ladder and had become consuls, Marius having been elected to the post no fewer than seven times.

Marius's first election as consul in 108 BC clearly demonstrated the importance and spread of literacy among legionaries during the republican period. His election was in large part due to a letter-writing campaign by his soldiers in Africa. According to one ancient historian, his troops were encouraged "to write to their connections in Rome about the war, attacking [his rival] Metellus in harsh terms, and to demand Marius as commander."[54]

The year 88 BC saw two momentous events in Roman history: the conclusion of the "Social War," in which Rome's Italian allies revolted against the Republic's refusal to grant their inhabitants full citizenship, and the previously discussed massacre of most of the Romans in Asia Minor by Mithridates VI. At the same time that the *comitia tributa* yielded to the Italian allies' demands and ended the conflict in the peninsula, it also gave the prestigious—and profitable—command of the Asia Minor expedition to Marius. This action enraged Sulla, who as consul felt entitled to the command and in fact had been promised it by the senate. When Sulla found out about Marius's appointment, his troops were encamped at Nola, near modern Naples, awaiting transshipment to Asia Minor. Sulla fired his men up by telling them that the *comitia tributa* was depriving them of their chance at Mithridates' booty; then he marched them to Rome to seize power and, along with it, command of the Asian campaign.[55]

Marius is best remembered for his army reform of 107 BC, during his first consulship. This reform did away entirely with the property requirement for enlistment and threw open legionary status to all free Roman males, who were then awarded land upon retirement. Marius's reforms also played their part in the Republic's demise; although no doubt a democratizing move, they opened up the army to the landless and also increased the loyalty of the legionaries to their commander, as opposed to the distant state.[56]

Following Sulla's eventual departure to Asia Minor, another consul, Lucius Cornelius Cinna, declared Sulla an outlaw and marched on Rome, then assembled an army to fight Sulla in Asia. His forces took the degree of violence in late republican Rome to a new level by displaying the heads of Roman citizens in the Forum.[57] The adventurism of Sulla and Cinna took the Republic yet one more step on the road to oblivion, and their examples would be followed in turn by Pompey, Julius Caesar, and, finally, Caesar's grand-nephew Octavian (later, Augustus): enormously wealthy and powerful commanders whose legionaries owed more fealty to them than to the Republic.

Finally, with the extension of full citizenship to most of Italy, those committed to republican government found themselves outgunned not only financially and militarily, but also in terms of communication and organizational resources. It was one thing to keep the Republic together when a large fraction of its citizens could be brought face-to-face in the assemblies; it was quite another when the vast majority, living weeks away from the Forum and Campus Martius, could not hope to communicate with each other. Even if a high proportion of ordinary citizens were literate, which they certainly weren't, they had no way of communicating and organizing; after about 100 BC, the only institution possessed of the literacy skills and a communications network adequate to span the now vast Republic, and after that the Empire, was the Roman army.

Even at the end of the Republic, literacy continued to provide an entrée to power to the relatively small percentage of ordinary Romans who could read and write; this was accomplished through the *libellus*—typically, a letter written to a magistrate or to the emperor. When the cabal of Cassius and Brutus murdered Julius Caesar in the senate on the Ides of March in 44 BC, he held in his hand several *libelli*, one of which warned him of the plot.[58]

Citizens also presented *libelli* to lesser officials, particularly provincial governors, who then might or might not forward them to the emperor, but the fact remains: the overwhelming majority of ordinary Romans could not read or write, and thus had no real way of influencing those in power.

Not for another three centuries after Sulla's march on Rome did an institution match the literacy and communications skills of the Roman legions: the early Christian Church. The Roman Empire's new Christians had reading and writing skills that allowed them first to survive and eventually to overcome and convert their Roman overlords. Nowhere was this process more apparent than among Egypt's lower classes, who benefited from a new script that would become the agent of subversion, revolt, and, in time, heresy.

By the first century, the Egyptians had absorbed millennia of conquerors: first the Hyksos, then the Persians under Cambyses, then Alexander's Greeks, and finally the Roman legions of Augustus, who appropriated wholesale the Greek-speaking Ptolemaic bureaucracy. In the time of the Greek Ptolemies, the old cursive Egyptian hieratic script used for everyday record keeping had given way to the simpler demotic, which as a fundamentally syllabic script was still too complex to be learned easily by ordinary people. The Greek alphabet of the Roman conquerors, while

easy to learn, lacked symbols for several phonemes in the ancient Egyptian tongue still spoken by the vast majority of Egypt's ordinary citizens.

Just as the Semites working at Serabit el-Khadim adapted monosyllabic characters from hieratic for their own use, so too in the first century
of the Christian era did Egyptians extract monosyllabic characters from
the demotic script. They appropriated just seven characters from demotic
that corresponded to their native Egyptian phonemes absent in Greek, and
the new amalgam of Greek and demotic characters—the Coptic alphabet—
greatly expanded popular literacy in Roman Egypt.[59]

The new Coptic alphabet, combined with the easy local availability of
papyrus, allowed the members of the Christian hierarchy to communicate
not only with one another but also with ordinary farmers and craftsmen
who did not understand Greek. The ability of Christianity's leaders to stay
in touch with their adherents allowed the religion to survive the Roman
pogroms and evolve a culture of martyrdom that long outlasted their persecutors.[60] In the words of historian Keith Hopkins,

> Literacy was not simply a passive technical skill; it was itself a cultural
> creation and a creator of culture. After all, the Roman Empire was
> conquered by the religious coherence of Christians a century before
> the western empire was conquered by invading barbarians.[61]

The first well-documented Christian bishop of Alexandria, Demetrius, was elected in AD 189, and almost immediately, the persecutions
began. (Egyptian Christians simply referred to the bishop of Alexandria as
father, or *pappas*—that is, "pope.") Conducted under Emperor Septimius
Severus, the first persecution lasted from 202 to 206, and the second, under
Decius, ran from 249 to 251.

The bureaucratic Romans, proficient in Greek and Latin, system-
atized the repression of the Christians by requiring Egyptians to sacrifice
to Roman pagan gods; they issued certificates to all who complied, and
imprisoned and tortured those who did not, until they either recanted or
succumbed. The punishment for failure to offer sacrifice often exceeded
even ancient standards of barbarity: disembowelment and gouging out of
the eyes with a stick; being torn to pieces, burned, or dragged through the
streets and flayed alive; or even dissolution in alkali. Wealthier Christians

often slid by—they had their slaves offer sacrifice in their place, or they bribed an official for a counterfeit certificate.[62]

Throughout the eastern Mediterranean, most of the senior Christian leaders met these gruesome fates, but a few escaped, most notably Dionysius, the sitting Alexandrian pope, and Cyprian, bishop of Carthage. While in hiding or on the run, these leaders directed church affairs with written instructions.

Dionysius and Cyprian paid a political price for their success. Those who forthrightly met the Roman wrath and survived earned special credibility—*charisma*—denied to the members of the hierarchy who went to ground. To deal with his lack of credibility, Dionysius concocted a transparent tale that his followers had forcibly led him from Alexandria. In a similar vein, Cyprian said that not being a martyr allowed him to write letters that kept the flock together "in spirit."[63]

The Decian persecution lasted only a few years, but worse was to come. The "crisis of the third century" saw the effective breakup of the Roman Empire among two dozen emperors and claimants between 235 and 284 before Diocletian brought the chaos to an end. By that period, most emperors no longer hailed from the Italian peninsula—Diocletian was born as Diocles, from the culturally and linguistically Greek province of Dalmatia, on what is now the coast of Croatia. After his ascension in 284, he expanded and reorganized the Empire's military and civilian administration. He also came down hard on dissident groups, especially Christians: the "Great Persecution," which began in 303.

Historically, the Romans easily tolerated a wide variety of theologies throughout the Empire; only when dissident groups challenged the authority of the Empire did they act.[64] Unfortunately for Christians, Diocletian desired to reunify the Empire not only administratively and economically, but religiously as well. With the paranoia inherent in turbulent times, he imagined that those making the sign of the cross somehow interfered with his own attempts to appease the Roman gods. It also did not help that in 297 Alexandrians had revolted against his new taxes.

In February 303 Diocletian decreed the destruction of churches, the burning of scriptures, and the revocation of believers' social rank. And as occurred under Decius, all inhabitants of the Empire, from Spain to Mesopotamia, were required, under threat of imprisonment, torture, and death, to sacrifice to the Roman gods.

Once again, the Egyptian prelate, Pope Peter, found himself constantly on the move, from Palestine to Syria to Mesopotamia. Along the way he emitted a constant stream of inspirational and organizational epistles to his flock.

The persecutions continued unabated for almost a decade under Diocletian and his successors. Still, like Dionysius and Cyprian before him, Peter paid the political costs of flight; under Diocletian and Galerius, the Romans had jailed and murdered a large number of the clergy, including four of Peter's bishops. His lame scriptural defense, "When they persecute you from this town, flee to the next" (Matthew 10:23), failed to impress those left behind to face the wrath of Rome.

One bishop, Melitius, was particularly distressed by his boss's lack of courage and devotion; in Peter's absence, he ordained several bishops to replace the imprisoned ones, who, in their turn, just before their executions, wrote letters under duress condemning Melitius's actions. When Melitius ordained two more bishops, Peter excommunicated him. In the end, the Romans finally caught, tortured, and executed Peter and so supplied the Church with the requisite top-level martyrdom.[65]

In Egypt, the literacy-borne organizational skills of the Christian Church proved equal to those of the Roman Empire, which the Church effectively conquered a few short years later with the conversion of Constantine to Christianity. Once again, the scroll proved more nimble and effective than the sword. The Egyptian story matters because the combination of its dry, preservative climate; its abundant papyrus; the literacy skills of the Coptic Christians; and the library in Alexandria, with its scholarly and literate heritage, focused a bright historical light on the Roman-Christian struggle of the early Common Era.[66]

Not all religious dissidents fared as well as the Egyptian Christians. The Gnostics—in Greek, literally "those in the know"—disappeared entirely. For centuries, Western scholars puzzled over the Church's fulminations against this obscure heretical group. The claims about the Gnostics' blasphemy and licentious behavior were so outlandish as to obscure the sect's actual belief system. Archaeologists have uncovered a few original Gnostic documents, but their low quality and scant quantity did not shed much light on the group's beliefs.

That changed in 1945 with the discovery of the Nag Hammadi Library. The word "library" fits this collection even less than the term applied to the collection at Alexandria. The collection was found in a jar, uncovered by a labor crew chief named Mohammed Ali while digging for nitrate deposits. Mohammed Ali pried open the container, which had been carefully sealed, and found inside some leather-bound books. Thinking that his underlings might want a cut of the action, he ripped the books up and distributed them, but his charges said no thanks, so he took the pieces home to his wife, who burned some of them as kindling.

Subsequently, Ali became involved in a blood feud. Among other activities, he and his brother cut out the heart of one of their enemies and then ate the still-beating organ. Unfortunately, the victim turned out to be the son of the local sheriff. Ali realized that his house was about to be searched and that the books might be worth something, so he had the local Coptic priest hide them. The priest's better-educated in-laws recognized the provenance of the books, which soon provided modern historians with the key to the Gnostic belief system.[67]

Even now, it is difficult to ascertain whether the origins of Gnosticism are Christian, Jewish, or both. One thing, though, is certain: the sect believed that the almighty God in charge of this world was a bad actor indeed, who loosed upon humankind a never-ending stream of illness, calumny, and evil. He did so intentionally. The Gnostics believed, in essence, that somewhere out there, above this world, was another one ruled by the true, benevolent God, and that only those who knew its secrets could escape to it. The Old Testament, it seems, was written by a sort of intermediate God, neither wholly good nor wholly evil; Christ functioned as the true God's conduit to believers stuck on this Earth.[68]

Why did the Gnostics disappear? They cannot have been entirely snuffed out by the early Christian Church alone. Just as the might of the Roman Empire could not suppress Christianity, Christianity could not easily do the same to a compelling heresy (as indeed the Reformation later demonstrated). The scarcity of primary Gnostic documents supplies the essential clue: the believers were possibly not literate enough, or not technically adept enough, at publishing and organizing in order to survive and spread. Admittedly, it is difficult to separate out cause and effect; it is equally possible that they failed to spread and grow for some other reason, and thus did not leave behind a great deal of documentation.

Gnosticism may or may not have failed because of its practitioners' imperfect mastery of literacy, but clearly, Egyptian Christians, and presumably Christians elsewhere, thrived because of it. In both remote and late antiquity, few could read or write, and those institutions that could maintain their literacy—the legions and the Church—amassed power.

Slaves commanded no organized power beyond their sporadic uprisings. In most cases, these revolts were perpetrated by gladiators, who, being largely illiterate, could not hope to overcome the sophisticated command-and-control system of the literate legions. Compared with modern slavery, particularly that of black Africans in the New World, the ancient institution was far more fluid; an untalented or unlucky free citizen could easily find himself—and his family—enslaved, especially by victorious foreigners, while the literate slave often achieved freedom and assimilation, and thus lost his slave identity.

It would not be until well after AD 1000 that literacy began to slowly spread in western Europe, not only on the wings of the new paper and printing technologies, but also with subtle yet powerful improvements in word spacing and punctuation—advances that would ever so gradually level the playing field between the rulers and the ruled.

4

BEFORE GUTENBERG

Not without reason has it pleased Almighty God that holy scripture should be secret in certain places, lest, if it were plainly apparent to all men, perchance it would be little esteemed and subject to disrespect, or it might be falsely understood by those of mediocre learning and lead to error. —Pope Gregory VII, AD 1079[1]

Before Gutenberg, books, along with their powerful magic, were utterly inaccessible to those occupying the bottom rungs of power. For starters, writing material was in such short supply as to render it prohibitively expensive; in AD 1022, Pope Benedict VIII issued the last papal bull written on Egyptian papyrus. During the medieval era, literacy was so thin on the ground that the Continent's scribes could make a handsome living copying books; one fourteenth-century monk earned thirty-six solidos—a year or two of income for a skilled worker—for reproducing a single manuscript, perhaps a few months' work.[2]

The catch was that learning the scribal craft required an ecclesiastical education, the only kind available in Europe at the time, and many a would-be cleric found himself co-opted into the secure living of scribbling. In 1050, a Lombard named Anselm advised, "You ought to write many books to obtain money with which to buy yourself off from those having claims on you."[3]

Since both paper and papyrus documents decompose over time, particularly when handled, the survival of antiquity's intellectual treasures depended on a daisy chain of copyists who reproduced them over and over throughout the centuries. In Europe's damp climate and unstable political environment, the problems of decomposition and destruction were particularly acute, and monks engaged in the Sisyphean struggle against them in monasteries whose hilltop locations offered a modicum of physical security. By contrast, in the Muslim East the politics and climate were more favorable, yet its enviable repository of Greek literature still had to survive serial translations through Arabic, Syriac (a dialect of Aramaic), Greek again, and finally Latin.

Historians of the codex, the bound pages that we today call a "book," traditionally date the process of bookbinding to Cassiodorus, a monk of the late fifth century who hailed from a politically powerful and literate Greek family in southern Italy. In the chaos following the fall of Rome, the ruling Goths found his literacy skills invaluable, and he advanced rapidly through the bureaucracy that the victorious Germanic tribes superimposed on the Roman one. He ultimately became a consul—a term that in Gothic Rome meant a minion of the Germanic rulers, with little actual authority. The conquerors, for example, commissioned one of Cassiodorus's early assignments, the propagandistic *History of the Goths,* to enhance their legitimacy in Italy.

The codex had several advantages over the scroll. Written on both sides, it conserved papyrus and parchment; it could be stacked and arranged on shelves, where individual volumes could be more easily recognized; since the pages were more tightly packed together, they survived longer; and when the pages were damaged, they could be replaced fairly easily. Yet one advantage of the codex towered over all others: unlike the scroll, which had to be read consecutively, the codex could be skipped through, browsed, and, eventually, indexed by page. Readers could peek at the ending, too.

Around the same time as Cassiodorus began to bind books, Benedict of Nursia established a dozen monasteries outside Rome, followed by one at Monte Cassino farther south, whose *scriptoria*—literally, "writing rooms"—established the Benedictine practice of manuscript copying that was to spread throughout the rest of Europe.

By the time of Cassiodorus and Benedict, literacy had been mankind's leading-edge communications technology for more than three thousand years; the *scriptoria* would occupy the forefront of literacy for nearly another thousand. As late as 1400, the *scriptoria*'s near-monopoly on reading and writing in Europe served to concentrate their stranglehold on knowledge and power. The Benedictine tradition became a particular focus of literacy in western Europe; this, in turn, concentrated power in the Church hierarchy throughout the so-called Dark Ages. It would take several new technologies to alter that state of affairs.

*   *   *

As is commonly known today, the "invention" of movable type by Gutenberg in the mid-fifteenth century quickly triggered an explosion of book production and literacy. The use of printing presses long predated Gutenberg, and he was not even the first to use movable type. This does not detract in any way from his innovations, which represented the final step in a technological and intellectual chain more than a thousand years in the making. This complex sequence of events wove together five separate but overlapping strands: the evolution and spread of word separation in written script; the founding of Europe's first great universities; the industrialization of paper manufacture; the invention of steel punches and counterpunches to manufacture the type moulds; and finally, advances in mining technology and metallurgy that allowed the development of durable yet malleable alloys to fill those moulds. Without each of these, Gutenberg's wondrous machine would have been either useless or impossible.

Gutenberg's major impact on literacy, religion, culture, and politics, after all, was simply to make books and pamphlets *cheaper*. Without the introduction of word spacing into Latin script by Irish monks, few would have been able to read easily and silently the inexpensive output of the new presses; without the intellectual community fostered by the great universities, literacy would not have spread; without inexpensive paper, the new printing technology would not have greatly reduced the cost of books and pamphlets; and without steel punches and counterpunches and the newly available alloys of lead, tin, and antimony, Gutenberg would not have been able to cast his malleable yet durable type blocks. The entire sequence was so multifaceted and complex that two chapters will deal with all five threads. This chapter covers three often ignored, yet remarkable stories: word separation, the intellectual ferment at the founding of the first great western European universities, and paper manufacture.

The proto-Semitic script adapted successively by the Phoenicians, Hebrews, Aramaeans, and Arabs removed the first major barrier between the written page and fluent comprehension: the overly complex Egyptian and Mesopotamian syllabic systems. A thousand years later, the Greeks introduced vowels and thus eliminated the next major barrier: the phonemic ambiguity of the consonant-only systems derived from proto-Semitic.

Paradoxically, Greek vowels removed one barrier but introduced another: *scriptura continua*. It is nearly impossible to decipher a script in the absence of both vowels *and* word spaces, as the Phoenicians and Hebrews well knew. But vowels make it possible—just barely—to read without word breaks. Why, then, did the Greeks and the Romans fail to separate their written words?

Strange as it may seem to the adult modern reader, *scriptura continua* seems to be hardwired into our brains: newly literate children, for example, tend to write without word spaces. Early on, the Romans did adopt the hedera—a letter-like symbol indicating a word break. They also developed the interpunct, a vertically centered dot that served the same purpose—the interpunct can still occasionally be seen inscribed on nineteenth-century buildings—but they discarded these two devices by the second century of the Christian era.

Why did they do this? Modern neuropsychological research reveals that the eye depends on spaces to separate words; electronically recorded eye movements demonstrate that reading *scriptura continua* greatly narrows the brain's focus on the page, producing a sort of tunnel vision.

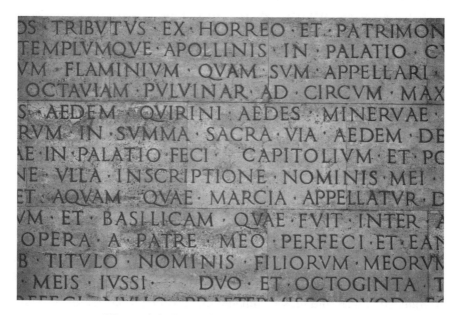

Figure 4-1. Separating words with interpuncts.

Compared with separated script, *scriptura continua* requires approximately double the number of saccades, or jumps, that the reader's eye must make to comprehend each sentence. The lack of word separation and of punctuation decreases comprehension; this is why both children and adults automatically sound out unseparated words.[4]

In *Confessions*, Saint Augustine wondered at a peculiar ability of his mentor, Ambrose, bishop of Milan:

> When he was reading, his eye glided over the pages, and his heart searched out the sense, but his voice and tongue were at rest. Oft times when we had come . . . we saw him reading to himself, and never otherwise. . . . Perhaps he feared that lest if the author he read should deliver anything obscurely, some attentive or perplexed hearer should desire him to expound it, or to discuss some of the harder questions, so that his time being thus spent, he could not turn over so many volumes as he desired, although the preserving of his voice . . . might be the truer reason for his reading to himself.[5]

Augustine's amazement is palpable: here was a man who read silently, *to himself*. Why did he do this? So as not to be interrupted? To prevent laryngitis? Whatever the reason, such a singular talent clearly impressed even the remarkable Augustine, for in the fourth and fifth centuries after Christ, extracting meaning from *scriptura continua* demanded every ounce of sensory input the reader could muster: not just the eyes, but also the voice and the moving finger. Ambrose's ability to read by sight alone, Augustine thought, surely signified superhuman powers.

Ambrose may have read silently, but he could not have read rapidly. Because of *scriptura continua*, few in the early Christian era could read fluently, and even fewer silently. To give an idea of just how slowly and laboriously *scriptura continua* reads, I've rendered Augustine's quote into it:

whenhewasreadinghiseyeglidedoverthepagesandhisheartsearchedout
thesensebuthisvoiceandtonguewereatrestofttimeswhenwehadcome
wesawhimreadingtohimselfandneverotherwiseperhapshefearedthat
lestiftheauthorhereadshoulddeliveranythingobscurelysomeattentive
orperplexedhearershoulddesirehimtoexpounditortodiscusssomeofthe
harderquestionssothathistimebeingthusspentthecouldnotturnoverso
manyvolumesashedesiredalthoughthepreservingofhisvoicemight
bethetruerreasonforhisreadingtohimself

While the above paragraph is difficult to read most readers will be able to decipher it. Taking things one step further, in order to demonstrate why Phoenician, Hebrew, Aramaic, and Arabic had to require word breaks or ending letter forms from the outset, I've next eliminated all of the paragraph's vowels, to produce this undecipherable letter salad:

whnhwsrdnghsyglddvrthpgsndhshrtsrchdtthsnsbthsvcndtngwrtrst
fttmswhnwhdcmwswhmrdngthmslfndnvrthrwsprhpshfrdthtlstf
ththrhrdshlddlvrnythngbscrlysmttntvrprplxdhrrshlddsrhmtxpndtrtd
scsssmfthhrdrqstnssththstmbngthsspnthcldnttrnvrsmnyvlmsshd
srdlthghthprsrvngfhsvcmghtbthtrrrsnfrhsrdngthmslf

Recall that Aramaeans were the first to apply word separation to the vowelless proto-Semitic-derived alphabet; this fact would certainly argue against widespread literacy in Phoenicia and Judea.

In approximately the seventh century, Irish monks began to experiment with different forms of word separation, including the use of spaces. Why Ireland? Apparently, its monks had acquired an extensive collection of documents written in Syriac, an offshoot of vowel-less Aramaic, and thus word-separated, script. These documents made obvious the advantages of word separation, and it soon spread: first to England, then to the Continent, and finally to Romania, the most distant region from Ireland using Latin script, half a millennium later.[6]

Not only could Europe's monks now read more rapidly, but they could do so in close proximity, seated in rows of desks to which librarians chained the precious manuscripts. Previously, libraries had crackled with the noise of monks reading aloud; the advent of silent reading marked the beginning of the modern library's culture of quiet.

Just as *scriptura continua* impeded reading and comprehension, so too did it make composition more difficult; this at least partly explains why classical authors were so fond of dictation. With *scriptura continua,* copying required two specialists: the scribe, who took down the dictation; and the monk, who read to him.

The introduction of word spacing and silent reading allowed one person to do the work formerly done by two. For the first time, spaced script let an author compose and write simultaneously. During the early medieval and ancient periods, paintings usually depicted authors dictating to scribes; after about the eleventh century, paintings began to show authors writing alone.

In addition to halving the number of required personnel, word spacing further streamlined manuscript production, since it enabled copying to be done by less well-trained personnel who did not necessarily need to understand what they were transcribing, and who often worked alone, silently, at furniture specifically designed for the task, much as a modern transcriptionist does.

The empowerment afforded by solitary silent reading is hard to overestimate. In the world of *scriptura continua,* the monk or scholar had to read aloud, usually as a member of a group, affording him no opportunity to stop, consider, or analyze. The silent reader had not only all these advantages, but also the ability to compose, fluently, in spaced writing. Most critically, having to dictate to a scribe took away the author's privacy, since it required two participants. Eliminating the need for scribes gave rise to the newly widespread expression of seditious

Figure 4-2. Livy's *History of Rome,* written in *scriptura continua.*

and sexual content. In the world of *scriptura continua,* Church authorities could control the reading of controversial texts. By contrast, silent reading of spaced text allowed scholars and monks at-will access to and independent analysis of these works. Spaced text snatched access to books from abbots or bishops and handed it to the monk, the student, and the researcher, who could peruse knowledge while keeping their thoughts to themselves.

Some of these thoughts were carnal, and the autonomy afforded by the new texts yielded predictable results. In the twelfth century, a French abbot, Guibert of Nogent, embarked on a prolific writing career that included accounts of his dreams, a controversial interpretation of Genesis, and last but not least erotica, which he rationalized as an abstraction, and not representing his state of mind at the time of composition. Toward the end of his life, blindness forced him to dictate, which he bitterly resented. By the fifteenth century, even religious texts contained sexually explicit images, especially in miniatures; one favorite theme was of David spying on Bathsheba at her bath, and ecclesiastical calendar books specialized in naked characters engaging in both heterosexual and homosexual embraces and fondling.

Solitary writing not only increased the power of individuals, but also improved their ability to impart ideas and knowledge to students, and it especially transformed the educational process. The classroom of *scriptura continua* involved reading aloud on a grand scale. The new spaced script enabled the educator to separate the lecture from the text; in the fourteenth century, French universities provided students with history's first known lecture notes.

The sum total of things wrought by the humble blank space between words—the ease of both reading and composition; the improved efficiency of copying and of education; and the control, autonomy, and privacy afforded the individual—is such that the Reformation and Enlightenment would scarcely have been possible without it.[7] All that was needed was the means to print the words surrounding those spaces, and the paper to print them on.

Along with the development of spaced words came the rise of Europe's great universities, initially in Bologna, Paris, Oxford, and Prague. Curiously, in Renaissance Italy, these institutions focused primarily on law and medicine, whereas north of the Alps, they were set up mainly as training grounds for the clergy. In the late fifteenth century, during the height of the Italian Renaissance, Bologna boasted about seventy-five professors of medicine, law, mathematics, logic, and philosophy, but had none in theology; Oxford and Heidelberg typically employed dozens of theologians but only a few professors of law and medicine. The student populations naturally reflected this distribution: the Italians graduated doctors and lawyers, whereas the English and Germans graduated priests.[8] This north–south dichotomy was fraught with religious and cultural portent, for while the southerners were content to manufacture working professionals, the northerners produced an ideologically focused cadre of theologians such as John Wycliffe and later Martin Luther, who applied their skills in Aristotelian logic to challenge the inconsistencies and corruption that had accrued in the Mother Church during the prior one-and-a-half millennia.

In both the north and the south, universities inherited the Benedictine mandate for manuscript copying. In particular, the University of Paris benefited from Carolingian minuscule, a highly uniform script developed in response to the bureaucratic needs of the new Frankish Christian kingdoms that had arisen north and west of the Alps in the ninth and tenth centuries.

Naturally, the medieval book markets congregated in these university towns. By the thirteenth century, Paris became Europe's undisputed bookmaking capital. Students overcame the pre-Gutenberg printing inefficiencies and expenses with the *pecia* system, under which the university faculties carefully vetted copies of works from booksellers for accuracy and then authorized their rental to students, who would reproduce them in the new Carolingian script. This resulted in a fairly uniform product, although it was not uncommon for wide variations to result when frugal students avoided paying the rental fee by making copies of copies.[9]

Even given all the advances in writing technique developed by Europeans, they still suffered from one overwhelming handicap: a lack of inexpensive material on which to deploy their new craft. For that, they would need to look east.

Since Mother Nature did not endow China with either abundant or easily malleable clay, as she did Mesopotamia, or papyrus, as she did Egypt, it is perhaps not surprising that the Chinese invented paper.

Most paleographers believe that in China writing evolved indepen-dently from that in Mesopotamia and Egypt; the scarcity in China of media upon which to incise and paint may have caused its 1,500-year lag behind the West. (The alternative hypothesis, that writing diffused slowly from the Fertile Crescent to the Orient by way of nomadic herders, is largely discounted by philologists and paleographers.)

At first, the Chinese made do with what they had: the first specimens of writing found in China date to approximately 1500 BC, and they were incised most commonly on the shoulder bones of oxen or on tortoiseshells, and less often on bronze and jade.[10] Next came bamboo and silk, neither of which provided a workable solution for records; the former had to be laboriously sewn together from narrow strips, while the latter was too ex-pensive for everyday use. A more practicable answer was needed; sometime around the dawn of the Common Era, somewhere in southern China, an unknown inventor noticed that a mass of hemp or other plant fiber, when pounded into a pulp and strained through a screen, left a flat, dense residue of cellulose, which was then dried into the first primitive sheet of paper.[11] Chinese mythology credits the invention to a royal courtier named Tshai Lun in approximately AD 105, during the Han dynasty, but this is belied by the presence of paper specimens in northwest China predating this by at least two centuries.[12]

Geography and climate becloud the origins of paper and printing in China, and the above-noted difficulty of dating paper's invention typifies this situation. The technologies of Eastern literacy almost certainly origi-nated and developed in southern China, with its relatively easy availability of textiles and cellulose-rich plant life, but researchers are far more likely to uncover ancient specimens where they will have survived the millennia in the country's dry north and west. In 1900, for example, a Buddhist monk stumbled across a cache of over thirty thousand religious texts dating to around AD 700 in Dunhuang, in China's desert northwest.[13]

Whatever the precise origins of papermaking, the Chinese were the first to unlock its basic technology: the separation of cellulose—a fibrous, essentially indigestible polymer that links thousands of sugar molecules—from plant products, and then its collection in a strainer, or mould. (Many readers may dimly remember the classic elementary-school science dem-onstration in which toilet paper is soaked, beaten, and filtered through a screen, then dried into "paper.")

Any source of cellulose will do. Cloth is relatively precious, and the Chinese early on learned how to extract cellulose from various plants and trees, most particularly from *Broussonetia papyrifera*—the paper mulberry. The Europeans and Americans, on the other hand, did not decode the secrets of extracting cellulose from their harder native woods until the industrial era; instead, for centuries after Gutenberg, they depended on rag-derived paper to feed their hungry presses.

Over the next two thousand years, advances in papermaking technology evolved from East to West. The first problem to be solved was early paper's blotter-like absorbency. The Chinese overcame this by "sizing," impregnating it with gypsum or rice starch. In the West, initially, Muslims and Europeans had used locally grown wheat that tended to attract cockroaches.

Only in China's dry north, with its sparse plant life, did Chinese papermakers favor rag-based methods. Buddhist monks and traders plying the Silk Road, which originated in northern China, probably carried the rag-based paper technology eastward into Muslim lands, and then eventually to Europe; by the eighth century, roughly coincident with the Battle of Talas, Chinese-inscribed trading records appeared as far west as the Russian Caucasus.

Once introduced into Asia's Muslim communities, the new medium spread rapidly along the region's expansive maritime and overland trade routes. The world of medieval Islam can be thought of as a vast free-trade area connected physically by fast-moving overland caravan roads and monsoon-driven maritime routes that linked outposts from Canton and Malacca in the east to Spain in the west and held together institutionally by a legal structure derived from the Prophet. Muhammad, after all, was a trader. Infidel Europeans needed not apply, except at the conveyor belt's western end, where the Venetians and Genoese got rich from the scraps, mainly spices and silk.[14]

By the time Muslims brought paper to Europe, both they and the Chinese had raised its manufacture to a high art; for a time, Baghdad produced large pure white sheets, known as *Baghdadi*, while in China, papermakers lifted, to the beat of drums, sheets fifty feet long from a vat fashioned from the hull of a ship. The Egyptians developed the technology to the point that by AD 950, the overwhelming majority of their documents were written on paper, not on their native papyrus.

Despite these advances, the cost of paper was hardly trivial; in tenth-century Egypt, an ounce of gold, enough to sustain a middle-class family for several months, bought only about 150 sheets. (In current terms, this is equivalent to approximately eight dollars per page.) Like later Europeans and Americans, medieval Arabs went to legendary extremes to conserve paper; one imam typically wrote letters on three-inch-square pieces and left just enough blank space around the edges for the recipient to reply. A letter received in an envelope was a rare luxury, since the envelope could be cut up and reused.[15] One Yemeni observer commented,

> The economy of paper in Imamdom reaches the sublime. Seldom one sees an envelope, seldom a full sheet of stationery—the scrap is the rule, and very rare is the exception. . . . Evidently the Imam Yahya, who won "a wealth" of guns and cannons from the Turks, turned their archives also into service. Books, coupons, petitions, documents of every sort, they have all been cut into scraps to be used in every department of the Government.[16]

By around AD 1000, paper mills operated in Muslim Spain, and when Christian forces took Toledo in 1085, the technology fell into their hands. And not a moment too soon: the lightning victories of Islam in the seventh century had cut off Europe from its supplies of Egyptian papyrus. Before about 680, the Merovingian courts of France and Germany were well supplied with papyrus imported into both Mediterranean and Atlantic ports; after this date, these ceased, and their Carolingian successors, and the monasteries in their territories, wrote mainly on parchment and vellum.[17] The modern reader may have trouble imagining a book whose leaves consist of what amounts to leather, but parchment, and particularly vellum, could be manufactured to a thickness not much greater than modern paper. Further, these materials had the advantage of allowing repair work with a needle and thread. Their main disadvantage, of course, was their staggering cost.

The Spaniards pioneered the paper industry on European soil. Spanish papermaking centered on the kingdom of Aragon, which at its greatest extent comprised not only southeastern Spain, but also Sicily, Sardinia, and Naples. Before long, papermaking became established on the Ligurian coast near Genoa, but it would be the town of Fabriano, near Ancona on Italy's Adriatic coast, that would define the European industry and would dominate it for the next few centuries. Fine paper is still manufactured there today.

Historians are uncertain whether the Fabrianese adapted the methods of the Ligurian papermakers or those they encountered in Palestine during the Crusades. But whatever influenced them, they developed three techniques that greatly improved paper quality and decreased its cost.

First, they pioneered the use of gelatin from animal hooves to size the paper. Second, they invented the hydraulic press to work the pulp, the most labor-intensive part of the process in premodern societies. Muslim and European papermakers, like other medieval industries, made extensive use of water power—hence the very term paper mill. While the continuous rotary motion of a water mill can efficiently grind grain, it is less suited for the hammering of pulp. Mechanical cams can transform rotary power to trip-hammers, but not efficiently. The Fabrianese solved this problem with the use of specially designed geared camshafts that delivered the maximum available water power to the hammerheads, in which they embedded metal studs—a specialty of the local metalsmiths— that pounded the pulp into a fine cellulose mesh.[18]

Third, the Fabrianese replaced the wood- and fabric-based moulds with ones made of finely drawn wire copper mesh, which yielded a smoother final sheet of paper. Since the mould leaves a fine impression on the dried paper, Fabrianese factories began using them to inscribe identifying marks into the paper—the first watermarks.

The new watermarks, while not contributing to the efficiency of the process, had two beneficial effects. First, they served to "brand" the high-quality products of the different factories; second, they made life a lot easier for paper historians, who used them to trace the trade in European specimens. Paper from Chinese and Muslim sources is much more difficult to trace because it lacks these distinctive patterns. Watermark analysis shows that the sheer volume of the higher-quality and less expensive Fabrianese paper soon overwhelmed the domestic products of Spain, Egypt, and even Baghdad, where fourteenth-century imams debated the sanctity of Korans printed on European paper.

As would happen later with print, such a portable skill could not long remain the monopoly of a single town. Paper manufacture required fast-flowing, pure water to provide power for the mills and a good substrate for clear, white paper, so the mills naturally gravitated toward the hill and mountain towns of northern Italy; the Lake Garda area, which was under the control of Venice, would later become critical to that city's burgeoning print industry.[19]

The period between 1000 and 1400 thus saw first the revolution in word spacing and second the availability of relatively inexpensive paper. These two events and the establishment of Europe's first great universities all influenced the balance of power among Western religion, politics, and culture at least as much as the advent of Gutenberg's movable type, around 1450.

Europe's first flowering of literacy-driven dissent took place in the twelfth century in eastern France, far from its great cities and teaching institutions, where there resided a businessman most commonly known to history as "Peter Waldo," after whom the movement he spawned—Waldensianism—was named.

Scholars have since concluded that his actual surname in the Franco-Provençal language was Vaudès, but whatever his real name, he read and wrote well enough to handle the finances of the archbishopric of Lyon, a city made rich from its trade connections along the Rhône River. Legend has it that on his wedding night Vaudès gave up his worldly goods and persuaded his bride to embrace chastity; clothed in rags, he fled the city alone. More likely, he simply feared, as did many wealthy men of the period, for his eternal soul, for in those days, Jesus's famous injunction from the Book of Saint Matthew, "It is easier for a camel to go through the eye of a needle than for someone who is rich to enter the kingdom of God," carried far more freight than it does today.[20]

Just as impressive to Vaudès was Jesus's final command from the Book of Matthew, to "make disciples of all nations . . . teaching them to obey everything I have commanded you."[21] These two mandates made clear to Vaudès his mission in life: to embrace poverty and to spread the literal truth of God as revealed in the scriptures.

This would require the translation of the Bible and the sayings of the saints from the Vulgate—the official fourth-century Latin version by Saint Jerome—into the Franco-Provençal language. Another factor mandated the translations: Vaudès' inability to read and write Latin. The timing of his voluntary impoverishment and the translations would prove tricky, since commissioning vernacular parchment copies of the Word required no small expense.

These two biblical mandates—poverty and proselytizing—became the foundation of a movement that spread throughout western and central Europe over the ensuing three centuries. The "Poor of Lyon," as they called themselves, were almost exclusively laypeople, whose preaching therefore directly challenged the traditional monopoly and authority of the Roman Catholic Church. These sermons from the Bible defied church doctrine, which maintained that only the clergy could interpret scripture.

In early medieval Europe, a largely illiterate society, the central religious institution certainly was not the Bible, which was written, moreover, in Latin. Rather, it was the Mass, conducted in Latin by priests with their backs turned to the congregation so as to inspire awe and obedience: a magical ritual in which ordinary bread and wine were transmuted into the flesh and blood of the savior. Attendance by the congregants, whose immortal souls hung in the balance, was hardly optional.

If, in Lord Acton's overused aphorism, power corrupts, and absolute power corrupts absolutely, then the power of the medieval Church over its flock and its own ensuing corruption could hardly have been more absolute. Understandably, the Church did not welcome these Lyonnaise challenges to the awesome power of the word of God and of the Mass. The Poor of Lyon committed other affronts as well, among which were baptizing of converts and preaching by women members; most insufferable of all was the sect's worship of poverty, which constituted a stinging rebuke to the luxury and wealth enjoyed at the Church's upper echelons.[22]

The foremost scholar of the Waldensian movement, Guido Audisio, leaves little doubt as to the source of Church's wealth and power:

> We should remember that only about 10 percent of the population was literate. . . . In such a context, the clergy enjoyed unequalled privilege. . . . In their hands were concentrated all the powers that gave access to both reading and writing. They were the official bearers of the holy scriptures and represented the one and only means to have access to them. They alone could interpret the word of God. As a result, they monopolized public speaking.[23]

Audisio might have added that the literacy-empowered clergy monopolized the most important commodity in the medieval world: access to the hereafter.

The Church would not tolerate this challenge, and it quickly counterattacked; in 1184, it excommunicated Vaudès, and sometime after his death in approximately 1206, the archbishopric drove his flock out of Lyon. This was an enormous strategic blunder, since exile metastasized the dissenters, along with their subversive ideology, throughout Europe—an error that the Church would repeat many times over the centuries in its battles against heretics.

At first, the Church depended upon secular authorities to enforce theological purity; paradoxically, it was the cruelty of lay judges, particularly in Provence, where mass burnings came into vogue, that led the Vatican in 1231 to establish a more evenhanded due process for heretics, the Holy Office—that is, the Inquisition—which was initially entrusted to the Dominican order.

Historians have been known to cynically observe, "Thank goodness for the Inquisition; had it not existed we would not have its precious archives teaching us virtually all we know about those whom the Church hounded from its doors."[24] And so it was that the Inquisition provided posterity with almost all of the existing documentation of the cat-and-mouse game it played with the Waldensian movement. The Waldensian proselytizers themselves left little documentation, not because they were illiterate, for quite the opposite was true. Rather, they observed the strict clandestine tradecraft required by their perilous mission, in which possession of a single incriminating document could condemn its owner to burn. Indeed, inquisitorial records plot the sect's irrepressible spread over most of western Europe; by 1266, the Holy Office detailed prosecutions in nearly all of France, as well as in what is now northern Italy, Germany, Austria, and Czechoslovakia.

The Waldensians went by many names: in Lyon, the Poor; in German lands, the Brothers; in the rest of France, *barbes*—roughly, "elders." Their lifestyle anticipated a John le Carré novel: they traveled from town to town, often covering thousands of miles in a year; they stayed neither so briefly as to arouse suspicion, nor so long as to increase the risk of detection. The new paper technology was the microfilm of the era and allowed for much more portable and thus more easily hidden documents and miniature books. Again, Professor Audisio:

> It is truly moving to be able to turn the pages of the five booklets which belonged to the *barbes*, conserved at the library in Geneva, bearing in mind the distances they had covered, the adventure they had met with and the narrow escapes endured by these little, motionless witnesses which are so endearing, dumb, and yet so eloquent.[25]

To minimize the risk of betrayal, the Poor discouraged large formal meetings. Groups of *barbes* congregated only briefly in the larger towns, where they recruited the most promising candidates, whom they instructed in reading, writing, and the scriptures, particularly the gospels of John and Matthew, for a few months each winter over a three- or four-year period. After this training was completed, the sect assigned each novitiate to a senior *barbe*, a preacher literate in the vernacular (but only rarely in Latin). These pairs formed the smallest and thus most secure of cadres; they then set out on their peripatetic missions, with the senior *barbes* slowly imparting their literacy and pastoral skills to their apprentices, who in time would acquire their own charges.

Inquisitorial records of the interrogations of one pair, named simply Martin and Jean, reveal that around 1492 they traveled thousands of miles across both southern France and northern Italy. The authorities finally captured the two in the small town of Oulx on the modern Alpine French-Italian border, beyond which they had planned yet more ambitious travel.

The *barbes* spun their theological magic in clandestine nocturnal meetings in local believers' homes, where they baptized, heard confessions, and granted absolution. Crucially, they preached sermons to their initially illiterate followers; it seems likely that they may have imparted a modicum of literacy to their peasant flock, for, as grudgingly acknowledged by one Dominican inquisitor:

> All of them, men and women, big and small, learn and teach incessantly day and night. Such is their eagerness that they scarcely have time to pray. . . . The lukewarmness of our doctors should make them blush with shame for not spreading the truth of the Catholic faith with the same zeal as the faithless Waldensians show in spreading their errors and unbelief![26]

Indeed, the inquisitors often found Bibles in the homes of heretic peasants, despite the fact that in medieval Europe, peasants usually did not own books. While ordinary illiterate Waldensians may simply have kept their Bibles as religious totems, which they could not comprehend, or perhaps the inquisitors planted them in their houses, finding them suggests a far higher degree of literacy among ordinary Waldensians than among their more orthodox peers.[27] Although Waldensian preaching was for the most part an oral performance delivered in an oral society, the literacy of the *barbes* was critical to the success of the sect, since the *barbes* wrote out these sermons so as to deliver a consistent message throughout their wide peregrinations, which continued well into the time of Martin Luther. In the end, the Waldensians could not decisively overcome the power of Mother Church, but their mere survival for centuries was triumph enough.

Word spacing and inexpensive paper enabled dissent elsewhere. Roughly coincident with the Waldensian dissent, the third factor, the rise of the great European universities, was added to this explosive mixture in two highly interconnected intellectual uprisings at Oxford and Prague.

The events in Oxford were fostered by perhaps the most towering intellectual figure in fourteenth-century Christendom, John Wycliffe, and his followers. Wycliffe was born in Yorkshire sometime around 1330, and little is known of his background; he appears to have sprung from a large family of middling yeomen, and his academic talents became apparent early.[28] In medieval Europe, the road out of poverty lay in patronage by the wealthy, for in those days the purchase of scholarships by feudal overlords came relatively cheap, and it often provided a generous long-term capital return to the lord when his scholarly lads ripened into princes of the Church.

Accordingly, Wycliffe attracted the attention of the Duke of Lancaster, who resided at his castle near the Midlands town of Leicester. The Duke was better known as John of Gaunt, uncle to Richard II. In about 1344, Wycliffe had matriculated at Oxford under the patronage of Gaunt, who was also the benefactor of Chaucer.

The medieval academic greasy pole normally consumed decades and culminated in a doctor of divinity (DD) degree and mastership of a college. This long road was usually interspersed with financially replenishing stints in university administration and parish priesthoods. Wycliffe, typically, did not receive his DD until age forty-three, nearly thirty years after he had arrived at Oxford. In those days, scholars measured academic accomplishment according to mastery of the sterile intricacies of Aristotelian deduction; from the moment the medieval student matriculated, he engaged in ever more complex logically oriented "disputations." (The modern cynic might observe that this was not greatly different from today's academic meritocracy, in which accomplishment in most fields is measured according to the volume of equally sterile, jargon-laden—or in the social sciences, formula-laden—publications.)

Today, Aristotelian deductive constructs are derided as "logic chopping," but they did sharpen minds and encourage deviation from orthodoxy, and by the fourteenth century Oxford had become, if not exactly a hotbed of sedition, at least an incubator of dissent.

Wycliffe's teachers and peers soon recognized his prodigious talent, "the flower of Oxford, second to none, without rival in the discipline of the schools."[29] Since the university's primary function was to produce priests, and since the priesthood was the primary repository of literacy in medieval Europe, the crown routinely scoured Oxford's student body for administrative talent. Fatefully, Wycliffe did not escape notice; he was tapped for diplomatic and judicial tasks, and his often controversial written opinions on matters both temporal and spiritual became objects of scrutiny.

Fortunately for Wycliffe, about the time he achieved the pinnacle of his academic and temporal career, the power of the papacy was hamstrung by the Great Schism. At the beginning of the fourteenth century, the Vatican had fled the political instability of the Italian peninsula and moved to Avignon, France, where it grew increasingly corrupt. When Gregory XI, who had begun to pursue Wycliffe for his belief that the Church should not accumulate riches, died in 1378, the cardinals elected the weak and ineffectual Urban VI, and the papacy returned to Rome. The cardinals soon regretted their choice of Urban, and a large number of them left Rome for Avignon and elected Clement VII, the first antipope.

The Schism was not the sole, or even the major, cause of Wycliffe's truculence. In 1374, as crown representative in negotiations with the Pope's minions at Bruges, he had seen firsthand the material excesses of the Vatican; this likely radicalized his opinion of the corrupt Church and strengthened his belief that Christians owed their allegiance to God, not to the priesthood. Envy and pique at having been passed over for higher office may have also spiced his anger: as succinctly and cynically put by a prominent modern Wycliffe scholar, K. B. McFarlane, "The first steps towards reformation were thus taken by men whose consciousness of abuses was sharpest when they were deprived of the ability to commit them themselves."[30]

Whatever its wellspring, Wycliffe's righteous anger at the Church embroiled Christendom for more than a century. First and foremost, Wycliffe asserted, Christianity's ultimate authority lay in scripture, not in the clergy; anyone, down to the most ignorant but literate believer, could interpret the Bible as he read it. He concluded, as had Vaudès two centuries before and half a continent away, that it was imperative that the scriptures be translated into the vernacular so that all believers could read them. Second, since only God and Christ knew who they would receive into the kingdom of heaven, no one could know who among the clergy, including the Holy Father, was so blessed. Therefore, believers could not trust even the Pope. This reasoning was a direct challenge to the authority of the Church.

The sale of clerical offices and indulgences (forgiveness for a sin in return for a specific donation to the Church) and the greed of the pope, cardinals, bishops, and even members of the lower clergy such as abbots and archdeacons, whose lifestyles a secular aristocrat might envy, particularly aroused Wycliffe's ire. So, too, did other, more arcane, issues move him, such as precisely what happens to the bread and wine during Holy Communion. The precise nature of the Eucharist (the ceremonial transubstantiation of bread and wine into the flesh and blood of Christ), while seemingly obscure to the modern reader, caused many a medieval heretic to burn.

The combination of Oxford's Aristotelian rigor, Wycliffe's steel-trap mind and his anger toward the Church, and pen, paper, parchment, and growing literacy gave rise to an explosive ideology that would span the farthest reaches of the Continent. It would also lay the intellectual foundation of the Reformation in a way that the simple Waldensian preachers could not.

Wycliffe's heresy, which he propounded in a series of manuscripts circulated at Oxford, inevitably provoked titanic clashes with the hierarchy, led by the Archbishop of Canterbury, William Courtenay, an equally arrogant and brilliant clergyman.[31]

In the spring of 1382, a London synod condemned Wycliffe's teachings, but the Great Schism, Wycliffe's reputation and prestige at Oxford, his support in Parliament, and particularly the support of his old patron, John of Gaunt, kept him from the stake, and even from excommunication. Instead, the synod simply banished him to his old pastoral appointment at Lutterworth, in the rural Midlands north of London. By that point, he had been broken by a stroke; within two years, he was dead.[32]

Notwithstanding his disability and exile, those two years were not quiet ones; such was his prestige and following that sleepy Lutterworth became a sort of medieval Dharamsala, to which the faithful trekked to join the prophet in his great, final effort—the translation of the Bible into vernacular English.

The battle begun by Wycliffe, and taken up posthumously by academic and lay acolytes, the so-called Lollards (a pejorative term roughly meaning "heretic"), revolved around nothing more and nothing less than the ultimate source of all power in the medieval West: the ability to interpret the Bible.[33]

The Church in Rome, and for a time in Avignon as well, maintained this monopoly on scripture through brute force. In 1407, for example, the Archbishop of Canterbury, Thomas Arundel, who was well aware of the explosive potential of a vernacular Bible, explicitly forbade its translation, or even the reading of any translation made during or after the time of Wycliffe.[34]

The Church, then as now, was not possessed of great wellsprings of intellectual honesty and self-awareness; it rationalized forbidding the lay reading of scripture on the basis of an enlightened interest in its flock's well-being, as expressed by Pope Gregory VII three centuries before Wycliffe in this chapter's epigraph.

Modern paper technology obscures the sheer mass of the Bible—the Old Testament and New Testament total about 593,000 and 181,000 words, respectively. In Cassiodorus's day, this would have consumed about nine large vellum folios; by the medieval period, scribes had miniaturized their handwriting to the point that only two folios, along with untold thousands of man-hours of labor, were required.

Certainly, Wycliffe was not the first to translate scriptures into English. Within a century of Saint Augustine's introduction of Christianity into the British Isles around 596, portions of it were being translated into the various languages of the Angles and Saxons; the most famous of these translations is the Lindisfarne Gospels, whose gorgeous illuminated pages are on display at the British Library.

While by 1400, scholars had translated large segments of the Bible, particularly the Psalms, into various vernaculars, none before Wycliffe had attempted the complete Bible. Curiously, such was the ailing scholar's other-worldliness that he decided on a word-for-word translation from the Vulgate, which retained even the Latin word order. Driven by his long-running battle with the popes in both Avignon and Rome, Wycliffe clearly intended this first volume not for ordinary people, but as an appeal to the English church, and perhaps, as well, to a few highly educated politicians, such as John of Gaunt.[35] This peculiar translation technique, combined with the fabulous expense of a massive parchment Bible, guaranteed that it would be inaccessible to all but the best-educated and wealthiest of laypersons.

Such was the force of Wycliffe's intellect and writing that he not only left behind a cadre of dissenters at Oxford, but also attracted a following at Lutterworth and in Leicester, the stronghold of John of Gaunt. Most, if not all, of the initial, literal, Lollard translation was done by a group that included John Purvey, Wycliffe's faithful secretary, who followed him to Lutterworth; and Wycliffe's former colleagues who remained at Oxford.

In approximately 1395, perhaps a decade after the first complete, literal English translation by Wycliffe, Purvey, and their associates, a second appeared, which was much more freely written and came with an explanatory prologue, and was thus clearly aimed at the lay audience. Since by the time of its publication, the authorities had eliminated nearly all of Wycliffe's earlier supporters save Purvey, scholars have concluded that Purvey must have written it.[36]

The Lollards put up spirited resistance to Church persecution. The high-water mark of dissent occurred in January 1395, when a group of Wycliffite aristocrats and knights concocted a document that described the sect's inflammatory main beliefs, the "Twelve Conclusions of the Lollards," which they not only read in Parliament but also nailed to the doors of Saint Paul's Cathedral and Westminster Abbey. This elicited a yet more vigorous reaction from Archbishop Arundel; by the early 1400s, he had neutralized most of the Wycliffite opposition through execution, jailing, exile, or recantation. (Purvey recanted in 1401, and Nicholas Hereford, an Oxford colleague of Wycliffe who helped with the initial literal Bible translation, was tortured by the Inquisition after inadvisably returning from exile. He not only recanted, but also joined the inquisitors.) Arundel personally mopped up the Oxford Wycliffites at a synod there in late 1407, where he proclaimed the above-mentioned prohibition on Bible translation.[37]

After the elimination of Lollard dissent at Oxford, the movement's center of gravity shifted to Gaunt's stronghold in the Midlands, where it was taken up by a mixture of clergymen, peasants, and not a few aristocrats. Among the latter was Sir John Oldcastle, a swashbuckling military hero and old comrade in arms of Prince Henry, the future King Henry V, and heir to a large manor on the Welsh border, which afforded him a barony and a seat in Parliament.

At some point in his military career, this seeming paragon of the English ruling elite came under the sway of a Wycliffite chaplain known to history only as "John," who, after some inquiries from Archbishop Courtenay, quickly disappeared from view. Afterward the archbishop pointedly enjoined Oldcastle against further heresies.

Oldcastle did not heed Courtenay's warnings; when the Archbishop came into possession of some heretical illuminations from a printer's shop belonging to Oldcastle, he summoned the baron to the royal chambers of his old comrade, now Henry V, and demanded an explanation. An innocent mistake, dissembled Oldcastle; a simple soldier, he had not realized the documents' theological significance. In actuality, by that point the baron had become the benefactor and collaborator of many Lollard clerics, some of whom he had hidden in his castles.

This soon became apparent to all involved. Yet the king bent over backward to avoid moving against Oldcastle, whom he urged to recant. By this point, the old warrior made overt his heresy, and in September 1413 Courtenay and the king had him imprisoned in the Tower, where he underwent extensive interrogation: Did he think it necessary to be absolved of his sins by a priest? Did he believe in transubstantiation? Alas, he did neither: the bread remained unchanged after the Eucharist, and he was responsible only to God for his sins, not to the clergy. Courtenay's line of inquiry so provoked Oldcastle that he proceeded to rail against the pope as the Antichrist and against the devil's tails he imagined on the bishops and friars. He then condemned his accusers to hell.

Oldcastle had been given every opportunity to save himself, and he had refused, ostensibly giving himself up to the mercies of his accusers.

Yet again, Courtenay and the king gave him one more chance: a forty-day cooling-off period in which to reconsider his intemperate testimony.

The recalcitrant baron used the breathing space to escape from the Tower and then hide in the houses of his supporters, from where he plotted a harebrained plan to capture the king and his brothers. While Oldcastle was obviously a formidable military presence, the Lollards who followed him most certainly were not, and their plot was soon betrayed. The king traditionally spent Christmas at Eltham Palace, in modern southeast London, where the conspirators expected to find him. Instead, he and his brothers set up their headquarters at Westminster, and on the night of January 10, 1414, thousands of Lollard peasants, their numbers swelled by Oldcastle's military reputation, streamed into their rendezvous point in Saint Giles Fields in London, where they were easily rolled up by Henry's troops. Within weeks, most of the leaders had been executed, but Oldcastle, ever the brilliant tactician, escaped the net and remained at large until he was finally cornered and captured three years later. On December 14, 1417, he was led before Parliament; he apparently remained mute to his accusers, and on that same day he received the usual punishment meted out to high-level English heretics of that era: hanging to death followed by burning.[38]

The lengths to which the authorities would go to avoid such an end for heretics is illustrated by another case overseen by Prince Henry before the Oldcastle episode: that of John Badby, a Lollard tailor who in 1409 was tried and convicted for denying transubstantiation. Held in prison for more than a year, he was put to the stake alive in 1410. At the stake, the prince begged him to recant and save himself. The tailor refused, and the flames were lit. Writhing in pain, he cried out, "Mercy!" This was misinterpreted by Henry as repentance. Pulled half-alive from the pyre, Badby once again declined to repent, and so was reattached to the stake and finished off.[39]

Oddly, Wycliffe's personal story did not end with his death in 1384. His popularity at Oxford and his ill health and premature demise cheated the Inquisition of his burning during his lifetime, but in 1428, by one of history's more bizarre papal orders, his body was exhumed and burned, and his ashes cast into the River Swift at Lutterworth.

Like the Waldensians, the Lollard movement simmered underground for the next few centuries; inquisitorial records report numerous trials, recantations, and burnings for at least a century after Oldcastle. Paradoxically, it would be half a continent away from Oxford, in Prague, that Wycliffite dissent would loom the largest, as ordinary men and women fought to read the Bible in their own language and interpret it free of interference from the Church.

Few great national movements can be laid at the feet of a princess, but such was the case with the rise of Christian dissent in Bohemia and with it, Czech nationalism.

With the death of Wycliffe and the defeat of his protégés, the Lollards, the center of anticlerical dissent shifted to Czechoslovakia. The conduit of Lollard heresies from England to central Europe was Princess Anne of Bohemia, the daughter of Charles IV, the French-educated king of Bohemia and the Holy Roman Emperor.

In 1347 Charles, who was literate in five languages (Latin, Italian, French, German, and Czech), established Prague University, which very rapidly took its place among the other great schools at Bologna, Paris, and, most fatefully, Oxford. He also redesigned much of Prague, and his ambitious building campaign produced the city's architecture and layout that to this day delights its modern residents and tourists alike: Hradčany Castle, the Charles Bridge, and New Town. In 1366 he fathered Anne, whose hand was given in a highly controversial dynastic marriage to England's Richard II in 1381. Both were fifteen.

The marriage of Richard and Anne provoked much criticism in her new home, as she brought no dowry. Richard actually had to pay her brother, King Wenceslas IV, 20,000 florins for her hand. During the Great Schism, the resultant combined support of the Germans, Bohemians, and English for the Roman papacy seems to have fostered the marital union as a way of isolating the French, who naturally supported the pope in Avignon. (The Bohemians had, however, previously offered Anne's hand to the dauphin, the heir to the French throne, and approached Richard only after negotiations with the French had broken down.)

Anne brought with her a retinue of chaplains and ladies-in-waiting; whether or not any of them had contact with Wycliffe, who died three years after her marriage, or his writings is unknown, but there is no question that in the decades following Wycliffe's death, a number of scholars from Prague arrived in Oxford, where they drank in the Lollard doctrines.[40]

For example, two Czech academics, Mikuláš Faulfiš and Jiříz Kněhnic, traveled to England to copy Wycliffe's texts; at Oxford, they obtained affidavits of the master's good character as well as a patently false one attesting that he had never been convicted of heresy, and at Lutterworth they visited his grave, where, as might any tourist in any age, they dutifully chipped off a piece of his tombstone as a souvenir.

Scholars have found large caches of Wycliffe and Lollard manuscripts in Prague, and a close examination of Czech-language manuscripts shows an uncanny ideological, and at times even grammatical, resemblance to those of Wycliffe and the Lollards. A brisk communication between Czech and English reformers even included a letter of encouragement sent from John Oldcastle to the leader of the Czech movement, Jan Hus, who himself had repeatedly and effusively expressed his admiration for Wycliffe.

The initial contacts between the Czechs and the English must have taken place in Latin, Europe's scholastic lingua franca and the language of Wycliffe's scholarly works, but the Bohemian visitors soon translated these into Czech. Ironically, owing to the Inquisition's destruction of Wycliffe's works in Britain, far more copies exist in Prague and other central European cities than in England.[41]

Hubris, corruption, greed, and sloth were as much a feature of the Bohemian clergy as of the Italian, French, and English clergies. Even before Anne wed Richard, the Waldensians and their anticlerical opinions were well known in Bohemia, and the rank-and-file clergy began to agitate against the hierarchy. In the late fourteenth century, one priest, John Milič, delivered daily three fiery anticlerical sermons to overflow congregations in three different churches—one sermon each in Latin, German, and Czech. (Most famously, Milič purchased a brothel, converted it into a religious hospice for the two hundred women working there, dressed them in nun's habits, and established a church on the site, outraging the Church hierarchy.)

Milič intuitively understood the importance of written sermons, not only as propaganda, but also in terms of achieving a uniform, reproducible product, or, as we might say today, of "keeping the team on message." He drilled into his students the importance of writing in the pastoral mission and circulated even first drafts of his sermons to students and colleagues. Collections of such preachings abound in the historical record and must have been an essential part of the dissident movement's toolbox.[42]

Milič's spiritual successor, Matthew of Janov, inveighed against the corruption of the Avignon papacy and helped organize the translation of the Bible into both German and Czech. Anne took portions of this translation with her to England.[43] The best-known Czech reformer, Jan Hus, born around 1369 in rural Bohemia, was Janov's junior by about fourteen years. Hus was fortunate to live close to the regional commercial center, Prachatice; there he attended an elementary school where he was taught the basics: grammar, rhetoric, and logic. He then matriculated at the University of Prague. At that point, Prague was engulfed by the turbulence of the Great Schism. Later, he would recall a resolution he made during his student years:

> Whenever I discern a sounder opinion in any matter whatsoever, I gladly and humbly abandon the earlier one. For I know that those things I have learned are but the least in comparison to what I do not know.[44]

Such rationalism was vanishingly rare in pre-Enlightenment Europe, the continent of blind faith and obedience to the Church. By the time Hus embarked upon his advanced studies sometime after 1390, the intellectual exchange between Oxford and Prague was in full swing; Wycliffe influenced many members of the university faculty, and they must have made an impression on the open-minded Hus. Probably the most influential of these was the scholar known to history as Jerome of Prague, who attended Oxford from 1399 to 1401, copied Wycliffe's most important works, and brought them back home, where he became Hus's close friend.

By 1396 Hus was lecturing on Aristotle at the university, and in 1402 he was made rector and preacher at Prague's Bethlehem Church, which had been founded by Milič's followers in reaction against the corruption of the mainstream clergy. There, Hus preached over three thousand sermons.[45] Like Milič, he understood the key role played by written sermons in amplifying his message and made them a central part of his instruction.[46] And like Wycliffe and the Lollards, he realized that in order to make scriptures available to the masses, their Latin forms would have to be both transliterated and then translated into the vernacular. Unfortunately, the medieval Czech script was not up to the transliterations, and so, like the Semites at Serabit el-Khadim and the Copts in Egypt, he invented new letters, which are still used today in several Slavic alphabets.

Inevitably Hus, like the Waldensians and Lollards, drew the attention of the authorities, particularly Zbyněk Zajíc, the Archbishop of Prague, who in 1410 burned two hundred of Hus's books in his castle's courtyard. The Lollards quickly replaced these with a shipment from England. Zbyněk then excommunicated Hus twice, in 1411 and 1412, arousing vigorous protests at the university. One popular ditty (which rhymes in Czech) ran:

Bishop Zbyněk ABC
burned books although he
knew not what they contained.[47]

Repeatedly warned, threatened, and excommunicated, Hus continued to preach. The attacks on him culminated in 1415, when he was lured with a safe-conduct pass from Sigismund, Anne's brother, to the Council of Constance, in modern-day Konstanz, Germany. The Church had called the council primarily to resolve the Great Schism, but it also pursued heretics; there, Hus was again convicted of heresy. On July 6, 1415, the presiding officials stripped him of his vestments, cut his tonsure with scissors, and placed on his head a paper crown depicting three devils and bearing the inscription, "This is a heresiarch" (the inventor or founder of a heresy). Hus then mounted a table, wood and straw were piled up to his chin, and the fire was lit. So terrified was the Vatican of Hus that Church officials deprived the Czechs even of relics from the burning. Accordingly, executioners burned him twice, removed his heart and burned it, too, and threw his ashes into the Rhine. A year later, Hus's colleague and friend Jerome of Prague would suffer the same fate in precisely the same location, today marked by a large boulder.[48] (Besides settling the Great Schism and burning Hus and Jerome, the Council of Constance is also remembered for Sigismund's memorable reply to a cardinal who corrected his Latin: "I am the Roman Emperor, and above grammar."[49])

Bohemia's German overlords, the nominal rulers of the Holy Roman Empire, strongly drove the suppression of Hussite ideology. Wycliffe's criticisms of the Church thus resonated especially strongly in Prague, where they became a touchstone not only of religious reform but also of Czech nationalism, whose spirit burns brightly to this day.

The executions of Hus and Jerome, along with growing Bohemian nationalism, raised the tensions between the Vatican and the Czech citizenry to the breaking point. In 1419 King Wenceslaus IV, brother to Anne and the son of the beloved Charles IV, died and was replaced with Sigismund, who had betrayed Hus; this triggered a full-scale armed rebellion. The Vatican and the Holy Roman Empire attempted to smash the rebels and were repeatedly thrown back; by 1428, the Bohemians had countered, and they invaded the Holy Roman Empire in territory that is now Poland and Slovakia.

To the very end, the conflicts over the vernacular Bible and the interpretation of the Eucharist burned heretics and changed the fates of nations. The Hussite movement was divided between two main factions: the Utraquists, who believed that laypeople could consume both the bread and the wine at Communion (instead of only the bread); and the Taborites, a zealous, apocalyptic sect that espoused a particularly radical interpretation of Hus's ideology. By the 1430s, the Church realized that it could not defeat the Hussites; it made the necessary theological accommodations with the Utraquists, and the resultant Catholic-Utraquist alliance made quick work of the Taborites and thus ended the rebellion.[50]

The Roman Catholic Church all too well understood the relationship between heresy and literacy; not only did literacy encourage heresy, but, as the education of Waldensian peasants demonstrated, heresy begat literacy. Within a few years of his 1407 ban on English Bible translation, Archbishop Arundel, in an effort to appropriate the tools of the Lollards, authorized and approved translation of the Church's own propaganda into English; the Bible, however, was still too hot for the Church to handle.[51]

All three movements—the Waldensians, Lollards, and Hussites— survived into the Reformation, because, in the words of one scholar, "A book is more easily hidden than a man."[52] The English movement greatly influenced the Czech movements. Abundant evidence indicates that the Waldensians, Lollards, and Hussites had established contact with one another and, after 1520, with the forces of the Reformation itself.[53]

What finally became of the Waldensians, Lollards, and Hussites? It is not too much of an oversimplification to say that all three groups became Protestants, and thus lost their original identity (although to this day, some

Protestants in central Europe still identify themselves as Waldensians). It seems that Protestantism, whose eloquent antipapal ideology, with its three ideological pillars—believers as priests, the infallibility of the Bible, and justification by faith and not by hierarchy—proved irresistible to western European religious dissidents of almost all stripes.

From the Catholic perspective as well, little separated the Reformation from the three older ideologies. When, in the mid-sixteenth century, the forces of the Counter-Reformation cataloged the Waldensian men, women, and children they had slaughtered in southern Italy, they listed them as "Protestants."[54]

Of the three movements, only the Hussites survived in the open, and only by making theological concessions to the Church. The era's lack of mass communication technology hobbled the Waldensians and Lollards; this situation would change when the Reformation exploited the power of Gutenberg's invention to break the Vatican's monopoly on faith in Europe.

Hus, the Waldensians, and the Lollards were not alone in popularizing their respective vernaculars and so augmenting literacy. This was also the age of Chaucer and Dante, who wrote in their native tongues and thereby legitimized them.

By the time of Gutenberg, the Church had lost its stranglehold on literacy, and thus on power. All over Europe in the wake of the Great Schism and then the Black Death, an increasingly wealthy and literate merchant class challenged the Church's domination of everyday life. The substitution of English, French, Italian, German, and Czech for Latin broke the clergy's Latin monopoly on the written word and became the keystone of the rise of secular society in Europe.

Between 1000 and 1500, word spacing, inexpensive paper, and the rise of the universities gave dissidents the power to challenge the Church. By making the Bible commonplace, the Waldensians, Lollards, and Hussites stripped it of its magic and so deprived the Church of its monopoly on scriptural interpretation.

Although these groups had dented the Church's power, they could not overcome it. In the fifteenth century, an obscure mirror maker from Mainz would take advantage of recent advances in mining and metallurgy to devise a technology that, when combined with word spacing and cheap paper, would enable later dissidents to complete the mission undertaken by Vaudès, Wycliffe, and Hus.

5

Punch and Counterpunch

In Victor Hugo's *Notre-Dame de Paris* (better-known in English as *The Hunchback of Notre Dame*), Claude Frollo, the church's archdeacon, gazes alternately at the massive cathedral and the book on his desk and intones sadly, "Alas! The one will kill the other!"[1] Hugo set the novel in 1482, barely a generation after the Gutenberg revolution, and he could not have been clearer: mass-produced books would undermine and ultimately destroy the Roman Catholic Church—the most powerful religious and political force in Europe. As the historian Johannes Janssen put it,

> This invention, the mightiest and most important in the history of civilization, gave, as it were, "wings to the human mind," and supplied the best means of preserving, multiplying, and disseminating every product of the intellect.[2]

Janssen might well have added that the printing press also gave wings to dissent, endowing it with an amplifying power that enabled ordinary people to successfully challenge the might of the greatest power on the Continent—the Church. Most dangerously of all, the printing press put the holy scriptures into the hands of the masses and so allowed them to interpret the Word for themselves, and thus deprived the Church of its greatest asset: its millennium-old monopoly on the gates of heaven.

By the beginning of the fifteenth century, many roadblocks to mass communication had been cleared: the elimination of *scriptura continua* had enabled silent reading, the first great universities had become both repositories and marketplaces for books, and paper mills had began to appear north of the Alps. The first of these mills was built near Nuremberg around 1390, followed in the coming decades by mills in a half dozen other cities. It cannot have been a coincidence that paper mills appeared in Basel and Strasbourg just a few years before Gutenberg and his associates manufactured their presses.[3] Indeed, when Gutenberg printed his initial Bibles on vellum, they were nearly as expensive as the handwritten copies they were meant to replace. Absent the new paper technology being developed in Fabriano, the name Gutenberg and his marvelous invention might have disappeared from history.

Great inventors, almost by definition, rarely start out in the fields that made them famous; rather, they spring from those that provided them with the tools to invent in the first place: Thomas Edison began as a telegraph operator, the Wright brothers as bicycle mechanics, and James Watt as an instrument maker.

So it was with Johannes Gutenberg, who trained in metalworking at a time of great advances in both metallurgy and mining, that held the key to the production of movable cast type. Had Gutenberg been born a century or two before, these advanced technologies, critical to his types, would not have been available.

While the Romans had excelled at deep mining techniques—they had sunk shafts as deep as six hundred feet in a lead mine near Spain's Mediterranean coast—their mining techniques, like most of advanced Roman civil engineering technology, were lost for nearly a millennium after AD 476. In addition, the Romans had played out most of their mines, so it would be in the areas north of the Danube, which the Romans had not occupied, that the descendants of their Germanic conquerors would develop the metals and alloys central to Gutenberg's success. Most critically, Europeans did not begin to mine antimony, a key ingredient of movable type, until the late medieval period.

The mountainous forests of central Europe—with their rich veins of silver, lead, copper, and antimony; plenteous wood with which to smelt it; and abundant running water to power the foundries' bellows and hammers—would midwife the metallurgical advances that made movable type and the Continent's later economic growth possible. As always, the search for precious metals, particularly silver, drove Europe's mining entrepreneurs. Miners usually find silver ores alongside ores of lead and copper, and advances in the extraction and smelting of all three went hand in hand.

The miner, particularly in northern Europe's wet climate, constantly battles water; any shaft dug below the water table will soon be flooded and in need of drainage. The Romans had drained their deep mines with human power, but this did not suffice in northern Europe's deep, damp mines. In approximately the thirteenth century, German miners began to conduct horses down specially designed spiral paths hewn into solid rock to turn intricately geared pumps. At Schemnitz in the Carpathians, ninety-six horses powered three separate devices.

In medieval Europe, academics such as Georgius Agricola, author of *De re metallica* ("On the Nature of Metals"), began to examine systematically the science of metallurgy, and soon metal factories, known as *Saigerhütten*, that applied the new techniques to separate copper and silver began to appear along streams near the mines.

The new metals-based industries had far-reaching effects that modern historians are only now beginning to plumb. On the one hand, German and Bohemian peasants penetrated deep into the hinterlands to seek their fortunes in the mines, and in doing so they freed themselves of their former overlords in "new economic zones" unblemished by the feudal system. On the other hand, since ancient times, the state had assumed political control, and sometimes direct ownership, of strategic mines, as did Athens at its rich silver deposits at Laurion. In France and England, only the national governments possessed the technical and financial expertise to oversee the mines, and so spurred the rise of these two critical nation-states.

The net effect of the new metals industry was to strengthen both the individual and the national governments at the expense of the old feudal overlords. Mechanical printing and the attendant expansion of literacy added to this brew yet one more ingredient that would remake the Continent in the coming centuries.[4]

Today's casual observer conceives of printing in its entirety: the blindingly fast mechanical press ravenously consuming a ton of paper every minute or two. While Gutenberg and his contemporaries could not imagine this modern reality, the concept of portable type that impressed its form onto a writing medium was hardly a new one; the Mesopotamians employed cylinder seals as primitive printing presses into which they inserted different characters—the first movable type. More than a millennium before Gutenberg, both Cicero and Saint Jerome conceived of printing frames filled with portable alphabetic type.[5] Centuries before Gutenberg, the Chinese became adept at woodblock printing for both written characters and images, and they even used movable wooden character blocks. Finally, the Koreans, who had developed an alphabetic script, beat the Europeans to movable alphabetic metallic type by at least several decades.[6]

To be sure, a number of other problems would have prevented either the Chinese or the Koreans from completely scooping Gutenberg. Technological barriers, such as the thinness of their inks, made printing with metallic type nigh impossible. Cultural barriers also impeded the development of presses in the East; in particular, the Asian fondness for fine calligraphy decreased the demand for and appreciation of print. Even had the Asians overcome these problems, printing requires prodigious capital investment, and the near-absence of functioning capital markets in the East would have throttled any nascent Chinese or Korean printing enterprises.[7]

Further, the mere invention of a press to deploy movable type would not have been enough. The page you are reading contains approximately two thousand separate characters, so even the simplest of print shops would require tens of thousands of pieces of type; the manufacture of such quantities of type lay well beyond the capacity of all but kings and emperors, in the East or West. Finally, even the manufacture of pieces of type in large numbers would itself be insufficient, for the pieces had to be so precisely crafted that thousands would fit together perfectly in absolutely straight lines.

Gutenberg's contribution to mechanical printing was thus not the concept of movable type, or even its implementation, but rather the mass production of individual bits of letter type so finely made that the few thousand blocks required for the average page fitted perfectly together. For centuries the impediment to practicable *alphabetic* movable type had been the precision required, for if the type caster does not produce it accurately and uniformly enough, the resulting page looks something like this:[8]

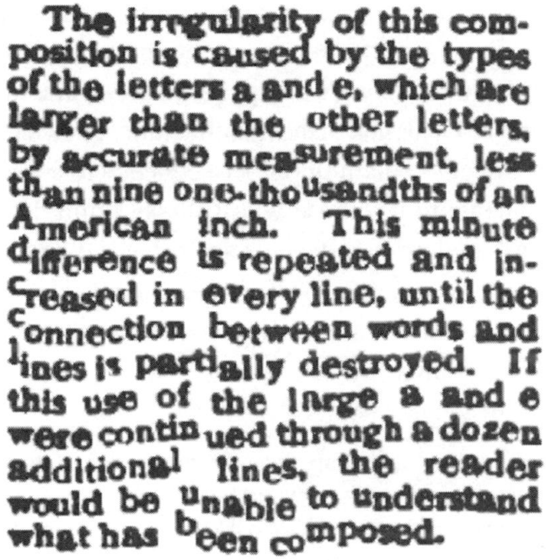

The irregularity of this composition is caused by the types of the letters a and e, which are larger than the other letters, by accurate measurement, less than nine one-thousandths of an American inch. This minute difference is repeated and increased in every line, until the connection between words and lines is partially destroyed. If this use of the large a and e were continued through a dozen additional lines, the reader would be unable to understand what has been composed.

Figure 5-1. Appearance of print from poorly cast type.

Notice how the misalignment, while barely noticeable in the first line, worsens with each succeeding one. Unless the type caster manufactures all the type blocks so that the printer can align them exactly, the result will be an unreadable jumble before the bottom of the page is reached. The key barrier, then, to industrial printing was not in the production of the presses or even of the formes into which the type fitted, *but rather in the precise and rapid casting of the tiny blocks of letter type themselves.*

In the words of Theodore De Vinne, a nineteenth-century American printer and preeminent historian of print:

> This invention does not belong to him who first thought of the advantages of types, or even to him who first made them by impracticable methods. Its honors are really due to the man to whose sagacity and patience in experiment we are indebted for the type-mould, for he was the first to make types which would be used with advantage.[9]

That man might have been Gutenberg, or just as likely a contemporary lost to history. Gutenberg did not invent any of the techniques central to casting type—the use of the punch, counterpunch, and mould to create type blocks. By 1450, these were all applied, at one time or another, in the stamping of coins and seals and in the manufacture of pewter items.[10] Rather, he was the first to deploy them in proper sequence to *efficiently* cast type.

Neither Gutenberg nor those who followed him described the process in any detail, and print historians are forced to deduce it from later sources, prime among which is the eighteenth-century bible of type casting, Pierre-Simon Fournier's *Manuel typographique*, in which he elegantly summarized the craftsman's job:

> to know the best possible shape that can be given to letters, and their proper relation to one another, and to be able to reproduce them upon steel so that they may be struck into copper to make the matrices by means of which the letters can ever after be cast in any numbers.[11]

The method described by Fournier probably became established within about a century of Gutenberg and remained essentially unchanged until the advent of the mechanized steam-driven press in the nineteenth century, and Fournier's dense paragraph summarizing it needs some unpacking.

The first concept to master is that of the "counter," the hollow space within most letters. The simplest letter of all is the lowercase "o," for which the counter is a simple circle or oval inside the "o." The punch cutter can either gouge out the counter with a sharp file or stamp it with a specially designed punch—the so-called counterpunch. Although making a counterpunch takes much more time than gouging out a single counter, it is more than worth the effort, since the counterpunch can rapidly and consistently strike the counters of many punches, as opposed to individually gouging out counters of nonuniform size and shape.

Now, let's consider a more complex letter, the capital "H," and its counter, shown in Figure 5-2.

Theoretically, there are two ways to produce a punch for this letter. The punch cutter could start by filing away the flat face of the blank punch so as to shape the outer edges of the "H" (the outer black areas of the "H" in Figure 5-2), then drive in the counterpunch to produce the letter's final

Figure 5-2. Capital H and its counter.

form. The problem with doing so is that if he drives the counterpunch even slightly off center, he has wasted the painstaking effort of first filing the outer letter margins.

Given the high risk involved in striking the counterpunch as the second step, it is far more efficient to *first* drive the counterpunch into the unfinished flat punch face. If, and only if, the punch cutter is satisfied with this counterpunch strike will he then meticulously grind away at the outer edge of the punch, first with a coarse file, then with succeeding finer ones, to make a perfect "H," as shown in Figure 5-3.

Figure 5-3. From left to right, blank punch face, counterpunch, unfinished punch face after counterpunch strike, and finished punch face after filing away of outside edges.

In practice, the process is a bit more complex than that; the punch cutter produces the tapered counterpunch from soft steel. The finished product is hardened—"annealed"—so that it can be driven into the soft flat steel of the blank punch, which is then filed away from the outside to produce the finished "H." At the end of the process, the punch, too, is hardened so that it can perform the next step in the process, the production of the mould.

The critical piece of equipment, then, in the artisan's panoply is the counterpunch. The lowercase letters in this paragraph, for example, contain only, depending on the font and preference of the punch cutter, several different counters: those for the h, n, and u, and sometimes the m as well, are identical, as are those for the p, q, d, and b; many letters, such as the l and r, do not require a counter at all. Further, because the counterpunch is in the shape of a tapered prism or cone, driving it to different depths allows it to be used for letters of different sizes, whereas the letters require a different punch for each font size. For this reason, museums of printing technology contain thousands of specimens of medieval-era punches, but only a few dozen of the critical counterpunches survive.[12]

Once the punch cutter has made a punch containing the face of the letter, it could easily be used in the printing process; properly inked, it would produce a perfect letter image on paper. In fact, steel punches had been produced for centuries, if not millennia, before Gutenberg, and no doubt some had stamped ink or another pigment on paper or papyrus.

The problem, as already mentioned, is the requirement for thousands of pieces of type, and the process just described is far too laborious for making type in such large numbers. Gutenberg's special genius, then, was devising a method for mass-producing type: the type-mould process.

The artisan begins by hardening the soft-steel letter punch, then driving it into a thick sheet of copper, producing a "matrix," such as for the capital "H," shown in Figure 5-4.

The artisan next cuts the matrix down to size, so that it fits in the steel mould, shown in Figure 5-5.

Note how the sides of the mould are adjustable. Each type size requires its own specially sized mould, but for a given type size—say 12-point—different characters can have greatly different widths, which require moving the lateral walls in or out. A capital "W," for example, is several times wider than a period.

Figure 5-4. Copper matrix for capital H, before it has been cut down to size to fit in mould.

Figure 5-5. Type mould. For clarity, a finished type for capital H has been placed in the location where the copper matrix shown above, after cutting down to size, would go.

In essence, the matrix-mould complex is a five-sided rectangular box whose width is adjusted to the character being produced: the matrix forms the box's bottom; the mould, its four sides. The type caster then pours molten metal into the open top of the box.

As daunting as punch cutting was, no task was more demanding or specialized than that of the type caster, who held the crucible of molten alloy in his right hand and the finished mould in his left. At the instant that he poured the alloy with his right hand, he jerked the mould rapidly upward with his left to force the alloy into its interstices before it cooled. He next removed the matrix from the bottom of the mould and with a toss ejected the type with its letter formed and ready for printing. Finally, he replaced the matrix and repeated the process; a skilled type caster could, in this manner, produce several type pieces per minute—up to three thousand per day. According to De Vinne, "Long practice enabled the type-caster to do this work with apparent carelessness; but the trick of making this throw or cast of the left hand, at the correct time in the correct manner, was slowly acquired—and by some strong men, never acquired at all."[13] In contrast, print historians estimate that an experienced punch cutter could produce only two to four punches per week.[14]

The construction of the press itself, which could easily be adapted from a winepress or fabric-printing press, presented little technical difficulty; nor was there much challenge in the construction of the forme, the box in which the compositor mounted the type. Sometime after 1445, Gutenberg cast his first type, which he then must have quickly married to an existing winepress or fabric press and an easily manufactured forme: the first practicable movable-type press.

The printing process itself was a two-man affair: one man to fit the paper sheet onto the bottom of the press, another to ink the mounted type with a ball of leather and tighten the press's screw. The paper sheet was typically a "folio," on which four page impressions were made—two on each side. ("Folio" refers to a sheet that is folded in half and sewn into the spine along the fold. A "quarto" is folded twice, receiving eight impressions; an "octavo" is folded thrice; receiving sixteen impressions; and a "sexto decimo" is folded four times, receiving thirty-two impressions, each on progressively smaller pages and in smaller type sizes.)

The controversy surrounding Gutenberg's claim to having invented the first metallic alphabetic movable type is familiar enough to most

Figure 5-6. Dangerous work: type caster, ca. 1683. Note the crucible in the right hand, type mould in left.

readers. Tellingly, we know far more of his multifaceted legal and financial troubles than of the details of the first printing presses; scholars have gleaned almost all of what we do know about the birth of movable-type printing either from the records of the lawsuits against Gutenberg or from scientific analysis of his printed products.[15]

The absence of effective patent law, particularly in the politically fragmented world of the Holy Roman Empire, made secrecy imperative, and this secrecy hides the origins of Gutenberg's technique from the historian's view. Furthermore, the practice of affixing the publisher's name to a book or pamphlet did not begin until about a decade after Gutenberg printed his first Bibles—a fact that creates yet more historical difficulty.

So we are likely never to know for sure who the inventor was. Nor are we likely ever to know what precise techniques he initially used. Were the first punches and moulds made of metal, or were wooden punches perhaps employed to make impressions in clay or sand? If the first punches and moulds were metal, were the first types mainly lead-based, or made primarily from a different metal? And so forth.[16]

From now on, we shall assume for the sake of argument that Johannes Gutenberg indeed deserved that honor. To the extent that historians can ever really identify the "inventor" of any device, it was the great good fortune of Gutenberg that the metallurgical techniques equal to the manufacture of high-precision type first came together in the early industrial crucible of mid-fifteenth-century central Europe.

Before proceeding further, it is important to set the historical scene in which the drama of Gutenberg's printing press takes place—the late Holy Roman Empire. The successor state to Charlemagne's empire, it was, as Voltaire put it, neither holy, nor Roman, nor an empire. It occupied, very roughly speaking, most of modern Germany, Austria, Czechoslovakia, Switzerland, northern Italy, Belgium, and the Netherlands, and the most common vernacular was German. By the time of Gutenberg and Martin Luther, the Holy Roman Empire had degenerated into hundreds of small autonomous dukedoms, counties, principalities, and city-states of which the emperor himself was only a titular head.

Born in Mainz, one of the Empire's largest cities, into a family of goldsmiths sometime in the last few years of the fourteenth century, Gutenberg received a monastic education. He spent his late thirties and early forties in Strasbourg, where he produced mirrors made of speculum—a bronze-like alloy of copper and tin. His mirrors also contained a smidgen of antimony to lighten their color, a fact of no small importance to the history of print. In that credulous era, mirrors were a hot item in the western empire: pilgrims to Aachen believed that they could use the devices to collect reflections from the city's holy relics to take back home. Mirror making required no small expertise in the casting of molten alloys, whose secrets Gutenberg, or one of his contemporaries, used to unlock the mystery of manufacturing movable type.

While making mirrors, Gutenberg may have either conceived of creating movable type with the new alloys himself, or heard about it from others. The burgeoning understanding of the science of metals, and their easy availability, provided the raw materials necessary for high-volume type manufacture.

Note how Gutenberg's technique moved from harder to softer materials: hard steel punches that impressed his typefaces into softer copper, which was then used to mold the yet softer type metal. The composition of the type metal must have involved extensive experimentation with various alloys, in a search for one wear-resistant enough to overcome lead's problems with both corrosion and poor durability, yet with a low enough melting point to be easily cast. None of Gutenberg's presses or cast types survived, but specimens from the same region from a generation later showed them to be approximately 60 percent lead, 25 percent antimony, and 15 percent tin.[17] (Lead and antimony were locally available, while tin probably had to be imported from Brittany or Cornwall.)

The optimal metallic composition of the type was only one of many metallurgical challenges presented by printing. The most difficult part of the process involved the production of hardened steel punches used to create the soft copper moulds that the type was cast in, and the punch's quality was the most critical aspect of the process, since one punch, if properly constructed, employed, and maintained, could produce as many as a million moulds, each of which could, in turn, yield approximately a million pieces of type, each of which might yield tens or hundreds of thousands of printed letters. The simple, highly personalized act of writing, which for thousands of years had been performed by hand, character by character, had become industrialized, and with a vengeance: a single steel punch had the theoretical potential to bequeath, through a chain of expertly crafted moulds and type blocks, its images to trillions or even quadrillions of letters printed on paper. In the digital age, we call this amplification of output "scalabilty," and in any age, it is a primary engine of power: the ability of a person or organization to influence events.

Around 1450, Gutenberg cut his teeth on small printed works, most likely the *Sibyllenbuch* (a longish poem printed in quarto form); calendars; the *Donatus*, a grammar textbook; and probably indulgences. Only when he had removed the kinks from the process with these smaller works did he attempt his first run of 180 Bibles of 1,282 pages each, a massive undertaking that would consume about two years.

Although Gutenberg could theoretically have gotten by with just fifty-two types—twenty-six lowercase and uppercase each—he aimed to make a book indistinguishable from the only Bible that he and his customers knew: the handwritten Vulgate Latin manuscript. Neither Gutenberg nor any of his immediate followers could conceive of the streamlined mechanical print-like font appearance so familiar in the modern world. They strove, rather, to produce volumes identical to those the scribes had copied and illuminated for a millennium. Therefore, Gutenberg designed and manufactured 290 different, and, to the modern eye, ornate, typefaces of varying sizes for his Bible.

Historians have determined from legal documents that by about 1454 he had manufactured six presses. Since each page contained approximately 2,750 characters, and at least two sides of a folio had to be set at any one point, Gutenberg needed approximately 100,000 bits of cast type to keep the day-to-day process running smoothly. Further, to keep the six presses in operation, he had to hire at least two dozen typesetters and pressmen to finish the 230,760 impressions required to make 180 of the 1,282-page Bibles. Historians estimate that each press could make not much more than a dozen page impressions per hour, so this would take, allowing for some wastage, about two years. The 40 vellum copies consumed about 3,200 calf hides, and the 140 paper Bibles required the purchase of approximately 70,000 folio sheets, a massive expenditure in those days.[18]

In addition, a considerable amount of handwork went into the first books: woodblock images, hand-illuminated pictures, and special letterings. The nascent printing industry employed an entire corps of highly specialized "rubricators" who inserted large red capital letters and normal-size lettering for phrases in need of special emphasis.[19]

Printing thus required a huge capital investment, magnified by the long time period separating the initial purchase of labor and material and the subsequent cash flows; this regularly led to litigation between the printer and his creditors. That Gutenberg had particular problems in this area is suggested by an earlier venture in the year 1438 or 1439, when he produced 32,000 mirrors for a pilgrimage to Aachen. As far as we know, these were of exemplary quality, the only problem being that the pilgrimage did not start until 1440.[20] Gutenberg would need help with funding, and to his misfortune he turned to Johann Fust, a brilliant, ruthless financier. Fust knew that the Bibles' production would tie up his money for two years, but the selling prices of the Bibles—fifty gulden for a vellum copy and twenty for a paper copy, at a time when a skilled craftsman earned about twenty-five per year—meant that they would sell slowly and thus send Gutenberg into bankruptcy.

Fust consequently demanded draconian terms for the project's financing: Immediately upon publication in 1455, he demanded that Gutenberg repay his loan, and when Gutenberg defaulted, the courts awarded Fust the presses and punches. Perhaps even more valuable to Fust was Peter Schoeffer, Gutenberg's chief pressman and punch cutter, who brought with him a set of his most advanced punches and counterpunches. Schoeffer eventually married Fust's daughter Christine and inherited the business. The courts allowed Gutenberg to keep an older set of punches, but from this point on he was lacking his own presses, his best technician, and his most advanced punches, and his career sputtered out. (Nor did it help that a decade later Mainz, where he had returned after the catastrophic judgment, was sacked.)[21]

Even viewed from more than five centuries later, Gutenberg's press represented a quantum leap in the ability of humankind to communicate, on a par with the invention of writing by the Sumerians and Egyptians, the invention of a workable alphabet by the early Semites and Phoenicians, and later the development of the telegraph, radio, television, and Internet. A few bits of historical data suffice: in 1480, the Florentine Ripoli Press could produce a print run of 1,025 quinternos (five sheets, usually of octavo, which would yield a document of eighty pages) for three florins; a scribe charged one florin for a single quinterno. Thus, even the first primitive presses cut the price of document production by an amazing 97 percent.[22]

Gutenberg's Bibles were a sensation, not so much because of the method of manufacture as because of their near-absolute mechanical perfection and the readability of the design, with its large type, forty-two-line page, and wide margins. One priest, Enea Silvio Piccolomini, who later became Pope Pius II, wrote to a colleague in Rome that he had met a "remarkable man" who had shown him a section of a Gutenberg Bible that could be easily read without spectacles. These volumes soon became so treasured that an amazing 49 of the original 180 survive today, four of which are complete vellum copies (belonging, respectively, to the Library of Congress, the libraries of Frankfurt and Göttingen, and Paris's Biliothèque Nationale).[23] Although mechanically produced, after printing all had color woodblock capital letters added by hand and were graced with often spectacular illuminations, so no two are alike. (Readers can view the beautifully illuminated Göttingen version in its entirety at http://www. gutenbergdigital.de/gudi/dframes/index.htm.)[24]

German-language versions soon followed, and so the printing press for the first time allowed, at least theoretically, ordinary people to own and read their own Bible, which had previously been the purview of the clergy, the aristocracy, and the wealthiest of citizens. The German Church, unlike its counterparts in France, Italy, and England, did not object to vernacular scripture, but this was only because before 1455 large-scale reproduction was not possible, and the small number of handwritten vernacular Bibles constituted little threat. The printing press changed everything, and the German Church was not slow to perceive the danger Gutenberg's machine posed to the clergy's near-monopoly on scripture. In 1485, the Archbishop of Mainz wrote of the new vernacular Bibles infesting his diocese:

> Although people may come to acquire erudition thanks to the so-called divine art of printing by turning to the books of the various sciences which are readily available in ample measure, we have nevertheless heard how certain men, tempted by greed after fame and fortune, have misused this art. . . . Then [scriptures] translated from Latin into German [fell] into the hands of common folk, not without dishonor to our religion. . . . We command that no work, whatever its kind and to whichever science, art, and knowledge it refers, that has been or shall be translated from Greek, Latin, or any other language into German, publicly or secretly, directly or indirectly, shall be printed or such printing offered for sale, without [the appropriate authorities] being allowed to examine it and issue a permit for it to be printed or offered for sale.[25]

In other words, the archbishop permitted no printed works—not just books, but also pamphlets and leaflets—to be produced or sold without his approval. As Martin Luther would prove a few decades later, the archbishop and the Church were whistling in the wind.

Too many people had been involved with the invention of the printing press to keep its technology a secret for long, the most famous example being Gutenberg's hugely successful head pressman, Peter Schoeffer, and then Schoeffer's offspring. The sensation print caused and the increasing knowledge of its methods triggered a pell-mell rush that left a trail of financial ruin, particularly among those who did not fully appreciate the full extent of the start-up costs of machinery, labor, and paper.[26]

The Englishman William Caxton began to experiment with Gutenberg's invention soon after it arrived in Bruges, and in 1473 he produced English-language books; in 1476 he returned to Westminster, where he set up the first British press. By the same year, dozens more had been established in Italy, and by 1500, sixty-four cities and towns in Germany and central Europe alone had presses, with dozens more in France and the Low Countries.

At first, many of these presses thrived, particularly in Paris, long a center of its university-associated manuscript trade, and in Venice, bolstered by the large number of surrounding paper mills. During the late fifteenth century, *la Serenissima* had become one of the largest cities in Europe, with over a hundred thousand residents. Most critically, Venice was the arrival port for the precious classical manuscripts that poured forth from Constantinople after its fall to the Turks in 1453. Venetian presses flooded a continent hungry for the wisdom of Plato, Aristotle, Seneca, and Plutarch with thousands upon thousands of copies of their newly arrived works, and this flow in turn triggered Europe's intellectual Renaissance.

Alas, as with the crazes for railroad, radio, and Internet companies in the nineteenth and twentieth centuries, initial enthusiasm over the new presses, and the resulting production overcapacity, swamped the demand of a largely illiterate continent. Within several years of the introduction of print into Venice, eight of its twelve presses closed. Many small towns, which never should have seen print shops in the first place, lost theirs.

Like all revolutionary technologies, the printing press outraged practitioners of the crafts it displaced—in this case, scribes whose hopelessly uneconomical manuscripts suddenly became expensive curiosities. One scribal victim, Filippo de Strata, a Benedictine monk living on the Venetian island of Murano, implored the doge to punish the printers, for

> They shamelessly print, at negligible cost, material which may, alas, inflame impressionable youths, while a true writer dies of hunger [and] a young girl reads Ovid to learn sinfulness. . . . Writing indeed, which brings gold for us, should be respected and held to be nobler than all goods, unless she has suffered degradation in the brothel of the printing presses. She is a maiden with a pen, a harlot in print.[27]

Not for the last time did the democratization of a previously rare communication skill provoke proclamations of doom among a privileged professional class. While the doge did not grant Strata's desire to curtail the new presses, market forces largely did. As with all new inventions, Darwinian competition winnowed out weak business and technological models and allowed the strong ones to survive. One survivor, Frenchman Nicolas Jenson, illustrates the process well. Before 1458, he was master of the French royal mint at Tours; in that year the French king, Charles VII, ordered him to Mainz to learn the art of type casting, perhaps under Gutenberg's tutelage. When Charles, whose favor Jenson had, died and was succeeded by Louis XI, whose favor he had not, Jenson found his way to Venice, where he set up his own press.

His venture did not share the sorry fate of most other Venetian presses in the late fifteenth century, for two reasons: First, he secured a financial partnership with a pair of deep-pocketed German merchants, whose support saw him through the inevitable cash flow lulls that killed off so many of his competitors. Second, rather than aiming production at a largely illiterate and fickle general audience, he catered to a specialized clientele of doctors, lawyers, and clergymen. Their desire for a steady supply of professional reading material led to his establishment of the first of a long line of small, quiet specialist publishing fortunes that continues to the present day.

Jenson, though, is best remembered for an innovation that, while not critical to his success, secured him everlasting fame: the Roman style font ubiquitous in today's books and computer monitors. While Gutenberg had accomplished one of history's great acts of technological legerdemain, his goal was the faithful mechanical reproduction of that era's conception of the "book," meaning handwritten manuscripts.

Not only could the public read simple, streamlined font types such as Roman more easily, but craftsmen could manufacture their punches and counterpunches more quickly and economically. Whether Jenson understood these advantages before or after he created the font, however, is another question, for its initial design seemingly had more to do with his simple desire to mimic the beloved script of Roman antiquity.[28] Whatever its original inspiration, within a few short decades after Gutenberg, Jenson had produced a remarkably modern-appearing font, which was soon acclaimed for its beauty and simplicity (though evidently not by

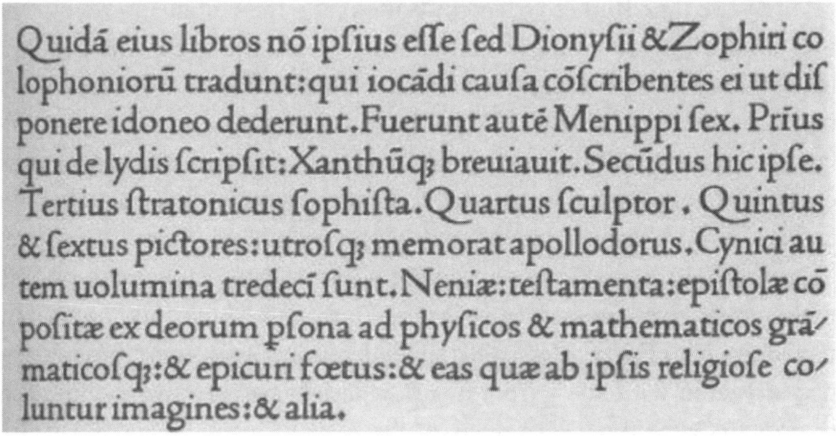

> Quidā eius libros nō ipſius eſſe ſed Dionyſii &Zophiri co
> lophoniorū tradunt:qui iocādi cauſa cōſcribentes ei ut diſ
> ponere idoneo dederunt.Fuerunt autē Menippi ſex. Prius
> qui de lydis ſcripſit:Xanthūq҆ breuiauit.Secūdus hic ipſe.
> Tertius ſtratonicus ſophiſta.Quartus ſculptor. Quintus
> & ſextus pictores:utroſq҆ memorat apollodorus.Cynici au
> tem uolumina tredecī ſunt.Neniæ:teſtamenta:epiſtolæ cō
> poſitæ ex deorum pſona ad phyſicos & mathematicos grā́
> maticoſq҆:& epicuri fœtus:& eas quæ ab ipſis religioſe co´
> luntur imagines:& alia.

Figure 5-7. Gutenberg and his successors strove to produce a print appearance indistinguishable from written manuscripts. Jenson's remarkably modern appearing Roman font, ca. 1470, changed that paradigm to fonts that were easy to read.

Jenson's jurist customers, who preferred the more traditional mimicry of handwriting).[29]

Another factor that improved the chance of a press's survival was association with a great university, as happened in Paris. Yet it would be Wittenberg—a tiny town halfway between Leipzig and Berlin that hosted a humble teaching institution—where access to this powerful new technology would turn the medieval world power structure upside down.

In 1485, Ernst, the Elector of Saxony (that is, its ruler, whose powers included a vote in the election of the Holy Roman Emperor), divided Saxony into two parts: the Duchy of Saxony, which he assigned to his brother Albert; and a smaller section, the "Ernestine Electorate," which he ruled. The next year Ernst died, and his son Frederick the Wise inherited the Electorate. Since Saxony's only university at Leipzig lay in the Duchy, Frederick decided to establish another one in Wittenberg, a sleepy town of just two thousand in 1502.[30]

The founding of the University of Wittenberg brought together the three critical ingredients for the Reformation: Martin Luther; Frederick, who was fiercely protective of his new university, and especially of Luther, its brightest academic star; and the half-century-old printing press, the key technology of the Reformation.

By the time Luther arrived in Wittenberg, the Gutenberg revolution had been in full swing for more than fifty years, and even after the late-fifteenth-century printing press shakeout, more than a thousand of the machines operated in Europe. While the Wittenberg presses usually got first crack at most of Luther's works, the difficulty of transportation and non-existence of copyright law mandated that multiple German cities became centers of Lutheran publishing and, along with it, Lutheran ideology.[31]

In 1503 the first commencement address at the University of Wittenberg was given by a professor named Nicolaus Marschalk; he so happened to be a printer. Marschalk specialized in Greek literature, and he had arrived in Wittenberg from Erfurt, where he became the first German to print in Greek type. Like many of the early printers, he had classicist-humanist leanings, and these soon landed him in trouble with Church authorities. Frederick backed Marschalk, but at this early juncture was not yet powerful enough to prevent Marschalk's expulsion.

Marschalk left, but his equipment remained and, via a roundabout route, found its way into the hands of another Wittenberg printer, Johannes Rhau-Grunenberg, sometime around 1508—the same year a young lecturer in philosophy who would later become known to the world as Martin Luther also arrived in town.

These postings of both Luther and Rhau-Grunenberg to Wittenberg may not have been a coincidence; both were German Augustinians and took their orders from Johann von Staupitz, the religious order's leader. For years before Luther's heresy, Grunenberg's presses had turned out a high volume of titles, many of which were graced with woodcut prints of an artist named Lucas Cranach the Elder.

The first printers aimed their product squarely at the educated elite; before 1500, three-quarters of their output was in Latin, most of that religious, with only a smattering of French, German, and Italian. Grunenberg, in fact, published exclusively in Latin and Greek. Since the dawn of print coincided with the flood of Greek books precipitated by the fall of Constantinople, both Marschalk and Grunenberg struck Greek fonts. At the top of the academic pyramid resided those rare scholars who could read Latin, Greek, *and* Hebrew: the vaunted *homo trilinguis*. For such *rara avises*, an even smaller number of printers cast Hebrew fonts so they could better understand the Old Testament in its original language. Around 1516, Luther contracted Grunenberg to produce a few

Figure 5-8. Johannes Rhau-Grunenberg, Luther's first printer. That both he and Luther had been sent to Wittenberg in 1508 by their superior, Johann von Staupitz, may not have been a coincidence.

works in German and thus began a shift to the vernacular that would forever change western Christendom.[32]

Luther might have had a long and peaceful academic career had it not been for the fiscal needs of the Vatican. After Saint Peter was crucified in AD 64 (upside-down, it is said, because he did not consider himself worthy of Christ's upright death), he was buried just across the Tiber from the Circus Maximus; when the Empire adopted Christianity in the fourth century, it built a basilica on the spot. Following a thousand years of shoddy maintenance and neglect, Pope Julius II decided in 1505 to demolish it and replace it with a far grander structure. The project—the present-day Saint Peter's Basilica—took well over a century to complete and involved some of the greatest names of the Renaissance: Donato Bramante, Raphael, Michelangelo, Giacomo della Porta, and Gianlorenzo Bernini, among others.

Saint Peter's construction and decoration consumed stupendous amounts of capital, and in that era, the most effective way of raising such funds was through the sale of indulgences. In 1515 Pope Leo X propounded the bull *Sacrosanctus salvatoris et redemptoris*, which applied to Mainz,

Magdeburg, and all of Brandenberg and allowed absolution for almost all sins, including theft and adultery, through the purchase of the appropriate indulgence. Nor was this all: in order to better flog the indulgences, the bull ordered priests to suspend all sermons on other topics, and the Holy Father threatened any interference with the bull with severe punishment. The most enthusiastic of the papal rainmakers was Albrecht, the archbishop of Mainz and Magdeberg, who deputized a commissary for indulgences, a Dominican preacher named Johann Tetzel, whose ceaseless activities finally attracted Luther's attention.[33] Luther began to research the scriptural basis of the indulgences; finding none, the Wittenberg preacher and professor decided to act.

The earliest printers grew wealthy by printing indulgences by the millions, commissioned, paid for in advance, and sold in bulk to the Church. Before embarking on his famous Bible, Gutenberg probably perfected his techniques on these. The ultimate irony of the Reformation may well be that just as the power of the printing press helped provoke Luther's anger at mass-produced indulgences, it also provided him with the tools to foment a mass revolution against them, and ultimately, against the Roman Catholic Church itself.

The modern image of Luther depicts a fiery preacher nailing the ninety-five theses to the door of Wittenberg Castle's church on October 31, 1517. Alas, no documentation exists of his handling of minor carpentry implements to such effect. One possibility is that he respectfully handed his written proclamation in person to his immediate superior, and prime offender, Archbishop Albrecht. More probably, he simply proceeded, in workaday academic fashion, to attack Church practices in the dry, legalistic fashion of the era by circulating his conjectures and heresies, cloaked in soporific Aristotelian formality, among colleagues and students.

On that day, he did make one undeniable departure from normal procedures by signing his letter to Albrecht "Luther" for the first time. (His original surname was Luder.) On at least one prior occasion, he also used the similar-sounding surname Eleutherius, which means "the free one" in Latin. His adoption of "Luther" was thus most likely a conscious decision to stress either his freedom of thought or his freedom from the authority of the Church.[34]

The listing of ninety-five conjectures constituted nothing unusual; he had previously drawn up numerous theses for disputation on other topics, and one Italian theologian, Giovanni Pico della Mirandola, famously offered nine hundred such tidbits at one sitting. Further, in those days the huge door of the castle church functioned as the de facto university bulletin board; in other words, the ninety-five theses probably started out as nothing more than a notice for a graduate-level seminar.

Apparently, the event never took place, perhaps for lack of interest. In the words of Renaissance scholar Paul Grendler,

> Had it occurred, attendance would have been limited to members of the university community and a few outsiders who understood Latin and were interested enough to attend a disputation on abstract theological points. Professor, students, and bystanders would have engaged in a noisy debate lasting several hours and settling nothing, just like sessions at the annual meeting of the Renaissance Society of America, except that today's scholars are less garrulous and more polite.[35]

No authentic copy of Luther's original disputation notice survives. What began as an academic exercise mushroomed on the strength of its own internal logic, Luther's force of personality, and his considerable literary ability. Nevertheless, before Gutenberg, those factors would not have been enough, for Luther's sermons, no matter how fiery and moving, would have been heard by few. In the event, it would have mattered little had Luther preached only in Latin and stuttered badly, because, as we well know today, he wrote extremely well. In addition, he quickly garnered a large part of the Holy Roman Empire's printing capacity, and it did not hurt that Cranach, one of the finest artists of his day, engraved pictures for Luther's works.

Leo X did not take kindly to Luther's heresies, and within a few months he sent Cardinal Cajetan to examine him at Augsburg. Cajetan ordered Frederick to hand him over to the Vatican; Frederick refused. Two years later Luther engaged in a disputation at Leipzig with two other theologians, in which he rejected nearly every last shred of Church authority beyond that explicitly documented in scripture, which wasn't much; this so enraged Pope Leo that he threatened Luther with excommunication if he did not recant all ninety-five theses. Luther responded with three of his best-known essays: *An Address to the Christian Nobility of the German Nation*, *On the Babylonian Captivity of the Church of God*, and *On the Liberty of a Christian Man*. The papal nuncio ordered the burning of these works and the excommunication of Luther, who in turn burned the bull proclaiming them.

In 1521 Holy Roman Emperor Charles V summoned Luther to the Diet of Worms, where, in characteristic fashion, he faced down his accusers. Frederick, who had negotiated a safe-conduct for Luther both to and from the Diet, "seized" him and cleverly hid him in Wartburg Castle after the Diet ordered him arrested. Charles, soon distracted by military matters elsewhere on the Continent, in time forgot about him.

Luther succeeded in challenging the Church's authority because he was the first to realize and exploit fully the power of Gutenberg's invention; he possessed what we today call the "first mover advantage." It is not far short of the truth to say that for decades after 1517, he and his supporters effectively controlled the dominant communications tool of the era, an advantage that most of his orthodox opponents at first only dimly grasped.

To be fair, a few in the orthodox Catholic clergy and hierarchy did appreciate the press's communicative power; in 1470, just a few decades after Gutenberg, one German preacher, Werner Rolevinck, noted that the printed sermon afforded far greater exposure than sermons delivered from the pulpit. Later, Johann Dobneck (better known to history by his Latin surname, Cochlaeus), perhaps Luther's most formidable intellectual opponent, called the press mankind's most beneficial creation.

Sadly, print could reach the masses only in the vernacular, and the Church's allegiance to Latin proved a ball and chain in the contest with the press-empowered dissidents. Almost a century after Gutenberg, the printing press continued to inspire awe. As put by one of Luther's supporters, "Much time can be saved, and in a single day two men can set and print off more than twenty or more [sic] were previously able to write in several years." Another exclaimed, "Printing is truly an art communicated by God to mankind."[36]

Today, publishers produce books and pamphlets in large printing presses and transport them to readers across the country and around the world. In contrast, in the medieval period land conveyance was unreliable, dangerous, and above all extremely expensive. In addition, paper consumed half of a book's production cost, and labor ate up much of the rest. This meant that medieval printing did not benefit from any real economy of scale; a print run of several thousand books would not yield much greater profit per unit than a run of several hundred.[37] Under such circumstances, it made far more sense for books to be copied, reedited, and reprinted in each city.

Luther's prodigious written output soon overwhelmed the capacity of Grunenberg's tiny shop, which apparently did not meet Luther's standards:

> You would not believe how I regret and how I am disgusted by his work. If only I had never sent him anything in the vernacular! He has printed these things so shoddily, so carelessly, so confusedly that I keep these scruffy types and paper hidden away. Johann the printer never gets any better![38]

Luther soon employed other Wittenberg printers: Melchior Lotter, followed by the formidable partnership of goldsmith Christian Döring and artist Lucas Cranach the Elder, the former supplying financial strength, the latter artistic talent in what was still primarily an oral and visual age. Luther's literary output soon overwhelmed even Lotter, Döring, and Cranach, and over the next few decades of his life, he added at least a half dozen more printers in Wittenberg alone.

Luther seemed to worry little about the profits from these operations, and he certainly made little, if any, money himself; he did, however, care deeply about the quality of his printed tracts, which could be quite slapdash. In that era, speed carried greater economic freight than did accuracy and appearance, so proofreading constituted the most expensive of luxuries; while Luther's grammar was superb, errors of spelling, page numbering, and page heading inevitably crept into his books, and this greatly exercised the Wittenberg professor. *Nachdruck*—what we today call pirating—bothered Luther not as much for its economic costs as because it denied him quality control; for example, one scholar estimates that between 1522 and 1526, for every edition of Luther's works produced in Wittenberg, presumably under his watchful eyes, five were printed carelessly elsewhere. On one occasion Luther lamented,

> I started work on [a manuscript], and then some rogue steps in, a compositor who lives off the sweat of our brow, steals my manuscript before I have finished it, takes it away and has printed it somewhere else, ignoring our expenditure and our labor.[39]

To combat such piracy, Luther pioneered a minor advance in intellectual property protection, the use of two trademarks: the "lamb, chalice, and flag" and the "Luther rose," which graced approved editions. Even so, one scholar estimates that of seventy known early-sixteenth-century German printers, forty-five worked with Luther at one time or another. While caring little for profit himself, he made many printers wealthy: Melchior Lotter and another Wittenberg printer, Hans Lufft, numbered among the town's most prosperous citizens, the latter becoming burgomaster.

In late 1521, while still in hiding at Wartburg Castle, Luther embarked on the project that would consume much of the rest of his life: a German translation of both the Old and the New Testaments. As already noted, the Holy Roman Empire did not forbid vernacular Bibles, so his was not the first. Prior to Luther, German printers had produced no fewer than nineteen different German translations.

In just eleven weeks, he finished his German New Testament from Erasmus's Greek version and adorned it with twenty-one spectacular

Dis zeichen sey zeuge / das solche bucher durch
meine hand gangen sind / den des falschē druckēs
vnd bucher verderbens / vleyssigen sich ytzt viel

Gedruckt zu Wittemberg.

Figure 5-9. The "lamb, chalice and flag," and "Luther rose" served as Luther's symbols of authenticity, assuring readers that a book or pamphlet had been printed under his supervision.

Cranach woodcuts. He accomplished all this in the greatest of secrecy, so as to avoid piracy. In an era when literacy was still limited, the images may have carried greater ideological impact than the quality of the text. The most inflammatory and memorable of these illustrations was "The Whore of Babylon," which prominently featured a papal tiara and contributed mightily to the marketing buzz. *Das Neue Testament Deutsch* may have sold as many as a million copies, a remarkable figure when we consider that Europe had only about fifteen million German-speakers at the time.[40] Price too was a factor; copies sold, depending upon the quality of the printing and binding, for about a gulden each, or about two months' wages for a skilled worker; certainly a major consumer purchase, but for the first time well within reach of a burgher concerned about the state of his immortal soul.[41] Lamented Cochlaeus,

> So many copies of Luther's New Testament had been brought out and distributed by the printers that even tailors and shoemakers, even women and other simple folk who had ever learned to read a bit of German, read it with great eagerness as though it were the fount of all truth. Some clutched it to their breasts and learned it by heart.[42]

The Old Testament, three times bigger and translated from the original Hebrew, took Luther a bit longer—eleven years, to be exact. (Appropriately enough, the Book of Job provided the biggest stumbling block.) The delay allowed others to step into the breach, and by 1529, it was possible to assemble a complete German translation stitched together from the parts completed by Luther, with the gaps in his work filled in by others. The most famous such "patchwork Bible" was produced by Peter Schoeffer (the son of his namesake father, Fust's partner).

Before 1517, printers turned out only about one hundred German-language books each year. The Reformation proved a wellspring of vernacular publication: by 1520, over five hundred were produced; and by 1523, nearly a thousand. Tiny Wittenberg became a publishing powerhouse, with approximately thirty-seven German-language printers, a number exceeded only in far larger Cologne, Nuremberg, Strasbourg, and Basel.[43]

Before Gutenberg, the high price of handwritten manuscripts restricted readership to the wealthiest and most powerful—in other words, Latin-speakers. When the printing press brought reading material into the price range of ordinary people, and when Luther gave them something to read, market forces almost automatically shifted publication into the vernacular. One year after the ninety-five theses, in 1518, the Strasbourg printers ran off approximately equal numbers of German and Latin pamphlets; by 1522, 90 percent were in German.

While it is fascinating to study how the printing press moved public opinion in the Reformation's ground zero, Wittenberg, Luther's physical presence there colors events. To get a more accurate picture of how Luther's writings were amplified by the printing press, it is better to look outside Wittenberg's small and fevered confines.

One useful vantage point was in nearby Leipzig, where the printers made a tidy living by reprinting Luther's tracts until 1521, when Georg the Bearded, Duke of Saxony (son of Albert and thus Frederick's cousin) decided to forbid the printing of Luther's heresies. The city council petitioned on behalf of the printers, noting, "What they have in abundance [Catholic tracts] is desired by no one and cannot even be given away."[44]

Another useful vantage point is Strasbourg. After 1480, the city's print shops, hungry for compositors and editors, attracted Europe's best and brightest; after Martin Luther, the Reformation heirs of this intellectual tradition established the Continent's first truly public primary school system so that its population could benefit from scriptures firsthand; the Church, ever eager to maintain its monopoly on holy writ, opposed this proposal.[45]

In Strasbourg, the Reformation's main weapons were not Luther's longer texts or even the vernacular Bible, but rather *Flugschriften*—"flying writings"—most of which were quite short, averaging just four folded quarto sheets, that is, thirty-two printed pages. Printers could turn these out quickly and cheaply with small, simple type sets and minimal adornment or illustrations, typically for about two pfennig per quarto, or eight pfennig for the average tract—a small fraction of a day's wage, or approximately the price of a kilogram of meat. For the first time in history, average citizens could purchase tracts pertaining to religious matters, the news, and politics.

Even more ephemeral, and nearly invisible to later history because of their physical fragility, were single-sheet printed placards and handbills that may have been the real ideological weapons in the sixteenth-century religious conflict between Protestants and the Roman Catholic Church. Typically hung on town gates or church doors, these fly sheets had lifetimes measured in weeks, days, or even hours, and printers churned them out by the millions. One of the few well-recorded episodes involving them, the 1534 *affaire des placards*, featured pamphlets denouncing the Mass, apparently produced by a single Neuchâtel printer, that appeared that year all over France, even at the bedchamber door of Francis I, and resulted in a brutal royal repression of religious dissent.

In our information-saturated age, it is hard to imagine the sensation this new technology must have caused. Throughout the Middle Ages, literacy remained low—certainly less than 10 percent. The average citizen, then, experienced Luther's writings read aloud, particularly by sympathetic preachers.

Even so, the printing press very likely provided a tremendous impetus to literacy. Perhaps the closest analogy in the modern era would be the sudden increase of "computer literacy" brought about by the advent of cheap computers. A generation ago, only a tiny percentage of the population had a working grasp of hardware, software, random-access memory, disk drives, microprocessors, file system architecture, and application formats, concepts that are second nature to most citizens of today's developed nations. In much the same way, the advent of the two-pfennig quarto must have greatly encouraged European peasants and craftsmen to learn to read.

These pamphlets and handbills became the bread and butter of most small presses, since they could be quickly produced and sold. Scholars estimate that before 1530 German presses cranked out about ten thousand different *Flugschriften* editions, three-quarters of them in the decade following the ninety-five theses; Luther alone wrote approximately two thousand of them. That 20 percent of sixteenth-century German-language print output—more than twice that of all other evangelical writers, such as Zurich's Huldrych Zwingli, combined—came from one man is testament to Luther's literary and ideological power. *To the Christian Nobility of the German Nation,* to give an example, sold four thousand copies in just three weeks and went through thirteen printings in the subsequent two years. So popular were some of Luther's tracts that they were, in the words of one contemporary, "not so much sold as seized."[46] Those who seek the source of Luther's charisma and persuasive power need look no further: never before had any one person's message reached so many people in so many places so quickly, and neither before nor after has anyone so dominated publishing in a major European language. J. K. Rowling, eat your heart out.

At an average print run of 1,000 to 1,500, Luther's pamphlets reached at least two million citizens when read aloud, resold, or simply recirculated to family, friends, and acquaintances, more than enough to reach all the world's German speakers. While the Waldensians had the capacity to spread their theology across thousands of miles, this took years, and the message still had to be transmitted aloud, person to person. The printing press gave, for the first time, anyone able to write compelling prose the power to reach a whole nation within days or weeks. Luther consciously arranged his priorities accordingly; when one of his Reformation colleagues, Martin Bucer of Strasbourg, criticized him for not getting around and about to preach, Luther curtly replied, "We do that with our books."[47]

The Roman Catholic Church initially responded to the onslaught in the only way it knew—through censorship, intimidation, and punishment. The aforementioned Georg the Bearded bought as many of Luther's New Testaments as he could, for burning. A series of Catholic proscription lists, edicts, and commissions failed to stanch the flow; in 1527 Georg even had one unfortunate printer, Hans Hergot of Nuremburg, put to the sword. In 1579 the Holy Roman Emperor finally set up an Imperial Book Commission in Frankfurt. It, too, fell well short of its goal. If the authorities had problems stopping Luther's ponderous Bible and tracts, the pamphlets, which were more easily printed and hidden, proved impossible. For every Catholic city in which the printing of Lutheran tracts was forbidden, printers in a Protestant town stood ready to meet the need.

The numerous small German states—some Protestant, some Catholic, and all jealously independent—made overt censorship a fool's errand. Even Catholic France, with a relatively unified government, at least for that period, could not turn the tide. While royal edicts set out detailed and draconian rules regulating publications of all types, in the absence of efficient communication and a national security apparatus, evading them was doable, if dangerous.

For starters, the wise French printer omitted his address, and sometimes his name, from the title page. Authors and editors could bury heresies in an orthodox-appearing text. Printers, like modern drug kingpins, learned to shift legal risk from themselves to others, particularly to the *colporteurs*, itinerant booksellers who smuggled cargoes of illicit books to all corners of the kingdom and through the gates of Paris itself. While many of these small fry were arrested and burned, the printers themselves only rarely faced judgment. In any case, by 1530 the censorship game was over for the French crown, for in that year the fiery preacher William Farel entered Neuchâtel, expelled the priests, abolished the Mass, and then set up a Protestant press. Five years later he set up another press in Geneva, and thereafter he inundated France with Reformation propaganda with impunity.[48]

The printing of such prodigious numbers of books in a vernacular accessible to the masses was carried out in a highly decentralized fashion, and printers all over Europe pirated these works. The wide availability of this new technology had given a powerful advantage to the dissidents in their struggles with the Catholic Church. Simply put, neither the ecclesiastical nor the temporal authorities could control all, or even a substantial majority, of any nation's presses. While the Catholic Church was not entirely helpless, it no longer possessed an overwhelming superiority born of brute force and a near-monopoly on the written word, to say nothing of the gates to heaven and hell. Before Gutenberg, anyone who challenged the church's authority was usually doomed to fail. The mirror maker from Mainz considerably improved the odds for the challengers, though he did not completely level the playing field.

It took the Catholic forces decades to respond intelligently to the new technology. Although the Church had far greater resources, the rebels outpublished it by as much as five to one; moreover, about half of Catholic output was in Latin, hardly the best way to reach the hearts and minds of the general populace. Unless the local ruler censored one side or the other, most cities, and many of their printers, happily did business with both Catholics and Lutherans. Strasbourg, one of the major Lutheran printing centers, also turned out a large volume of Catholic tracts. Even when the local ruler did censor his city's presses, the political bandwagon could turn on a dime, as happened when Georg the Bearded died in 1539; Leipzig joined the dissident camp, and its printers happily began producing Lutheran tracts again.[49]

It is a gross exaggeration to say, as some do, that the Reformation was Gutenberg's child—after all, the Waldensians, Lollards, and Hussites proclaimed reformation aplenty. Equally clearly, had any of these three movements had the printing press, they likely would have brought widespread Protestantism, or something very close to it, into being centuries earlier than Luther did. In the event, fate, in the person of Johann von Staupitz, assigned Martin Luther to a flyspeck of a town that just happened to have both a university and a printing press, endowing him with a megaphone that his English, French, Italian, German, and Czech predecessors could but envy; had Luther never penned his ninety-five theses, the printing press might soon enough have allowed some other dissident to do the job, for the Catholic Church was ripe for reform. As put by historian Elizabeth Eisenstein,

> Even if Luther, Zwingli, and others had died in their cradles, it seems likely that some reformers would still have turned to the presses to implement long-lived pastoral concerns and evangelical claims.[50]

The final chapter in the story of technology and religious reform in the sixteenth century revolves around an English contemporary of Luther's, whose familiarity with foreign tongues left an indelible mark on his native one.

Even among the rarefied ranks of the *homo trilinguis*, William Tyndale punched well above his weight. Born around 1494 in the rolling hills of the Cotswolds—the vale of Gloucestershire, perhaps the finest sheep country in England—he grew up among the area's shepherds and, more important, among its merchants, both local and foreign. England's trade in its preeminent manufactured export good, wool, made young William aware, in a way that most of his countrymen were not, of the world beyond England's shores and the languages spoken there. In due course he mastered not only the three classical tongues, but the four great languages of European commerce as well—French, German, Spanish, and Italian.

In order to grasp the critical talents that Tyndale brought to the translation of scripture, and the impact this had on English religious politics, we need to understand the Bible's linguistic history. The New Testament was originally written almost entirely in the lingua franca of the eastern Roman Empire, Greek, although it also had a smattering of passages in Aramaic and Hebrew. Confusingly, the oldest surviving Old Testament, the second- or third-century BC Septuagint, is also written in Greek, but its source language was Hebrew, again with some Aramaic bits.

Even more confusingly, the oldest surviving substantive copy of the Old Testament in its native Hebrew dates to the ninth or tenth century of the Christian era, more than fifteen centuries after its first portions had been composed, and twelve centuries after Alexandria's scholars had produced its far-better-known Greek version. This Hebrew text was produced in early medieval Palestine and Babylon by the Masoretes, scholars who were renowned for their editorial rigor (and who invented the Hebrew vowel points discussed in this book's Introduction). Although written more than a thousand years after the Greek-language Septuagint, the Masoretic text squares nicely with the few existing pre-Christian Hebrew biblical fragments, such as the Dead Sea Scrolls.

The most accurate and pleasing translations derive as directly as possible from the original native-language texts—for any vernacular Old Testament, then, in any language, the Hebrew Masoretic text is the place to start, as is the earliest Greek version for any vernacular version of the New Testament. The best translators can think and compose fluidly in both the source and the target languages, criteria that Tyndale met as well as anyone. Wycliffe, in contrast, translated his Bible indirectly through a third language—the Vulgate Latin of Jerome—and stiffly at that. Luther translated directly into German from Erasmus's Greek Old Testament and the Masoretic Hebrew Old Testament, and while the former did not give him trouble, the latter quite obviously did.

In much the same way that Chicago's role as the hub of American transportation endowed its inhabitants with an accent and dialect pleasing to the rest of the nation—a characteristic highly prized in radio and television announcers—so too did Gloucestershire's position as a hub of trade enable Tyndale to make the Greek of the Old Testament and the Hebrew of the New sing in a rich yet neutral English cherished by most of his countrymen, no matter what their dialect.

Gloucestershire had also proved fertile ground for the ideology of Wycliffe and the Lollards, and the Tyndale family's commercial links gave William the wherewithal to attend Oxford, Wycliffe's old turf, and to connect with continental dissidents, including, briefly, Luther himself in Wittenberg. (Tyndale's brother Edward was said to be the wealthiest and most powerful merchant in the Gloucestershire vale.)

After he completed his master's degree at Oxford in 1515, the same year that Leo X issued the infamous bull on indulgences, Tyndale returned home to Gloucestershire to serve as an ordinary house chaplain for a local notable, Sir John Walsh, and to tutor Walsh's children. By all accounts,

Tyndale charmed his new patron with his erudition and piety, and particularly with his translation of a minor Latin theological work by Erasmus. This in turn drew the enmity of the older and less gifted clergy displaced from Walsh's sumptuous table by Tyndale's talents.[51]

Tyndale responded in kind against this old guard, calling them "unlearned priests, being rude and ignorant, God knoweth; which have seen no more Latin than that only which they read in their [prayer books]."[52] In 1522 the older castoffs had him called before a local chancellor to face trumped-up charges of heresy; he beat them back easily.

Tyndale was not alone in his dim opinion of his predecessors. A survey by one reforming bishop, John Hooper, found numerous priests who did not know the number of commandments or where in the Bible they were located; more than a few could not even recite the Lord's Prayer. Wycliffe fought against a politically grasping hierarchy; Luther, against a greedy one; and Tyndale, apparently, against a dense one. Tyndale, at least initially, harbored no grand design to depose the authority of the clergy; he wished only to allow the common man access to the scriptures and, as an added bonus, to make England's priests less dim-witted. Foxe's *Book of Martyrs,* a late medieval Protestant propaganda tract, famously recounts how Tyndale engaged in a disputation with an orthodox priest who posited that the pope's law was more important than the Lord's, to which Tyndale replied:

> I defy the Pope and all his laws; if God spare my life, ere many years, I will cause a boy that driveth the plough to know more of the scripture than you do.[53]

Tyndale had already produced some English translations of scripture and religious tracts, but translating the full Bible would require not only financial resources but political cover as well, for it would no doubt draw the ire of the hierarchy. The Bishop of London, Cuthbert Tunstall, seemed the most likely source of support for Tyndale: a fellow Greek scholar, Tunstall had studied not only at Oxford with some of the Roman Catholic Church's intellectual heavyweights, including Thomas More, but also at Padua, where he had befriended Aldus Manutius, founder of one of Venice's great presses. Were that not enough, Tunstall was also a formidable mathematician, and he was known for his empathy and kindness;

his dioceses saw almost no burnings at the stake, even under the notorious Queen Mary I.

Tunstall turned Tyndale down, albeit in characteristically polite fashion. Exactly why he did so is uncertain, but most likely, situated as he was in the middle of England's turbulent politics—he was also Lord Privy Seal—he simply had a full plate and did not wish to take on unnecessary political risk in the person of a zealous, young, and unknown cleric, no matter how talented.[54]

Tunstall's refusal puzzled and distressed Tyndale; after all, by 1523 the Bible had been translated into German dozens of times, culminating the year before with Luther's wildly successful New Testament; the French, the Dutch, the Spanish, and even that most sclerotic hierarchy of all, the Portuguese, had by that time allowed vernacular versions as well. It offended Tyndale's sensibilities as a skilled translator that his own church should be so backward as to forbid an English Bible.

By 1523, news of Luther, and of his German New Testament, had reached London. Tyndale probably had contact, through his family connections, with the colony of German cloth merchants who lived near the Tower. At this stage, he was not much of a dissenter; he would travel to Germany inspired by Luther's translations and printings, not by his ideology.[55] Tyndale spent the next decade wandering around northern Europe, translating, publishing, and fleeing his English persecutors.

He had another reason for departing England for Germany: even had Tunstall taken Tyndale under his wing, the few Englishmen who took up the print trade after William Caxton's death in 1491 could not turn out the handsome volumes that thrilled readers on the Continent.[56] Tyndale traveled, then, to the northern Continent's great merchant cities that housed both a vigorous textile commerce, with its attendant connections to his Gloucestershire home, and an advanced printing industry.

First on Tydale's itinerary was Cologne, where he immediately ran into a bit of bad luck: he and his assistant, William Roye, chose the print shop of one Peter Quentell, who also happened to publish for Cochlaeus, Luther's most vociferous academic critic. Cochlaeus got a few of Quentell's pressmen in their cups, and they revealed that Tyndale and Roye had paid them to print three thousand copies of an English New Testament. Word was quickly gotten to Henry VIII, who had the authorities in Cologne seize the as yet unfinished work. The two apostates, in all likelihood forewarned, fled up the Rhine to Worms with a pile of quarto sheets ending abruptly in the middle of the Book of Matthew. There, they completed their New Testament, which was published by Peter Schoeffer in 1526.

This first Tyndale New Testament, printed in both Greek and English, was a relatively plain, unadorned affair; its richness, rather, lay in Tyndale's everyday English prose. It contains many expressions still in common usage: "Seek and ye shall find." "No man can serve two masters." "Ask and it shall be given to you."[57]

His New Testament began to reach England in 1526, and was followed two years later by *The Parable of the Wicked Mammon*, a sermon in which he for the first time went after the Roman Catholic Church on doctrinal grounds, albeit obliquely: the road to salvation, said Tyndale, lay in faith, not good works.

His books proved wildly popular: not just forbidden fruit, but beautifully written forbidden fruit whose small quarto sheets could be easily smuggled into England, most commonly one by one within the leaves of larger folio books, and then reassembled. The printing, piecemeal smuggling, and selling of these hand-size volumes made minor fortunes for their German printers and English dealers, delighted their readers, and infuriated both the clerical and the temporal hierarchies.

The entire high command of the English Church—not just the archbishop, William Warham; but also the politically powerful lord high chancellor, Cardinal Thomas Wolsey; and even Tunstall—demanded that the Holy Roman Emperor seize Tyndale, Roye, and a businessman named Richard Herman. In the event, the authorities arrested only the unfortunate Herman. Those in England fared far worse: anyone caught with a copy of either Tyndale's New Testament or his *Parable* risked a hideous death, which might include extensive racking, live burial, or being burned alive, the last of which had been heretofore rare even for common criminals. All this disturbed Tyndale, safely ensconced in Antwerp, but what truly shocked him was the mass burning of his books, particularly his New Testament: he could not believe that the English Church would burn the very word of God.[58]

Even more agitated was Tunstall, frustrated by his inability to control Tyndale's scandalous output. The bishop is said to have visited Antwerp and complained to an English merchant, Augustine Packington, about the torrent of heretical literature flowing from the Continent to England. Packington, no doubt with a twinkle in his eye, said that he knew where Tunstall could buy all he wanted for burning. The merchant relayed the bishop's intent to Tyndale, and it pleased him no end. Replied Tyndale,

> I shall get money of him for these books, to bring myself out of debt, and the whole world shall cry out upon the burning of God's word. And the overplus of the money, that shall remain with me, shall make me more studious to the correct said New Testament, and so newly imprint the same once again.

Alas, no sooner had the bishop bought and burned his scriptural cargo then yet more Tyndale New Testaments appeared on England's shores. When the bishop called on Packington to explain how this could happen, the merchant observed neutrally that more had obviously been printed, and suggested that Tunstall consider purchasing the punches and type. Realizing that he had been snookered, Tunstall let the matter go with a testy, "Well, Packington, well."[59]

Almost as soon as he had arrived on the Continent, Tyndale began to translate the Old Testament, but he, like Luther, found it a much more formidable task. He quickly realized that he probably did not command its main source language, Hebrew, well enough for the task, for in the early 1500s, England contained but a few scattered Hebrew texts.

The logical place for Tyndale to acquire Hebrew was Wittenberg, which Luther had made a center of scholarship in that ancient language so as to facilitate his own effort to translate the Old Testament into German. Tantalizing evidence exists that Tyndale indeed did travel to Wittenberg not long after leaving England, perhaps in 1525. It seems that Luther and Tyndale must have met, but although a number of historians record the event, neither of the principals do, and the truth of the matter will probably never be known for certain.

Despite Luther's head start with Hebrew, Tyndale possessed two advantages over his German colleague: first, he was a preternaturally talented linguist. Second, unlike German, Greek, Latin, and the Romance languages, English shares with Hebrew a very similar syntax. This is curious, since Hebrew is related to English much more distantly than Greek and the other European languages.

In any case, this similarity often enables a nearly word-for-word translation that transmits the moving Hebrew prose of the Old Testament, polished to a high sheen over the centuries by the ancient Israelites and medieval Masoretes, into equally moving English. Tyndale himself exclaimed at how pleasingly Hebrew translated into English:

> The properties of the Hebrew tongue agreeth a thousand times more with the English than the Latin. The manner of speaking is both one; so that in a thousand places thou needest but to translate into the English, word for word. . . . A thousand parts better may it be translated into the English, than into the Latin.[60]

For this reason, so many phrases from Tyndale's Old Testament (much of which was transmitted almost intact to the later Authorized Version of the King James Bible), suffuse the English language today that we hardly recognize their source: a broken heart; a drop in the bucket; a fly in the ointment; my brother's keeper; old as the hills; white as snow; a leopard cannot change its spots; and so forth.[61] In the words of Tyndale's most authoritative modern biographer, David Danieil, "Reading Leviticus in Tyndale . . . is like seeing a road ahead through a windscreen that has been suddenly wiped."[62]

While working on his English Bible, Tyndale increasingly found himself in conflict with Sir Thomas More. In 1521, Henry VIII called on More for assistance in his propaganda war against Luther, whose heresies had just reached England's shores. The battle between Henry and Luther grew in volume and temperature, for at one point, Luther called the king a "pig, dolt, and liar," and More responded by labeling Luther an ape and drunkard.

By the late 1520s, England's religious and political landscape changed with "The King's Great Matter," the pope's refusal to allow Henry a divorce from Catherine of Aragon after she failed to produce a male heir, which propelled More into the position of high chancellor.

By this point, Tyndale had appeared on More's radar alongside Luther; in 1531–1532, the two exchanged written polemics, one volley from More running to half a million words. More lost favor in 1532 when he refused to support Henry's declaration of primacy over the Vatican; in 1535 More lost his head, and the nation entered its long and wild oscillation between Protestantism and Catholicism.[63] Meanwhile, on the Continent, Tyndale continued to work on both the Old Testament and a revision of his previous New Testament; he completed the latter around 1534, and soon it began to flood England.

By the spring of 1535, Tyndale was living in the "English House" in Antwerp, a boarding facility for British merchants and other itinerants, and still working on the Old Testament. By that time, political England was no longer unanimously out for his blood. With a little luck, he would have lived to a peaceful old age, but he fell afoul of a dissolute son of the aristocracy, Henry Phillips, who stole a fortune from his father and lost it gambling, and then betrayed Tyndale to the agents of Holy Roman Emperor Charles V in order to make good his debts. After Tyndale had spent fifteen months in prison near Brussels, a Catholic stronghold of the emperor, his captors ritually stripped him of the marks of priesthood, strangled him, and then burned his body. While the orthodox Charles V had reason enough to eliminate Tyndale, there is strong suspicion that either Phillips or the emperor's agents had been tipped off by John Stokesley, the unrepentantly papist Bishop of London.[64]

At the time of his death, Tyndale had, in addition to his authoritative re-editing of the New Testament, translated and published the first five books of the Old Testament (the Pentateuch, that is, the Torah). In addition, he had probably translated, but never published himself, at least half of the rest. He did not, alas, make it to the Psalms, and in consequence the world's literature is a poorer place.

Soon after his death, many complete printed English Bibles appeared in England, all derived mainly from Tyndale's translations. The most famous of these was the "Great Bible" (so called because of its massive size, housing complete English and Latin Vulgate versions) printed by Miles Coverdale, by then Bishop of Exeter. Coverdale knew neither Hebrew nor Greek and used, wherever he could, Tyndale's translations, published and unpublished; what Tyndale had not completed, Coverdale had translated from Luther's German Bible.

Two decades after the deaths of Tyndale and More, England would see a Protestant archbishop, Thomas Cranmer, widely disseminate Tyndale-derived Bibles. The rabidly Catholic Queen Mary I committed Cranmer to the flames, and a few short years after his martyrdom, the new queen, Elizabeth I, brought the pendulum to rest more or less halfway between the two poles: henceforth, England would have bishops and archbishops, but no pope.

When James I ascended to the English throne in 1603, he commanded the publication of a fully "authorized" King James Version (KJV) of the Bible, which was finally published in 1611. This Bible, with a 1769 reediting, remains the standard version to the present day. Scholars estimate that approximately 80 percent of the KJV's wording descends directly from Tyndale's translations of 1522–1535.[65]

Both Luther and Tyndale harnessed the "hard power" of the era's leading-edge communication technology, the printing press, to challenge the existing religious and political order. This alone, however, did not suffice. Both men also possessed in ample measure "soft power": in Luther's case, exceptional literary talent; and in Tyndale's, a mynah bird ear for languages. In modern terms, both content and media were necessary, and the printing press's industrialization of the writing process allowed Luther and Tyndale to amplify their compelling content in a way that the Waldensians, Lollards, and Hussites could not.

Luther, of course, used this combination of hard and soft powers to help defeat the most potent political force in Europe, the Roman Catholic Church. In addition to his dissenting tracts, Luther, by translating the Bible into German, prised from the Church's grasp its most jealously guarded prerogative: the monopoly on scriptural interpretation, and with it, control of the gates to the afterlife.

Tyndale did the same for English readers. More subtly, but just as powerfully, he changed the very written language itself. "No Tyndale, No Shakespeare"; without Tyndale, the Bard would have carried far less punch, and spoken English today would be much the poorer.[66]

The stories of Luther and Tyndale demonstrate another principle: access to the power of the press depends upon political geography. In the fractured and decentralized environment of Europe, and particularly of the Holy Roman Empire, no one ruler could control all the presses. If Duke Georg, or even Henry VIII did not allow printers in his realm to turn out seditious pamphlets and books, then *colporteurs* and smugglers could easily spirit them in from more tolerant venues.

Luther's and Tyndale's stories also make yet another point: the extreme ability of the printing press to "scale up" communications, and thus its power, highlights the importance of a medium's potential to amplify a message; a single printing press in the hands of a political or religious dissident imparted to him or her the ability to "outshout" the powers that be.

This is true, of course, of all the other communications advances described in this book. While a handwritten pamphlet or manuscript may not appear to have much "amplification," compared with word of mouth, it most certainly does. A single sheet of papyrus can be read by thousands of people over the centuries, and a laboriously made stone inscription by millions over the millennia. Going forward, even simple modern duplicating technologies such as linked tape recorders and carbon paper, while capable of making only a few copies at a time, can exponentially amplify a message over multiple cycles; ultimately, access is about amplification.

In the modern world, despots ruling over large unitary states with relatively well sealed borders, such as China, the Soviet Union, and Nazi Germany, had a far easier time stopping the modern high-speed presses. The next great technology to affect the world's political balance, the electronic encoding of written and spoken language, proved even easier for totalitarian states to control than Gutenberg's marvelous invention, with disastrous consequences for citizens of those benighted nations, and for the world at large.

6

THE CAPTIVE PRESS

The splashiest news item of 1492 was not the departure of Columbus on his voyage of discovery, or even the expulsion of Jews from Spain, but rather the arrival of a 260-pound meteorite near the village of Ensisheim in the Alsace region, history's first well-described extraterrestrial impact. Over the centuries, museums around the world would acquire chunks of it; about 100 pounds or so of the rock still reside in the Ensisheim town hall.

The fame of the shooting star stemmed from a broadsheet published by a German humanist, Sebastian Brant; it consisted of a woodcut depiction of the object's west-to-east trajectory accompanied by Latin and German text describing the event. The portion in Latin, being the language of scholarship, discussed recent, related natural phenomena and meteorites from antiquity, while the vernacular portion exhorted the Holy Roman Emperor, Maximilian I, to direct the meteorite's ill tidings toward the French king, Charles VIII, who had reneged on his contract of marriage with Maximilian's daughter.

Eventually, Columbus's written report did circulate publicly after his return to the Continent in 1493, but unlike the Ensisheim meteorite, it did not make much of an impact; late-fifteenth-century European explorers regularly discovered "new islands," and Spain was not exactly the publishing capital of Europe. Brant did not bother to report Columbus's first voyage until 1497.

The Florentine nobleman Amerigo Vespucci, who sailed four times to the Western Hemisphere between 1499 and 1503 for both Portugal and Spain, received much better press. He did not return to Florence after his voyages but rather remained in Spain and Portugal, from where he wrote back home to his family's old patron, Lorenzo de' Medici, and to another nobleman, Piero Soderini. Italy was much closer to the publishing centers of Europe, and Vespucci's letters drew more attention than Columbus's reports. Consequently, the Western Hemisphere continents are today called North and South America, and not North and South Columbia.[1]

The differing treatments afforded Columbus's and Vespucci's exploits highlight the central problem of the news business. To the extent that newspapers wield power, it resides primarily in the prerogative of choosing what to print. But in the information-starved premodern period, there were not many stories to pick from; far from being the all-powerful colossus of, say, Hearst or Annenberg, the premodern newspaper toiled at the mercy of those who supplied it with information, mainly overland travelers and crews from incoming merchant and military vessels.

Further, for four centuries after Gutenberg, printed material remained an expensive luxury. The average citizen might manage the purchase of a family Bible or even a calendar, but a newspaper, to be discarded after a week or a month, was an unattainable extravagance; while it might attract enough of a readership of wealthy artisans and merchants, a newspaper just as often had to fall back on direct government subsidies or, as in the United States, indirect subsidies in the form of advertising from the political parties and the local governments they controlled. And since premodern newspapers were dependent on scarce information, where did this leave their readerships?

Newspapers, by their very nature, consume vast amounts of capital, and this constraint limits their number. For the first few hundred years following their birth in medieval Europe, their production remained easily under the thumb of the ruling elites, and even the purchase of individual broadsheets remained the prerogative of the wealthy.

In the nineteenth century, cheap wood-pulp paper and steam-driven high-speed presses, along with burgeoning literacy, made newspapers accessible, for the first time, to the average citizen. Ironically, the higher costs of this new newspaper technology marginalized ordinary citizens, who could not hope to compete with printing facilities capable of churning out tens of thousands of copies per hour. The expense of the new presses put them well out of reach of the average citizen and made it even easier for the state to control the relatively small number of newspapers, as would occur particularly in both the Soviet Union and Nazi Germany.

* * *

What exactly is a newspaper? By modern standards, certainly not the odd pamphlet describing a shooting star or the discovery of a new island, or even a new land. Closer to the modern newspaper may have been the "courants," semi-regularly or even regularly appearing pamphlets that began to circulate in seventeenth-century northern Europe, particularly in the Netherlands.

Most chroniclers of modern print credit a French physician, Théophraste Renaudot, with Europe's first regular comprehensive newspaper coverage. The history of his publication, the *Gazette,* demonstrates the nexus between power and access to print in Europe's best-organized nation-state of that period, France, and in particular, how easily the crown could control the period's nascent press.

Although trained in medicine at provincial Montpellier, in 1606 Renaudot moved his practice to Paris—no mean trick in those days. There, he caught the attention of Cardinal Richelieu, the brilliant first minister of Louis XIII. He soon became physician to both cardinal and king.

He quickly exploited his influence at court to deploy many advanced social schemes, among which were an expansion of aid to the poor, including free medical care, and the *bureau d'adresse et de rencontre,* which functioned as an employment agency for people in Paris who were out of work. Even more impressively for that era, under the auspices of the *bureau,* he held a series of weekly academic conferences that focused on medicine and the sciences. Renaudot intended these seminars, open to the public, as a general intellectual tonic for the body politic, which he likened to a staving man confronted with a choice between real food—that is, the facts—and nutritionally worthless wax facsimiles: rumor and innuendo.[2]

In short, history could not have hoped for a more open-minded, generous, and public-spirited individual to run its first real newspaper. Although Renaudot himself served the nation, the *Gazette* served only the powerful.

At the *Gazette*'s founding, several kinds of print periodicals regularly circulated in France: official announcements from the royal printer, whose workers were chosen for the high level of technical skill required for these documents; the *canard,* an ad hoc account of current events and court gossip, the more lurid, the better; the *relation,* similar to the *canard,* but usually concerning diplomatic events and aimed at a more specialized audience; and finally, the *annuel,* a more informal account of events at court.

Richelieu, no mean writer himself, well understood the potential of the pen and press, and in deputizing Renaudot as his propaganda lieutenant, he chose well; with the explicit backing of the cardinal and the implicit support of the king, the first issue of the *Gazette* appeared on May 30, 1631. Six months later the royal backing became explicit when Louis granted Renaudot the national newspaper monopoly. Although it took Renaudot a few years to suppress his competitors, by 1635 he had become the preeminent press baron of his time, churning out not only the weekly *Gazette* but numerous other weekly and monthly publications as well, including the above-mentioned *relations,* the accounts of his weekly educational conferences, and the irregular *extraordinaires,* warranted by late-breaking events.

These publications did not come cheaply: when the *Gazette* hit the streets each Saturday, its twelve pages set readers back four sous—about the price of two kilos of plain bread, enough to feed a family for a day. While this might strike the modern reader as a bit steep, remember that Renaudot's publications represented the leading edge of that era's media technology. Those on a tight budget could rent out the *Gazette* for a monthly fee at shops or stands, the most popular of which was on Pont Neuf.[3]

Renaudot's reportage would have done the North Korean Central News Agency proud. Someone who wanted to learn about the *fronde* (the revolt of the local governments and aristocrats against the king), the deteriorating state of Louis XIII's health, and his many military disasters was not going to find them in the *Gazette*. It happily reported, of course, civil disorders abroad, especially in England. Likewise, while French atrocities against its foes went unmentioned, those of the nation's enemies generally warranted their own *extraordinaire.* Natural disasters represented a special case; in general, they were ignored unless they affected the court in some way, as when a deadly flood in the provinces delayed some ladies-in-waiting crossing the stricken region.

In short, the *Gazette* was all the king, all the time. Renaudot devoted entire issues to the marvelous state of Louis's health, his ability to heal the sick with his mere touch, or the remarkable attraction of his castle windows for white doves. The *Gazette* especially favored the royal ballet, in which the king on one memorable evening danced three separate times, each in a different costume, "always with the delight inseparable from all the exercises to which His Majesty applies himself."[4]

France, it seems, had learned the hard lesson taught by Luther: if not properly overseen, the power of the era's most advanced print technology could become profoundly subversive, and the king proved fairly successful at controlling it. In England, things began in much the same way under the absolutist Stuart monarchy of the same period. Having come through the turbulence of the Civil War, the newly reestablished Stuarts, in the person of King Charles II, were in no mood to coddle the press, and so rammed through Parliament the Licensing Act of 1662. Roger L'Estrange, appointed licenser—that is, censor—put it bluntly:

> No man denyes the necessity of suppressing licentious and unlawful pamphlets, and of regulating the press; but in what manner, and by what means this may be effected, that's the question.[5]

L'Estrange wasted no time on this rhetorical question: for a few decades, brute censorship and incarceration of errant printers served the English monarchy nearly as well as these measures served France's kings.

How did the French and English monarchs maintain control over their presses, when the pope and the Holy Roman Emperor could not? The answer is that outside France and Spain, most of the Continent was a patchwork of thousands of small states with porous borders; even if a local duke maintained an iron grip on his duchy's printers, he could not prevent the flow of pamphlets and books from the adjoining principalities and cities. England and France, on the other hand, were large enough, and land transport costs high enough, that effective censorship was possible.

At least at first. The English political climate changed abruptly with the overthrow of James II by a Dutch in-law of the royal family, William of Orange. In this upheaval, known in England as the Glorious Revolution of 1688, the monarchy's wings were clipped by the first real stirrings of constitutional government, and in 1693, Parliament allowed the Licensing Act to expire. Once committed to the path of increasing civil liberties, England then saw fit to allow private individuals the power of the press, ushering in a flowering of press freedom that began with truly independent periodicals from the likes of Daniel Defoe (*A Weekly Review of the Affairs of France,* or more simply, the *Review*), Richard Steele (*Tatler*), and Joseph Addison (with Steele, *The Spectator*). Yet even in postrevolutionary

England, freedom of the press arrived only gradually; the ruling aristocracy vigorously reserved the right to suppress criticism of ministers and of the monarchy. When Defoe unwisely published a tract attacking the Church of England in 1703, he was placed in the pillory for three days, then jailed. Merely selling a copy of Thomas Paine's 1791 tract, *Rights of Man,* could earn an Englishman a minimum sentence of four years, in addition to a crippling fine and surety bond.[6]

The crown also imposed a heavy levy on paper—the stamp tax—to raise revenue and to throttle newspaper sales. The typical periodical of the time sold for around a shilling, to which a stamp tax of up to one-third was added. English progressives labeled this a "tax on knowledge" but could do nothing about it. On the other side of the Atlantic, readers did not tolerate the colonial stamp tax and won its repeal within five months of its institution in 1765 with the cry, "No taxation without representation."

Although today we recall early modern England as the cradle of liberal democracy, as late as the nineteenth century, judges and juries condemned authors, printers, and booksellers for "seditious libel" for even the mere possession or sale of a single unknowingly suspicious tract. A remnant of this practice even surfaced in the newly independent United States, when John Adams, during the duress of the naval conflict with France, signed the Sedition Act into law in 1798. Under it, a handful of American printers were tried and convicted. The act contributed significantly to Adams's defeat in the 1800 election; the hated act expired the day before he left office. This unfortunate interlude aside, historically, Americans have enjoyed far more freedom of the press than their English cousins.[7]

Until the 1800s, Englishmen viewed a strict editorial respect for monarch and minister as a key tool for maintaining societal order. The modern concept of "freedom of the press" struck them more as "license to treason" than as an essential element of the "rights of Englishmen," the ringing phrase applied to the freedoms acquired under centuries of common law and cemented by the Revolutionary Settlement of 1689 and, on the other side of the pond, resurrected by American revolutionaries nearly a century later.

England deployed not only the stick, with censorship, taxes, and prosecution for seditious libel, but also the carrot, in the form of subsidies—bribes, in reality—to publications that toadied to the ruling party. These incentives proved highly effective; the newspaper of the eighteenth century was hardly the all-purpose news source that readers

know today, but rather a financially tenuous grab bag of shipping information and commercial advertising, whose opinions, such as they were,
could easily be bought.

Even so, Parliament itself could not be seen openly suborning journalists, and so left the dirty work to the Treasury's "secret service" budget,
dedicated to fighting subversion both at home and abroad. Typically, in
1782, Parliament appropriated £10,000 to this pool, with a fair portion
going to support cooperative newspaper publishers. In normal times, perhaps half this budget went to press subsidies and could take multifarious
forms—not just direct grants, but also payments and pensions for writers,
advertising, and postal concessions. During the 1790s, as the specter of the
French Revolution haunted Engand's ruling class, this amount swelled.[8]
Thus, as late as the dawn of the nineteenth century, the English press
remained, generally, a tool of government.

Curiously, in America the first newspapers sprang from the Boston
post office, whose postmaster considered among his duties the dissemination of news, particularly concerning shipping. (He possessed another,
unspoken, advantage in the news business: the ability to snoop discreetly
on the mail.)[9] One postmaster, John Campbell, began by having his brother
transcribe the news by hand, but in 1704 the Campbells switched to the
printing press. They named the newspaper the *Boston News-Letter*.

Issues of the *News-Letter* never sold more than 250 copies, and in
1719 a succeeding postmaster, William Brooker, established the *Boston
Gazette,* which engaged as its printer James Franklin, who then apprenticed
his younger brother Benjamin. When the Franklins lost the *Gazette* account,
they took on the *New-England Courant,* which prided itself on its editorial
content; the younger Franklin contributed his first article at age sixteen.

After several years of toiling for his older brother, the disenchanted
Benjamin ran away to Philadelphia to start the publishing empire from
which his wealth, influence, and fame sprang. While Ben Franklin's chosen
profession might strike the modern reader as quaint, it must be remembered
that printing was the leading-edge communications technology of the era,
and Franklin's position as its most successful colonial practitioner made
him an eighteenth-century amalgam of Rupert Murdoch and Steve Jobs.

Since the Americans had started their journalism nearly from scratch,
they established a slightly hardier tradition of independence than that in
the mother country. As in England, the colonial authorities prosecuted for

seditious libel. In 1735, John Peter Zenger, publisher of the *New York Weekly Journal,* was brought to trial for his attacks on the governor. Despite the vigorous efforts of both the governor and the prosecutors, the jury acquitted Zenger, to mixed effect. While the colonial government's failure to convict sent shock waves across the Atlantic, in the colonies themselves, Zenger's prosecution intimidated even the bravest of printers. Said one of his colleagues, "I once thought a little *Politics* now and then thrown out among our Readers might whet their Appetites, but upon Second thoughts we had as good let that alone." In the event, Zenger made no more trouble, and later meekly took the government's advertising along with its implied silence.[10]

The Americans schooled the English in the workings of a truly independent press in other ways, as the careers of two transatlantic pamphleteers, Thomas Paine and William Cobbett, demonstrate.

Paine, "a corset maker by trade, a journalist by profession, and a propagandist by inclination," did not emigrate to the colonies until age thirty-seven. He sailed to America in 1774, on the suggestion of another transatlantic commuter, Benjamin Franklin, whom he had met in London. In early 1776, Paine published *Common Sense,* which sold more than a hundred thousand copies; it was easily the most effective propaganda piece of the American Revolution. He left the United States in 1787 and thereafter spent much of his time in England and France.[11]

Meanwhile, back in England, the battle between the government and the printing press played out in the stories of three pioneer journalists: William Cobbett, William Hone, and Richard Carlile, each of whom, to some degree, felt the heavy hand of the state on his shoulders.

William Cobbett imitated Paine's transatlantic peregrinations, and in due course he, too, faced the prosecutorial wrath of English censorship that Paine had sidestepped. Born in 1763 as the son of a humble tavern keeper, Cobbett enlisted in the British army in 1784, and soon found himself in the Canadian wilds of New Brunswick, garrisoned against the ex-colonials to the south. He patrolled through hundreds of miles of trackless forest, and when winter curtailed mobility, he read voraciously.

His intellectual and physical abilities brought him rapid promotion to sergeant major over dozens of more senior candidates. His new rank put him in charge of regimental accounts, and he soon tumbled to the embezzlement of army funds by his commanding officers—a routine event in any military organization of that era.

Despite warnings from his fellow NCOs, Cobbett naively pressed charges. The accused officers easily stymied his efforts to bring them to justice, so he bided his time until he returned to England in 1791, and then once again pursued them. To his astonishment, the military authorities entrusted Cobbett's incriminating evidence to the officers themselves, and in short order Cobbett found himself the target of trumped-up charges that he had toasted with friends the destruction of the royal family.[12]

Facing certain conviction and transport to Australia, he fled to Philadelphia, where he taught English to Frenchmen and wrote pro-British tracts under the pseudonym Peter Porcupine. He specialized in gossip columns, and when he set after the famous physician Benjamin Rush for his inept treatment of victims of a yellow fever epidemic, the good doctor obtained a ruinous $5,000 libel judgment—approximately $500,000 in today's currency. Cobbett thought it better to face criminal prosecution in England than bankruptcy in America, and fled back to the mother country in 1800.[13]

Luckily, he had never been formally charged. Sometime during that return journey, his spine stiffened. In 1802, he began to report on parliamentary debates from his printing shop on Fleet Street. This took some courage; decades before, in 1728, as a case in point, the House of Commons had fined and imprisoned a correspondent for reporting its deliberations. By the 1770s, the Commons grudgingly admitted reporters, but it forbade note-taking, a crippling barrier until the *Morning Chronicle* deployed its secret weapon: William "Memory" Woodfall, who could reproduce with perfect recall hours of debate.

Before Cobbett, no one had risked a publication devoted exclusively to comprehensive coverage of activities in the Commons. His periodical, *Parliamentary Debates,* was later renamed *Hansard* (after Thomas Hansard, Cobbett's printer and the eventual owner of *Debates*), which remains to this day Parliament's official record. At nearly the same time, he also founded the *Weekly Political Register,* which covered extra-parliamentary activity.

In those days, any sort of political reporting constituted an open invitation to a seditious libel tribunal, and the powers that be were not long in obliging Cobbett. When, in 1803, the *Register* reported on the government's bungled handling of an Irish rebellion, the crown prosecuted him.

The proceedings fairly dripped with upper-class disdain for the lowborn gadfly. The prosecutor, Spencer Perceval, delivered part of his address in Latin, not only because Cobbett could not understand it, but also to underline the fact that the defendant stood accused of libeling his betters; he asked of Cobbett, *"Quis homo hic est? Quo patre natus?"* (Who is this man? Who is his father?) Perceval's righteous anger seemed most exercised by the liberties taken by Cobbett's reference to Prime Minister Henry Addington by the nickname "the doctor" (which referred to his father's profession); the English may be fond of nicknames, but not those uttered by one's inferiors.

The judge's instructions to the jury spoke volumes about the freedom of the British press at that time. English law theoretically allowed criticism of royalty and government ministers, but, as the presiding judge instructed Cobbett's jury, if "individual feelings are violated, there the line of interdiction begins, and the offense becomes the subject of penal visitation." To wit: injure the tender sensibilities of a prince or minister, and we'll toss you into prison. The jury deliberated precisely ten minutes before delivering a guilty verdict. In the event, Cobbett paid a hefty £500 fine, but avoided jail.[14]

Cobbett continued to skirmish with the government. As an ex-NCO, he took seriously the welfare of British enlisted men, and just two years later, when two successive mistresses of the Duke of York, George III's second son and commander in chief of the army, were caught selling commissions, the *Register* rang with indignation at soldiers' lives and welfare being put at risk by inexperienced, corrupt officers. The government responded by attacking him in the subsidized press. Shortly thereafter, when some troops in Cambridgeshire protested against missed pay and short rations and were subjected to five hundred lashes each, the *Register* howled. Cobbett knew from his army days the barbarity of the lash and exploded in sarcastic anger:

> *Five hundred lashes* each! Aye, that is right! Flog them: flog them: flog them! They deserve it, and a good deal more. They deserve a flogging at every meal-time. "Lash them daily, lash them duly." What, shall the rascals dare to *mutiny*, and that too, when the German Legion is so near at hand.[15]

The attorney general immediately served him with a writ, but delayed prosecuting him for several months. Cobbett might have avoided a trial had not he continued to harass the government over other military affairs. Nor did it help his case that his old nemesis, Perceval, became British prime minister in October 1809 (and less than three years later would become the only one to be assassinated). Again, the judge severely charged the jurors, who this time returned a guilty verdict in just five minutes, not even having retired to their chamber.

This time, Cobbett was not so lucky; he would spend two years in Newgate prison, his circumstances there ameliorated by his modest wealth and good credit, which allowed him to borrow and spend the more than twenty guineas per week (about $3,000 in today's money) to purchase a decent room and palatable food.

Newgate gave Cobbett, if anything, time to think about newspapering. The problem, he realized, was that the public lacked, and sorely needed, an affordable news source. In 1816, several years after his release, he published a smaller, cheaper version of the *Register*. The original ran to twelve pages and cost a shilling, plus the state's substantial stamp tax. The "second *Register*" consisted of only a single sheet limited to Cobbett's leading editorial in the regular *Register* and was not, because of its small size, subject to the stamp tax; it cost only twopence. This was a political masterstroke. Ordinary workingmen could not afford the regular *Register*, but a twopenny version was well within their reach, and its circulation soon ran to a highly influential forty thousand.

The publication of the twopenny *Register* coincided with Cobbett's collaboration with a reform activist, Henry Hunt, and the combination of the muckraking journalist and the fiery orator frightened the government no end. Its fears were confirmed by the January 1817 mob attack on the coach of the Prince Regent; a month later, the government clamped down on dissent and suspended habeas corpus.

The government spent tens of thousands of pounds attacking Cobbett in the subsidized press; it failed miserably. It then offered him a substantial pension if only he would stop writing. Cobbett refused, and with the suspension of habeas corpus fresh in his mind and knowing what was next, he slipped quietly out of Liverpool harbor in March 1817, bound again for New York.[16]

Absent Cobbett, the government settled on another target, William Hone. Cobbett's junior by nearly two decades, Hone had been born into, and subsequently married into, comfortable circumstances. Unhappy with a legal clerkship in London's Gray's Inn, he established a print shop–cum–lending library on Fleet Street. Wealth often endows its possessors with a light touch, while poverty often results in a hard edge, as with Cobbett. Hone's prosperous upbringing consequently imbued his writings with a graceful humor that Cobbett's lacked.

Consider Hone's "Catechism of a Ministerial Member," which he adapted from an unpublished essay by John Wilkes, a radical politician of the previous decades (and the first person legally allowed to report Commons proceedings). The pamphlet presented itself as a sort of Machiavellian primer for English politicians, set to biblical verse; it offered this mangling of the Lord's Prayer:

> Oh lord, who art in the Treasury, whatsoever be thy name, thy power be prolonged, thy will be done throughout the empire, as it is in each session. Give us our usual sops, and forgive us our occasional absences on divisions; as we promise not to forgive them that divide against thee. Turn us not out of our Places; but keep us in the House of Commons, the Land of Pensions and Plenty; and deliver us from the People. Amen[17]

Hone also provided what may have been the most devastating, and certainly the most delicious, deconstruction of the "rotten borough" inequities in the Commons, whereby equal representation was given to all boroughs, whether rural fiefs of a few dwellings or urban slums of tens of thousands. He suggested that the Prince Regent make a visit to Sir Mark Wood, lord of the Surrey borough of Gatton, which had sent two MPs to London each session between 1450 until the 1832 Reform. Their conversation, Hone thought, would go something like this:

> Prince Regent: You are the proprietor of this borough, Sir Mark?
> Wood: I am, may it please your Royal Highness.
> PR: How many members does it send to Parliament?
> W: Two, Sir.
> PR: Who are they?
> W: Myself and my son.
> PR: You are much beloved, then, in the borough, Sir Mark?
> W: There are not many who tell me otherwise, your Royal Highness.
> PR: Were there any opposition candidates?
> W: None, Sir.

PR: What is the qualification for an elector?

W: Being an inhabitant and paying scot and lot [property tax].

PR: Only six electors, then? For I see you have only six houses in the place?

W: Only one elector, please your Royal Highness.

PR: What! One elector and two members? How is that? But what becomes of the other five householders?

W: By buying the borough, I am the freeholder of the six houses; I let five by the week, pay the taxes myself, live in the other; and thus, being the only elector, return myself and my son as members at the election.[18]

In April 1817, the prosecutor filed three charges of seditious libel against Hone; in May, Hone was confined to jail; he was not tried for seven months thereafter. The jury, evidently as charmed by his whimsy as it was repulsed by the government's transparent maliciousness, returned three verdicts of not guilty within fifteen minutes.[19]

Historians consider Hone's trial a significant victory in the battle for freedom of the English press, but this was not apparent at the time. The authorities did indeed learn that the most rapid and certain road to ridicule lay in the prosecution of parody, a mistake they never again made. Still, although they had met their match in the agreeable, charismatic Hone, neither censorship nor political repression died with his acquittal.

On August 16, 1819, Cobbett's colleague Henry Hunt addressed a crowd estimated in excess of sixty thousand in a field adjacent to Saint Peter's Church in Manchester. The protestors had intended to hold a mock election of Hunt as a reformist MP. Its organizers conducted the meeting peacefully and so confused the authorities, who, expecting violence, panicked and perversely reasoned that because so many had gathered, Hunt had to be arrested by force. Swinging truncheons and sabers, mounted troops cleared a path toward Hunt, killing eleven and injuring hundreds in the process, a donnybrook that quickly became known as the Peterloo Massacre.[20]

Also scheduled to speak in Saint Peter's field that day was Richard Carlile, a printer, who, as had Cobbett and Hone, maintained a shop on Fleet Street. Like Cobbett, and unlike Hone, he came from straitened circumstances, apprenticing as a tinsmith, a vocation which he despised, but which proved an asset in the printing business. His unprivileged background imparted a bitter, self-righteous edge to his work, as it had to Cobbett's. The economic downturn following the Napoleonic Wars had radicalized Carlile. The extreme suffering it visited on England's poor was not only the natural effect of an economic depression, but also the conscious result of repressive policies, such as the corn laws, which dramatically increased the price of bread and caused widespread starvation. England's ruling aristocracy, particularly the Tory party, had turned a deaf ear to this misery.

Carlile lacked education, even of the self-taught variety acquired by Cobbett, and so wrote relatively little himself. Rather, he mainly sold the works of others in *Sherwin's Political Register,* a publication born of his partnership with printer William Sherwin. Founded just a few months before Peterloo, Sherwin's *Register* prominently featured pirated essays by Paine and Hone, which did not earn Carlile friends in the radical community—on one occasion, Hone even threatened him with legal action over the *Register*'s literary theft. Nevertheless, what Carlile lacked in creative ability he more than made up for in zeal, buying up radical pamphlets and peddling them around town at a minuscule profit. In his own words, he on "many a day traversed thirty miles for a profit of eighteen-pence."[21]

On that day at Saint Peter's Field, Carlile never got to speak. He escaped, hid with fellow travelers, and later returned to London, where he published the first eyewitness account of the events under the title "Horrid Massacres at Manchester." The government promptly closed his paper.

Within three months after Peterloo, Carlile found himself on trial for, of all things, blasphemy, a charge on which the government's prosecutors thought it easiest to earn a conviction. Among the works Carlile had reprinted was Paine's *The Age of Reason,* a workaday rehash of the doctrine of deism, which postulated a God who had created the universe and then stood back, a master clockmaker who did not interfere with human affairs, and whose worship, or at least recognition, did not require organized religion of any sort.

The government had many political allies in its prosecution of Carlile, and none was as curious as the abolitionist William Wilberforce, who seemed to draw a distinction between freedom for slaves and freedom of the press. Wherever Carlile's prosecutors could be found, so too could members of Wilberforce's Society for the Prevention of Vice, drawn by their hatred of Carlile's manifest impiety.

Even more remarkably, by the early nineteenth century, deism was old hat to the educated elite; Carlile's crime, it seems, lay in introducing the concept to the lower orders. After a few days of Monty Python dialogue with judge and prosecutor and set-piece speechifying, Carlile found himself duly sentenced, imprisoned, and fined.[22] When he refused to pay, troops raided his shop and confiscated his equipment and supplies.

It did not help Carlile that during his first prison stint, he segued from deism to outright atheism. All the while he continued to feed pieces to the *Republican* (essentially, his old *Sherwin's Political Register,* renamed), now under the direction of his highly competent wife, Jane. His incarceration well suited both their relationship and their professional enterprise, for the two did not get along personally and had agreed to separate even before the Peterloo Massacre; the husband's imprisonment allowed them to collaborate without having to share each other's company.

Ultimately, the courts sentenced Jane and imprisoned her for two years, at which point Richard's sister took over publication, and when she was duly sent up, the *Republican*'s workers took up the cudgel. The courts ultimately jailed eight employees and approximately 150 newspaper sellers for printing and hawking the *Republican*.

The Carlile affair also demonstrated the real purpose of the stamp tax. While he was in prison, Parliament passed two Press Acts that imposed a levy, as well as surety bonds, on all atheistic, deistic, or republican publications, while specifically exempting publications defending Christianity and the constitution. Naturally, the *Republican* thumbed its nose at the new acts.

The prosecutorial victory over Carlile and his wife, sister, employees, and newspaper sellers proved Pyrrhic; with each conviction, the *Republican*'s circulation grew. The government never learned that in publishing, there is no bad publicity; it would have been far wiser to leave Carlile alone. In early 1824, opposition to the government, and especially revulsion against the heavy-handed opposition of Wilberforce's Society for the Prevention of Vice, began to feed on itself. In May of that year, Carlile put out a call from jail to freethinkers everywhere to volunteer to sell books in his shop as an act of civil disobedience.

It worked. The arrest and trial of dozens of volunteers backfired. The lord chief justice, Charles Abbott, finally admitted defeat: Open trials only made Carlile stronger, and Abbott ordered that all prosecutions cease (although Prime Minister Peel insisted that the employees and volunteers serve out their terms). As put by Sir Joseph Arnould, the biographer of Attorney General Lord Thomas Denman,

> It was [Denman's] firm opinion, founded on experience, that a political libeler thirsted for nothing more than the valuable advertisement of a public trial in a Court of Justice. Triumph there made him rich, and defeat gave him all the honours of martyrdom.[23]

In 1825, the government released Carlile; in the words of Guy Aldred, his foremost biographer, "The quitting of jail meant no more to him mentally than a change of lodging." Five years later, in a spasm of institutional amnesia, the government again jailed him for several months for inciting farmworkers to strike; all in all, Carlile spent nearly a decade behind bars before he finally died a pauper in 1843.[24]

Successive governments also continued to pressure Cobbett, who had again returned to England soon after Peterloo in 1819. In 1830, he stood accused of inciting starving farmworkers to burn a landowner's barn. In a spectacular show consisting of both legal defense and political theater, Cobbett and his lawyer thoroughly discredited the government's chief witness—Thomas Goodman, who had set the fire, was sentenced to hang, then was pardoned after fingering Cobbett—and laid bare the government's duplicitous prosecution. When the 1832 Reform Act abolished the system of "rotten boroughs" and broadened the franchise, Cobbett easily won a seat in Commons, having stood unsuccessfully for election on several occasions prior to Reform.[25] Over the ensuing decades, England gradually repealed the "tax on knowledge"; it reduced the newspaper stamp tax to a penny in 1836 and abolished it completely in 1855. Finally, in 1861 the tax on paper itself disappeared.[26]

Historians generally date the achievement of freedom of the British press as coincident with the Reform Act of 1832. Yet, no discrete legislation granted it; rather, legislators, ministers, prosecutors, and judges came to the collective realization that in an increasingly prosperous and literate society, the prevention of what was, from the government's perspective at least, blasphemy and seditious libel spewing from widely available hand presses was futile.[27]

Critically, the deed had been accomplished by men and women dedicated to reform, and of no great means, who operated machinery not far advanced from that used by Gutenberg four centuries earlier. In the decades leading up to the early nineteenth century, in Europe and in North America, access by ordinary people to what had been the world's most advanced communications technology for four hundred years had become a formidable tool for democratic development.

Viewed from the broadest possible perspective, the two great premodern communications technologies—simple literacy and mechanical printing—initially followed the same historical paths. In the case of literacy, access broadened slowly as simpler writing systems endowed an ever-greater proportion of the population with the ability to read and write, which forced open both political and religious systems, at least in those societies that took the expansion of literacy seriously. Most critically, with the advent of public education on both sides of the Atlantic, literacy became more widespread, and neither the state nor religion could effectively control its use by ordinary citizens. This was also true of the hand-operated printing press for the first four centuries of its existence.

In the ancient world, anyone who could write—at first a small group—could publish effectively, one copy at a time. Access to Gutenberg's press was limited to those who could afford one of the many thousands of small printers' shops that dotted Europe in the preindustrial age, but as the preceding pages have amply shown, in the Anglo-Saxon world after 1700, ordinary men and women, if sufficiently motivated, could employ the hand press to do battle with the powers that be.

In the mid-nineteenth century, the familiar world of the hand press and the horse-drawn transport of both information and goods would disappear far behind the leading edge of the new printing and communications methods. These innovative technologies would not come cheaply, and their control by an increasingly constricted, rich, and powerful elite would change the political process in ways that Renaudot, Franklin, Cobbett, Hone, and Carlile could not even begin to imagine.

To repeat, the enterprises of these pioneers did not deploy a technology much different from that invented by Gutenberg. In the three centuries following his first printed indulgences and Bibles, the only significant improvements in technique involved the slow replacement of wood by iron in the presses, especially in the screw threading, and perhaps some changes in type metallurgy. In 1798, Gutenberg's human-powered technology reached its pinnacle, and a dead end as well, when Charles, Earl of Stanhope, eliminated the last bit of wood from his press. While his all-iron machine slightly improved the speed and quality of printing, the compositor still had to fill the formes by hand, and pressmen still had to feed each sheet individually into the machine. The Stanhope iron press could at best turn out but 250 pages per hour, a rate not too much greater than that of Gutenberg's immediate successors.

In the mid-nineteenth century, steam wrought changes in daily life that have no parallel in history. Those impressed with the rapid pace of technological change today should consider that people, goods, and information do not travel materially faster than they did fifty years ago; were the average citizen of 1963 magically transported forward to the current year, the Internet and personal computers might need a bit of explaining, but automobiles and jet airliners would be entirely familiar concepts. Now consider a time traveler who crosses the half century from 1825 to 1875. In the former year, almost nothing moved faster than the horse; by the latter year, the speed of maximum human transport and information had increased severalfold. Even more impressively, in the intervening five decades the world had just been wired with what author Tom Standage called the "Victorian Internet"—a global telegraph system that flashed critical information across the globe in a matter of minutes.[28] By 1925, the electrical and electronic revolutions would yield improvements in the speed and per-unit costs of communications technology that were arguably greater than those seen in the previous five millennia, and their impact on the political process would not always be positive. (There were two exceptions to this premodern speed limit. The first was smoke and semaphore signaling, which had been in use since ancient times, most famously the system established in France by Claude Chappe beginning in the late eighteenth century. These systems could transmit messages, depending on their length, at speeds exceeding one hundred miles per hour, but only at very great expense. The second was homing pigeons, used at least as early as 500 BC, with a service range of around five hundred miles at an average speed of about fifty miles per hour.)[29]

For thousands of years, humans had harnessed steam technology for novelty uses, such as opening and closing temple doors. By the late seventeenth century, several English inventors had demonstrated low-efficiency engines, and around 1712 Thomas Newcomen built one that worked well enough to drain mines, but whose high fuel consumption rendered it economically viable only atop a coal shaft.

In 1764, James Watt, an instrument maker at Glasgow University, was asked to repair a model Newcomen engine. Its high fuel consumption vexed him, and while strolling one day on Glasgow Green, he tumbled to the root of the problem: with each stroke, the cylinder alternately heated with compression and then cooled with expansion, wasting an enormous amount of energy. Condensing the steam *outside* the engine's cylinder, Watt realized, would bypass this limitation. Over the ensuing decades, Watt's engines so improved fuel efficiency that, for the first time, steam power could be applied to almost any purpose.[30]

Print was one of those purposes. By the early 1800s the circulation of *The Times* of London had grown to the unheard-of volume of five thousand daily copies; at this level of output, simply buying yet more Stanhope-type hand presses and hiring yet more compositors and pressmen became both financially and logistically impossible.

Around 1800, Friedrich Koenig, a German immigrant to London, applied himself to the problem. In his initial attempt, he first mounted a Watt engine onto a Stanhope-type screw press, a clumsy marriage that failed miserably. Next, he adapted an idea patented by fellow inventor William Nicholson: a cylindrical forme into which the type was mounted, similar in concept to the cylindrical seals of remote antiquity. An adjacent roller continuously applied ink to the print cylinders, but a pressmen still had to feed each sheet into the device by hand. A breakthrough, nonetheless: Koenig's first roller presses could crank out a thousand sheets per hour, quadruple the rate of a Stanhope machine.

By 1840, the circulation of *The Times* had reached forty thousand, and inventors kept up with demand by stacking multiple rollers onto a single engine: first "two-rollers," then "four-rollers," on up to gargantuan "ten-rollers" capable of twenty thousand impressions per hour, and frenzied teams of pressmen slaked its ravenous thirst for paper. One such monster, whose cylinders were stacked vertically, rose to a dizzying height, and by a contemporary account featured

a wilderness of wheels, and cylinders, and straps and . . . a deafening thunder that accompanies the storm of sheets pouring down on all sides faster than the eye can follow them, or the mind can realize their number.[31]

In the late 1860s, papermakers began to supply newspapers with large rolls of newsprint that could be fed continuously into the maw of printing cylinders. At the same time, European and American paper manufacturers finally unlocked the secret of producing paper from hard European wood pulp, and thus broke free of their dependence on increasingly scarce rags. In the United States, the price of paper fell by nearly 90 percent between 1866 and 1900, while in Britain, the same revolution in paper technology saw a sixtyfold increase in paper production over the course of the nineteenth century.[32]

The elimination of these two expensive barriers—the crews of human sheet feeders and rag-based paper—merely moved the bottleneck to another step, the composition of type, which still had to be done by hand, the same way as in Gutenberg's time. Initially, inventors simply mechanized the centuries-old process of selecting the type and placing it into the formes. The first practical version of such a machine, designed by Robert Hattersley, allowed the operator to select keys, similar to those on an ordinary qwerty keyboard, that triggered the extraction of the appropriate type from a bin and slotted it into the forme. These devices proved notoriously difficult to maintain, and even when they were in good working order, they could do the work of only two or three manual compositors.

It fell to a German immigrant to America, Ottmar Mergenthaler, to revolutionize composition. Mergenthaler's genius lay in the realization that casting type a *line* at a time required the storage of only a relatively small number of letter and punctuation matrices that could be reassembled with each new line. His device, then, produced a hot type slug for a whole line, which after each print run could be fed back into the machine, remelted, and recast into a new line. As a bonus, each "line o' type" (hence the name of the machine) was fresh and unworn, and this eliminated the metallurgical requirement for durability that had hobbled type casters and printers since Gutenberg. Closely related to Merganthaler's Linotype machine was the so-called Monotype device, which continuously cast single characters. While the Linotype produced faster and cleaner drafts, pressmen could correct a Monotype forme much more easily than a Linotype forme, fixing a misspelled word rather than a whole line.

The basic Linotype/cylinder printer/feeder assembly described above survived for nearly a century, and the machines themselves proved remarkably durable. For example, *The Guardian* purchased its first two Linotypes in 1893; both remained in nearly continuous use, with only minor modifications, until they completely wore out in 1948.

The application of steam power, and later electrical power, to the printing process ominously changed the political calculus of technological control. For four centuries after Gutenberg, any merchant, craftsman, or burgher with modest wealth or good credit could start a press; consequently, thousands of presses blossomed on the Continent and in the New World. Koenig and Merganthaler forever transformed this relatively arcadian publishing world into a landscape dominated by far fewer, highly capital-intensive, large newspapers and printers. Previously, the powerful few could not completely control the older, cheaper, and thus more widely available hand presses. The new concentration of printing capacity into fewer, bigger, and more expensive facilities placed them more easily under the thumb of the aspiring demagogue or despot, or even of ostensibly democratic political institutions.

In colonial America, before the time of Koenig and Mergenthaler, the line between journalism and political propaganda, and between newspaper and revolutionary government, was a fine one indeed; it was often impossible to detect just where the American political apparatus left off and the newspapers began. As a case in point, the Committees of Correspondence, the revolution's first political organizations, spread the news about Concord and Lexington, and Committee members often ran the newspapers.[33] This patriotic cooperative publishing endeavor found itself enshrined in the new nation's Post Office Act of 1792.[34] The newspapers themselves also created their own private postal networks, that the government would commandeer from time to time.

While the press was deeply woven into the fabric of the Revolution, it exercised little independent influence, but rather was the creature of its opposing sides. In the words of press historian Thomas Leonard,

> Editors printed only what the king's army or the patriot militia allowed. The peace was brutally selective. The taint of loyalism was

fatal. The *Massachusetts Gazette* shut down when the redcoats left Boston. In New York, Hugh Gaine and James Rivington gave up their important print shops when the British forces sailed. Most newspapers were not strong enough to survive the death of a proprietor.[35]

The American newspapers *were* a power, but that power was captive to their sources of information. As the postrevolutionary "Era of Good Feelings" gave way to intense political partisanship after 1824, the newspapers served as the obedient foot soldiers of one side or the other; Daniel Webster noted that the typical Whig Party newspaper was "our natural field marshal." Those alarmed by today's political polarization might consider an editorial in one Democratic Party paper stating that anyone outside the party "has no right to live."[36]

It could not be any other way. The typical paper of the era cost about six cents at a time when the average daily wage was less than a dollar, and so could be easily afforded only by merchants and other notables. The first and last pages contained what these readers were looking for: shipping news and government notices, the latter of which explained the papers' dependence on party patronage. The second page contained editorials that duly reflected the views of the party in power, while the third contained the actual news. The very names of these "six-penny" papers reflected their constituencies: the *Boston Daily Advertiser,* the *Baltimore Federal Republican,* and the all-inclusive *Baltimore Patriot and Mercantile Advertiser.*[37]

The business model of the American six-penny papers was thus very similar to that of their English cousins: dependence on subscriptions from regular commercial customers. It was nearly impossible for a citizen on the street to purchase a single copy, except at the printer's shop. Editors and publishers often spent more time collecting subscription fees from their tardy customers than they did collecting, writing, and printing the news, and in hard times their offices often bulged with goods taken in barter.

At approximately the same time that the steam-driven press and hot-lead composition dramatically decreased per-unit production costs and increased the output of the newspapers, they also became the recipients—and often rather uncomfortable ones—of an increasing input from the first electronic medium: the telegraph. Consider this brief notice to readers of the *New York Gazette* on December 17, 1747, a century before the telegraph was introduced:

> The Philadelphia Post not coming in last week at the appointed Time,
> and the Weather setting in very cold, has occasioned both the Boston
> and Philadelphia Posts, to set out a Week sooner than they had de-
> signed, to perform their Stages but once a Fortnight.—We have very
> little News and the Post not expected in till next Saturday.[38]

Recall that the new nation's postmasters became its first de facto newspaper publishers. They all felt acutely the paucity of information flow across the vast, empty distances of the new continent, and they banded together to form the nation's first "press agency," a common agreement to circulate their papers among themselves post-free, a mechanism formalized by the first colonial postmasters general, Benjamin Franklin and William Hunter, in the 1750s.

The informational constraints faced by newspapers at the beginning of the telegraph era are scarcely imaginable today. As in England, the newly independent United States government practiced secrecy in some of its most basic processes; the Senate closed its doors to the public and press for the first six years of its existence. Even more amazingly, the nine delegates to the Constitutional Convention of 1787 who took notes withheld them for at least thirty years, and the best-known record, that of James Madison, was not made public for half a century.[39]

The tyranny of distance also strangled the flow of news to the papers. A sense of the scarcity and preciousness of information can be gathered by following the entry of a regular packet ship into New York Harbor in the early nineteenth century. The packets, the fastest, sleekest ships of the era, with average Atlantic crossing times of under three weeks, carried passengers and only the most valuable of cargoes, and since they conveyed the freshest news from Britain and the Continent, newspapers sought them out eagerly. So widely anticipated were new installments of Dickens' major novels that in the winter of 1841 American fans waited at the docks for the packets and cried out to the crew of an incoming ship, "Is little Nell dead?"[40]

Packet ships were required to use pilots for harbor entrance. Pilots usually spied the boats from their base on Staten Island; the first to reach a ship earned not only the inbound job, but, by tradition, the outbound one as well. As the piloted packet ship approached the Narrows, it was next met by customs and health officials who detained cargo, passengers, and crew for inspection; suspected contraband or disease could incur a quarantine and a month's delay. Mail pouches and regular newspaper shipments usually shared these delays.

One item received VIP treatment. For the approaching passengers and crew, the first sign of impending landfall was usually the "news boat" bobbing through the fog, often encountered up to a hundred miles out. These craft lay offshore more or less permanently in wait for the packet ships' special pouches, which were exempt from postal and customs regulations and entrusted to designated ship's officers by London editors for conveyance to their colleagues in New York.[41] These news boats helped to overcome the tyranny of distance and sped the news from abroad to the waiting presses.

Around the same time that Mergenthaler built his first steam-driven cylindrical presses, a different group of men began to experiment with the electronic transmission of information. Since prehistory, mankind had been aware of both the bioelectricity produced by certain fish and the artificial electricity produced from rubbing amber with cloth. In 1746, a French abbé, Jean-Antoine Nollet, accomplished the first electronic data transmission—of sorts—when he linked two hundred monks with twenty-five-foot iron bars, and spaced them out over a mile. When he shocked the first monk, he was amazed to see that the last monk felt the shock simultaneously with the first, demonstrating the instantaneous nature of the phenomenon.[42]

But whether an experimenter used copper wire or monks, electronic transmission depended upon a more reliable source of electricity than that from rubbed amber or electric eels, a problem not solved until Alessandro Volta invented his first zinc/copper and zinc/silver pile batteries in 1800.[43] It took several more decades before the likes of the American Samuel Morse and Englishmen William Cooke and Charles Wheatstone produced functional telegraph lines. In 1844, Morse dramatically signaled the results of the Whig convention in Baltimore to Washington more than an hour in advance of their arrival by horseback in the capital. By 1848, the United States had strung two thousand miles of telegraph lines; two years later, it had twelve thousand; and on October 24, 1861, the transcontinental line was complete. Two days later, the Pony Express went out of business.[44]

In 1858, an Anglo-American governmental consortium laid the first transatlantic cable and astounded the planet with instantaneous communication between the New World and the Old World; as New Yorker George Templeton Strong famously wrote in his diary:

> Yesterday's [New York] *Herald* said that the cable is undoubtedly the Angel in the Book of Revelation with one foot in the sea and one foot on land, proclaiming that time is no longer. Moderate people merely say that this is the greatest human achievement in history.[45]

Strong did not exaggerate: otherwise rational observers, astounded by the sudden, transformative advance in communications technology, thought it capable of establishing peace among nations and peoples. In the months following the completion of the first transatlantic cable, Charles Briggs and Augustus Maverick rushed into print *The Story of the Telegraph and a History of the Great Atlantic Cable,* in which they breathlessly proclaimed,

> How potent a power, then, is the telegraphic destined to become in the civilization of the world! This binds together by a vital cord all the nations of the earth. It is impossible that old prejudices and hostilities should longer exist, while such an instrument has been created for an exchange of thought between all the nations of the earth.[46]

Sadly, the new technology did not bring world peace, and that expectation was a mistake that would be repeated with each new communications advance over the next century and a half. In any event, the poorly designed transatlantic line sputtered out after only a month. The Civil War prevented the next attempts, but by 1866, two more reliable transatlantic links functioned. In 1870 and 1871, the Asian trunk line reached India and Australia, respectively. At a stroke, terrestrial and submarine telegraph lines compressed communication times that had previously consumed the better part of a year down to minutes or hours.[47]

This network represented the ultimate in expensive, low-access technology. Its routine use was beyond the means of the ordinary citizen, and its *control* was completely beyond the financial resources of the average person. In Europe, the telegraph systems soon came under government aegis, while in the United States, one company, Western Union, had gobbled up most of the smaller lines by 1880.

Britons paid about a shilling per message—approximately twenty-five American cents, perhaps half of an English laborer's average daily wage.[48] Initially, Americans paid about a dollar per message, but by 1879 the price had fallen to forty cents, at a time when the average American daily wage was slightly more than a dollar. (Observe from the above numbers that Englishmen earned about half the wage of Americans. In the late nineteenth century and the early twentieth, Europeans did not flock to America for anything so extravagant as streets paved with gold; on a continent starved for labor, the doubling of the paycheck proved incentive enough.)

Contemporary observers noted that even given the high costs of telegraphy, usage by ordinary people was more common in the government-run European systems, which early on abandoned their association with rail lines and located themselves conveniently in post offices. The American system, by contrast, remained closely associated with its rail system for one simple reason: while the geographically dense European routes were generally double-track, all but the busiest American routes were single-track and required close telegraphic control. Consequently, before 1880 few Americans outside the railroad and financial industries ever saw the inside of a telegraph office.

In addition, in much the same way that modern start-up software companies aim at an exit strategy of voluntary or involuntary absorption into Microsoft or Google, so too did almost all successful American telegraph start-ups become part of Western Union. Buying out these smaller companies required a constant flow of new capital, and after 1870 Western Union was loath to reduce its rates. Public dissatisfaction with Western Union's prices reached the point that a remarkable attorney, Gardiner G. Hubbard, the father-in-law of Alexander Graham Bell and a cofounder of Bell Telephone, spearheaded an unsuccessful effort to nationalize Western Union.[49]

The telegraph became the newspaper's lifeblood and extinguished the world of horse couriers, news packet boats, and carrier pigeons. By the mid-nineteenth century, newspapers on both sides of the Atlantic found themselves dependent on the telegraph monopolies to supply the information they printed. While the great clattering cylindrical presses and Linotype machines overwhelmed the senses and sensibilities of observers, the essential fact remained that this impressive apparatus produced *news*, whose sources the newspapers did not control. In 1851, the *Springfield* [Massachusetts] *Republican* optimistically observed:

> Nothing can be more evident to the public, and nothing certainly is more evident to publishers of newspapers, than that there is a great deal more news nowadays than there used to be. . . . Publishers of country weeklies used to fish with considerable anxiety in a shallow sea, for matter sufficient to fill their sheets, while dailies only dreamed of an existence in larger cities. . . . The railroad car, the steamboat, and the magnetic telegraph have made neighborhood among widely disserved states. . . . These active and almost miraculous agencies have brought the whole civilized world in contact. The editor sits in his sanctum, and his obedient messengers are the lightning and the fire.[50]

The reality was that in the United States "the lightning and the fire" of the telegraph were hardly anyone's obedient servants. Rather, the telegraph was for all intents and purposes the ward of a rapacious Western Union, which thus controlled the flow of the lifeblood of information to the newspapers. As had occurred before, and would occur again, an advanced, expensive, and cumbersome communications technology was commanded by the very few who controlled the flow of information to the population at large.

In 1833, a New York printer, Benjamin Day, took William Cobbett's concept of an inexpensive mass-market newspaper one step further when he founded the first American one-penny paper, the *Sun*. Day intended it as a purely advertising venture, but in 1835, his overly imaginative editor, Richard Adams Locke, published the purported observation of people, crops, and animals living on the moon. The competing *New York Herald* soon exposed the hoax, but by then, readers could not get enough of the *Sun,* and Day soon brought in the nation's first steam presses to keep up with demand.

In 1846, the *Sun* and the *Herald*, with three other New York papers, banded together to form the Associated Press (AP) in order to share the high costs of telegraph, boat, and horse messenger service from the Mexican-American War front. The new consortium would go on to sell high-quality reporting to papers around the nation; similar organizations, most notably the United Press syndicate, would join it.

By the late nineteenth century, the telegraph had given the newspapers more to report, and the rotary press and inexpensive paper allowed them to print more of it much more cheaply. The old thin six-penny paper, beholden to a given party and aimed at the mercantile class, gave way to the likes of the thicker one-penny *Sun* and *Herald,* stuffed with scandal and patent medicine advertisements to titillate and tempt the mass literate societies of the West.[51] The names of the penny papers reflected the change: in New York City the names *Sun, Herald,* and *Tribune* suggested publications that, respectively, illuminated, cried out, and protected the downtrodden.

For a while, the six-penny and one-penny presses coexisted, the former railing against the scandalmongering and fraudulent advertising of the latter, the latter trumpeting its independence. In the words of James Gordon Bennett, founder of the *New York Herald,* only the one-penny press could be trusted "simply because it is subservient to none of its readers."[52] The typical six-penny publication rarely had more than a few thousand regular subscribers. The one-penny papers, by contrast, sold thousands of copies at news shops—Bennett's *Herald* sold 20,000 per day just a few years after its 1835 founding; and by the eve of the Civil War, it sold 77,000.[53]

The six-penny press, with its limited circulation and its dependence on the municipal and state political apparatus and commercial interests, remained local and had little national influence. The one-penny press suffered no such constraints; borne on the wings of the telegraph, cheap paper, high-speed rotary presses, and the Linotype, it quickly grew to national importance. The stories of two men—one an incarnation of the Horatio Alger myth, the other a scion of wealth—colorfully illustrate the birth of the national press chain, as well as the limitations of its power and influence in the late nineteenth century and early twentieth.

The Hungarian Joseph Pulitzer was born into prosperity in 1847, the progeny of a Jewish grain merchant. His father died in 1858, and the business bankrupted soon after, leaving the family penniless. Rejected by the Austrian, French, and British armies because of his poor eyesight and fragile physique, Pulitzer finally began his military career in 1864 by signing on with Union Army recruiters in Hamburg, who would enlist any man with a pulse.

Although fluent in French, German, and Hungarian, he spoke little English. This was of little import in an army with many immigrant units, Pulitzer's being composed mainly of Germans. After Appomattox, he went west. At that time, the logical choice for an ambitious young middle European was Saint Louis, which had a large German population and was the bustling gateway to the open spaces beyond the Mississippi River. There, he worked at a number of jobs, finally landing one as a reporter at the German-language *Westliche Post,* where he polished both his journalistic craft and his English.

Fortune smiles on the prepared. Pulitzer not only reported but practiced law and served in the state legislature, and when he came into a small inheritance, he speculated successfully in bankrupt newspapers, over time gaining possession of two in Saint Louis, the *Post* and the *Dispatch,* which he combined into a single business.

Pulitzer by that point had acquired a sharp sense of the reading public's taste, as evidenced by this typical *Post and Dispatch* headline:

SOME GLIMPSES AT THE ST. LOUIS
GAMBLER'S RING

HE ALLEGES HE MADE THE GOVERNOR
DRUNK AND PUT HIM TO BED

The paper exposed brothels and published the tax returns of the wealthy; the city's prostitutes feared the former but treasured the latter, since it provided them a more accurate appraisal of their customers' net worth. Scandalmongering was not only good business for Pulitzer, but catharsis as well. When the city's Democratic Party denied him its congressional candidacy, he set after its leadership with glee and exposed corruption in the city's real estate dealings and streetcar monopolies, and its extortion of money from private companies. In that era, the guilty often expressed little public remorse. Commented one public official caught red-handed by the *Post and Dispatch*: "It'll be an advertisement of my business. . . . De people dat didn't know afore dat dere was anything corroked in de House of Delegates knows it now, an' if dey wants anything done dey'll pony up a dime or two."[54]

At the time of Pulitzer's death in 1911, his holdings remained largely confined to his Saint Louis and New York papers. He left $2,000,000 to Columbia University to found its Graduate School of Journalism; in 1917 the university would also establish the prizes that bear his name. In life, he inspired the career of another publisher, William Randolph Hearst, who would go on to found the nation's first truly national newspaper chain.

Hearst sprang from even more exotic stock than Pulitzer. In 1850, his father, George, trekked west from Missouri with the gold rush and nearly died of cholera along the way. Verging on bankruptcy, he struck a remarkable series of silver veins that catapulted him from the depths of poverty to the pinnacle of wealth.

Money did not add polish to the unhygienic, foul-mouthed Missouri farm boy. When he returned home in 1860 to attend his mother's last days, he shocked family and friends by courting a local schoolteacher, Phoebe Apperson, a refined young woman twenty years his junior who spoke passable French, a rarity in that part of the world. Despite George's many shortcomings, he was at heart a kind man, and rich to boot. He and Phoebe finally married in 1862, and then left for California.

In the days before the transcontinental railroad, two paths led to California. The poor risked hardship and death overland, as had George on his first voyage west, while the wealthy went by ship, portaging across Panama, a somewhat safer though no less arduous route. The combination of rough Pacific seas and pregnancy sickened Phoebe horribly, and upon beholding the Golden Gate she proclaimed, "I intend to live on these hills where I can always see the bay."[55] On April 29, 1863, she gave birth to a son named William Randolph, whom fortune blessed with his mother's intelligence and refinement, and with the personal strengths of both parents.

Willie traversed no ordinary childhood. The young toughs in Willie's class worried his mother so much that she had servants escort him home from school; she relented when Willie demanded to walk home alone like everyone else. When Willie was ten, he and his mother left on a European grand tour, where they perfected their German and French, visited every imaginable museum, dined with American diplomats, and met the pope. Meanwhile, George entered the ranks of America's wealthiest men with remarkable mineral strikes in North Dakota and Montana, founding the Homestake and Anaconda companies.

In 1880, just before young Willie went off to Harvard, George purchased the *Examiner,* San Francisco's "Democratic" newspaper, which focused on keeping the party faithful informed about issues, getting out the vote, and persistently losing money. Nearly illiterate, George desperately needed editorial help, and when Harvard finally tossed Willie out for one too many high-spirited pranks—to wit, giving his professors chamber pots with their names inscribed on the inside—the younger Hearst took over the paper.[56]

Willie's ignominious scholastic career did not greatly discomfit him. By that point, he knew he would be running the *Examiner*, and while at Harvard, he had sharpened his entrepreneurial skill as the business manager of its student humor newspaper, the *Lampoon*. He also had a role model: in 1883 Joseph Pulitzer had purchased the *New York World* from financier Jay Gould. Pulitzer, along with the *Herald*'s James Gordon Bennett, had "connected the dots" in the brave new world of American journalism: The old, low-volume commercially and politically oriented six-penny papers had yielded, thanks to the new high-speed presses and streamlined Linotype composition, to an independent, scandalmongering, patent-medicine-selling penny press. The telegraph, in its turn, allowed entrepreneurs to knit together individual newspapers into national chains. Needless to say, only the wealthiest and most powerful could wield the high-output presses and telegraph networks essential to this new nationwide medium.

The ground zero for this revolution was the nation's largest market, New York City, not its smaller regional cities. Also gone with the six-penny press was the reliable cash flow of the subscription model; now street-corner newsboys and news shops hawked each day's issue, the size of which varied according to the day's news. The temptation to manufacture events out of whole cloth often proved irresistible for penny-paper publishers, especially Hearst.

While Pulitzer was turning the *World* into New York's newspaper powerhouse, Hearst started with his own small-bore version in San Francisco, the *Examiner*, on which his father had been losing money for years. Well, initially not exactly *in* San Francisco. In March 1887, as his father was traveling east to assume his duties as a United States senator, Willie, age twenty-four, headed west with his mistress, a Cambridge waitress named Tessie Powers; the two took up residence in sunny, pleasant Sausalito, just across the Golden Gate; the *Examiner*'s offices temporarily moved there as well.

Hearst took the sleepy world of San Francisco's six-penny press by storm. He purchased the license for the superb national and international coverage of Bennett's *Herald* by telegraph; just as he exploited his family's capital resources, he tapped its political connections as well, cajoling his rich, and now powerful, father to steer advertising revenue from the competing *Chronicle* to his own paper.

Hearst also had an eye for talent; he imported a platoon of writers from Cambridge and New York, and also closer to home, most famously the wickedly funny and penetrating Ambrose Bierce. In classic style, the grizzled journalist recalled his first meeting with the tyro publisher:

> "O," I said, "you come from Mr. Hearst."
>   Then, that unearthly child lifted its blue eyes and cooed, "I am Mr. Hearst."[57]

At the *Examiner,* Hearst developed one of his signature methods, stunt journalism. An early example of this technique was the paper's investigation of wrongdoing at the city's mental hospital. Hearst directed one of his reporters, Winifred Black, to dress in rags, dilate her pupils with belladonna, and stagger and fall on Kearny Street. Quickly, she gained admission to the mental asylum, and once inside documented its many abuses.[58]

Over the coming decade, Hearst regaled San Francisco with nonstop, lurid coverage of mayhem, murder, lust, and corruption in high places, a style that became known as "yellow journalism" (a term whose roots have been variously ascribed to the Yellow Kid, the first nationally famous comic strip character, and to the lack of intellectual courage of journalists who manufactured stories out of thin air). On any given day, the *Examiner* would sport half a dozen or more such headlines and subheads:

> KILLED FOR HIS MONEY. The Horrible Crime to Which a
> Young Villain Has Confessed.
> A Man Decapitated.
> Insanity of the Victim's Widow—
> The Murderer's Mother Greatly Affected.[59]

Although Hearst's contemporaries accused him of unfairly throwing his father's wealth around, he well understood old George's saw that it takes a mine to make a mine—that in most businesses, deep capitalization often provides an unassailable advantage. Hearst prospered mightily and followed Pulitzer's earlier example by purchasing New York's *Morning*

Journal in 1895, and renaming it the *New York Journal.* The next year, another aggressive young Chattanooga newspaperman, Adolph Ochs, moved to New York City and purchased the *Times.*

A full-fledged newspaper war ensued, and the competing coverage of the Spanish-American War, which would begin just a few years after Hearst's and Ochs's purchases, illustrated both the extent and the limitations of the power of the fledgling industry.

After acquiring the *Journal,* Hearst sent two men—reporter Richard Harding Davis and artist Frederic Remington—to Cuba to cover the insurgency against the Spanish. The local colonial authorities barred them from the combat zones, and with nothing to report, Remington cabled Hearst, "Everything is quiet. There is no trouble here. There will be no war. Wish to return." Hearst supposedly cabled back, "Please remain. You furnish the pictures and I'll furnish the war." (Hearst's famous reply is probably apocryphal, and whatever the nature of his boss's instructions, Remington left the island.)[60]

In February 1897, Davis wired home a story about Spanish police strip-searching some Cuban women on the American ship *Olivette,* bound for Key West. The story was inflammatory enough—the headline read, "Does Our Flag Protect Women? Indignities Practiced by Spanish Officials on Board American Vessels"—but its best-remembered feature was Remington's drawing of a naked woman surrounded by leering Spanish policemen. Never mind that the artist drew the scene from New York, or that the women had actually been searched by matrons; William Randolph Hearst indeed seemed set on influencing events and furnishing a war.

Damsels in distress sold papers; the *Journal*'s next escapade in Cuban romantic adventure involved eighteen-year-old Evangelina Cisneros. In late 1897, the paper reported that the young woman, the daughter of an aristocratic Cuban family, had landed in a Havana jail cell for resisting the advances of an aide to the infamous Spanish General Valeriano Weyler (better known to Hearst's readers as "The Butcher"). The *Journal*'s man on the scene, George Bryson, described her cell as worse than a pit. The Spanish supposedly had treated her father at least as badly and had transported him across the Atlantic for incarceration near Gibraltar.

At this point, Hearst replaced Bryson with Karl Decker, a dashing Virginian chosen not only for a skill set uniquely appropriate to the Cisneros story, but also to curry favor with the U.S. consul in Havana, another Virginian. Decker set up shop across the street from Evangelina's cell, and after a few unsuccessful attempts finally managed to harness a coach to its window bars; the tender young woman did her part by faking a toothache and obtaining enough opium to render both her jailers and her cellmates comatose.

After being freed by Decker, Evangelina cut her hair to male length, disguised herself in a sailor's suit, and insouciantly strolled to Havana's wharf, where Decker placed her on a ship bound for the United States. The *Journal*'s headline would make Fox News blush: "An American Newspaper Accomplishes at a Single Stroke What the Best Efforts of Diplomacy Failed Utterly to Bring About in Many Months."

When she arrived in New York, Hearst put Evangelina up in a suite in the Waldorf, dressed her in virginal white, and paraded her around town, where she thanked Decker and the great nation that had freed and protected her; tears welled in the eyes of all. The truth, unearthed by Pulitzer's *World,* proved more ambiguous: her father was in reality a revolutionary leader and was incarcerated not in Europe but on Cuba's Isle of Pines. While visiting him in prison, Evangelina had used her feminine wiles to entice the facility's commander to her father's rooms, where his compatriots attempted to slit the commander's throat. For this treachery, the Spaniards threw her into a Havana jail, where she had a spacious suite, not the hellhole described by Bryson. And so on. By that point, however, Hearst's lurid, manufactured Cuban stories had acquired a momentum all their own, and few paid much attention to Pulitzer's more factual reportage.

The situation in Cuba slid inexorably toward conflict; in early 1898 the *Journal* published a letter in which Dupuy de Lome, Spain's ambassador in Washington, had made indiscreet, though hardly shocking, comments about President McKinley. Thundered the *Journal,* "THE WORST INSULT TO THE UNITED STATES IN ITS HISTORY." Already in possession of the letter for more than a year, Hearst had waited patiently for the most propitious moment to print it; de Lome subsequently resigned. Spain and America moved closer to war, and it finally came on February 15, 1898, when the *Maine* blew up in Havana harbor. Americans blamed a Spanish mine or torpedo, but a far greater likelihood was an accidental ammunition explosion, a not uncommon warship mishap in those days.[61]

Looking back more than a century later, we might conclude that a single man, empowered by his command of the telegraph and high-speed press, had brought two of the world's great nations to Armageddon. Hearst as much as said so: in May 1898, his New York paper asked on its front page, "How do you like the *Journal*'s war?"[62]

Yet, in reality, Hearst wielded less influence than his ownership of his rapidly expanding empire of major papers would suggest. The most careful analysis of the Spanish-American War suggests that the press did little to precipitate it beyond reporting the facts. To wit, a foreign power was conducting a brutal, nearly genocidal repression of a native population on an island just off America's shores. And not just any foreign power, but the most hated and corrupt of the European ancien régimes, Spain. Add to this the fact that the United States had just closed its western frontier; thus, the only soil on which it could exercise its manifest destiny was foreign. Even without Hearst's antics, war would have come.[63] (The ultimate irony of the Cuban insurgency and Spanish-American War was that the major factor triggering the rebellion was the damage to the local economy done by American sugar tariffs.)[64]

In the realm of foreign policy, the American president operated—and still operates today—with a degree of autonomy that would have been envied by most European monarchs.[65] President McKinley deeply resented Hearst's interference, and had he lived longer, he might have taken on Hearst.

In the event, that job was left to his successor, Theodore Roosevelt, who decided that the presidency's revenge on the flamboyant newspaperman would be served cold. After the war, Hearst was elected as a Democrat to two terms in Congress; he also ran twice unsuccessfully for mayor of New York City and once, in 1906, for governor against Charles Evans Hughes. Roosevelt chose the gubernatorial election as the venue for his attack on the press baron; it was likely no accident that the New York governorship was the president's old billet.

The president deputized his secretary of state, Elihu Root, for the task. In spite of the fact that he had just returned from an exhausting tour of South America, Root rose to the challenge. On November 1, 1906, just five days before the election, the secretary spoke in Utica, New York, a few miles from his hometown, Clinton. The text of the speech had already been published and had attracted a horde of Hearst's backers. One of them heckled Root, and when Hughes' supporters moved to throw him out, Root raised his hand and announced in a booming voice, "No, let him stay and learn!"

Root then proceeded to deliver the speech, the most famous of the era, painting Hearst as a demagogue of the worst sort, a sordid example of the power of the evil corporate trusts that Roosevelt was bent on breaking up, and a wealthy, callous dilettante who had missed 90 percent of congressional roll calls and absented himself on 95 percent of legislative days.

Root was only winding up. Then, he detonated a daisy-cutter that no one expected: Hearst's papers' vile attacks on McKinley, and most of all, the ghoulish cartoons of the president, made Hearst complicit in the president's murder. Of Leon Czolgosz, the assassin, Root noted,

> He was answering the lesson he had learned, that it was a service to mankind to rid the earth of a monster; and the foremost of the teachers of these lessons to him and his kind was and is William Randolph Hearst with his yellow journals.[66]

Root ended his speech by making clear the ultimate fount of his sentiments:

> Do you believe in President Roosevelt? Do you agree with his policy in pursuing and preventing corporate wrongdoing? . . . I say to you with his authority that he desires the election of Mr. Hughes as Governor of the State of New York; I say to you, with his authority, that he regards Mr. Hearst as wholly unfit to be Governor, as an insincere, self-seeking demagogue.[67]

The speech effectively ended Hearst's political career. His defeat was the only major Democratic loss in the New York 1906 midterm election; after that date, he could probably not have been elected sanitation commissioner. In the words of one commentator of the era, "Behind the editorial page he can accomplish much. In the open he can fool no one."[68] The speech in Utica considerably burnished Root's already excellent reputation; but for the fact that he sprang from the now out-of-favor field of corporate law, Root's performance would have made him the obvious choice for the 1908 Republican presidential nomination. Ironically, only a tenuous connection existed between Hearst and McKinley's assassin, Leon Czolgosz, whose motivation stemmed from his anarchism and concern with American social inequality.[69]

Hearst's newspaper career lasted a remarkable six decades, almost until his death in 1951, and spanned the tenure of ten presidents. His expansive operations and lifestyle included financing both the acting career of his mistress Marion Davies and the castle at Sam Simeon, and on at least one occasion his extravagance swept him over the brink of bankruptcy. He controlled thirty major American newspapers, and to this day, the Hearst Corporation maintains a formidable publishing empire. And yet, he wielded so little power that he could not hold on to political office, and other national figures often used him as a foil, as did both Roosevelts.[70]

Moreover, Hearst was defeated not so much by the political establishment as by the evolution of journalism into a profession. It is no fairer to judge Hearst by today's journalistic standards than it would be to measure the behavior of a Roman legion commander according to the rules of the Geneva Convention. In the Hearst era, the concept of journalism as a profession (that is, a commitment to dispassionate objectivity and attention to fact) was nearly unknown. Just as law students are taught to separate out the letter and logic of the law from their emotions and opinions, and as medical students learn to isolate their emotional reactions to patients and their conditions, so do reputable journalists strive to double-source and distance themselves from their subjects and interviewees.

Just why journalists, whose responsibility to the public is less direct and obvious, should strive for a high degree of professionalism is not always clear. Lawyers and doctors, after all, have a direct and compelling responsibility to their clients and patients, respectively; journalists cannot easily make the same ethical case. Yet, over the past century, journalism has become a highly professionalized craft, replete with standards of performance, and even ethical imperatives that in extreme circumstances demand that a reporter refuse to reveal the identity of a source and so serve jail time.

In the early twentieth century, journalist Walter Lippmann wrote an influential essay in the *Yale Review,* which recapitulated much of the story told in this chapter: the evolution of newspapers through three stages: direct government control (Renaudot, England under the Licensing Act before 1695); party and commercial control (roughly, the six-penny press); and dependence on appeal to the mass market (the penny press and Hearst's yellow journalism).[71]

In the 1970s, Denise Schmandt-Besserat deduced that the ubiquitous small clay tokens scattered around Sumerian archaeological sites represented the precursors of the first cuneiform writing. Courtesy of Denise Schmandt-Besserat.

Bisitun relief: Note inscribed panels below and to the left and man at lower right panel for scale. Source: *Wonders of the Past: The Romance of Antiquity and its Splendours,* Sir John Alexander Hammerton, Ed., G.P. Putnam's Sons, 1924.

Drawing of Bisitun Relief: Darius gives thanks to the God Ahura Mazda for victory over the vanquished under foot and to his right. Source: *Wonders of the Past: The Romance of Antiquity and its Splendours,* Sir John Alexander Hammerton, Ed., G.P. Putnam's Sons, 1924.

Researcher on a ledge at Bisitun inscription. Source: *Wonders of the Past: The Romance of Antiquity and its Splendours,* Sir John Alexander Hammerton, Ed., G.P. Putnam's Sons, 1924.

Early Sumerian sales contract for field and house, ca. 2600 BC, from Shuruppak. Note multiple circular and semicircular markings indicating numbers. Louvre, Paris, France, The Bridgeman Art Library.

Sir Henry Rawlinson, decoder of the cuneiform inscriptions at Bisitun. Source: *George Rawlinson, A Memoir of Major-General Sir Henry Creswicke Rawlinson,* Longmans, Green & Co, 1898.

Hilda and Flinders Petrie, who came across the earliest known alphabetic script at an abandoned turquoise mine at Serabit el-Khadim in the Sinai Desert. Source: *Flinders Petrie,* by Margaret S. Drower, Victor Gollancz/Orion Publishing. Republication permission kindly granted by Richenda Kramer and Judy Kramer Gueive.

This birthday greeting from Claudia Severa to Sulpicia Lepidina survived in the cold, damp soil of the Vindolanda site for nearly two millennia. Note that it is written in multiple hands and has no word spacing.

One of the first depictions of silent reading, from Jacque Le Grand's *Livre des bonnes moeurs*, a mid-fifteenth century manuscript.

European papermakers were the first to add wire images to their moulds to produce identifying watermarks, such as this 1389 camel design from a French artisan.

English academic John Wycliffe, left, the Czech Jan Hus, center, and Martin Luther, right, challenged the Church's legitimacy in the fourteenth, fifteenth, and sixteenth centuries, respectively. Because Luther had access to the printing press, he succeeded; because Wycliffe and Hus did not, they failed.

Because of Johannes Gutenberg's intense desire to keep secret the technology behind his invention, his only substantive historical traces lie in the legal difficulties strewed in his wake. This 1600 portrait, which hangs in Mainz's Gutenberg Museum, is fictional. Source: Johannes Gutenberg (1398–1468) in a 16th century copper engraving; Kupferstich; 16th century, by Michael Schönitzer, *Die großen Deutschen im Bilde (1936)*.

The complete original B42 type set used in the Gutenberg Bible. The earliest printers strove to make their books and pamphlets indistinguishable from printed manuscripts, not to make them easy to read.

Gutenberg's Illustrator, Lucas Cranach the Elder, drew *The Whore of Babylon* (riding a seven-headed monster), an allusion to the corruption of the Church, from Luther's New Testament.

Woodcut of Luther in "captivity" at Wartburg Castle by Lucas Cranach the Elder.

Matthias Huss's 1499 woodcut, *Danse Macabre*, in which Death claims a print shop's workers. This print provides one of the earliest—and perhaps darkest—images of Gutenberg's invention.

William Tyndale's unique linguistic talents allowed him to translate the Old Testament's well-polished original Hebrew into an English version that colors the language to the present day.

How the news traveled in 1504: Frontispiece of publication of Amerigo Vespucci's letter to his patron Piero Solderini in Florence. At the time of the first New World voyages, Spain lay far from the center of European publishing, so news of Columbus's discoveries did not spread widely or rapidly. Vespucci's letters are the reason the Western Hemisphere's continents were named after him, and not Columbus. Source: *The Soderini Letter 1504 in Facsimile*, *(Princeton, NJ, 1916)*.

The first media tycoon: Théophraste Renaudot founded multiple Paris publications, including the groundbreaking *Gazette*, the *People* magazine of the seventeenth century.

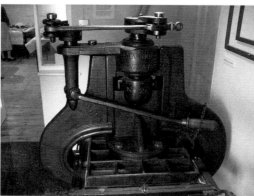

The last of the line: The all-iron, hand-operated Stanhope Press, capable of producing two hundred impressions per hour. After 1850, steam-powered high-speed presses shifted the locus of state-of-the-art printing technology from small- and medium-sized entrepreneurs like Cobbett, Hone, Carlile, and Franklin to companies large and wealthy enough to afford the expensive new technology. Republished by permission of Peter Chasseaud, Director, The Tom Paine Printing Press Museum, http://www.tompaineprintingpress.com.

Joseph Pulitzer, left, the son of a bankrupt Hungarian grain merchant, had such poor eyesight and general health that no European army would enlist him, and so he signed on with a Union Army recruiter in Hamburg in 1864. After the Civil War, he practiced law, served in the state legislature, and eventually bought two Saint Louis newspapers, the *Post* and *Dispatch*, and later, the *New York World*. At Harvard, the privileged William Randolph Hearst, right, decided to emulate Pulitzer's budding national chain.

SPANIARDS SEARCH WOMEN ON AMERICAN STEAMERS

"You furnish the pictures and I'll furnish the war." Although Hearst's supposed instructions were probably apocryphal, Frederick Remington carried them out to a tee with this illustration of the strip-searching of a Cuban damsel by Spanish police on the U.S.–flagged vessel. Source: *"Spaniards Search Women on American Steamers."* Illustration for an article entitled "Does our Flag Shield Women?" by Richard Harding Davis. *New York Journal*, February 12, 1897, 1–2.

The aristocratic Walter Lippmann foresaw and encouraged the development of journalism as an honorable, objective profession, no different from the law or medicine. Source: Alfred Eisenstaedt, photographer, © 1933.

The beautiful Evangelina Cisneros, whom Hearst employee Karl Decker sprang from a Cuban prison. Hearst had her paraded in virginal white around New York, where she profusely thanked the U.S. for her freedom. The truth was less than pristine. Source: *New York Journal*, October 1897.

Heinrich Hertz, the physicist who devised the first radio transmitting/receiving system.

Guglielmo Marconi around 1896 with his apparatus, some of which is enclosed in a "secret box." Source: *Wireless: From Marconi's Black-Box to the Audion,* by Sungook Hong, figure of the young G. Marconi, page 37, © 2001 Massachusetts Institute of Technology, by permission of the MIT Press

Lee de Forest (left), a brilliant electrical engineer who pushed the limits of financial propriety and patent law. Source: *Empire of the Air: The Men Who Made Radio,* by Tom Lewis, HarperCollins © 1992.

Transmitter in Brant Rock, Massachusetts, from which engineer Reginald Fessenden broadcast a recorded Handel aria, his own violin solo, and a Bible reading in 1906, which was heard by astounded listeners hundreds of miles away.

Like many late nineteenth and early twentieth century communications entrepreneurs, the young David Sarnoff started out as a telegraph operator. His first employer, the Commercial Cable Company, which fired him for observing the Jewish High Holidays. His telegraph skills then landed him a job at the Marconi Company, where he later wrote the famous "radio music box memo," which foresaw the rise of radio as a commercial entertainment medium.

The master at work. Few contemporary politicians could match Franklin Roosevelt's deliberate, soothing radio style, a talent that contributed in no small way to his persuasive power and four presidential electoral victories. Courtesy of the Franklin D. Roosevelt Presidential Library/Roosevelt Reproductions.

The bitter, cynical Joseph Paul Goebbels, at the microphone. Like Roosevelt, he grasped the persuasive power of radio early on, and made it Nazi Germany's primary communications media. Courtesy of the German National Archives. Berlin-Lustgarten. Joseph Goebbels bei Rede von Mikrophon: Juli 1932, Photographer O. Ang.

Idealized Third Reich working-class family; note the inexpensive *Volksempfänger* ("people's set") on the right. Courtesy of the Bundesarchiv (Federal Archives of Germany), Berlin-Lustgarten. Joseph Goebbels bei Rede vor Milsrophon; July 1932, photograph by O. Ang.

The Belgian Georges Ruggiu, incited Rwandan Hutus to murder their Tutsi countrymen over RTLM (Radio-Télévision Libre des Milles Collines). He is shown here on trial at the International Criminal Tribunal for Rwanda. Sentenced to twelve years imprisonment by the court, he was illegally released by his Italian jailers after only fourteen months.

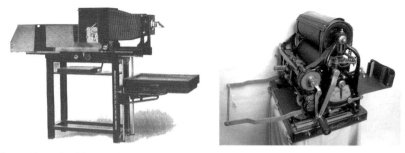

In the early and mid-twentieth century, copying could be done either on cumbersome, smelly photographic devices that produced high-quality images on expensive photographic paper, such as this 1918 Photostat machine (left), or inexpensive but low-quality images on paper with stencil devices, such as this 1950's vintage Gestetner Duplicator (right). Source: Gestetner Duplicator from Museum of Technology, http://www.museumoftechnology.org.uk/expand.php?key=241.

The 1966 trial of Andrei Sinyavsky, left, and Yuli Daniel, right, illustrated how personal communications technology enabled dissident activity. Friends and family of the accused drew in foreign correspondents, whose stories were broadcast back to the USSR on the Voices, attracting yet more visitors and reporters. This process, along with smuggled tape recordings of the trial produced a daisy chain of prosecutions that undermined the legitimacy of the regime both domestically and abroad.

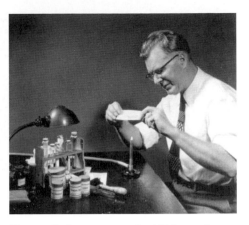

Chester Carlson reenacts the 1938 experiment
in which he produced the world's first
xerographic image on plain paper, which
he holds in his hand over a Bunsen burner.
Courtesy of Xerox, Inc.

Lech Walesa learns of his 1983 Nobel
Peace Prize from Radio Free Europe.

Mikhail Gorbachev and family return from Foros after the 1991 coup. The coup plotters
thought that they had cut off the Soviet president from outside news at his Black Sea
Villa, but they were mistaken; access to foreign radio broadcasts stiffened his resolve to
resist the plotter's demand that he resign. Source: Mikhail Gorbachev returning with his
family from Foros. August, 22 1991, The International Foundation for Socio-Economic
and Political Studies (The Gorbachev Foundation), *Raisa Gorbachev, Biography,* http://
www.gorby.ru/en/gorbacheva/biography/.

The Internet did not become a practical mass communication channel until around 1990, when Timothy Berners-Lee invented the first browser. Courtesy of the World Wide Web Consortium, Copyright © 2012 W3C ® (MIT, ERCIM, Keio).

Early advertisement for the Xerox 914. Courtesy of Xerox, Inc.

By the mid-1990s the popular use of the Web had exploded, but navigating its exponentially increasing breadth remained problematic. Stanford grad students Larry Page and Sergei Brin (left) created an algorithm that successfully identified relevant, and usually authoritative, search results, which eventually became Google.com. Not long after, Blogger and Twitter, the creations of Evan Williams (right) surmounted the final hurdles to making the Web the world's first two-way, mass-access communications medium. Sources: For Mssrs. Page and Brin, promotional photograph courtesy of Google, Inc.; and for Mr. Williams, http://flickr.com/photos/joi/2118601809/, December 18, 2007. Photo by Joi Ito licensed under a Creative Commons Attribution License.

Lippmann, the anti-Hearst, hailed from the intellectually oriented aristocracy of German-American Jewry. He studied at Harvard under the likes of George Santayana and William James, graduated in three years, and became arguably the century's most influential public intellectual.

Lippmann had a surprising sympathy for the yellow press. After all, pandering to a base and gullible public at least freed newspapers from their previous reliance on political parties. The yellow press was, in his words, "the first politically independent press the world had known."[72] Further, by constantly titillating and shocking, it inevitably sowed the seeds of its own destruction:

> The method soon exhausts itself. When everything is dramatic, noth-
> ing after a while is dramatic; when everything is highly spiced, nothing
> after a while has much flavor; when everything is new and startling,
> the human mind just ceases to be startled. But that is not all. As the
> readers of this press live longer in the world, and as their personal
> responsibilities increase, they begin to feel the need of being genuinely
> informed rather than of being merely amused and excited.[73]

That well may be, but the objective impartiality of modern journalism had another source, namely, the drive for subscription and advertising revenue; a large, general-audience newspaper could hardly afford to offend half of its subscribers, and advertisers certainly did not want to alienate half of their potential customers by backing a partisan publication. Professional journalism, in short, became "a grand bargain between all the different players," according to journalism professor Jay Rosen.[74]

Lippmann postulated a four-stage paradigm that explains the historical relationship between the power of the press and the power of the state. In Lippmann's stage one, the era of Renaudot and of the seventeenth-century English Licensing Act, the two were one and the same, and the power of the press as an agent of the state was constrained by low levels of literacy and the expense of newspapers. In Lippmann's stage two, the eras of the subsidized press in England and of the party-oriented six-penny press in the United States, political control of the press was only slightly less direct.

In Lippmann's stage three, Pulitzer and Hearst hit upon a model that not only allowed but demanded freedom from political control: the constant stimulation of a reading public addicted to mayhem, sex, and scandal. Without the ability to provide this stimulation and to attract more readers, the new mass-market press could not afford to function, and even had the government or political parties attempted to commandeer a particular newspaper, the less appealing fare would have soon placed it at a competitive disadvantage.

In the years following World War I, Lippmann saw American newspapers evolving into a fourth stage, that dominated by the professional journalist. To the new "fourth-stage" journalists, Hearst was an anathema, and his loss of credibility and of influence stemmed as much from the disdain of his peers as from opposition by Root, the Roosevelts, and others.

While today's tabloid journalists would seem to contradict Lippmann's optimistic perspective, it's well to remember that even today's yellow press cannot completely ignore the strictures of objectivity and breadth of coverage. (At least on this side of the Atlantic. American readers can rejoice that no major American newspaper has, as far as we yet know, behaved as badly as *News of the World*.)

Things did not evolve this happily in Germany. By the late 1920s, western Europe also had a thriving, diverse press, nowhere more so than in Germany, which boasted over four thousand daily and weekly papers. Berlin alone had twenty; Hamburg had ten; Stuttgart had eight.[75] Then, the political and economic chaos created in the wake of World War I and exacerbated by the Great Depression allowed the Nazis to acquire dominance over the German press with a surprising facility. This was a frightening demonstration of just how easy it was, under the proper circumstances, to commandeer a communications medium controlled by relatively few men.

In *Mein Kampf,* Adolf Hitler set out his philosophy of the role of the press in the Nazi future. He divided the public into three classes: the vast majority of the credulous, who believe everything they read; a substantial minority of the cynical, who believe nothing; and a tiny minority of the intellectually rigorous, who critically weigh information and form their own opinions accordingly.

In modern societies, even those that are relatively nondemocratic, Hitler reasoned, the opinion of the first group, the largest, was the most important:

> Nowadays when the voting papers of the masses are the deciding factor, the decision lies in the hands of the numerically strongest group, the crowd of simpletons and the credulous. It is an all-important

interest of the State and a national duty to prevent these people from falling into the hands of false, ignorant, or evil-minded teachers. . . . Particular attention should be paid to the Press, for its influence on these people is by far the strongest and most penetrating of all. . . . With ruthless determination the State must keep control of this instrument of popular education and place it at the service of the State and the Nation.[76]

Accordingly, the Nazis began to acquire control of the press long before they grabbed political power. Two economic catastrophes—World War I and the punitive Versailles Treaty—made this task relatively easy for them. By 1925, the Nazi Party had purchased for a song Eher Verlag, one of the proudest names in German publishing, and made its flagship Munich newspaper, the *Völkischer Beobachter*, the official party organ. Listed on the masthead as publisher: Adolf Hitler.

The combination of a Nazi government and fire-sale prices allowed Eher Verlag to gobble up hundreds of local newspapers and close hundreds more. Jewish-owned, socialist, and communist papers were the first to fall into Eher Verlag's hands, but even the all-powerful Nazi Party could not purchase all of Germany's newspapers—at least not all at once.

Theoretically, like all privately and publicly held companies, those papers not owned directly by the Nazi Party functioned independently in a market economy. In fact, a market economy cannot exist in the absence of rule of law and secure property rights guaranteed by an independent judiciary; the Nazis had shredded both concepts almost as soon as they took power.

In the twentieth century, the high cost of producing a newspaper meant that only a relative few could own and maintain one. Even in Germany, with its thousands of periodicals, controlling them proved all too easy. By the war's end, Eher Verlag wound up owing 82.5 percent of Germany's newspapers.[77]

The next great communications advance, radio, proved even easier to dominate; because the transmitters were so expensive, it was an almost exclusively one-way medium. That ease of control, along with radio's emotive power, further contributed to the rise of totalitarianism in the early twentieth century, leaving repression, suffering, and mounds of corpses in its wake.

7

WITH A MACHETE IN ONE HAND
AND A RADIO IN THE OTHER

Wars are not fought for territory, but for words. . . . Man's deadliest weapon is language. He is susceptible to being hypnotized by slogans as he is to infectious diseases. And where there is an epidemic, the group-mind takes over. —Arthur Koestler[1]

The ear accepts; accepts and believes.—Archibald MacLeish[2]

Of all the communications technologies discussed in this book, radio and television are the most hierarchical; no preceding media could reach so many people so instantaneously and with so little feedback in the opposite direction. From the outset, the near-monopoly control of these two media troubled both the public and lawmakers; in 1934 during the U.S. Congressional debate surrounding the establishment of the Federal Communications Commission, Representative Louis McFadden thundered against the "radio trust" in words that still sound fresh: "The strong hand of influence is drying up independent broadcasting stations in the United States and the whole thing is tending towards centralization of control."[3]

McFadden's concerns about the concentration of media power were well founded. As discussed in the Introduction, the advent of commercial radio around 1920 coincided with a quantifiable increase in the number of despotic governments around the world. Obviously, other factors were also at work, including the catastrophe of World War I and the subsequent global depression. Nonetheless, the triumph of the one-way media—radio and, later, television—contributed mightily to the worldwide spread of totalitarian governments in the mid-twentieth century. Even within the democratic framework of the United States, whose government, unlike those in the rest of the world, did not own or operate domestic radio stations, President Franklin Roosevelt masterfully manipulated this new medium. Elsewhere, the totalitarian effects of radio would prove much more potent.

Since prehistoric times mankind had unknowingly propagated radio waves by discharging static electricity, as occurs when a dog's fur is rubbed on a dry winter day and sparks fly. In 1842, an American, Joseph Henry, who later became the Smithsonian Institution's first secretary, assembled an apparatus that detected radio waves produced by a spark source thirty feet away, but scientists still lacked an overarching theory that would enable wireless electrical transmission and reception of information—that is, "radio."

At roughly the same time, Englishman Michael Faraday was conducting experiments on the magnetic fields that surround electrical currents. In 1846, he postulated that light was a disturbance in these fields, and in 1864, his fellow countryman James Clerk Maxwell developed a theory that radio waves and light were essentially the same thing: "electromagnetic waves" differing only in their frequency and wavelength. He would develop an elegant mathematical framework—Maxwell's equations—that described the relationships among light, magnetism, and electrical current.

The essence of science is the generation and subsequent testing of hypotheses. What separates science from pseudoscience, both premodern and New Age, is this testability; a hypothesis that makes no testable predictions is worthless. Maxwell's equations predicted three things: that an acceleration of an electrical field, such as occurs when a spark jumps a gap, produces electromagnetic waves; that these waves travel through space; and, most astoundingly, that they do so at the speed of light. Over the prior two centuries, scientists had measured the velocity of light with increasing accuracy; since light and radio waves represented the same electromagnetic phenomena, Maxwell's equations predicted that radio waves should travel at the same speed.[4]

Beautiful as Maxwell's theory was, it lacked substantial real-world verification until German physicist Heinrich Hertz, in a series of carefully crafted experiments in the late 1880s, transmitted and received radio waves for the first time. With clever measurements and precise computations, he determined the velocity of radio waves of a known wavelength. As predicted by Maxwell, the speed of radio waves matched that of light.

Hertz produced his radio waves in so-called Leyden jars, glass containers whose inner and outer surfaces were lined with tinfoil and could hold an electrical charge (in modern terms, capacitors). These contraptions could be electrostatically charged by rubbing, as in the ancient fur-and-amber-wand technique, or, as in the case of Benjamin Franklin, by thunderstorm and kite. Both methods create the necessary sparks—hence the radio static produced by thunderstorms. Initially, these jars provided scientists with a reliable source of electricity. Hertz found that by varying the shape and size of his jars, he could also vary the wavelength produced.[5]

At about the same time, in England, Oliver Lodge demonstrated that antenna size affected the wavelength received; familiar with telegraphy and initially unaware of Hertz's work, Lodge transmitted his radio waves along wires, and not through the open air, as had Hertz. It fell to his more imaginative fellow countryman, William Crookes, to realize that:

> Rays of light will not pierce through a wall, nor, as we know only too well, through a London fog. But the electrical vibrations of a yard or more in wave-length [i.e., a frequency of less than 300 million hertz, or cycles per second] of which I have spoken will easily pierce such mediums, which to them will be transparent. Here, then, is revealed the bewildering possibility of telegraphy without wires, posts, cables, or any of our present costly appliances.[6]

In other words, the work of Lodge and Hertz had made possible what even in the late nineteenth century must have seemed a miracle: instantaneous communication not just through walls but across vast expanses of empty space using invisible waves.

Today's highly congested radio frequency spectrum stretches from waves of very low frequency (3,000 cycles per second) used for submarine communication to waves of super high frequency (30 billion cycles per second) used for satellite-based operations. This entire range is densely packed with traffic, and successful operation requires precise tuning at both ends so that distant receivers and transmitters can connect among the cacophony of many, many other signals. By contrast, at the dawn of the radio age, this spectrum was a desert that necessitated a broad, sloppy

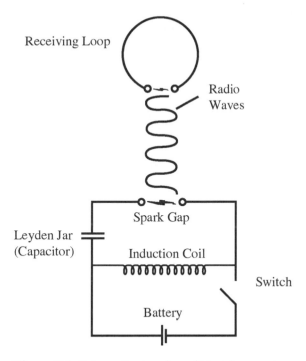

Figure 7-1. Schematic drawing of Hertz' apparatus.

broadcast signal and imprecise tuning so that the first crude transmitters and receivers could find each other.

Like Hertz, Maxwell, and Faraday, Lodge was more interested in the scientific pursuit of pure knowledge than in commercial gain. In 1897, he filed the key patent that described the practical basis of tuning for the transmission and the reception of radio signals—known in those days by the more euphonious term "syntony"—but left to more aggressive souls its commercialization.[7] Lodge knew that the lot of the technological entrepreneur, then as now, involved continual litigation, a fate he clearly did not desire:

> The instinct of the scientific worker is to publish everything, to hope that any useful aspect of it may be as quickly as possible utilised, and to trust to the instinct of fair play that he shall not be the loser when the thing becomes commercially profitable. To grant him a monopoly is to grant him a more than doubtful boon; to grant him the privilege

of fighting for his monopoly is to grant him a pernicious privilege, which will sap his energy, waste his time, and destroy the power of future production.[8]

Sometime around 1800, a Scotsman, Andrew Jameson, migrated to Dublin to engage in that most Scottish of industries, the manufacture of fine whiskey. He was following in the footsteps of his older brother John, whose brand of Irish whiskey survives to this day. Andrew's business prospered, and he sired a daughter, Annie, who was endowed with a singing voice that reduced listeners to joyous tears. Covent Garden Opera House offered Annie an engagement that her father forbade her to accept on the grounds that it was not a proper venue for a respectable young woman. In consolation, he sent her on a grand tour of Italy.

Annie stayed with family business associates in Bologna, where she fell in love with Giuseppe Marconi, the widowed son-in-law of her hosts. He proposed, she accepted, but her father, outraged at her romance with an Italian widower seventeen years her senior, once more smothered her dreams and forbade the union. Brokenhearted, she returned to Ireland; passionate letters were smuggled in both directions, and when Annie came of age in 1864, she stole away across the Channel to France, where the two married. The couple returned to Bologna, where a year later they produced a son, Alfonso, and nine years after that, another, Guglielmo.[9]

Guglielmo had what we would today call a nontraditional upbringing. His parents put little academic pressure on the lad, who attended local schools only when the mood struck him, and by the time he reached college age he found himself unqualified to attend Bologna's famous university. The story of how this superficially unimpressive young man surpassed his older and more illustrious competitors in radio communication, not only in England, but also on the Continent, in the United States, in Russia, and elsewhere evokes the unconventional paths followed by many of today's high-tech pioneers.

From the first, Guglielmo took a shine to physics and chemistry; when the family summered in the Italian Alps in 1894, he carried with him a biography of Hertz. Astutely, he realized the communications potential of Hertz's work on radio waves, and when he returned home he outfitted the vacant attic of the family mansion, Villa Griffone, for his experiments.[10]

Aside from a conveniently empty upper floor, the villa possessed another advantage: a neighbor, Augusto Righi, who was a giant in early electromagnetism research. Access to Righi's library proved far more valuable than access to his laboratory, for the equipment used to generate and detect microwaves, Righi's specialty, is very different from that for radio waves.

Grudgingly, Marconi's tightfisted father financed his son's early efforts, and this drove Guglielmo relentlessly toward commercial application, which in practice meant the propagation of radio waves over increasingly long distances. Whereas Hertz, Lodge, Righi, and their colleagues focused mainly on precise tuning, Marconi virtually ignored it. As he tinkered with his receivers and transmitters, he kept only those adjustments that increased transmission distance. After exhausting the range of the villa's attic, Guglielmo expanded his experiments over the surrounding hills. Typically, he would transmit from the attic the letter "s"—three short dots that came across as three brief movements of the hammer on the receiver. At a distance of a few hundred meters, his brother Alfonso or a local tenant farmer named Mignani signaled with a kerchief the reception of the "s." At one kilometer, Marconi could no longer see the kerchief, and so he instructed his assistants to fire a rifle shot instead when they received the signal; on a fateful day in 1895, he transmitted the "s" and almost immediately heard a shot that rang across the hills.[11]

While Hertz and Lodge had learned that radio transmissions generally travel over longer distances at longer wavelengths than at shorter wavelengths, Marconi had not. He may not even have been aware of a related key fact well known to Hertz and Lodge: that longer antennae resonated at longer wavelengths. All he knew was that the bigger he made his antennae, the more successful he was at transmitting over long distances. Marconi found that if he oriented the antennae of both transmitter and receiver vertically and buried their bottom ends in the ground, a technique abhorred by Lodge because it threw the tuning off, the signals could carry for miles across the Italian countryside. (When Marconi executed his first transatlantic transmission in 1901, his antennae at both ends extended from deep underground to high in the air on kites.)

In 1895, he offered his new technology to the Italian government, which politely refused it; his mother Annie's British-Scottish family connections and England's naval power made Britain the next likely customer.

A year later, he traveled to Britain, accompanied by two formidable accessories: his radio frequency equipment, consisting of crude receiving and transmitting devices, not materially different from those designed by Lodge; and his mother. In remarkably short order, he garnered political and financial support from England's technological and financial elite, including the post office's chief engineer, William Preece, and the name Marconi became synonymous with early radio technology.

In 1897, the same year that Lodge acquired his patent, Her Majesty's government also awarded one to Marconi for his devices. His machines utterly lacked tuning precision; they constituted, in the words of historian Hugh Aitken, "a practical system of wireless telegraphy only as long as there was very little wireless telegraphy."[12]

The post office fully expected to operate England's radio business, as it did the telegraph, but the government bureaucracy moved too slowly for Marconi; Preece's support served merely to attract more nimble private capital. In July 1897 Marconi and his investors incorporated the Wireless Telegraph and Signal Company Ltd., which three years later changed its name to Marconi's Wireless Telegraph Company. Many Britons felt that the company had unfairly capitalized on Preece's endorsement of Marconi's technology; this would stick in the government's craw for decades thereafter.

Marconi continued his focus on pushing radio's geographic range as far and as fast as possible. By 1897, he could throw his signals only a few miles. While the company's spurning of the post office's support evoked public anger, opprobrium never seemed to attach to Marconi personally, for both the public and the press lionized this inventor as the "wizard of wireless." Marconi polished this image with a continuous stream of publicity-attracting stunts: connecting the coastal town of Bournemouth with the Isle of Wight in January 1898; connecting Bournemouth with London shortly thereafter; keeping Queen Victoria in touch with Prince Edward while he was recuperating from an appendectomy on the royal yacht when a storm blew down the telegraph lines; and last but not least, transmitting the single letter "s" across the Atlantic in December 1901.[13] In the course of maximizing range, Marconi did make one major scientific discovery: the ionosphere, off of which he could bounce shortwave signals over great distances.

At the turn of the twentieth century, Marconi's company very much resembled any modern Internet start-up with a whizbang product but no obvious source of revenue. For one thing, the new devices could transmit only brief bursts of signals, which could not encode the sound of the human voice, or anything else for that matter. Marconi certainly did not, as is commonly supposed, invent the modern radio. To the extent that he invented anything, it was the concept of marrying the telegraph key to the spark-generated signal; the only information he transmitted was the on-off of standard telegraph key Morse code.

To compound matters, Marconi's first receivers were crude "coherers": glass tubes with electrodes at either end and filled with metal filings that had to be reset through mechanical tapping after each message. Opportunistically, he soon pirated Lodge's tuning circuits. In character, Lodge did not promptly sue. In 1911, Marconi settled the matter by buying Lodge's unsuccessful company and, critically, its patents for transmitting and receiving antennae.

The major drawback of wireless telegraphy was far more prosaic: the telegraph already provided nearly instantaneous communication that, while far from cheap, was much more inexpensive, and reliable, than wireless communication. By the turn of the century, the global transoceanic submarine cable network had functioned well for a generation, and fourteen undersea cables spanned the Atlantic Ocean.

Early radio technology held a potential advantage in only one area: ship-to-shore and ship-to-ship telegraphy. Lloyd's, the British marine insurance underwriters' consortium, closely monitored shipping inbound on the "Western Approaches" off Ireland's southern tip. Because of fog, the ships often could not be sighted from shore, but generally could be seen from Rathlin Island, which lay a few miles south of the Irish mainland and which could be reached more cheaply by wireless signals than with a submarine cable. Alas, Marconi's company received no contracts for a few years after filing the 1897 patents; even when he successfully passed a signal across the English Channel in 1899, it attracted no business.

Given the uncertain financial prospects of Marconi's venture, private incorporation served it well; the company was largely controlled by Marconi and his family, who did not clamor, as public shareholders or government sponsors are wont to do, for immediate dividends. The capital structure of the

Marconi Wireless Telegraph Company allowed it to plow all of its revenues back into the business for longer-term gain. Soon, the family's patience paid off; the Admiralty signed on in 1900, followed by Lloyd's in 1901.

So attractive was marine telegraphy to Lloyd's that it agreed to lease, not buy, Marconi's equipment, which Lloyd's employees then operated. (Marconi forbade Lloyd's employees from communicating with stations and ships not equipped by him.) In an early demonstration of "network externality," in which the value of a service grows exponentially with the number of users, the company's business boomed; by 1907 it served virtually all of the world's ocean liners. This effective monopoly, which the company's contracts specified would last until 1915, produced a backlash in the form of the 1907 International Convention on Wireless Communication at Sea, which prematurely broke the company's stranglehold the next year, seven years in advance of the 1915 contract date.[14]

Marconi's seemingly magical transmissions of messages over ever-longer gaps of empty space electrified the public imagination, but this did not impact the life of the average citizen, who was not likely to employ Marconi's specialized services, let alone purchase an extremely expensive radio transmitter or receiver. Until 1906, no one had figured out how to encode sounds into radio waves, as Alexander Graham Bell had done in 1876 with the telephone. Not until after World War I did reliable and inexpensive vacuum tubes for transmitting and receiving sounds via radio waves become available.

While radio emerged to play a substantial role in military communications on both sides in World War I, at that time it carried little political or cultural freight. As so often happens with exciting new technologies with as yet uncertain application, self-promoters and con men stepped into the breach. In the first category was Lee de Forest, a talented, single-minded, but egomaniacal inventor. He had studied under the great physicist J. Willard Gibbs at Yale and earned a PhD in electrical engineering in 1899. De Forest's innovative ability sprang from the happy combination of lab bench skill and a habit—inculcated at Yale—of assiduous surveillance of the scientific literature. For both better and worse, he associated with Abraham White, a Texas-born fraudster whom de Forest tapped for start-up capital.

In 1902, White incorporated the De Forest Wireless Telegraph Company in New Jersey with $1 million of investors' seed money, soon followed by nearly $20 million in ever-larger stock offerings under different names.[15] White feted "investors" at elaborate Potemkin village "executive of- fices" and "research facilities," and his impressive "radio towers" were constructed at locations convenient for sales, but not for aerial transmis- sion. When de Forest lost a patent suit in 1906, White froze him out by transferring all the assets of the largest of the companies, American De Forest Wireless Telegraph, to White's own wireless company, United Wireless Technology, whose revenues consisted almost entirely of bogus stock flotations. Four years later, postal inspectors closed it down.[16] It would not be the last time that de Forest's poor judgment of character undid his efforts.

De Forest also had the bad habit of appropriating the inventions of others. His attention to scientific journals provided him with a steady stream of new potential devices, the most notable of which was the Fleming valve, the precursor to the vacuum tube. In 1883, John Ambrose Fleming, while working for Thomas Edison, took an interest in a particular variation in one of his boss's incandescent bulbs; it had the interesting charactcristic of transmitting an electrical current across its vacuum—something that seemed impossible. The current, it turned out, consisted of electrons, whose existence would eventually be proved by physicist J. J. Thomson, but not for more than another decade: without realizing it, Edison and Fleming had invented a device that would, with subsequent modification, allow radio waves to transmit sounds, including the human voice.

Edison, a profoundly practical, untheoretically-minded man, inex- plicably missed its potential. Instead, he directed Fleming's attention to more commercial applications, but Fleming did not forget the unusual behavior of their curious bulb. When Fleming came into the employ of the Marconi Company, he investigated its use in the reception of radio waves and found it highly promising. Once more, Fleming's superiors ordered him to work on other projects. Fleming then compounded both of his bosses' initial misjudgments by making an innocent but fatal mistake of his own: he published his results in a highly respected academic journal, *Proceedings of the Royal Society.*

Just a few months after the article appeared, an assistant of de Forest brought a bulb to the New York factory of Henry McCandless, a manu- facturer of automobile lights, with instructions to duplicate it. The bulb, the assistant unthinkingly informed McCandless, was a Fleming valve.

Several weeks after that, de Forest took out a patent on it, conveniently relabeling it a "static valve for wireless telegraph systems," and he followed this piracy several weeks afterward with a similar patent that gave the valve a catchier name reflecting its ability to decode broadcast sounds: the "audion."

The audion was not altogether a theft: de Forest modified and improved Edison and Fleming's original design by adding a third wire between the filament and the plate. Even so, one of McCandless's assistants made the critical suggestion: the bending of the third wire into a zigzag shape, thereafter called the "grid." Because he had "borrowed" a large part of its design, de Forest did not understand how the audion worked, and he later demonstrated his confusion all too clearly on the witness stand in patent infringement suits.

The audion, as noted above, gave rise to the vacuum tube, which may well have been one of modern man's most important inventions. The

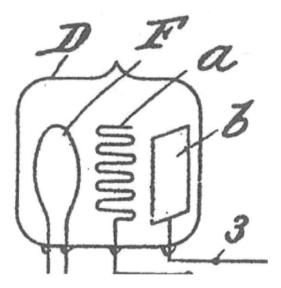

Figure 7-2. Detail from de Forest's 1907 patent application for the audion. [F] represents the filament and [b] the plate, whose basic design he "borrowed" from a scientific publication by John Fleming, an employee of Thomas Edison. The "grid" [a] between the two was probably de Forest's idea; an assistant of his bulb manufacturer, Henry McCandless, suggested bending the grid into its zig-zag shape.

vacuum tube made possible the almost infinite amplification and regulation of electrical currents: a small lever linked through a vacuum tube could vary the output of a thousand-horsepower motor. Even more critically, the tubes could effect this amplification *instantaneously* and thus completely eliminate the need for human intervention; instead of moving a lever, the tube could respond to tiny changes in force, temperature, speed, frequency, brightness, or any other measurement that could be transmuted into an electrical current. These completely automatic processes were first fully realized in the Manhattan Project and with the radar control of antiaircraft fire in World War II, then became nearly ubiquitous in factory processes, and finally spread to automobiles and household appliances.

By World War I, technological innovation had ceased being the product of lone geniuses; it had shifted to corporations large enough to undertake ever more expensive research. The names involved, while well-remembered among engineering historians—Reginald Fessenden, Charles Steinmetz, and Edwin Armstrong, among others—do not resonate historically like those of Edison, Bell, and Marconi. This new generation of radio entrepreneurs would have done well to heed Lodge's warning, for litigation took its toll on most of them. Armstrong, who invented FM broadcasting and the superheterodyne receiver used in nearly all modern televisions and radios, was perhaps the greatest radio engineer who ever lived. Ultimately, he jumped to his death in despair over unfavorable patent rulings and abuse at the hands of RCA, the successor to the Marconi Company. The opportunist de Forest, by comparison, got off lucky: he merely died broke.[17]

Nonetheless, during the early twentieth century, these less well-known innovators dramatically improved the amplification ability of vacuum tubes to the point that they could easily pull in weak signals from distant continents. At the same time, the new tubes also enabled high-frequency transmitters capable of encoding the human voice and music.

On Christmas Eve 1906, Reginald Fessenden broadcast from a transmitter in Brant Rock, Massachusetts, Handel's aria "Ombra maifu," followed by his own violin solo and Bible reading; the words and music could be heard hundreds of miles away.[18] Even so, this first public voice broadcast thrilled only radio enthusiasts and hobbyists, whose heads were squeezed by earphones tight enough to cut off the blood flow and whose backs were hunched over temperamental homemade mineral and cat's whisker receivers. The equipment at both ends—particularly the receivers—was still far too expensive and unreliable for general use.

Another ingredient necessary for the popular adoption of radio was lacking as well: commercial vision. As obvious as its mass-market communication potential is today, in the years surrounding World War I it took a special kind of imagination to conceive of radio as a consumer enterprise, let alone to envision the form it would eventually take. None of the inventions discussed in this book, from writing onward, were designed with mass communication in mind; their development hinged for the most part on limited commercial, governmental, and military uses, and in some cases on intellectual and technological curiosity alone; Gutenberg, after all, printed only 180 Bibles, and the creators of the telegraph had mainly railroad and financial applications in mind.

Nowhere was this truer than with radio. Faraday and Hertz conceived no commercial designs at all, and Lodge's came mainly as an afterthought. Even the visionary Marconi focused almost entirely on shipping companies, insurers, and navies. As late as the beginning of World War I, no one imagined the average consumer using a radio receiver for any purpose. That transformation would fall to one of the most singular characters in American business history, David Sarnoff.

Born in 1891, Sarnoff hailed from the desperate poverty of the tiny Jewish shtetl of Uzlian in western Russia; when he was five, his father, Abraham, already ill from tuberculosis, emigrated alone to New York City. The rest of the family joined him four years later, and during that interim David was consigned to the care of a rabbinical granduncle, the head of his mother's deeply scholarly and religious extended family.

Each day, young David had to memorize two thousand words of biblical Hebrew or Talmudic Aramaic; failure meant going to bed hungry. This left him with both a singular power of concentration and a burning desire to avoid any further religious study.

From nearly the moment he stepped onto American soil at age nine, David served as head of the family; within a few years he had built a string of newspaper stands that employed his brothers. When he turned fifteen, his father became bedridden, and so he went looking for a higher-paying job.

By that point, David had benefited not only from New York's educational system, but also from the Educational Alliance, a secular East Side organization that served the immigrant community and taught him to write and debate in fluent English. Inspired by the city's burgeoning penny newspaper industry, he imagined himself the next William Randolph Hearst or the next James Gordon Bennett of the *New York Herald*. In September 1906, he strode confidently into what he thought was the lobby of Bennett's newspaper in Herald Square and announced to the lobby clerk that he wanted to work for the paper. The attendant replied, "You're in the wrong place. This is the Commercial Cable Company, not the *Herald*. But we're looking for a messenger boy. Can you handle it?"[19]

Soon enough, like the young Thomas Edison, David became fearsomely competent at Morse code. Several months later, just before his father died, Commercial Cable refused to allow him time off for Rosh Hashanah and Yom Kippur; he protested and was fired. The hand of fate next sent him to the Marconi Company.

On such serendipity does history pivot. At Marconi he, more than any other human being before or since, shaped how the world saw and heard itself, and so determined the fates of nations. Sarnoff spent the next decade at Marconi rising through the ranks. The company assigned him to venues as varied as arctic seal-hunting expeditions and Marconi's station atop New York's Wanamaker Building, where he handled the sparse radio traffic between the Philadelphia and New York stores. The glassed-in facility was, in fact, a publicity stunt cooked up by the Marconi and Wanamaker companies; Sarnoff's job there was to expound the magic of radio to visitors.

This agreeable public relations gig abruptly turned deadly serious on the night of April 14–15, 1912, when the *Titanic* sank, and the Wanamaker office swarmed with frantic relatives awaiting survivors' names from the rescue ship *Carpathia*. Ironically, the White Star Line had offered the famous Marconi free passage on the ship, but he declined. He traveled instead on the *Lusitania*, whose stenographer he preferred.[20] (Three years after an iceberg sank the *Titanic,* a German submarine would sink the *Lusitania*.)

The U.S. Senate later grilled Marconi over the slow release of information that evening by Sarnoff and others, but, as usual, Marconi came up smelling like a rose, the genius whose invention "saved" hundreds of lives.

The next year Sarnoff, by now the company's chief inspector, and three other Marconi engineers visited the radio laboratories of Columbia University, where Edwin Armstrong showed them a prototype of his remarkably sensitive vacuum-tube receiver, and in the coming months, Sarnoff and his colleagues convinced themselves of its commercial usefulness. Marconi himself, who by this time had returned to England, also investigated Armstrong's receivers, but he was not as impressed. Mass communication was just too much of a stretch even for the company's visionary founder; after all, his wireless telegraph company transmitted messages between individuals, where secrecy was usually of the highest concern. Only Sarnoff realized that the ease of intercepting radio signals, far from being a drawback, could be exploited to great benefit. In 1915, he sent his famous "radio music box memo" to his immediate supervisor, Edward Nally:

> I have in mind a plan of development which would make radio a "household utility" in the same sense as the piano or phonograph. The idea is to bring music into the house by wireless.
> While this has been tried in the past by wires, it has been a failure because wires do not lend themselves to this scheme. With radio, however, it would seem to be entirely feasible. For example—a radio telephone transmitter having a range of say 25 to 50 miles can be installed at a fixed point where instrumental or vocal music or both are produced. The problem of transmitting music has already been solved in principle and therefore all the receivers attuned to the transmitting wave length should be capable of receiving such music. The receiver can be designed in the form of a simple "Radio Music Box" and arranged for several different wave lengths, which should be changeable with the throwing of a single switch or pressing of a single button.[21]

Sarnoff's vision would not come easily, for in 1915, neither the American Marconi Company nor any other commercial operation possessed the wherewithal to erect the broadcasting network and build the millions of radios to receive its signals. During World War I, the U.S. Navy, which coveted Marconi's huge transmitters, had taken over not only all radio production, but the patents themselves. At war's end, the Marconi Company wanted to purchase the most advanced GE alternator-driven transmitters, but both the navy and Congress argued that it should be prohibited from doing so, since it was incorporated in Britain. In addition, when the war ended, the navy had no desire to relinquish the turf it had acquired: in December 1918, Secretary of the Navy Josephus Daniels testified before Congress, "It is my profound conviction, as is the conviction of every person I have talked with in this country and abroad who has studied the question, that [radio] must be a monopoly."[22] Daniels did not need to mention who the monopoly holder would be. (In the 1920s, the cohabitation of the American radio frequency spectrum by both the navy and hobbyists resulted in a series of spectacular, and far from harmless, practical jokes as pranksters posing as admirals sent cruisers and battle-ships scurrying across the seven seas on bogus missions.)[23]

But by the end of the war, the American public was heartily sick of government control of anything, so a compromise was reached: the divisions of General Electric that manufactured the high-powered transmitters would merge with the Marconi Company to form a new entity, Radio Corporation of America (RCA), which was incorporated on October 17, 1919. As a sop to the navy, its chief of communications, Rear Admiral William Bullard, received a seat on the new RCA board. Additionally, the government granted RCA and AT&T monopoly status for the manufacture of the critical superheterodyne radio tubes and for telephone transmission, respectively.[24] In 1926, RCA would cooperate with GE, Westinghouse, AT&T, and United Fruit to form the National Broadcasting Company (NBC).

Soon after, in 1920, the nation's first commercial radio stations began operations—KDKA in Pittsburgh, WWJ in Detroit—and the price of reliable, commercially produced radio sets slowly fell. Just as David Sarnoff had predicted, the radio became the ornate mahogany god of the American living room: there were three million sets in 1924, thirty million in 1936, and fifty million by 1940, by which time a simple radio could be had for less than ten dollars. Network externality, chicken-and-egg yet once more: the increasing number of sets fed the demand for more stations, which grew to 275 in 1935 and then 882 in 1941; more stations begat yet more demand for radio sets.

In our current information-soaked age, it is difficult to imagine the thrill of bringing Jack Benny, Fred Allen, and Bob Hope into the living room for the first time, let alone a onetime event like the Joe Louis–Max Schmeling boxing match. By the mid-1930s, the average American spent more hours listening to the radio than reading newspapers or attending movie theaters, concerts, and plays combined; social workers reported that families did without beds and iceboxes to purchase a radio set.

The above sales figures understate radio's penetration, since programs were not just a family event; they often involved neighbors as well. By 1935, only a few of the 127 million Americans could not at least cadge an invitation to listen from a neighbor, friend, or family member.[25]

Just as Martin Luther intuitively grasped, at a time when few of his ecclesiastical opponents did, the persuasive power of the printing press, so too
did Franklin Roosevelt appreciate, at a time when few of his ideological
opponents did, the persuasive power of radio. He understood, well before
any other American politician, Archibald MacLeish's injunction in this
chapter's epigraph about the gullibility of the ear.

At the time of the 1932 election, Roosevelt had a communications
problem: his ideological opponents largely controlled the nation's newspapers. Although nominally a Democrat, Hearst opposed nearly all of
Roosevelt's policies; an even more serious threat to the New Deal was the
archconservative publisher of the *Chicago Tribune,* Robert McCormick.
Not only did radio offer Roosevelt wide-open access, but in that innocent
age, the president of the United States could draw an audience share on a
par with Benny, Hope, Louis-Schmeling, or a New York Yankees game.[26]

In proficient hands, radio possesses enormous emotive power, in no
small part because, especially during its first decades, it was usually experienced in a social environment. The first two presidents to broadcast, alas,
did not emote. Calvin Coolidge's nasal voice put off audiences. Herbert
Hoover, in contrast, seemingly possessed a huge advantage with the new
medium, since his engineering background gave him a special interest
in the field. As Coolidge's secretary of commerce, he devised a system
for awarding frequencies, chaired the 1927 International Radio Conference, wrote treaties governing global radio traffic, and played a key role
in the establishment of the Federal Radio Commission, the forerunner of
the Federal Communications Commission (FCC). Regrettably, Hoover's
emotionless delivery put listeners to sleep; even more seriously, he did not
know when to stop talking. During the 1932 election campaign, he gave
an address that was to last exactly one hour and end just before the start
of the enormously popular Ed Wynn vaudeville show. His speech was a
disaster. According to an account in *The Nation*:

> Even Americans will rebel if things go too far. At eight-thirty on
> a recent evening, the populace of the United States, respectful if
> dubious, tuned in on Mr. Hoover's portentous speech in Iowa. At
> nine-thirty, accustomed to the prompt intervention of the omnipotent
> announcer, the listeners confidently awaited the President's conclud-
> ing words. . . . But Mr. Hoover had only arrived at point number

two of his twelve-point program. The populace shifted in its myriad
seats; wives looked at husbands; children, allowed to remain up till
ten on Tuesdays, looked with alarm at the clock; twenty thousand
votes shifted to Franklin Roosevelt. Nine-forty-five: Mr. Hoover had
arrived at point four; five million Americans consulted their radio
programs and discovered that Ed Wynn's time had not been altered
or canceled; two million switched off their instruments and sent their
children to bed weeping; votes lost to Mr. Hoover multiplied too fast
for computation. . . . What did N.B.C. mean by this outrage? Whose
hour was it anyhow? Ten million husbands and wives retired to bed
in a mood of bitter rebellion; no votes left for Hoover.[27]

By contrast, Roosevelt's voice, demeanor, and temperament were
made for radio. He had no need to command Hoover's knowledge of the
technology, for he possessed a unique insight into the medium's political
potential. Most normal conversation occurs at a rate of about 300 words
per minute (wpm). Throughout history, experienced orators had slowed that
down to about 150 wpm, as did most radio announcers. Roosevelt rarely
exceeded 130 wpm, and the more important the speech, the more slowly
he talked; his address at the outbreak of World War II in September 1939
was clocked at 98 wpm; and his speech after Pearl Harbor at 88 wpm. To
today's ear his voice sounds aloof and aristocratic, as do most radio announcers and movie actors from the period, but in the 1930s, Roosevelt's
intonation struck listeners as down-to-earth, even slightly folksy. Radio
engineers loved him; so even were his timbre and modulation that they
rarely needed to touch their dials.

Roosevelt carefully crafted his delivery; although he benefited from
the best verbal stylists in his famous "brain trust," he wrote the texts himself
and then spent hours polishing them. He possessed as wide a vocabulary
as any Harvard graduate, but consciously restricted his content to the most
commonly used English words. His favorite slot was Sunday at ten PM,
when the public was "relaxed and in a benevolent mood."

The Princeton University psychologist Hadley Cantril recognized
that radio had caused an earthquake in the public mind-set, and that those
who understood it, such as Roosevelt, could wield enormous power. In
the early 1930s, he observed a unique "natural experiment" in public
speaking in Boston, where a popular evangelist gave an address. The hall
the evangelist had rented could not accommodate all who came, and the

overflow audience members were directed to a nearly identical hall on the floor below, where they listened to the preacher on a loudspeaker.

The in-person audience upstairs rocked the hall with tears, shouting, and laughter and filled the preacher's coffers, while the people listening to the loudspeaker in the lower hall fidgeted and left only a few copper coins. Cantril realized that the dynamics of the personal performance in the upper hall varied greatly from the more radio-like performance downstairs. In short, radio had turned the age-old art of oratory nearly on its head, for like the preacher's lower hall, it utterly lacked visual cues. While this is a disadvantage to the personally attractive and physically dynamic speaker, it greatly helps one who has a calm, soothing voice and who can keep a speech short; if, while speaking, he shuffles papers or fiddles, no one is any the wiser.[28] For every Roosevelt who profited from the new style, there was a Herbert Hoover who did not.[29]

Cantril noticed that the president's radio addresses rarely exceeded twenty minutes; although a particularly compelling speaker can command an audience's attention for up to a few hours, the attention span greatly shortens when a disembodied voice emanates from a loudspeaker without visual cues.[30] The psychologist was amazed by the ability of Huey Long, the populist governor of Louisiana and United States senator, to enlist thousands of his radio listeners as his coconspirators, having them call their friends and neighbors about his broadcasts, and by the way the anti-Semitic Catholic priest Charles Coughlin bowled over his audiences with ridiculously simplistic solutions to complex problems. Cantril drily remarked, "A sound argument is always less important for the demagogue than are weighted words."[31]

Roosevelt also intuitively understood how to take advantage of radio's highly centralized structure. Through the newly established FCC, he led a campaign to strictly separate newspaper and broadcast station ownership. While this no doubt served the public interest by diffusing control of the media, it served Roosevelt even better, for it excluded the likes of his political foes, McCormick and Hearst, from the airwaves—the latter having already begun to use his wealth to accumulate a radio empire.

Roosevelt, in addition, made a tacit deal with the leaders of the nascent broadcast industry, who must have cast a nervous eye on state ownership of radio across the Atlantic and on the emergency economic conditions at home: I'll keep my hands off your stations as long as you provide me with access

and deny it to my opponents. The president generously allowed radio reporters into press conferences, and in exchange the networks gave Roosevelt
instantaneous, on-demand entrée to the airwaves. The president especially
cultivated popular commentators such as the brilliant Dorothy Thompson
and the nasty, bitter Walter Winchell. In exchange for scoops, Roosevelt
expected, and received, favorable coverage for himself and for his policies.

Finally, radio offered Roosevelt yet one more advantage: as a purely
verbal medium, it hid his physical disability. As an inaugural gift, in 1933
NBC gave the president a microphone stand with special handlebars and
leg brace fittings.

Almost from the moment he took office on March 4, 1933, Roosevelt
commanded the airwaves. On March 9, with the nation in the midst of a
horrifying banking crisis, the president declared a bank holiday; three days
after that, he took to the microphone with a stirring address that calmed
the nation and largely restored faith in the financial system.[32] Will Rogers
opined that Roosevelt explained the machinery of banking so well "that
even bankers understood it."[33]

Over the twelve years of his presidency, as radio completed its penetration of American society, Roosevelt honed his technique. By 1941, a
typical fireside chat probably reached nearly three-quarters of the American public. An entire generation fell under the spell of Roosevelt's radio
mystique, including the young Jimmy Carter. As described by Carter's
biographer, James Wooten:

> The resonant tones of the President of the United States slicing crisply
> through the static from faraway Washington, would remain and endure
> for [the young Carter] as an oral symbol of authority and strength,
> leadership, and hope, a force in his life that he would never quite
> escape or outgrow.[34]

On only one occasion did Roosevelt's radio magic fail him: his ominous attempt to pack the Supreme Court. Frustrated by its obstruction
of key New Deal legislation, he proposed the appointment of one extra
associate justice for each serving justice over the age of seventy who had
sat for more than a decade.

The effort failed, but just barely. Polling data showed a bump in public
support for the packing bill with each fireside chat on the topic; after his

major address on the subject on March 9, 1937, 48 percent considered the proposal favorably, probably enough for passage.

Roosevelt failed to follow up his accumulating success with more broadcasts, and over the ensuing weeks the polling data deteriorated. The public also noticed that Charles Evans Hughes, who was now chief justice—a well-loved and respected figure—did not conform to Roosevelt's caricature of senior justices as decrepit old men. (Although Hughes worked behind the scenes to defeat the Supreme Court bill, he had previously polished his credibility regarding the issue by ruling most of the New Deal legislation to be constitutional.) By 1937, the political opposition had finally learned to use the airwaves, especially senators Burton Wheeler, Kenneth Burke, and Royal Copeland, who gave stirring radio addresses in opposition to packing the court. In particular, Burke's speech caught the public imagination by turning around Roosevelt's famous catchphrase to assert that if the president succeeded, "Constitutional democracy was facing a rendezvous with death."[35] In spite of Roosevelt's failure to alter the court through legislation, he succeeded through sheer longevity by appointing eight justices during his twelve years in office.

This one failure aside, it may not be an understatement to attribute Roosevelt's unprecedented four electoral victories largely to his command of the medium, nor an exaggeration to describe that command as hypnotic.[36] Unfortunately for Jimmy Carter, though he was smitten with Roosevelt's radio magic, none of it rubbed off on him. Ronald Reagan, who began his career as a radio sports announcer during the Roosevelt era, probably did learn from the master and used his talent to defeat Carter in the 1980 presidential election.

Franklin Roosevelt, the young Jimmy Carter, and Ronald Reagan were not the only Americans to understand the manipulative potential of radio. In 1938, Orson Welles, the enfant terrible of the American stage, inadvertently demonstrated the awesome power of the new medium not just to distort reality, but to invent its own.

Welles wasn't consciously trying to make trouble. H. G. Wells' *War of the Worlds,* a late-nineteenth-century short novel about an alien invasion, seemed like a good story for his Mercury Theater Radio to read on its regularly scheduled Sunday evening broadcast just before Halloween. The problem was that, as was his wont, Welles had modernized the script.

In this case the revisions were done by a talented screenwriter, Howard Koch, who moved the novel's action from London to Grover's Mill, New Jersey, halfway between New York City and Philadelphia. Koch then happily set about destroying much of the northeastern United States.[37] Welles' collaborator, actor John Houseman (whose signature role was his screen and television portrayal of an intimidating Harvard Law contracts professor in *Paper Chase*) worried that the production of the musty Victorian novel would put audiences to sleep.

It did not. The very first words out of the announcer's mouth clearly informed listeners that the Mercury Theater was presenting the H. G. Wells novel, and this remark was followed by a few minutes of fictional historical prologue not likely to scare anyone. The broadcast then segued to the sound of an imaginary orchestral program suddenly punctuated with, "Ladies and gentlemen, we interrupt this program of dance music to bring you a special bulletin from the Intercontinental Radio News."

There then followed some descriptions of mysterious explosions on Mars, and the arrival of shiny metal cylinders in Grover's Mill, all interspersed in the program of dance music. A few minutes later hideous slimy creatures arose from the cylinders and mounted huge traveling machines that fired death rays, emitted poison gas, and, in short order, defeated the army and its air arm, occupied New York City, and destroyed most human life in their general vicinity.

Welles' technique of dressing up old scripts in contemporary clothes amplified the credibility of his productions. When he staged *Macbeth,* he decked out his actors in 1930s fascist garb. In the *War of the Worlds* broadcast, the ill-fated New Jersey militia commander sounded suspiciously like General Douglas MacArthur; the smooth-talking secretary of the interior's delivery was nearly identical to FDR's; and the announcer's general tenor was modeled on the radio reportage of the earlier, all too real *Hindenburg* disaster and of the Munich crisis. All these factors contributed to the broadcast's terrifying impact.

During the Sunday night broadcast, tens of thousands of Americans fled their homes and crowded onto highways in a panic, flooded police stations with concerned phone calls, donned their World War I gas masks recovered from the attic, and even had hallucinations: some saw New York City burning on the horizon; not a few claimed to have seen the Martian fighting machines and flying cylinders.

Not more than ten minutes into the performance, it was apparent to nearly all stations broadcasting the program that there was trouble; most interrupted it with extra statements about its fictional nature; William Paley, the president of CBS, materialized at the Mercury Theater studio in his robe and slippers to investigate.

Welles also soon became aware of the sensation he was creating, but refused to break the story's flow with an extra announcement, telling one executive, "What do you mean interrupt? They're scared? Good, they're supposed to be scared. Now let me finish!"[38] Later, he unashamedly defended this refusal as a warning about the gullibility of the public to radio broadcasts.

A few years later, Professor Cantril produced an authoritative analysis of the event. He found that those audience members who mistook the broadcast for reality tended to have missed most of it, particularly the beginning, and to have lower socioeconomic status and educational levels; southerners were more easily fooled than northerners. Curiously, those who listened with friends were far more likely not to check the veracity of the story by tuning in other stations to discover that nothing was actually going on; Cantril interpreted this as the result of social reticence.[39]

In many respects, *War of the Worlds* constituted a perfect media storm: a brilliantly executed knockoff of a contemporary news broadcast–cum–fireside chat delivered during a time of high anxiety over national security. The inherently persuasive nature of radio as a stand-alone one-way medium controlled by a very few network officials heightened the effect; it is difficult to imagine television being able to assemble a package of both verbal and visual information into such a convincing hoax, particularly in the modern cable and Internet environment of thousands of simultaneously available outlets.

The broadcast would have done more damage but for the fact that it ran opposite the far more popular Charlie McCarthy show, named after its star, ventriloquist Edgar Bergen's wooden sidekick. One literary critic reached a conclusion different from Cantril's, writing to Welles: "This only goes to prove that the intelligent people were listening to a dummy, and all the dummies were listening to you."[40]

Cantril's analysis of the event brilliantly fingered the source of radio's hypnotic power:

> By its very nature radio is the medium par excellence for informing
> all segments of a population of current happenings, for arousing in
> them a common sense of fear or joy and for enticing them to similar
> reactions toward a single objective. . . . The radio audience consists
> essentially of thousands of small, congregant groups united in time
> and experiencing a common stimulus—altogether making possible
> the largest grouping of people ever known.[41]

Human beings are profoundly social creatures and constantly feed
off the emotions of those around them; the larger the group, the more
intense the experience, as anyone who has ever attended a professional
sporting event, a mass political rally, or even a moving lecture can attest.
A key factor in all these settings is the simultaneity of the event; while
radio does not assemble human beings in person, it made it possible, for
the first time, to assemble millions of them in time, as Franklin Roosevelt
had already discovered to his advantage.

Casting his eyes to the future and across the Atlantic, Cantril also
worried that:

> The day cannot be far off when men in every country of the globe
> will be able to listen at one time to the persuasions or commands of
> some wizard seated in a central palace of broadcasting, possessed of
> a power more fantastic than Aladdin.[42]

His concern proved horrifyingly prophetic, for in those parts of the world
lacking the institutional checks and balances of the United States Constitution, radio would amplify the potential of the world's totalitarian governments right up until the end of the twentieth century.

Paul Joseph Goebbels was born in 1897 to a poor, devout German Catholic
family. The Catholic Church early on recognized his intellectual talent, and,
having been rejected for military service because of his clubfoot, he was
able to earn a doctorate in literature from Heidelberg University in 1921.
His brilliance, physical deformity, short stature, and dusky complexion—
hardly an advertisement for the Nazi Teutonic ideal—combined to produce
a bitter, sarcastic personality and a genius for manipulating the minds of
men. Nazi press chief Max Amann called him "Mephistopheles."[43] Hitler

recognized his unique talent early, and in 1926 appointed him the Berlin party leader.

Berlin became Goebbels' propaganda laboratory. In the 1920s, in the aftermath of the Beer Hall Putsch, the Nazi Party was little more than a ragtag group, and he was forced to attract attention any way he could, most commonly by starting public brawls with communists and socialists. In Berlin, Goebbels also found his voice as an orator and learned to sway the masses he so despised.

Gradually, he learned that the voice convinced far better than the pen. Analytical to a fault, he studied history's great persuaders: Christ, Buddha, Zarathustra, Robespierre, Danton, Mussolini, and, of course, Lenin:

> Has Mussolini been a scribbler, or a great orator? Did Lenin, when arriving in St. Petersburg from Zürich, go from the railway to study and write a book, or did he instead address thousands of people?[44]

What better way to preach to thousands, or even millions, of people than radio? Even before the Nazis assumed power in January 1933, the Weimar government had put all radio stations under the control of a loose group of semipublic national and regional committees. In March 1933, Hitler appointed Goebbels head of the new Propaganda Ministry; five months later the new minister declared, "What the press was to the nineteenth century, radio will be to the twentieth."[45]

By the time the Nazis took power, Germany already had excellent radio coverage, but the receivers cost far too much for the average citizen. Goebbels remedied this with the *Volksempfänger*, or "people's set," which had weak long-wave and medium-wave reception and no shortwave band at all, and thus could not easily bring in foreign broadcasts. Its initial version sold for seventy-six marks—about twenty dollars, half the cost of the cheapest previous models. Subsequent variations sold for half again less.[46]

Little was left to chance. The Propaganda Ministry's broadcast office organized a network of "wireless wardens," tasked with directing the people's attention to the radio; arranging loudspeaker-equipped public listening areas; and, at the workplace, preventing anyone from leaving his or her desk while the Führer or Goebbels was speaking.[47] The government required that all radio dials display little red placards, which proclaimed, "Racial Comrades! You are Germans! It is your duty to not listen to foreign stations. Those who do so will be mercilessly punished." As indeed Germans were; merely listening could earn years of hard labor. Radio miscreants did not even have to be caught in the act—the discovery during a house search of a dial left tuned to a foreign station was enough to ruin one's life.[48] The Nazis dealt far more severely with those who repeated foreign broadcasts:

> The Nuremberg Special Court [not to be confused with the famous postwar trials of Nazi leaders] has sentenced the traitor Johann Wild of Nuremberg to death for two serious radio crimes. . . . He behaved as an enemy of the state and people by continuously listening to hostile broadcasts from abroad. Not content with that, he composed insulting tirades whose source was the enemy station. In these tirades he revealed his treachery to the people by vulgar abuse of the Leader.

Wild's punishment was far from rare; BBC editors were fond of scribbling on substandard copy, "Would you risk your life to listen to *this*?"[49]

In the 1930s, César Saerchinger was a member of the legendary CBS news team—the "Murrow Boys." Just before Edward R. Murrow replaced Saerchinger as the network's chief European correspondent, Saerchinger wrote a compelling description of the well-oiled Nazi radio machine in *Foreign Affairs*:

> In their hands the radio has become the most powerful political weapon the world has ever seen. Used with superlative showmanship, with complete intolerance of opposition, with ruthless disregard for truth, and inspired by a fervent belief that every act and thought must be made subservient to the national purpose, it suffuses all forms of political, social, cultural, and educational activity in the land.[50]

In 1937, Saerchinger reported on the Berlin May Day celebration. For several hours before its high point—Hitler's speech—the airwaves were filled with a hysterical narration of the arrival of each marching contingent, accompanied by thunderous cheering and martial music. As Hitler's car made its way through the city, it was followed by a truck from which an announcer broadcast the Führer's progress. As he left the vehicle and approached the platform, all Germany could hear the crowd rise to fever pitch, shouting *Der Mai ist gekommen, Heil Hitler!*

In contrast to Roosevelt, whose rhetoric ran to soft, measured ca-
dences designed to convey calm, Hitler's shrieks expressed his country's
anger at the "stab in the back," the idea that since in the final weeks of the
war, Germany appeared to be winning, its defeat must have been due to a
domestic fifth column—the communists and the Jews. His speeches were
almost rhythmically punctuated by the crowd's cheering, whose broadcast
volume radio technicians carefully modulated. Saerchinger remarked that
neither Hitler nor Mussolini ever spoke before a microphone in a quiet
studio or office, as did the American president.

When Hitler spoke, everyone, German or foreigner, stopped and
listened, whether he wanted to or not. Again, Saerchinger:

> Needless to say, there is no dissent; the use of radio, as of all vocal
> expression, is reserved exclusively for those who serve and inciden-
> tally own the state.[51]

Goebbels and Hitler could be subtle when subtlety suited their purposes. Just as they allowed the newspaper *Frankfurter Zeitung,* as an important international face of the regime, relatively free editorial rein, so, too,
did they not censor the radio and press reporting of foreign correspondents
in Germany, in marked contrast to the British, who did. This did not go
unnoticed by American reporters, who found that it was easier to get the
facts in Berlin than in London. In a similar vein, during the 1936 Olym-
pics (which had been awarded by the Olympic Committee long before
the Nazis came to power), the rabid anti-Semitism of the press and radio
was toned down.[52]

Saerchinger closed his piece by describing how the Nazis strove to
keep the populace from listening to the powerful French station in Strasbourg, not only by making the receiving of foreign broadcasts illegal but
also by jamming. He ended his essay on this somber note: "Only an incor-
rigible optimist would deny that in the last analysis this feverish building
of radio facilities is part of the general preparation for war."[53]

Goebbels and Hitler understood radio's immense centralized power
at least as well as Roosevelt, and they exploited it to far more nefarious,
and ultimately cataclysmic, ends. A half century later and a continent
away, history tragically repeated itself.

*   *   *

After 1960, multiple factors mitigated radio's totalitarian potential: the decreasing costs and increasing accessibility of telephone, fax, and personal printing and copying devices; the miniaturization of cheap long-range radio receivers capable of pulling in foreign broadcasts; and the growing importance of television. In one part of the world, however, these factors remained largely absent: Africa. As the twentieth century drew to a close, this lack of countervailing factors allowed a centrally controlled radio station to propagate one of history's worst genocides.

In the late nineteenth century, in an effort to catch up with England and France, a newly unified Germany set its sights on East Africa, including the tiny colony of Rwanda, which consisted of a majority Hutu population and a substantial minority of Tutsis.

During World War I, the Belgians displaced the Germans. Critically, both colonial powers were influenced by the British explorer John Hanning Speke, who put forward the "Hamitic hypothesis." This pseudoscientific racial theory postulated that lighter-skinned tribes with Caucasian-like facial features, such as the Tutsis, were superior to more Negroid-appearing tribes, such as the Hutus. (Ham, the accursed son of Noah, was said to have migrated south to Africa; Europeans, Americans, and Arabs frequently invoked this biblical curse as a justification for the slave trade.)

Before the 1950s, the Hutus and Tutsis had gotten along reasonably well, and because of frequent intermarriage it was often difficult to discern to which group an individual belonged. This did not stop the Belgians from issuing identity cards labeling Rwandans as one or the other, or from assigning the best jobs to the Tutsis, who were told, "You whip the Hutus or we will whip you."[54] The resultant Tutsi repression of the Hutus produced, for the first time in Rwandan history, widespread interethnic violence. The approach to independence in 1962 saw spasms of slaughter. Between 1959 and 1967, Hutus killed twenty thousand Tutsi, and hundreds of thousands of the latter fled.

Hard economic times typically breed political and racial conflict, as occurred in Germany in the 1930s. After 1967, life in Rwanda quieted down for a while, but in the late 1980s, prices for the nation's coffee and tea exports fell; the resultant economic dislocation heated up its simmering ethnic cauldron. Over time, the Hutus regained power, and in 1990, the Tutsi reaction to the new Hutu domination erupted into outright civil war, which pitted the forces of the Tutsi-led Rwandan Patriotic Front (RPF) rebels, mainly the children of those who had fled the slaughter of the early 1960s, against the Hutu-led national government of President Juvénal Habyarimana. There were similar events in neighboring Burundi, where in October 1993 Tutsi officers assassinated Melchior Ndadaye, the country's first democratically elected president—a Hutu—and triggered anxiety among Rwandan Hutus that their Tutsi countrymen would turn on them, too.

On April 6, 1994, Rwanda's President Habyarimana, Burundi's new leader, Cyprian Ntayamina, and several of the latter's cabinet were returning home from a regional trip on a Falcon 50 business jet. When the plane was on its final approach to the Kigali airport, witnesses saw two missile launches; both missiles struck the aircraft, which crashed into the presidential palace and killed all aboard.

The attack, which probably had been orchestrated by Hutu extremists, signaled the start of the genocide. During the initial phase of the civil war in 1990, Hutus had killed perhaps a few thousand Tutsis in isolated massacres, but within four months of the plane crash, approximately eight hundred thousand Rwandans—mostly Tutsi, but also Hutu "collaborators"—fell victim to one of history's most horrific slaughters. Initially interpreted by the outside world as a typical spasmodic outbreak of African tribal violence, it was no such thing; it had been planned years in advance by the Hutus. The killing began literally within minutes of the plane crash.[55]

In Rwanda, two media outlets drove the genocide. The first, *Kangura*, a militantly anti-Tutsi newspaper run by journalist Hassan Ngeze, gradually stirred the genocidal pot for several years prior to 1994. The paper's main message could be loosely translated as "Hutu-ness." Its credo, the Hutu ten commandments, laid out the seductive danger of Tutsi women, the dishonesty and treason of Tutsi men, the way the Tutsis secretly controlled the nation, and the actions to be taken against them. The most often quoted of the commandments, number eight, stated, "Hutus must stop having mercy on the Tutsis."[56]

The semiofficial Radio-Télévision Libre des Milles Collines ("Free Radio-Television of the Thousand Hills"), RTLM, triggered and directed the actual slaughter that followed the death of President Habyarimana. RTLM was set up as a private corporation with low-priced shares widely

held among the Hutu population; its programming, unlike that of the ponderous state-run Radio Rwanda, was laced with lively music, off-color
jokes, edgy disk jockeys and announcers, and interviews with ordinary
citizens. The station quickly commandeered listeners, personnel, and funding from its state-run sister station.

Its primary product, though, was a murderous hatred of Tutsis
nearly identical to *Kangura*'s. The spew could be diffuse and general:
the demonization of Tutsis as thieving, sexually and financially predatory
"cockroaches," usually coupled with exhortations for their murder, both
individually and en masse, such as the chilling, oft-repeated rhetorical
question, "The graves are only half filled. Who will help us fill them?"[57]

RTLM could also supply highly specific guidance: the Hutu guards
manning this particular checkpoint should be on the alert for a specific
Tutsi vehicle approaching it; that group of Tutsis had hidden on one specific
hill or another. After the targets had been murdered, the RTLM announcer
would congratulate the perpetrators. The radio station also warned Hutus
when foreign observers were about, and told them to refrain from killing until the all-clear was given.[58] The most popular announcer, Kantano
Habimana, harped constantly on the Tutsi's fondness for milk, riches, and
Hutu women; his mention of a specific Tutsi name was tantamount to a
death sentence. In the words of Major General Roméo Dallaire, the Canadian commander of the United Nations peacekeeping force, "The haunting
image of killers with a machete in one hand and a radio in the other never
leaves you."[59]

The outside world did almost nothing to stop the genocide, which
essentially ended, at least in Rwanda itself, only when the RPF, spurred
on by the murder of their fellow Tutsis, overran the last Hutu positions
around the capital, Kigali, in July 1994. Although the genocide largely
stopped within Rwanda's borders at that point, for two more years Hutus
continued to murder Tutsis in refugee camps in eastern Zaire, with the
knowing connivance of President Mobutu's government and the unwitting
support of Western aid agencies and the United Nations. Only when Zaire
began expelling and murdering its own indigenous Tutsis in 1996, did
Rwanda's new Tutsi president, Paul Kagame, decide he had had enough;
with assistance from Zairean insurgent Laurent Kabila, Rwandan troops
invaded eastern Zaire, cleared the murderous camps, and brought the
remaining Tutsis back home.[60]

Why did the world stand aside? First, it did not monitor RTLM closely and thus only dimly perceived the power of its murderous tone and content. One Westerner who understood was General Dallaire; he repeatedly and unsuccessfully asked for permission to jam it. Writing years later, he pointed out that if such tragedies are to be prevented in the future, international monitoring of radio broadcasts in civil war zones will prove key. One of his major regrets is that he did not destroy RTLM's transmitters.[61]

After April 6, 1994, the withdrawal of almost all Westerners from Rwanda compounded the tragedy. The memory of the gruesome deaths of eighteen United States soldiers in the Somalia "Blackhawk Down" incident, and the even more gruesome treatment of their bodies afterward, remained fresh in American minds. As early as January 1994, three months before the plane crash triggered the genocide, a Rwandan government informant revealed to Dallaire the outline of the Hutu strategy: they would provoke the murder of some Belgian troops, the backbone of the UN mission, and thus would trigger the withdrawal of the peacekeepers. Directed by the informant, the peacekeepers discovered several Hutu weapons caches.

In a famous "genocide fax" to his superiors in New York on January 11, 1994, three months before the fateful crash of the presidential plane, Dallaire outlined the plot and asked for permission to destroy the weapons caches; Kofi Annan, who at the time supervised UN peacekeeping activity, not only refused Dallaire's request but actually ordered Dallaire to betray the name of his informant to the then Hutu-led government. (Annan compounded his shame three years later, when, as secretary-general, he ordered Dallaire not to testify before the Belgian senate investigation into the UN's role in the catastrophe.)[62]

Events ran precisely according to the Hutu plan. After the shootdown, the Hutus fabricated the story that the Belgians had ordered it, and on this pretext hacked to death ten Belgian soldiers. The rest of the Belgians and, along with them, most of Dallaire's peacekeepers and almost the entirety of Rwanda's foreign population, then left. The UN ordered Dallaire's rump force not to protect Tutsis, but rather to guarantee the safe evacuation of foreigners.

The virtual absence of Western observers sealed the Tutsis' fate. At the time of the shoot-down, only a very few journalists—mainly freelancers—reported from Rwanda. Afterward, numerous correspondents did accompany RPF forces as they invaded, but their association with the RPF prevented them from directly witnessing any of the atrocities. One reporter did operate independently: Englishman Nick Hughes, who carried with him a small video camera. On April 11, 1994, he climbed to the roof of the French school in Kigali, and, unobserved by the Hutu militiamen below, he shot a heartrending recording of their cold-blooded, almost casual, murder of several captive men and women. This was one of only a small number of extant recordings of the actual genocide.[63]

Although Hughes' footage and other news of atrocities seeped out fairly early in the genocide, the Western media reported it as yet another example of spasmodic African tribal violence. At the time, they had bigger fish to fry; the genocide began just before the O. J. Simpson case broke. Even Tonya Harding, a disgraced American Olympic ice skater, got more airtime on American network TV than the events unfolding in Rwanda.[64]

Hughes described the significance of his footage with eloquence and poignancy:

> I know now that what I saw was human evil in majesty. Many of those who were there later felt a bond—a need to explain what had happened to anyone who would listen. . . . These images are among the only known pictures of the genocide and they are shocking. In a sense, they are the only reminders that this event really happened. If only there had been more such images.[65]

It's all too easy to assign a particular genocidal tendency to the Hutus, or for that matter to Germans, Serbs, or the Khmer Rouge. Sadly, under the appropriate circumstances, nearly all humans, and every race or ethnic group, may participate in genocide; one of the most bloodthirsty RTLF announcers was a Belgian, Georges Ruggiu.[66]

Hannah Arendt first called attention to this "banality of evil" in her famous *Eichmann in Jerusalem.* Laurence Rees, in *Auschwitz: A New History,* described in detail how a well-structured institutional environment can condition human beings to treat the industrialization of death as ordinary and even laudable, like the making of computer chips or fitness training. Rees found that death camp personnel, almost to a man or woman, considered themselves good people doing important work. In the 1960s and 1970s, psychologists Stanley Milgram and Philip Zimbardo cemented this concept with a series of experiments in which subjects were coaxed with frightening ease to administer brutal, and in some cases "fatal," punishment to innocent strangers.[67] Or, as put most simply by Holocaust survivor Primo Levi, "It happened, therefore it can happen again . . . and it can happen everywhere."[68]

In the mid-1990s, modern two-way communications technologies, such as fax machines, cell phones, and personal video cameras, were rapidly spreading throughout the developed world. Not so in Africa: in 1994 through 1996, video cameras were scarce in both Rwanda and Zaire, and, as Nick Hughes implied, the genocide might well have been stopped had more images gotten out. Rwanda's singular misfortune was that its 1990s genocide took place in a 1960s communications milieu.

Tragically, both the Nazis and the Rwandan Hutus well understood the despotic and murderous potential of radio. Behind the Iron Curtain, on the other hand, the Soviet Union mismanaged radio in so astounding a way that it would contribute to its eventual downfall.

8

THE COMRADES WHO COULDN'T
BROADCAST STRAIGHT

N. I. Stolyarova rushed in to report that a Russian edition of The First Circle *had appeared in the West; she also whispered in my ear that a way had been found to take a microfilm of the* Gulag *text abroad on Pentecost, in a week's time. Our hour was striking, high up on an invisible bell tower.*—Aleksandr Solzhenitsyn[1]

Would there be the earth without the sun?—Lech Walesa commenting on the role of Radio Free Europe in freeing Poland from communist rule.[2]

In the 1970s, most Russians did not question the safety of the nuclear power plants that sprouted around the Soviet Union. Their faith was not daunted by the near disaster at Three Mile Island in Pennsylvania in 1979, for they thought the Western media coverage was overblown. As a technician from the Ukrainian town of Pripyat, which housed the reactors, explained, "There is more emotion in fear of nuclear power plants than real danger. I work in white overalls. The air is clean and fresh; it's filtered most carefully."[3]

Later, by the spring of 1986, Pripyat, fifty miles north of Kiev, and its immediate environs bustled with nuclear power activity, and the boomtown and its surrounding area burgeoned to nearly fifty thousand people. The city's economic life centered on its four operating nuclear reactors and the construction sites of two more; when completed, the complex was to be the world's largest producer of electricity, capable of lighting every home in England.

Reduced to their essence, most nuclear power reactors are water heaters that produce steam that spins turbine blades that, through the magic of Maxwell's equations, yield electrical power. As long as the water is flowing, all is well. But in a cascade of accidents, poor planning, inadequate design and training, and simple bad luck, at 1:23 AM on Saturday, April 26, 1986, the water stopped in Pripyat. Uranium fuel rods overheated and melted; the facility officially known as the Chernobyl No. 4 reactor exploded and sent a fireball high into the night sky.

The human and technical dimensions of the tragedy—the dozens of firemen and technicians who died almost immediately after heroically keeping the blaze from reaching the other three reactors, the thousands more poisoned by radiation, and the vast swath of territory around Pripyat permanently abandoned—need no amplification here. For our purposes, the most remarkable aspect of the episode was the government's initial concealment of the explosion itself from the populace, and when that was no longer possible, the clumsy attempt to hide its catastrophic consequences.

The world first became aware of the nuclear accident when a radioactive plume borne on the prevailing southeasterly winds arrived thirty-six hours later over southern Sweden at an altitude of five thousand feet. The Swedish air force, which routinely swept the nation's skies for radioactivity, detected it first. Later, on the morning of April 28, a worker at a Swedish reactor detected radioactivity on his work boots; his coworker's clothing soon tested positive as well, and so the plant's managers ordered it evacuated, and motorists were kept away from its vicinity.

Soon enough, Swedish authorities measured radioactivity falling in snow and rain all over the country and deduced the Soviet Union as its source. Early on the evening of April 28, Swedish diplomats in Moscow made inquiries. The Soviets stonewalled them, but a few hours later a Moscow television news show made a brief four-line announcement, buried under several preceding upbeat economic stories, about "an accident" at Chernobyl. Although this apparent lack of emphasis amazed Western observers, Soviet citizens, attuned to the finer nuances of official pronouncements, clearly understood that the announcer's terse, grim delivery portended a major disaster.[4]

The tragically inadequate governmental response to the Chernobyl disaster flowed inevitably from the central characteristic of all communist regimes: the instinctual control of information. In response to the explosion, the plant's director, Viktor Bryukhanov, cut almost all telephone connections to the outside; on the day of the accident, in order to calm the public, news officials bragged that sixteen couples had been married in Pripyat. Satellite photos showing a soccer game in progress less than a mile from the burning reactor appalled American intelligence analysts.

The local apparatchiks did not even caution residents to remain indoors on April 26, and they did not evacuate Pripyat until the next day, April 27. Four days later, on May Day, Kiev's party leaders refused to cancel the traditional parade, in spite of the radioactive winds blowing toward the city. While Europeans a thousand miles away furiously rinsed and scrubbed produce, Soviet citizens a dozen miles away took no special precautions with their food, and almost no one, save for a few high-ranking party officials, was issued the potassium iodide tablets that would have prevented thousands of subsequent thyroid cancers. Not until two weeks had passed did General Secretary Gorbachev address the nation. Even then, he barely hinted at the full extent of the disaster.[5]

As usual, the general secretary was behind the curve; almost from the first, most Soviet citizens had learned the awful facts of the accident from "the Voices": the BBC, Radio Liberty, Voice of America, and Deutsche Welle.[6] Information about the accident also spread through informal domestic channels, especially in the scientific and engineering community.[7]

The Chernobyl disaster was merely a symptom of more serious rot at the core of the Soviet Union. Five years later, the country collapsed abruptly from within, surely one of the most singular, mystifying, and almost totally unpredicted events in modern political history. As such, the implosion is something of a Rorschach blot that reveals more about the observer than about the event.

To his admirers on the American right, Ronald Reagan deserves the lion's share of the credit. The Gipper, after all, had labeled the Soviet Union an "evil empire" and challenged Mikhail Gorbachev to "tear down this wall," thereby capturing the high moral ground. Reagan rapidly built up the United States' military might, initiated the "Star Wars" missile defense program, and, according to this narrative, snookered the Soviets into an arms race they could ill afford.

To be sure, most historians would single out the equally remarkable story of Gorbachev, who in 1985, following the deaths of Leonid Brezhnev, Yuri Andropov, and Konstantin Chernenko, became the fourth general secretary of the Communist Party within twenty-eight months. Gorbachev sincerely believed that the two policies of perestroika (roughly, restructuring) and glasnost (roughly, openness) would save communism; instead, these two initiatives hastened its end.

To the petroleum economist, the seminal events were the rapid rise in crude oil prices after the 1973 and 1979 oil crises, followed by the equally impressive fall in prices of crude in the early 1980s. The 1970s price rise pumped badly needed revenue into the Soviet Union and granted its tottering governmental system approximately a decade's reprieve; the 1980s price fall knocked the last remaining prop out from under it and rang the curtain down on the grand seventy-year experiment. The 1970s rise in oil prices treated eastern European satellite nations, which had to import Russian petroleum, less well. Although the Soviets did subsidize these imports, in the long run eastern Europe could not be insulated from the oil shock that affected the rest of the global economy, and so communism's end was hastened there as well.[8]

The military historian would surely focus on the cliff-hanging tactical events surrounding the August 1991 coup against Gorbachev by a small, incompetent group of KGB and army diehards. They neglected to arrest the Russian president, Yeltsin; did not completely secure the television and radio stations; and catastrophically failed to muzzle the media's rebellious reporters and producers. Had they been more scrupulous about these things, the Soviet Union might still be around today.

Finally, a political scientist or an aviation expert would point out the remarkable bit of airmanship executed by a wayward German youth, Matthias Rust. On May 28, 1987, Rust, with just fifty hours of flying experience, piloted a small Cessna with dicey internal fuel tanks the almost six hundred miles from Helsinki to Moscow and deftly landed the aircraft in Red Square, where he informed the crowd that he had come to see Gorbachev about world peace. Although the Soviet leader outwardly expressed rage at the incompetence of his military, Rust's stunt allowed him to sack much of the obstructionist, hard-line defense establishment and thus advance perestroika and glasnost.[9]

Reagan, Gorbachev, the price of oil, the incompetence of the coup plotters, and Rust all performed their part, but from the broader perspective, all the events that precipitated the fall of communism revolved around the control of communication, information, and news. Two simple technologies —carbon paper and shortwave receivers, both of which the Soviet command economy produced in incomprehensibly enormous quantities—lay at the core of the collapse of the Soviet Union and its eastern European empire.

The closer the observer was to the centers of Soviet power, the more strongly he or she emphasized the importance of the Voices. The sentiment of Lech Walesa expressed in one of this chapter's epigraphs is clear enough. Gorbachev told Margaret Thatcher that the impulse for reform came from the desire for freedom, which in turn came from the Voices. Boris Yeltsin spoke more specifically about Radio Liberty: "This radio station reports objectively and fully, and we are generally quite thankful to them." In the days leading up to the August 1991 coup, he had one of his aides fax a message to allies in Washington:

> The Russian Government [as opposed to that of the USSR] has NO way to address the people. All radio stations are under control. The following is [Boris Yeltsin's] address to the Army. Submit it to the U.S.I.A. [U.S. Information Agency]. Broadcast it over the country. Maybe "Voice of America." Do it! Urgent![10]

Václav Havel noted, "If my fellow citizens knew me before I became president, they did so because of these stations." When Radio Free Europe's funding got slashed in the 1990s and it could no longer afford its quarters in Germany, Havel gave it a home in Prague.[11] The irony of the almost universal reverence for the Voices behind the Iron Curtain is that many in the West distrusted them; Senator William Fulbright labeled them Cold War relics, creatures of the United States government and CIA, and tried to shut them down.[12]

The best place to begin any understanding of the fall of communism is a brief essay written by the Austrian economist Friedrich Hayek, recently elevated, along with Milton Friedman and Ayn Rand, to near-sainthood by the neoliberal right. His most brilliant insight was encapsulated in "The Use of Knowledge in Society," a short article published in *American Economic Review* in 1945. Its intellectual appeal extends far beyond libertarian circles.[13]

The problem in consciously structuring any economic system, Hayek saw, was that there are just too many moving pieces: a myriad of goods and services, each offered by diverse individuals and organizations. Consider just one industrial commodity: ball bearings. The world's largest national economies consume approximately one hundred thousand different kinds of the tiny spheres; the manufacture of each takes multiple steps. The total material ensemble of any economy is thus so numbingly complex that its efficient organization lies well beyond the smartest planners in possession of the most detailed data and wielding the most powerful computers and sophisticated software. As put by Hayek:

> The "data" from which the economic calculus starts are never for the whole society "given" to a single mind. . . . The [data] never exists in concentrated or integrated form, but solely as the dispersed bits of incomplete and frequently contradictory knowledge which all the separate individuals possess.[14]

Hayek's special genius lay in the realization that the millions of individuals participating in a smoothly running economy communicate by means of the information inherent in prices—the "price signal":

> Assume that somewhere in the world a new opportunity for the use of some raw material, say tin, has arisen, or that one of the sources of supply of tin has been eliminated. It does not matter for our purpose—and it is very significant that it does not matter—which of these two causes has made tin more scarce. All that the users of tin need to know is that some of the tin they used to consume is now more profitably employed elsewhere, and that in consequence they must economize tin.[15]

The cynic might say that all Hayek had done was to provide a fancy description of Adam Smith's famous "invisible hand," the ability of the markets to arrange automatically for the efficient provision of goods and services. Perhaps—but in 1945, capitalism's record over the previous two decades, especially during the worldwide Great Depression, did not inspire confidence. By contrast, the Soviet Union's economy, far from collapsing, seemed to be rapidly overtaking the free market economies of the liberal democracies. As late as 1975, the usually astute Daniel Patrick Moynihan wrote an essay that pronounced the capitalist liberal democracy an endangered species.[16] By the mid-twentieth century, the world desperately needed reminding of the existence of Smith's invisible hand and of how it worked.

In 1945, Hayek saw that the best way to determine the output of bread or steel was to allow producers to observe prices, and then simply let those prices guide output. If bread became more expensive, then bakers would automatically turn out more loaves; if steel became cheaper, then plant managers would, without prompting from anyone else, shut down some blast furnaces.

The Soviet economic system, in contrast, mandated a certain fixed level of output, and a fixed price, for every single commodity. The results were a shortage of wearable shoes, and bread loaves whose cost had not changed for decades and which consequently had become so relatively cheap that they were commonly (and illegally) fed to livestock. (Contrary to the popular image, the Soviet Union was actually the world's largest shoe manufacturer, but the shoes were of poor quality, style, and fit: "torture for the feet," in the words of one Russian acquaintance, who added, "Italian shoes made me feel like a Cinderella story miracle.")[17]

Western visitors to the Soviet Union marveled at the low prices of food staples, low rents, and low fares on public transport—prices that had, of course, been fixed by the authorities. What went unnoticed was that the state mandated even lower wages, and thus made these goods, when they were available, often unaffordable. In a normal market economy, wages constitute approximately two-thirds of gross domestic product; in the Soviet Union, wages constituted only one-third. The absence of a meaningful price signal proved especially damaging in the labor market, where a truck driver might be paid two to four times as much as a physician; in the sexist Russian society, this meant that highly skilled but poorly paid cognitive work, such as medicine, engineering, and teaching, became highly feminized. (The official pay of Russians often represented only a small portion of their actual recompense; access to consumer items was a key perquisite of party membership. Even for nonmembers, vocational access was a critical component of compensation: the teacher could solicit bribes from pupils' parents, the doctor from her patients; and the construction foreman could pilfer prodigious amounts of materials.)[18]

The communist nations thus attempted to run a system devoid of the price signal, and they failed miserably. Their governments demanded that factories crank out this many tons of steel and that many liters of cooking oil, whether these were needed or not, no matter what their quality, and whether or not they could even be transported to consumers. The result: milk that spoiled before it reached stores, steel so pocked with defects that it could not be used in cars, and soap supplies that swung between severe prolonged shortages and massive surpluses that saw mounds of it dissolving in the rain.[19]

Worse, the belief in an economy run by a planning elite in possession of the "complete" set of data inevitably leads those who control this vital information to deprive others of it, no matter how innocuous the information. In the Soviet Union, among the most sought-after items brought in by foreigners were street maps *of Soviet cities* created from Western satellite photos; the ones produced by the domestic cartographers had been intentionally distorted to the point of uselessness, presumably for military reasons. Increasingly, the official information itself was falsified, all too often rendering the planning process worse than worthless.[20] And if city maps were dangerous, then political opinions, or even literature, must surely carry mortal peril.

At the same time that Hayek wrote his famous essay, a mathematician, Norbert Wiener, considered the use of information in society from a somewhat different angle. Unlike Hayek, Wiener, who hailed from a highly intellectual midwestern Jewish-American background, held a jaundiced view of capitalism, which he saw as both inefficient and unjust. He earned a PhD in mathematics from Harvard at the astounding age of eighteen, and during World War II found himself working on the problem of the radar control of antiaircraft fire.

Researchers quickly realized that the solution to the problem of antiaircraft fire lay beyond even the sophisticated ballistic calculations normally used for artillery, and that automatic, rapid devices were called for: thus the first primitive electronic computers. Wiener recognized that such computational methods carried with them enormous implications for medicine, physiology, economics, and the very structure of human society. He gave the new field of study a name: cybernetics, the theory of information and control in human and animal systems.[21]

With stunning prescience, Wiener foresaw a "second industrial revolution," during which information, mediated by mass-produced computers, would become at least as important as manufactured goods. Wiener's foresight, in an era that had only a few room-size vacuum-tube computers tended by small armies of technicians, has worn well. While IBM's founder Thomas Watson, contrary to popular legend, probably never said, "I think there is a world market for about five computers," this apocryphal statement did accurately reflect the public perception of computers in the pre-PC era. In short, Wiener imagined a world in which

> That country will have the greatest security whose informational and scientific situation is adequate to meet the demands that may be put upon it. . . . In other words, no amount of scientific research, carefully recorded in books and papers, and then put into our libraries with labels of secrecy, will be adequate to protect us for any length of time in a world where the effective level of information is perpetually advancing. There is no Maginot line of the brain.[22]

Put into plain English, in a world where technological progress and military security depend on constant scientific advance, secrecy, far from maintaining national security, actually erodes it by preventing the intellectual cross-fertilization that characterizes open societies. While the anti-capitalist Wiener aimed his concerns about secrecy at what he saw as the absurd precautions of the American military-industrial complex, they applied in spades to the Soviet Union.

The Soviets well understood the ominous economic and political implications of Wiener's writings, which were enormously popular and influential in the West. As expected, the Russian propaganda machine inveighed mightily against the philosophical and economic aspects of cybernetics, which it labeled a "pseudoscience."[23] Outwardly, Stalin's henchmen mocked cybernetics:

> The process of production realized without workers, only with machines controlled by the gigantic brain of the computer! No strikes or strike movements, and moreover no revolutionary insurrections! Machines instead of the brain, machines without people! What an enticing perspective for capitalism![24]

Although the Soviets disdained Wiener's new science—it did not help that he was Jewish—his vision of a postindustrial world suffused with cheap, easily available information-crunching machines must have petrified them, since they could not help noticing the ability of the new devices to *copy* information. (While the Soviets dismissed Wiener's work publicly, they were not so thick as to prevent their military from incorporating cybernetic theory into their missile technology.)[25]

For centuries Russia, geographically far from the center of the European Enlightenment, found itself constantly playing intellectual, cultural, technological, and economic catch-up with the West. Periodically, visionary leaders such as Peter the Great and Catherine the Great attempted radical modernization. Peter traveled incognito through western Europe early in his reign as czar, visited the Sorbonne, and learned, among other things, the shipbuilding techniques of the Dutch East India Company; Catherine began her life as the highly educated daughter of a German prince and attempted to align Russian culture and government with the French model.

All modernizing Russian leaders, from Peter through Catherine to Gorbachev, faced the same problem, which historian James Billington called the "dilemma of the reforming despot":

> How can one retain absolute power and a hierarchical social system while at the same time introducing reforms and encouraging education? How can an absolute ruler hold out hope for improvement without confronting a "revolution of rising expectations?"[26]

After 1950, Billington's "revolution of rising expectations" slowly eroded communist regimes' grasp on absolute power on a variety of communications battlefronts. The relevant mechanisms ranged from the handwritten copying of seditious novels to the miniature shortwave radio that kept a captive Mikhail Gorbachev apprised of the coup plotters' weaknesses. In the second half of the twentieth century, the peculiar development of the Russian radio industry would combine with simple copying technologies to break the government's stranglehold on information in the Soviet Union and its eastern Europe satellites.

The contributions of carbon paper and radio to the downfall of communism in the Soviet Union and its eastern European satellites were not merely additive. These two media yielded political synergies that no one foresaw; their potent combination snowballed over the decades and exceeded the most optimistic hopes of these nations' repressed populations and the worst nightmares of their rulers.

The Soviet audience differed from that in the West, and particularly from that in the United States, in at least four essential ways. First, Russians take their authors and poets far more seriously, and these writers occupy a far loftier place in the public consciousness. When political expression is suppressed, literature becomes the main political outlet. As put by the Russian essayist Osip Mandelstam, "Only in our country is poetry respected—they'll kill you for it. Only in our country, and no other."[27] Shortly after he uttered this sentiment, he died for his writings.

Second, because the rulers of the Soviet Union restricted news from abroad, Russians became intensely interested in it, far more so than people in the United States, a nation in which almost no one—including at least one former president—knows the difference among Slovakia, Slovenia, and Slavonia.

Third, in Stalin's time the authorities generally granted ordinary workers more autonomy of thought and action than intellectuals and party officials. One famous story has a young woman factory worker being told by a panel of bosses that she must work overtime without pay. She turned her back to her seated bosses, lifted up her skirt, and said, "Comrade Stalin and all you can kiss me wherever it is most convenient for you." For a very long moment, the commissars sat pale, silent, and frozen with fear, until one elicited nervous laughter with, "Did you notice she didn't have any [under]pants on?"[28]

Fourth, after Stalin's death, the asking of "sharp questions"—a particularly Russian pastime—became more acceptable, even fashionable, particularly at the highest political levels and at elite universities. One American exchange student at Moscow University in the early 1960s, William Taubman, noted that students reserved the most acid ridicule for their peers who routinely mouthed Marxist cant; contrariwise, those who could flummox instructors and political officials with clever cross-examination earned high esteem.[29]

Along with radio and the dramatic steam- and electricity-driven improvements in printing, a quieter revolution in the reproduction of the written word was taking place that would destabilize the communist world: the development of inexpensive mechanical copying.

Technically speaking, the printing press is a *duplicating* machine, not a *copying* machine; the former makes multiple identical document copies from a mechanical template, whereas the latter makes copies of an original document that may often vary greatly among themselves. For thousands of years, cheap human clerical labor had provided the most economical way of making replicas of a letter, pamphlet, or book—that is, copying it by hand.

In 1603, a German Jesuit, Christoph Scheiner, built a device based on Euclidian geometry that made more or less exact duplicates, as well as enlargements and reductions, of writing and drawing; he named it the pantograph. Over the next two centuries, the temperamental, expensive device evolved in the hands of multiple inventors; its final form, the "polygraph," could produce up to five copies at once.

As late as the early nineteenth century, clerks still cost less than fickle, complex polygraphs and pantographs, which remained largely the province of enthusiastic first adopters such as Thomas Jefferson, who owned several pantographs. A prodigious inventor in his own right, he was obsessed with the fragility of the information chain in the preindustrial age. In a letter to historian Ebenezer Hazard, Jefferson fantasized:

> Time and accident are committing daily havoc on the originals deposited in our public offices. . . . Let us save what remains: not by vaults and locks which fence them from the public eye and use, in consigning them to the waste of time, but by such multiplication of copies as shall place them beyond the reach of accident.[30]

Jefferson would surely have mightily approved of the Xerox machine and the personal computer, devices that allow the nearly infinite copying of information, but in the late eighteenth century, the pantograph was all he had, and it was not up to the task.

Jefferson had no way of knowing just how prescient he was. Even in that era, scholars had noted how some documents yellowed, became brittle, and fell apart; by the early twentieth century document self-destruction reached epidemic proportions. Many observers blamed atmospheric pollution from industrial activity, but it fell to William Barrow, an autodidact who was worried that he would not be able to preserve family documents, to uncover the problem's multiple causes. Although he possessed only an associate degree, Barrow managed to acquire sophisticated mechanical testing equipment and assembled a talented team of materials scientists to solve the mystery of the decomposing books.

The trouble, Barrow found, began even before Gutenberg, when scribes, and then printers, gradually converted from carbon-based to iron gall inks. If the printer added too much tannic acid to the brew, the highly acidic written and printed letters would slowly eat through and shred the page. As high-quality cotton rags became more scarce, papermakers started to bleach their darker, dirtier raw materials with chlorine. This made for more acidic paper, which became increasingly brittle over time.

Nothing, though, savaged the integrity of books like the switch in the 1880s from cloth to wood pulp, which required the use of harsh chemicals that could yield either a highly acid, or, less commonly, a highly alkaline, product. In the late 1950s, Barrow examined five hundred books, one hundred from each decade between 1900 and 1950. The results stunned him; within decades, the paper became weak and brittle; sheets that could be folded hundreds of times when new cracked and tore when bent only half a dozen times. Barrow went on to invent a restorative process now used by librarians around the world, and he also helped develop today's industry standard acid-free paper.[31]

Other modern media suffer from even more severe problems. The earliest nitrate films spontaneously combusted; later acetate reels suffered from "vinegar syndrome," a term referring to the characteristic odor that accompanies their degradation; and Technicolor film generally fades into uselessness within a few decades. Film historians estimate that more than 90 percent of silent films, and more than half of films made after 1950, have been lost forever. (In addition, at least as many of the earliest films were lost by careless archiving and simple discarding as by degradation.)[32] Finally, as mentioned in Chapter 1, today's digital media may prove even more ephemeral, not only because of degradation but also because of format obsolescence.

History best remembers James Watt as the inventor of the first steam engine efficient enough for practical use, but he also devised the nineteenth century's preeminent copying method, whose use survived well into the twentieth century.

Watt, like any other successful businessman, desired duplicates of his letters, invoices, and internal records. For millennia, scribes had known that a freshly inked document, when compressed evenly against another piece of paper, will transfer a reversed image onto it. Watt realized that if thin, moist paper received an impression from the original, under sufficient pressure the ink would wick evenly and completely through to the opposite surface of the copy, and thus produce a normal nonreversed image. Through trial and error, he found that adding a bit of sugar to the ink improved the result, as did, under the appropriate conditions, either a screw press or a roller press. In 1780, he patented his first roller device, which sold for £6, or about $400 in today's currency. His devices, commonly known as "copying presses," succeeded wildly; nearly all of the founding fathers, including Jefferson, bought them. (Jefferson's purchases in 1789 for the nation's new State Department became the American government's first office copiers.)[33]

Copying presses grew in diversity and popularity. On the smallest scale, they could be primitive, portable devices consisting of blank pages and a small roller into which sequential copies could be impressed, compact enough to fit in a pocket. For high-volume office use, they could be large, complex machines. In the nineteenth century, the term "copying press" was applied, at one time or another, to nearly all of them. Today, the screw-operated copying press can easily be found in antique shops and on eBay.com, almost always mistakenly referred to as a "book press."

The late eighteenth century and the early nineteenth saw the appearance of four more copying technologies. The first, lithographic printing, came about in 1795 when the mother of Alois Senefelder, a young German playwright, asked him to record the clothes sent for laundering; not having any paper handy, he wrote the list on a piece of polished limestone, using a waxy ink he had been experimenting with.

In a stroke of genius, he realized that while nitric acid would etch away limestone, it would not erode the surface protected by the wax. When he bathed his limestone laundry list in the acid, he was left with a raised impression protected by the waxy writing about a hundredth of an inch thick, and with careful flat polishing of the stone and meticulous printing technique his method yielded fine, clean copies. The technique he patented, lithography, represents a vital intermediate technology between the printing press and the copying press, capable of yielding large numbers of copies of handwritten documents and pictures. (Early printing presses could not easily reproduce drawn figures, since these presses required laborious manual production of each image, while copying presses could not generate copies of any sort in volume.)[34]

The second copying system was stencil duplicating; for centuries, it had been known that ink could be applied through a cut template, or "stencil," to produce an image or writing. In the late nineteenth century, inventors discovered that writing with a stylus on waxed paper laid on a finely cut flat file plate yielded a punctuate image of drawings and letters. This technique was refined by multiple entrepreneurs, including Thomas Edison and a lumberman, Albert Blake Dick. The latter patented the famous mimeograph machine, whose trademark inscription "AB Dick" aroused giggles in generations of children allowed into the inner sanctum of their school's copying room.

Older readers will remember rough copies of exams or worksheets printed in purple ink. Although usually called "mimeographs," these copies were far more likely to have been examples of a third copying system, the hectograph. With this technique, originals were printed on paper with a thick wet ink, which was then applied to a moist flat gelatin plate. The ink that adhered to the plate could make scores of copies before it wore away; the term "hectograph" indicated that the plate could print up to a hundred copies, although this number was rarely achieved in practice.[35]

Russian and eastern European dissidents employed, at one time or another, all of the above copying technologies. Not infrequently, when none was easily available, they reverted to medieval scribal mode—hand copying. Among all copying technologies, however, a fourth nineteenth-century invention, carbon paper, deserves the greatest credit for bringing down communism.

The first primitive carbon paper was invented in 1806 by Ralph Wedgwood, grandson of the famous English potter Josiah Wedgwood. Ralph's product, intended as a writing aid for the blind, consisted of a complex system of plates, styluses, and ink-soaked paper. The process involved four sheets: the "original" sheet on top, underneath which were stacked two more sheets with the double-sided inked "carbon" between them, thus yielding an original, a normal copy, and a reversed copy. Smelly and messy, Wedgwood's technique found only scattered practical use.

But Wedgwood's invention did find favor with the reporters and editors of the Associated Press (AP). In 1868, the AP covered the twenty-first-birthday celebration of a greengrocer, Lebbus H. Rogers, deemed newsworthy because the young man climaxed the festivities with a balloon ascent. In an interview in the AP offices afterward, Rogers spied the carbon paper; intrigued by it, he gave up aeronautics to pursue its business potential.

Flimsy quill pens could not inscribe high-quality carbon copies, and Rogers' venture initially foundered. Sometime around 1873, he attended a demonstration of the first practicable commercial typewriter, manufactured by the gun and sewing machine maker E. Remington and Sons. Rogers found that the combination of carbon paper and typewriter could yield up to ten legible copies in expert hands; this method replaced the copying press, which by that point had served businessmen and writers around the world for more than a century. Even so, he had his work cut out for him, because by 1873, carbon paper technology had not evolved much beyond Wedgwood's technique; in the ensuing decades, Rogers developed, then mechanized, a process for applying dry carbon black to only one side of a thin, durable paper sheet. Ever the polymath, by the time he died in 1932, he had written sonnets, run a ranch, invented wire-casing machinery, and observed with pleasure that his invention had become a mainstay of office copying.[36]

Had Rogers lived two more generations, he would have seen the typewriter and carbon paper trigger amazing events in Russia, for this combination made possible the relatively rapid, decentralized production of large numbers of copies, in which each duplication cycle could exponentially increase a book's or a pamphlet's circulation.

The history of Russian dissident and underground publishing goes back centuries, as Russia's rulers understood, almost from the first, the subversive nature of words in totalitarian societies.[37] In 1790, the author and social observer Alexander Radishchev wrote an anti-serfdom tract titled *A Journey from St. Petersburg to Moscow*. Although the police confiscated all the print copies they could find, handwritten manuscripts circulated widely; during the Decembrist revolt of 1825, Pushkin and others kept a low profile by avoiding the printing press and circulating their writings only in manuscript form. Throughout the nineteenth century and the early twentieth, homemade manuscripts and books printed on foreign presses proliferated in czarist Russia. The most famous of the foreign presses was Free Russian Press, founded in London in 1852 by the Moscow-born intellectual Alexander Herzen.

Before the Bolshevik victory in 1917, the revolutionaries produced the first carbon-paper-derived "Underwood copies," named after the popular typewriter manufacturer. After the Bolsheviks gained power, they naturally suppressed this mode of copying. Carbon reproductions contributed to the 1938 death of Mandelstam, whose quote earlier in this Chapter about dying for poetry proved all too prophetic. The extreme repression of the Stalinist period made things too hot for even Underwood copies, and writers simply produced manuscripts *v yashchick* ("for the desk drawer"), to be read, if at all, by visitors to their homes.[38]

Aleksandr Solzhenitsyn, who was imprisoned from 1945 to 1953, best described the spirit of *v yashchick*:

> Without hesitation, without inner debate, I entered into the inheritance of every modern Russian writer intent on the truth: I must write simply to ensure that it was not forgotten, that posterity might someday come to know it. Publication in my own lifetime I must shut out of my mind, out of my dreams.[39]

Without pen and paper, the jailed Solzhenitsyn committed his novels, essays, and poems to memory, using beads and matchsticks as mnemonic aids. After Stalin's death in 1953, the repression relaxed, and in 1956, two momentous and countervailing events rocked the communist world: the Twentieth Congress of the Soviet Communist Party and the political uprisings in Poland and Hungary.

During the Twentieth Congress, Khrushchev delivered a blistering "secret speech" that exposed the horrors of the Stalinist era; it was followed over the next several years by a loosening of censorship, increased cultural ties with the West, and even some modest economic liberalization. The CIA almost immediately obtained a transcript of the "secret speech," which the Voices extensively rebroadcast; in response, the Soviets made its gist public after some delay, but they did not publish its full text until 1989, more than three decades later.

For several years after 1956, a literary and political thaw flourished under Nikita Khrushchev. In 1962 Solzhenitsyn used his bead-and-matchstick method to reconstruct and publish a novelistic account of prison life, *One Day in the Life of Ivan Denisovich*, in *Novy Mir*, an official literary magazine in the vanguard of liberalization. However, after Khrushchev fell from power in 1964, the gloves came off, and the authorities again began to pursue aggressively not only Solzhenitsyn, but other dissident writers as well.

Yuri Andropov, Russia's ambassador in Budapest during the Hungarian political uprising, never forgot the sight of his agents' bodies strung from the city's lampposts, nor did he forget being fired upon by the revolutionaries as he moved about the city. Andropov concluded that from this point forward, the first signs of dissent anywhere in the communist empire had to be quickly and firmly crushed; within two years Imre Nagy, Hungary's former premier, who had been promised a safe-conduct from his hiding place in the Yugoslav embassy in Budapest, was arrested, tried, and executed under the direction of the Soviets.

Over the coming decades these two paradigms—Khrushchev's liberalization and Andropov's repression—would do epic battle. The gradual ascendancy of the hard-liners was reflected in Andropov's rise; in 1967, he became KGB head, the position from which he directed the 1968 smothering of the Prague Spring and the 1979 invasion of Afghanistan. In 1982, he was elected general secretary of the Party.

Thus, 1964 represents a watershed in dissident publication, and most authorities date the history of underground dissident publishing—samizdat, humorously referred to as "overcoming Gutenberg"—from approximately that year.

The term "samizdat" was said to have been coined in the 1950s when a Moscow poet, Nikolai Glazkov, whimsically wrote the word *samsesbyaizdat*—"publishing house for oneself"—on the front of a typewritten collection of his work in the place where the name of the publishing house would normally appear.[40] The word can have multiple meanings: most narrowly, typewritten copies distributed from hand to hand; or more broadly, these plus copies made by other methods. Or, as the dissident Russian author Vladimir Bukovsky put it, "Write myself, edit myself, censor myself, publish myself, distribute myself, go to jail for it myself."[41]

Other words share the same root: *tamizdat,* foreign printing of a dissident work, literally, "published over there"; *radizdat,* any material, including music, broadcast abroad and copied at home; and *magnitizdat,* materials, usually music, recorded on tape or cassette. (State-run publishing organizations carried similar names: Gosizdat and Politizdat.)

Samizdat, *tamizdat, radizdat,* and *magnitizdat* became woven together in a self-reinforcing cycle: written material was smuggled and then published abroad, broadcast over foreign radio, and retranscribed and recopied by Russian listeners. Unless the police could intercept the process within the first few copies, stopping this cycle proved impossible.

Julius Telesin, a dissident Soviet writer who emigrated to the United Kingdom, provided the classic operating description of samizdat.[42] He begins his essay by playfully noting that the best place to plumb its murky beginnings would be in newspaper records of Stalinist trials, but unfortunately, the state "does not like its citizens to read old newspapers."[43]

He then describes how samizdat closely resembles publishing in capitalist countries, but with a twist: in order for a work to be extensively reproduced, not only must it be well written and of wide interest, but it must not be *too* dangerous:

> Samizdat is differentiated according to degrees and shades of danger. A man develops, consciously or intuitively, his own notion of the risk he is taking when he types out, gives people to read, or keeps at home, pieces of samizdat or tamizdat literature.[44]

Telesin then observes that the reader of samizdat copies, which are hand-produced and in high demand, may borrow his copy for only a few precious days at a time:

> It is natural that I should want to keep this work for myself. But I have to return the copy I was given, perhaps very soon, as someone else is waiting his turn to read it. Consequently, I have to start looking for a way to copy the work.[45]

Were the manuscript short—say, several pages—no great problems would hinder copying: the reader would simply sit down at his typewriter for a few hours and bang out carbons for himself and his friends. But what if the work is longer—say, even a novel? First, as a matter of basic courtesy, permission for copying must be obtained from the manuscript's source; second, a typist must be found; and finally, the manuscript will be needed for some extra days beyond the initially agreed-upon loan period:

> At this point a certain amount of bargaining usually begins. It emerges that, as a "fee," I must return the work plus three copies. The person who gave it to me wants one copy for himself; he will give another one to the person who gave it to him, but as the work belongs to a third person

> (as a rule names are not mentioned) the last wants an extra copy for himself (perhaps he will give it to someone as a birthday present). Then I declare that I am being "overcharged." My friend's typist can only do five copies—her old typewriter cannot "take" more. At the same time she wants a copy for herself, and my friend wants one too. Thus, if I give away three copies here and two there, what will be left for me?[46]

He bargains his source down to two copies; of the five he gets from the typist, she will—he hopes—take only one, thus leaving two for the original lender and two more for Telesin: one for himself, and one for "a certain person who is very much interested in the subject; besides, this person may be useful in getting hold of other things for me to read."[47]

Telesin praises the beauty of the system: typewriters are cheap and no longer have to be registered as in Stalin's time; plain paper and carbon paper, while occasionally in short supply, can be stockpiled. But since the mail is definitely not secure from the state's eyes, copies must be passed from hand to hand.

Soviet and eastern European police failed to control adequately access to both typewriters and carbon paper. For example, while government departments sent print samples from all typewriters to the KGB, officials did not require and monitor the private sale and use of typewriters. Instead, the authorities tried to control the dissidents themselves, but once the first batch of carbon paper copies had been distributed, Rogers' carbon paper genie had escaped the ink jar, no matter how many subsequent arrests were made.

Other techniques round out the samizdat process: to conserve precious paper, the typist employs a tiny font, single spacing, and the narrowest possible page margins. She—most typists were women—also uses onionskin paper that could yield as many as fifteen copies, the last of which was barely legible. In especially favorable circumstances, hectograph and mimeograph machines, sometimes homemade, were pressed into service as well. Once printed, a samizdat book or essay might even be bound; rarely, state printing facilities could be commandeered, and one group of Soviet Baptists even managed to run a clandestine printing press.[48]

The most critical phase of distribution involved the delivery of the copies into the hands of travelers and diplomats for publication abroad. Over time this proved the most effective channel of distribution, for it allowed the Voices to broadcast the most important samizdat texts into millions of homes, among which might be thousands more typists listening to and transcribing the broadcasts.

Even so, danger, expense, and shortage of trained and willing personnel dogged the process at every step: skilled typists, who could be easily intimidated with the threat of transfer to physical labor, were chronically in short supply, and printing and copying operations had to be shifted continually from location to location. All too often, those involved were repaid with arrest, beating, and imprisonment.

The final product was often threadbare and riddled with typographical and grammatical errors, yet this shabbiness lent the document a palpable credibility. As put by an anonymous Czech writer who went by the pseudonym Josef Strach (the surname translates as "fear"), samizdat publications were

> a medium of communication which looks poor and miserable beside the fantastic rotary press and color television, but which is an unusually powerful and indestructible force. . . . It is written by someone who has something to say. . . . When I take it in my hand, I know that it cost someone a good deal to write it, without an honorarium and at no little risk.[49]

The tattered paper; crude, uneven print; and typographical and grammatical mistakes, amplified by repeated copying, actually increased the appeal and legitimacy of samizdat. At the very least, it was forbidden fruit. The sway of this bohemian shabbiness was so great that it served to delegitimize the slicker official press: the more attractive a book, the less believable it was. A popular Russian anecdote from the 1970s tells of a woman unable to interest her granddaughter in *War and Peace* because it looked "too official"; the grandmother finally gets the girl to read it by laboriously retyping it on cheap paper.

As put by one apparatchik in a private letter to friends,

> A compulsory ideological diet is so tiring that today even an orthodox Soviet bureaucrat would read certain books if they happened to come into his hands. . . . What if *The Gulag Archipelago* was published. . . . How many would buy it? How many copies would be needed? Five, ten, maybe twenty million? A country of censorship does in truth pave the way for a whole army of thankful readers.[50]

Even the mere reading of samizdat could become a complex, conspiratorial activity. While the reproduction cycle for short essays might consume but a few hours, allowing the manufacture of thousands of copies in a week, the duplication of longer essays, novels, and nonfiction took more time; the resulting shortage of larger works led to nocturnal "reading parties" where pages would pass from hand to hand as they were read.[51]

In the Soviet Union, even during the repressive post-Khrushchev era, and particularly in the eastern European satellites, a younger generation— the students Taubman observed asking "sharp questions"—gradually assumed power from the old guard in the 1960s and 1970s. As this younger generation rose through the ranks, perhaps out of a feeling of guilt for their lack of courage compared with the dissidents, they gradually began to court their samizdat-empowered countrymen. By 1980, the process of democratic reform was nigh unstoppable.[52]

In 1956, *Novy Mir* refused to publish Boris Pasternak's masterful *Doctor Zhivago*, which the author had begun not long after the Bolshevik Revolution. The next year, he had it smuggled out of the country; it became a best seller in more than a dozen languages. What did it say about the Soviet Union that the nation's greatest living author had been forced to publish his finest work abroad, and what did that imply about what the Soviets did allow into print? If even the great Pasternak could not get *Doctor Zhivago* published in the Soviet Union, what hope did more daring novelists have of reaching the Russian audience by conventional means? When the authorities threatened Pasternak with expulsion and made him refuse the 1958 Nobel Prize, what did that say about the legitimacy of the regime itself?

Before the 1960s, Pasternak, Solzhenitsyn, and others like them attempted to work within the framework of the Writers' Union; when it finally threw Pasternak and Solzhenitsyn out, in 1958 and 1969, respectively, expulsion became a badge of honor among the Russian literary elite.[53]

The other communication technology that empowered the citizenry of the Soviet Union was radio. How did radio, a centrally controlled, one-way technology that promoted totalitarianism in Nazi Germany, encouraged and choreographed genocide in Rwanda, and arguably concentrated power in the hands of the few even in the United States, help liberate Russians and eastern Europeans?

Figure 8-1. *"I won the Nobel Prize for Literature. What was your crime?"*
Bill Mauldin did not win a Nobel for this 1958 cartoon, but it did earn him a
Pulitzer the next year.

The remarkable answer is that the Soviet Union and Eastern European communist regimes inexplicably flooded their nations with millions
of shortwave devices—machines that actually received foreign broadcasts
better than those transmitted from within their own territory.

Immediately after the 1917 Revolution, the fact that the Soviet
Union's population was largely illiterate mandated an oral means of mass
communication. It would take decades to deploy radio technology in Russia, so the leadership first pressed into service millions of "agitators": farm

and factory workers who served as unpaid, hardworking, problem-solving role models and regularly met with their peers to overcome production obstacles and to transmit the party line to the proletariat. In the 1920s and 1930s, while radio was burgeoning in America and Europe, agit-brigades crisscrossed Russia on agit-trains, performing musical numbers and plays at all stops.

In general, the agitators were neither highly literate nor ideologically sophisticated. They had little formal education; occasionally they might briefly attend special schools or meetings, but by and large they took their cues from party publications such as *Agitator,* which was aimed specifically at them.

In truth, the agitator was a throwback to an almost prehistoric "Dunbar's number" society, where communication occurred face-to-face; by the 1930s, the agitators should have disappeared, but in true Soviet style, this archaic institution persisted almost until the collapse of the Soviet Union.[54]

In the United States and Nazi Germany, by the 1930s radios were household appliances and broadcasts reached most of the population; in contrast, Soviet radio production remained minuscule until well after World War II. The Soviets had also ignored radio for another reason; they had wired farms, factories, and most public spaces with a massive loudspeaker propaganda system that peaked at around thirty-five million outlets in the mid-1960s.

While Stalin lived, few Russians owned radios, and as in Nazi Germany, those who did listened to foreign broadcasts at mortal peril. After Stalin's death, the authorities still frowned when citizens tuned in the Voices, but they rarely punished those who merely listened. To get arrested, a Soviet citizen usually had to take a step beyond simply hearing a foreign broadcast; depending upon the political pendulum, the repetition of foreign radio content, either orally or in print, might or might not result in prison time.[55]

Early in the Cold War, the Voices were of relative unimportance in the Soviet Union. When the Voice of America (VOA) began broadcasting to Russia in 1947, the country had only about 1.3 million shortwave receivers; as late as 1955, it had only about 6 million of them. Had the Soviets been smart, they would have kept it that way. Inexplicably, in the 1960s, they dramatically increased production. The precise reasons why they engaged in such a patently suicidal manufacturing enterprise may never be known. One possible explanation for the decision involves Russia's vast distances and the government's desire to minimize, for reasons of both cost and control, the number of radio transmitters. Alternatively, and more simply, massive centrally planned economies by their very nature tend to make massively irrational decisions; the commissars did not fully appreciate the downside to making the shortwave band the main broadcast conduit.

Whatever the reason, officials commanded the production of millions of sets per year, nearly all capable of receiving the Voices. The commissars had made a colossal, unbelievable blunder: they had given away their monopoly control of this powerful medium and supplied Western broadcast stations with a ready-made audience.

Recall that the Nazis designed only underpowered long- and medium-wave reception (150–1700 kHz) into their *Volksempfänger* and were smart enough not to include shortwave reception. To be sure, the Soviets prohibited the manufacture of sets capable of receiving some of the higher frequencies later used by the Voices, but in a nation amply endowed with engineers and hobbyists, anyone wishing to circumvent this prohibition had little problem doing so. The Bulgarian communist regime selected a devious middle course by offering radio owners free overhauls, after which the sets received only Radio Sofia.[56]

The Soviets compounded their error by developing a news service suffused with turgid ideological cant and so focused on controlling the information flow, particularly from abroad, that it provided the citizenry with almost nothing worth listening to. Frequently, news bulletins were written days or even weeks before being broadcast; why bother with the official radio station when the Voices provided both foreign and domestic news, with greater accuracy and currency?[57]

The West consciously took advantage of these circumstances. The BBC, which had begun its English international service in 1932, began to broadcast in Russian in 1946, and the United States soon followed with the creation of the Voice of America, the equivalent of the BBC foreign service, and "privately funded" services: Radio Free Europe (RFE), aimed at eastern Europe; and Radio Liberty (RL), aimed at the Soviet Union.

The eastern Europeans, being more prosperous and more technologically advanced than the Russians, adopted shortwave sooner. In 1956, workers at the Cegielski factory in Poznań, Poland, rose up and demanded higher wages and the departure of Russian troops. An end to radio jamming was clearly an unvoiced demand, since when the factory's workers took as their stronghold the local radio station, they smashed the transmitters used to jam Radio Free Europe and tossed the pieces out the window.

At the time, the head of RFE's Polish Service was Jan Nowak, the remarkable "courier from Warsaw" who during World War II engaged in a years-long death-defying sojourn among the major centers of resistance to Nazi rule in Poland and London, the seat of the Polish government in exile.[58] Nowak brilliantly handled Poland's informational link to the West during the Poznan revolt. As put by one reformist Communist Party official, "Had RFE not told our people to be calm, I am not sure whether we alone would have managed to cope with the situation."[59]

The events in Poland led to the return to power of the relatively liberal Wladyslaw Gomulka and inspired the Hungarians to implement similar changes; but when the Hungarians' popular reformist leader, Imre Nagy, moved toward a multiparty democracy, declared the nation's neutrality, and withdrew from the Warsaw Pact, the Soviets invaded. RFE served a similar role in Hungary as in Poland, but its Hungarian programming was not as tightly disciplined as that of Nowak's Polish Service; while RFE did not directly incite the violent uprising, many of its broadcasts were later interpreted as giving Hungarians the impression that help from the West was on the way. As put by one observer, "[Never before has radio been] the principal means of communicating internal as well as external facts during a major national uprising."[60]

In 1967, the American left-wing magazine *Ramparts* blew the cover off the funding of RFE and RL, which, in fact, had derived from the Central Intelligence Agency, just as the Soviets had long asserted. Far from discrediting RFE and RL, the CIA connection enhanced their credibility in communist nations, where intelligence services carried greater authority. (The revelation of CIA funding, however, did significant damage to morale at RFE and RL; as put by one staff member, "We were lied to." The revelations also gave opponents of RFE and RL, most notably Senator Fulbright, ammunition in their campaign to close them down. Fortunately, the more conservative members of the Senate Foreign Relations Committee, especially Jesse Helms, prevailed.)[61] Other Western sources penetrated behind the Iron Curtain, most prominently Deutsche Welle, Vatican Radio, and Radio in the American Sector (RIAS), which broadcast from West Berlin and West Germany. By 1975, the Russian factories had churned out an astounding fifty million shortwave sets, enough for nearly every household in the Soviet Union.

During the Cold War, Western governments and academics conducted surveys of visitors and emigrants from the Communist bloc that demonstrated that they trusted the Voices far more than the domestic media. These data were confirmed after 1991, when researchers gained access to secret internal Russian polls. Listeners were impressed with the speed and accuracy of Western broadcasts, and especially by their willingness to air unfavorable news. A classic example was a Bulgarian-language BBC report of an ink bottle thrown at Prime Minister Thatcher during a visit to West Germany: the story gained widespread currency among Bulgarian listeners, who could not imagine their domestic media reporting such an attack on one of their own leaders.[62]

The Communist bloc could respond to this barrage of outside broadcasts in one of three ways: by improving its own news coverage, by attempting to modify through diplomatic means the content of Western broadcasts, or by jamming the Voices. At one time or another, it tried all three.

The Soviets did gradually improve the timeliness and accuracy of their reporting, but as the Chernobyl meltdown demonstrated, this improvement was too little, too late.

Likewise, the Russians had little diplomatic leverage with which to tone down the Voices, and even if they could have done so, it would have done them little good, as the Voices derived most of their legitimacy from their evenhandedness. What did the most damage to the credibility of the Soviet Union and its satellites was not so much unfavorable news about them, but rather the glaring contrast in accuracy and promptness between the Voices and the domestic media. The more strident the programming, the less the credibility; among Hungarian listeners, 21 percent found the more hard-edged, CIA-funded RFE unreliable, versus only 4 percent for the VOA and 2 percent for the BBC.[63]

That left jamming the broadcasts, a measure to which the Soviets and Eastern Europeans devoted vast resources. The Soviets started interfering with the Voice of America almost as soon as it initiated its Russian-language service in 1947. Then they began jamming the other Voices as well. By 1958, the Russians were expending more resources on jamming than on their own domestic and foreign broadcasts. A report to the Central Committee dryly noted that while at any one time about 50 or 60 Voices stations were broadcasting to Russia, they were answered by 1,660 jamming stations with a total power output of over fifteen megawatts. (Ironically, history's first known jamming was aimed by the Nazis against *Soviet* war broadcasts. The Soviets' reports of the adulterous affairs of the Third Reich's leaders especially irked the Nazi hierarchy.)

Complete blocking of all the Voices' broadcasts proved impossible. As with any long-distance shortwave radio broadcast, jamming was accomplished with a sky wave bounced off the ionosphere; this method did cover a very wide area, but it was also spotty and relatively ineffective. Sky-wave jamming also suffered from "twilight immunity": late in the afternoon, broadcast signals of certain frequencies from the west, which was still in daylight, were bounced back to earth from the ionosphere, but the jamming signals in the east, transmitted in darkness, penetrated through the ionosphere, and thus allowed for an approximately two-hour period around sunset of relatively clear reception. Jammers also used a direct, line-of-sight ground wave; this was highly effective, but only over a small area.

In practice, the Soviets broadcast sky-wave jamming signals over the entire country, and ground-wave signals over urban areas, and even in the local rural areas where the more better-connected intelligentsia had their dachas.

The Soviets and their allies succeeded only in making radio reception of the Voices challenging enough to increase their appeal as forbidden fruit. The Voices could still be heard by several different techniques: listening at just the right time of day, changing channels every few minutes, or carrying a receiver into the countryside.[64] In the early 1950s, during the most intense period of jamming, researchers estimated that between 5 and 12 percent of broadcasts could be heard—just enough to increase the allure of tuning in and the perceived value of the programs that got through, but not enough to discourage citizens in the Eastern bloc from trying.

Of Soviet visitors to the 1958 Brussels World Fair—admittedly an elite, but also a loyal, communist group—92 percent admitted listening to the Voices. When Boris Pasternak, who had been made an unperson when he received the Nobel Prize for Literature in 1958, died in 1961, thousands of Russians, who had heard of his death from the BBC, streamed into the small writers' village of Peredelkino, where he had a dacha, to attend his funeral.[65]

Research by the KGB showed that the BBC and VOA could be heard even at certain locations in Moscow, Kiev, and Leningrad. The KGB report also lamented the massive production of shortwave receivers: "It is enough to point out that at present, up to 85 percent of shortwave receivers are located in the European part of the USSR, *where our own shortwave broadcasts cannot be heard and where it is possible to listen only to hostile radio*" (italics added). By the 1970s, the Voices could be easily heard throughout even the largest Russian cities.[66]

As if that were not enough, only 15 percent of German sets, and a minuscule 0.1 percent of American radio receivers, were equipped to receive Soviet shortwave broadcasts.[67] (The author's parents owned one of these rare American sets, which provided him with the occasional thrill of distant reception and reliable amusement at the constant stream of turgid Marxist rhetoric.)

The ebb and flow between Russian reformers and hard-liners and United States–Soviet Union relations dictated the intensity of jamming. Khrushchev dialed it down during his rule, only to temporarily ratchet it back up in May 1960 when Soviet missiles downed a U-2 spy plane. After that year, the Soviets again reduced jamming, and in particular allowed broadcasts when they wished their public to receive certain news that was too sensitive for domestic stations. For example, the Soviet Union did not report its own atmospheric nuclear tests, but intentionally allowed its citizens to hear about them from the Voices. Likewise, the Soviets despised the East Germans, but could not directly attack them in their own media; when the Voices broadcast news that reflected poorly on East Germany, the Soviets stopped jamming.

In June 1963, John Kennedy gave his famous American University speech calling for a de-escalation of the Cold War, after which all jamming ceased. At the same time, in an effort to compete with the Voices, the Soviets revamped their media, most notably with a round-the-clock news station, *Mayak,* and a few years later with increased television production and a lively TV news program, *Vremya* ("Time"), modeled on Western news shows.[68]

The Soviet Union's most bizarre competitive effort soon followed. By 1966 it had become apparent that radio and television had rendered the agitator obsolete. Rather than let the institution wither and die, the Soviets layered on top of it a new, improved version, the "politinformators":

literate, well-educated performers, under the direct supervision of party organs. They were specifically tasked with counteracting the Voices' influence. At least a million were "trained," but more often than not, workers perceived them as stooges of Central Committees, and their performances at meetings often consisted of verbatim readings from party newspapers. Soon, they became a laughingstock. Like the agitator, however, the politinformator persisted almost until the fall of the Soviet Union.[69] The Soviets calculated that livelier radio and TV broadcasting and politinformators would compete successfully with Western media. Instead, they set in motion a series of events that fatally crippled their credibility and, ultimately, communist rule in Europe.

In early 1964—months before Khrushchev's fall from power—the Soviet hard-liners fired the "opening shot" in their campaign against dissident literature with the trial of poet Joseph Brodsky. His work was both lyrical and entirely nonpolitical, and his trial was a Kafkaesque witch hunt famous for this exchange between the judge and the defendant:

> Judge: And what is your real trade?
> Brodsky: I'm a poet and a translator of poetry.
> Judge: Who has recognized you as a poet? Who has given you a place among the poets?
> Brodsky: No one. And who gave me a place among the human race?
> Judge: Did you learn that?
> Brodsky: What?
> Judge: To be poet. You didn't attempt to go to a university, where people are trained, where they're taught?
> Brodsky: I didn't think that could be done by training.
> Judge: By what, then?
> Brodsky: I thought that by God.[70]

But for the courage and determination of a woman named Frida Vigdorova, Brodsky's trial would never have come to light, and he might have disappeared into the Gulag without a trace. A small, timid woman, initially so meek and orthodox that she was elected to a regional party committee, she possessed a remarkable moral sense and fought for those she saw as wronged by the system: a battered woman, a family unfairly crammed into a tiny communal apartment, or a schoolboy unfairly smeared by lies. When asked why she helped the boy, she replied simply, "He is a person to me."

When, in February 1964, Brodsky, whom she did not know, went on trial, she attended. When the judge shouted at her to stop taking notes, Vigdorova replied that she was a journalist and a member of the Writers' Union. When the judge continued to shout at her, she took notes of that, too. Her transcript eventually found its way abroad, where it was broadcast by the Voices back to the Soviet Union.[71] A firestorm of protest from the cream of the Western intelligentsia, including Jean-Paul Sartre, ensued and resulted in Brodsky's release after eighteen months of hard labor in the Arctic north. In 1972 he was exiled to the West, and in 1987 he received the Nobel Prize for Literature.

Although Vigdorova's transcript made the Brodsky trial a high-profile event, it had relatively few long-lasting repercussions. At the time the poet was twenty-three years old and almost completely unknown, and the authorities prosecuted him not for the content of his poetry but for "social parasitism," a catchall Soviet phrase for the avoidance of useful work. The publication and broadcast of the transcript did not occur until after the trial was long over, and so could not provoke protest during the trial itself. Two years later, that would change with the trials of Andrei Sinyavsky and Yuli Daniel, which set in motion a sequence of trials and protests that destroyed what little remained of the regime's international and domestic credibility.

Sinyavsky was born in 1925; after serving in the Russian army in World War II, he studied at Moscow University. Like many Soviet citizens of his age, he began his young life as a dedicated communist, but in 1951 his father was arrested by the secret police. Five years later Sinyavsky, like many Russians, was moved to outrage by the revelations of Stalin's brutality in Khrushchev's "secret speech."

His disillusionment impelled him to write; under the pseudonym Abram Tertz, Sinyavsky produced the three works for which he was tried: *Lyubimov,* a gentle satire of a small-town Soviet demagogue; *On Socialist Realism,* a stuffy analysis of literary theory; and *The Trial Begins,* a phantasmagorical account of a tribunal modeled loosely on the Stalinist "Doctors' Plot," which was Stalin's final, paranoid act of persecution—the show trials of Jewish physicians on fabricated charges of conspiracy to kill the Soviet leadership.[72]

Yuli Daniel, also born in 1925, was Jewish and had served with distinction in the war, after which he was pensioned off because of a combat injury. Whereas Sinyavsky had published in the official media, including *Novy Mir,* Daniel was far less well known, having been unsuccessful in getting literary exposure in a "legal" venue. However, he did achieve several foreign publications via the samizdat-tamizdat route, under the pseudonym Nikolai Arzhak. One of these, a satire titled *This Is Moscow Speaking,* involved an official proclamation of "Murder Day," an eighteen-hour period during which each Soviet citizen was allowed to kill anyone, as long as the victim was not a policeman, a soldier, or an apparatchik. This story so enraged the prosecutors that they decided to try Daniel alongside the better-known Sinyavsky.

The authorities had both men arrested in September 1965, and tried five months later in the Supreme Court of the Russian Republic under the infamous Article 70 of the republic's code. Under this law, anyone could be prosecuted for "agitation or propaganda with the purpose of subverting or weakening the Soviet regime." Although the proceedings harked back to Stalin's show trials, three things about them were different. First, in spite of the authorities' attempt to pack the court with supporters of the regime, someone in the courtroom, perhaps a relative of one of the accused, had smuggled in a tape recorder, from which a nearly complete transcript was later assembled; second, the defendants pleaded not guilty; and third, unlike Brodsky, the two were tried for the *content* of their work. Never before had Soviet prosecutors gone after anyone for writing fiction (although to be sure, many writers, such as Mandelstam, had been exiled, imprisoned, and even executed under other pretexts).[73] After four days of farcical proceedings, the court duly convicted and sentenced them, Sinyavsky to seven years of "strict regime," Daniel to five.

Sinyavsky's and Daniel's real crime had been to publish their pseudonymous works abroad, and as with Brodsky, it would be from abroad that the blowback came, but with one essential difference: with Sinyavsky and Daniel, the protest came in real time. Almost from the moment of their arrest, their family and friends had tumbled to the fact that they could generate domestic support by conveying information via foreign correspondents to the Voices, which would then broadcast the story of the trial to the Soviet Union. The authorities, who had not fully absorbed that a high percentage of Russians regularly listened to the Voices, were faced with a unique, terrifying scenario: even on the trial's first day, about fifty supporters, drawn by the foreign radio broadcast coverage, converged on the courtroom. Each evening, Russians tuned into the Voices for news of the trial, and each successive morning, ever-larger crowds consisting of both supporters and foreign reporters assembled. From time to time, both groups would unobtrusively steal away to a local café where the former fed the latter *pelmeni*—delicious hot dumplings to fight both hunger and the bitter cold—and information.[74]

Further fireworks were not long in coming from abroad, where the greatest names in literature, respected in Russia in a way few Westerners understood, spoke out against the trial. So as not to alarm the authorities, when Daniel's wife Larisa visited him in prison, she veiled the strength of foreign support behind this message to her husband: "Grandmother Lillian Hellman asked me to say hello. Uncle Bert Russell also sends his regards. Your nephew, Günter Grass, talks about you a lot, and so does his younger brother, little Norman Mailer." Observed Daniel's guard, "It's nice that you Jewish people have such large families."[75]

Even the Western communist parties denounced the proceedings. Complained the leader of the British party, John Gollan, "Justice should not only be done but should be seen to be done. Unfortunately, this cannot be said in the case of this trial."[76]

Next came Taubman's students' "sharp questioners." When a professor at Moscow University affixed his name to a letter supporting the convictions, his students asked him whether he had signed under duress. Had he answered yes, they would have forgiven him; when he admitted that he had signed it voluntarily, they walked out of his class. Even the president of the court of the Soviet Union itself (as distinguished from that of the Russian Republic, which held the trial) criticized the tribunal's conduct.[77]

Two writers, Alexander Ginzburg and Yuri Galanskov, in their turn compiled *The White Book,* a samizdat four-hundred-page transcript of the Sinyavsky-Daniel trial proceedings, along with other related documents; in 1967, they and two associates found themselves prosecuted for these. The court sentenced all four to long terms the next year in a proceeding dubbed "The Trial of the Four." Ginzburg served his time and was later exiled to the United States, but Galanskov died after prison authorities ignored his bleeding ulcers; just before his demise he wrote home, "They are doing everything to hasten my death."[78]

The "Trial of the Four" duly attracted its own foreign broadcasts and domestic supporters, one of whom, the young dissident Vladimir Bukovsky, was himself arrested, tried, and sentenced to three years at forced labor for his efforts. Bukovsky, who was actually sentenced before "The Four," was by that point no stranger to the penal system, having been sent to various psychiatric facilities in 1965 for copying a book by the Yugoslav dissident Milovan Djilas and for demonstrating at the Sinyavsky-Daniel trial. Bukovsky conducted protests and hunger strikes in prison and was delighted when his guards relayed reports of his actions that they had heard a few days later on the BBC or RL.[79]

Apparently, prison personnel also listened avidly to the Voices. When dissident Andrei Amalrik wound up in the Gulag in the early 1970s, he became deathly ill with a severe ear infection and meningitis. The prison doctor took an instant dislike to Amalrik because of his political crimes and spoke poorly of him to the dispensary staff, who then relayed her comments back to Amalrik. When he confronted the doctor about her unprofessional behavior, she repeated her insults and then shouted at him, "Why does the Voice of America talk about you and not about me?"[80]

The Bukovsky trial eventually drew in a physicist named Pavel Litvinov. Even among Soviet dissidents of the period, Litvinov stood out: tall, good-looking, fearless, and—most gallingly of all to the authorities—a child of Soviet privilege with a venerated, instantly recognizable surname. In the 1930s, his grandfather Maxim Litvinov served as foreign minister. Almost alone among Soviet officials, Litvinov candidly offered Stalin his unfiltered opinions; immediately after Germany's June 1941 attack, he made a famous radio broadcast that all but upbraided Stalin for trusting Hitler. Even more remarkably, on another occasion he explicitly warned an American correspondent that acceding to Stalin's demands would only lead to others. Exactly how he survived, in fact, is something of a mystery. In the words of Molotov, "Litvinov remained among the living only by chance."[81]

Pavel inherited his grandfather's courage. Like most young people of his era, he was a committed Marxist. He was thirteen years old when Stalin died, and when older family members celebrated the tyrant's death and told jokes, Pavel ran from the room crying. While still a believer at age twenty, he befriended Alexander Ginzburg, and when Ginzburg was arrested seven years later, he felt the need to respond.[82] When Bukovsky and a codefendant were tried shortly thereafter, Litvinov transcribed the proceedings, and after being warned by a KGB agent not to publish them, he sent a transcript of his conversation with the KGB agent in question to *Isvestia* and multiple foreign newspapers. The agent told Litvinov, "Imagine what would happen if the entire world found out that the grandson of the great diplomat is involved in such affairs. That would mar his memory." Litvinov replied, "I don't think Grandfather would take offense. Am I free to leave?" The conversation with the agent didn't make it into any of the local newspapers, but millions of Russians heard about it over the Voices.[83]

By 1968, the Soviets were losing the radio battle with the West and so responded in the only way they knew: they resumed jamming. In the five years since jamming had stopped in 1963, the commissars had ordered the production of tens of millions more shortwave receivers. Interference with the Voices only increased their allure and credibility to Soviet citizens, almost all of who could now receive them.

As the 1960s gave way to the 1970s, the literary persecutions continued. In 1968, a Latvian collective farm chairman, Ivan Iakhimovich, wrote a samizdat essay protesting against the Ginzburg-Galanzkov trial and was sent to a psychiatric facility; Bukovsky wrote an essay about Iakhimovich's arrest in which he excoriated the practice of sending dissidents to lunatic asylums. When Bukovsky circulated it in samizdat and had it smuggled abroad, he was duly tried and imprisoned in 1972, all in the radio frequency glare of the Voices. A few years later, he cowrote *A Manual on Psychiatry for Dissenters,* which described how to behave in order to avoid commitment to the Gulag's asylums.[84]

The effect of the literary and journalistic storm that roiled the Soviet Union for nearly two decades after the Sinyavsky-Daniel trial is difficult to exaggerate. As put by Ludmilla Alexeyeva, a prominent dissident who was forced to emigrate in 1977, then returned to Russia in 1993 to continue her human rights work,

> Political trials in Moscow, Leningrad, Vilnius, and Kiev received coverage by virtually every Western news organization in the Soviet Union. Those dispatches were then broadcast back into the USSR over the Voice of America, Radio Liberty, the BBC, the Deutsche Welle, and other shortwave radio stations. Their listeners in the USSR numbered in the tens of millions. Thanks to those broadcasts, thousands of wronged and disaffected people nationwide learned that . . . it was possible to use our Moscow samizdat and our Western-press connections to bring *glasnost* to their struggles.[85]

At about the same time that the Sinyavsky-Daniel episode was mushrooming out of control, the samizdat/Voices echo chamber amplified other strains of dissent. One was the transformation of Aleksandr Solzhenitsyn into the national conscience of Russia. Like many of the Soviet Union's World War II veterans, he had been sent by Stalin's apparatus to the Gulag soon after discharge (in his case, for criticizing Stalin's wartime military strategy). After Solzhenitsyn's 1953 release into central Asian exile, he was told he had an advanced malignancy and had but a few weeks to live. He quickly scribbled his unwritten, memorized novels onto tiny scrolls, inserted them into a champagne bottle, and buried it in his garden; when his cancer unexpectedly entered remission, he recovered them.

Suddenly, he had the leisure to write out and keep whole drafts. Still, as an exile, he knew he would be searched, so he learned to microfilm. When he had finished an early manuscript that could not be published in the Soviet Union, he had a fellow exile, a surgeon with skilled hands, expertly insert the tiny film into the covers of a book.

At that early stage of his literary career, he had no contacts in the West, so he sent this book to the only person he could think of in the United States: Aleksandra Tolstoy, the great novelist's daughter. While most writers measured their output in words or pages, Solzhenitsyn measured his volume, quite literally, in cubic centimeters to be hidden, then destroyed after the microfilming was done.[86]

The government relentlessly pursued Solzhenitsyn, who had been working for some time on several books, most notably his massive three-volume history of Stalin's sprawling prison system, *The Gulag Archipelago.*

The publication of this landmark work is a saga unto itself; it took ten years to finish, and like all of the books Solzhenitsyn wrote in the decade after Khrushchev's ouster, it involved dozens of accomplices who edited, translated, typed carbon copies, and microfilmed the work in progress. By his own description, the clandestine process

> involved constant games of hide-and-seek: there were times when you could not deliver texts, places you could not leave them, telephones you must not use, and ceilings beneath which you were not supposed to speak. You could not keep the typed texts in your apartment, the used carbon paper had to be burned, and for all correspondence you had to depend on direct delivery by friends, since the regular mails were out of the question.[87]

By the late 1960s, the author had mastered the complex cloak-and-dagger tango that enabled him to complete the daunting project under the KGB's nose. In the guise of making social calls, he worked in numerous apartments and took care to make multiple, widely distributed fragmentary copies so that the entire effort would not be compromised in a single raid. While more advanced printing technologies were available to the author, he dared not risk their larger footprint; on one occasion, the famous cellist Mstislav Rostropovich, a personal friend, gave him a stencil duplicator. Solzhenitsyn simply referred to it with an exclamation point and italics, as a "*whirly printer!*" The contraption was too hot to handle: "We were at a loss about what to do with this whirly-thing of ours and had to think of someone we could give it to for printing leaflets." (Its eventual recipients, friends of friends, ultimately destroyed it, fearing a police raid.)[88]

Despite Solzhenitsyn's meticulous tradecraft, the authorities seized and tortured one of his typists, Elizaveta Voronyanskaya, who had falsely assured the author that she had destroyed a complete copy of *Gulag* after microfilming. Under torture, she produced the hidden copy; a few weeks after her August 1973 release from prison, she hanged herself.

By that point, *Gulag* had been finished for five years, but Solzhenitsyn had hesitated to publish it abroad for fear of exposing his collaborators. Voronyanskaya's arrest and suicide added urgency to publication, and the author quickly smuggled at least two copies abroad, where the first of three Russian-language volumes was published in Paris by the YMCA Press in late 1973, then translated into English and French in early 1974. Solzhenitsyn shortly found himself arrested once again, then deported. His main "courier," Natalya Stolyarova, smuggled manuscripts not only from Solzhenitsyn to the West before his deportation, but also *to* him in the West afterward.[89]

No single piece of literature did more to discredit the Soviet Union, either domestically or abroad, than *Gulag*. Almost immediately after Voronyanskaya's suicide, samizdat versions began to circulate in the Soviet Union, and after the YMCA Press's edition was issued, the Voices broadcast readings from it: Radio Free Europe and Radio Liberty did so almost continuously, although Voice of America, wishing not to appear too anti-Soviet, did so more sparingly. In turn, samizdat editions produced from these broadcasts began to circulate widely in the Soviet Union and eastern Europe; at least one listener was sentenced to a psychiatric facility for producing transcripts.[90]

The same year that *Gulag* was published in the West, a loosely organized group of intellectuals established *The Chronicle of Current Events*.
This publication, named after a Russian-language BBC program, specialized in exposing human rights violations, especially arrests, imprisonments,
and house searches. Except for an eighteen-month hiatus in the early 1970s,
it published more or less continuously until 1983; after a time, English-
language translations were often reproduced abroad, and today they are
available in the libraries of most large Western universities.

If the Soviets shot themselves in the right foot by producing too
many shortwave receivers, they then did so in the left foot by producing
too many tape recorders. Moderate-size reel-to-reel machines became
widely available in the West in the 1950s, and the Soviet Union followed
about a decade later; it produced over one hundred thousand in 1960, and
over one million in 1970.[91]

The most common type, the Yauza, was a characteristically clunky,
unreliable Soviet device, and the tape itself was similarly of low quality;
with even moderate use, it stretched and broke, and the Russian audiophile
necessarily acquired skill at splicing and repair. Still, a Yauza, or more accurately, Yauzas jacked together, constituted a potent copying mechanism;
whereas a skilled typist might produce several samizdat essay copies in a
day of intense labor, an unskilled audiophile could copy tape reels almost
automatically; better yet, the supply of Yauzas greatly exceeded that of
skilled and willing typists.[92]

Because of the ease of tape recording, the volume of *magnitizat* exceeded, likely by an order of magnitude, that of samizdat, but its message
was softer: songs, or more accurately, poetry sung by the poet accompanied
by an out-of-tune guitar and listened to late at night in cramped smoke-filled
apartments with friends. As with samizdat, the amateurishness of both the
content and the setting of *magnitizat* burnished its authority to a high gloss.

Typical of the medium was Alexander Galich. Born in approximately
1918, he began composing poetry as a youth, then took up acting. Early in
his career, during the war, he performed for frontline troops; later, he succeeded as a dramatist, and even became wealthy in the process. But as so
often happened in that era, he became disenchanted with Soviet society in
the wake of the "secret speech," and his poems took on a harder edge; in
1968, the authorities essentially banned this previously successful actor from
public performances, and in 1971 they expelled him from the Writers' Union.

He titled one typical song poem "Fame Is the Spur." It is a complex song within a song, in which he takes the role of a dissolute performer playing in an apartment for some friends. The performer tells a story reminiscent of Solzhenitsyn's *Cancer Ward* experience—an ex-prison guard and one of his ex-prisoners are slowly dying together in the hospital and form a bond: "Him, he used to be a screw, I a number / Now we can't get by without one another / We compare sarcomas, they run the show now / You were slippery, you were sly, you politicals / What a fool I must have been not to nail you!" The guard succumbs first; in faraway Moscow, the prisoner's son and the guard's daughter walk arm in arm through the snow. Then, Galich's song poem switches back to the scene in the apartment. The song within the song ends; the guests are silent for a minute, then continue drinking; the "outer song" ends with a KGB informant neighbor taping the activities on his recorder.[93]

Galich also could have a lighter touch: in the hilarious "Red Triangle," a union boss travels abroad, and her husband, who works at the same factory, cheats on her. Caught, he begs forgiveness, and she retorts, "No use eating humble pie, you'll be telling / Everything what's happened at the Party meeting!" Their comrades, after discussing socialism in Ghana, come around to their marital troubles, and "I confessed the rotten West had been sapping / The foundations of my moral conceptions." In the end, the committee lets the miscreant off with a mild reprimand and orders the couple to reconcile, and so they do, "We drank a toast (her wine, and me vodka) / to our model Soviet family relations!"[94]

The Communist Party did not, in general, take *magnitizat* as seriously as it did samizdat; when the police raided an apartment, they usually returned the former and kept the latter. The Voices certainly paid attention; Radio Liberty devoted several programs per week to *magnitizat* smuggled to it by tourists and émigrés.[95] The authorities did, on the other hand, view Galich seriously enough; in 1974 they gave him twenty-four hours to pack up and get out of the Soviet Union. The next year, he was electrocuted in Paris as he plugged in a new tape recorder at home. The French police labeled it an accident, but many Russians were not so sure.

How much *magnitizat* eroded the legitimacy of Soviet authority is anyone's guess, but one should never underestimate the power of poetry and music. An East German acquaintance explained his disenchantment with communism thus: The son of Greek communist parents who were forced to flee their native land in the late 1940s, he went with them to East Germany, where he grew up a dedicated socialist and trained as a journalist. East Germans had open access to West German radio and television, and as a young man he succumbed to the pull of capitalist music. One song in particular, the Beatles' "Come Together," caught his fancy, and he often listened for an entire week to enjoy a single playing. One day, he asked himself, "What is wrong with communism that it forbids me a simple rock and roll song?"[96] On that day, there was one less East German Marxist.

In the 1970s, the influence of samizdat grew as it traveled to Hungary, Poland, and Czechoslovakia, where it attained a degree of sophistication unimaginable in the more repressive and backward Soviet Union. Polish dissidents had access to printing presses; they even organized an insurance fund that paid off losses when police confiscated supplies and equipment.

Because of Poland's proximity to the West, its citizens had easier access to the Voices. In the early 1980s, the United States, operating under a National Security Decision Directive by Ronald Reagan, undertook the smuggling of small shortwave sets into Poland, where one device found its way into a unique hiding place: the extravagant beard of an imprisoned dissident, Alexander Malachowski, who tuned it to the BBC.[97] Lech Walesa also managed shortwave reception during his 1981–1982 incarceration under martial law. According to his wife, when she visited him,

> I was surprised to find that Lech had a shortwave radio on which he
> could listen to the Polish-language broadcasts from the West. He was
> constantly listening to Radio Free Europe, the Voice of America, the
> BBC, whatever he could get, and he drove the guards so crazy that
> after a while they announced that the radio was broken. . . . One of
> the guards complained that it gave him migraines. Lech sat at the
> radio all day long, fiddling with the knob.[98]

The guards had altered the radio to eliminate shortwave reception, but they forgot that Walesa was a master electrician; shortly thereafter, he was back listening to foreign broadcasts, this time on the long-wave band. Soon enough, he too became the recipient of one of Reagan's miniature shortwave radios.[99]

The Czechs also made extensive use of samizdat and shortwave radio. The roots of their ultimately successful dissidence lay in three events: the brutal repression of the Prague Spring by Soviet troops in August 1968; the Helsinki Accords signed in August 1975; and, bizarrely, a riotous wedding and a rock group named The Plastic People of the Universe.

On January 5, 1968, the reformist Alexander Dubcek rose to power; he quickly loosened the government's restraints on travel, speech, and political activity, and even promised to establish a multiparty democracy. The head of the KGB, Yuri Andropov, seared by his experience as the Soviet ambassador in Budapest in 1956, concocted a nonexistent conspiracy among the CIA, NATO, and Dubcek, which led to the August 1968 invasion of Czechoslovakia by the Warsaw Pact. It overthrew Dubcek, who was shuffled off to Turkey as ambassador.

Sporadic protests followed the invasion, most memorably in early 1969 when a student at Charles University, Jan Palach, immolated himself in Wenceslas Square. Around the same time, the newly organized Plastic People began playing gigs around Prague. Initially, the rock group imitated the then current vogue of Western psychedelic music, but it soon segued into religious and social commentary and so attracted official wrath.

When the group's artistic director, a poet and Charles University graduate named Ivan Jirous, celebrated his wedding in February 1976 in a small village south of Prague, the Plastic People and other rock musicians entertained the four hundred guests for twelve hours. It was all too much for the authorities, who interrogated about a hundred of the attendees and arrested twenty, including Jirous and the entire Plastic People band. A series of opera bouffe trials ensued, revolving mainly around allegations of the band's bathroom humor. The scope of the trials encompassed not only the wedding celebration, but also the band's prior performances; Jirous received an eighteen-month sentence, the saxophonist received eight months, and other band members were forced into exile.

Many of the nation's foremost intellectuals, including playwright Václav Havel, attended the rock band's trials; they were outraged, not only because the government had made a mockery of the law, but also because the tribunals directly contravened the recent Helsinki Accords. The agreement, which had been signed less than a year before, promised freedom of "thought, conscience, religion, or belief" in the Soviet Union and eastern Europe. (In return, it conferred legitimacy on Europe's 1945 borders, most significantly the westward shift of Poland and the Soviet

Union's 1940 occupation of the Baltic republics.) Havel and his colleagues drafted the Charter 77 initiative, which demanded that the communist leadership adhere to the Accords' human rights stipulations, to say nothing of the nation's own constitution and laws.

On the night of January 6, 1977—Twelfth Night—the Prague police intercepted an automobile driven by actor and playwright Pavel Pandovský and containing Havel, novelist Ludvík Vaculík, and 250 envelopes stuffed with copies of the group's manifesto awaiting the signatures of its members. The occupants were questioned and released, but the envelopes were seized.

No matter: Charter 77 reached its destinations the very next day via the *Frankfurter Allgemeine Zeitung* (the direct descendant of the newspaper the Nazis had left untouched until nearly the end of their regime), and thence through the Voices.[100]

In 1980, the Voices began broadcasting news of the labor strikes in Poland. The Soviets, who had once again stopped jamming in 1973, restarted it, but in vain: the broadcasts that got through led to similar strikes in factories and mines all over the Soviet Union. Comically, the Soviet leadership treated transcripts of the Western broadcasts as state secrets, in spite of the fact that they were heard through the interference by millions of Russians. Being on the government's circulation list of the transcripts, which were usually delivered by an armed guard, was considered a high honor; ironically, the people who were in the best position to effect reform were precisely the ones who got the reports. As put by historian Michael Nelson, "The fish rotted from the head."[101]

Indeed, by the 1970s, many Soviet leaders privately accepted Norbert Wiener's assertion, "[The] demand for secrecy is scarcely more than the wish of a sick civilization not to learn the progress of its own disease."[102] By this point, the more thoughtful Soviet Politburo and Central Committee members, even if they denied the need for expanding individual liberties, clearly saw that their economies were falling behind those in the West because of the way their societies handled information. Prime among these reformers was Andropov's protégé, Mikhail Gorbachev. Almost immediately after becoming general secretary in 1982, Andropov fell ill with kidney failure; although he had designated Gorbachev as his successor, he was so incapacitated during his last year of life that when he finally died in 1984, the Politburo was able to suppress his written political will and replace him with Konstantin Chernenko, who would serve for only thirteen months before his death finally allowed Gorbachev to assume power.

At first, the new general secretary acted cautiously; in August 1987 several thousand Latvians publicly mourned the forty-eighth anniversary of the infamous Molotov-Ribbentrop Pact, which had handed the Baltic republics over to Stalin. The demonstration's organizers credited the Voices with informing the populace of its time and place; said one, "Those who want to arrange a demonstration don't have the possibility to get out their information, so, of course, the role of the radios is very big."[103] Gorbachev responded by bitterly criticizing the Western radio stations.

Then, a few months later, Gorbachev opened the floodgates of glasnost: in October Senator Moynihan told 150 million Soviet television viewers that they lived in "human rights hell," and the jamming was ended for good.[104] Suddenly, the flow of reform in the communist block reversed: before 1987, it had flowed from west to east, from the rapidly reforming satellite countries, Poland and Hungary, to Russia; after 1987, it flowed from Russia to the more repressive regimes in Czechoslovakia, East Germany, Romania, and Bulgaria.

From that point on, revolution surged through ever more complex channels and more technologically advanced mass communication. By the mid-1980s, Hungary, like Poland, had liberalized its media coverage and Hungarian TV told East Germans the best escape routes. Viewers in Czechoslovakia began to tune in Soviet programming, which had suddenly become more appealing than their dull domestic fare.

A bizarre episode worthy of Czechoslovakia's talented novelists triggered the sudden end of communism in that nation. On November 17, 1989, thousands of students marched in Prague; unbeknownst to them, they had been infiltrated by a police lieutenant, Ludvik Zifcac, who led them into a dead-end trap. Hundreds were injured in the ensuing police riot, in which Zifcac faked his death by falling to the ground; his police compatriots covered his "body" with a blanket and carried him off.

The ruse backfired horribly. VOA and RFE both reported that a student had been killed, and their broadcasts brought hundreds of thousands of protesters out into the street in the following days. Eleven days later, the regime stepped down. (When Zifcac turned up very much alive, he was prosecuted by the nation's new democratic rulers for abusing his power as a police officer.)[105]

Meanwhile, the Romanian government, under the dictator Nicolae Ceauşescu, had not been liberalized. Romania was, however, home to three million Hungarians, many of whom could receive Hungarian radio and television broadcasts. When the uprising against Ceauşescu began in earnest in December 1989, a new personal communications tool made its appearance on the stage of history. When security forces came to arrest the Romanian reformist Father Lázló Tőkés at his church in Timisoara, a bloody battle ensued. To the horror of the regime, footage of the carnage at the church was almost instantaneously broadcast from Hungarian television to Romanian viewers. How, they wondered, had the Hungarians gotten hold of the footage? Simple: several months before, a Hungarian journalist had left a lightweight video camera with Father Tőkés, anticipating such an eventuality.

Two years later, the final curtain fell on communism in the Soviet Union. On August 19, 1991, Russian hard-line plotters rose up in a coup against Mikhail Gorbachev. They failed to realize that the media cards had been stacked against them. Although the conspirators had physically seized the television broadcast facilities at Ostankino, with its 1,770-foot tower, they did not command the hearts and souls of its journalists and producers, who had long since been captured by the spirit of glasnost.

The television spectacle that followed floored Soviet as well as international viewers. The plotters replaced the lively give-and-take that had come to characterize the new Soviet news programs with stilted announcements loaded with the Communist Party jargon of yesteryear. On the afternoon of August 19, the plotters, in an unexplainable lapse, appeared at a news conference, a format that itself was the child of glasnost.

Oddly, of the eight conspirators, its least powerful and most reluctant member, Gennady Yanaev, took most of the questions and so became a symbol of the old regime's illegitimacy. The television camera is a relentless, heartless engine that can, in the hands of a skilled practitioner, reduce complex events into a single, instant, telling image, as it did with Richard Nixon's five o'clock shadow during the 1960 presidential debate.

On the afternoon of August 19, 1991, Elena Pozdniak, *Vremya*'s experienced producer, made the best of this distinctive power of television. For years she had edited Leonid Brezhnev's tics, stutters, and visual miscues out of his appearances; this time, she would do the opposite to the conspirators. Although Yanaev had a booming, authoritative voice, his nose ran and his hands shook. Pozdniak framed Yanaev's image in a way that amplified those faults and so evoked the old Russian adage, "Trembling hands give away the chicken thief." The correspondents present piled on question upon question; one pointedly inquired as to the state of Yanaev's health; and another, Tatiana Malkina, even more brashly asked if the plotters fully understood that they had executed an illegal coup d'état. While Yanaev responded, Pozdniak switched to a close-up of Malkina's disdainful face.

KGB and army commanders watched this performance with incredulity; those sitting on the fence threw their weight to Gorbachev and Yeltsin, while many who supported the plotters realized that they had backed the wrong horse.

Vremya reporter Sergei Medvedev, in a television performance that would have done Dan Rather proud, strode to the Russian White House, where he covered Boris Yeltsin issuing defiant speeches to his supporters and preparing for the onslaught. Medvedev's editors spliced into his broadcast the now famous video of Yeltsin defiantly standing on top of tank No. 110, an image that evoked Lenin's 1917 Finland Station speech from atop an armored car. While Medvedev's cameramen had filmed a great deal of the footage from his Russian White House coverage, the tank clip had come from CNN.

The Voices kept up their own coverage, most prominently Radio Liberty, which maintained an office on the top floor of the Russian White House; during the coup, outside the big cities, most Russians stayed glued to their shortwave radios. The plotters exploded in anger at the station's head and ordered Medvedev demoted on the spot. Too little, too late; by midnight on August 19 television and the Voices had exposed the plotters as weak and illegitimate, and so decimated their shaky support among the army, the KGB, and the Soviet people.[106]

The next night, August 20, events came to a head at the barricades. The plotters ordered elite *spetznaz* troops to assault the Russian White House. Unfortunately for them, earlier that year Gorbachev had ordered the same units to execute a bloody assault on a television station in Vilnius, Lithuania. The brutal attack had produced a popular backlash, in response to which the government hung the *spetznaz* officers out to dry. When the

plotters ordered these units to attack the Russian White House, most of
the troops, from the commanders on down, simply refused to comply. (A
small minority did follow orders; these units made a few abortive sorties
that resulted in the three accidental deaths suffered during the coup.)

One more salient detail from the August coup: although the plotters thought they had isolated Gorbachev and his family from the outside
world at their Black Sea villa at Foros, they had not. The security guards
who remained loyal to Gorbachev were able to set up some jerry-rigged
radios, and his son-in-law Anatoli had a pocket Sony shortwave receiver,
with which the Gorbachev family obtained news from the Voices. These
foreign broadcasts informed Gorbachev just how inept and weak the coup
forces were, and thus fortified his will to resist their demand that he resign
for reasons of "ill health."[107]

The refusal of the *spetznaz* troops to fire on the defenders at the Russian White House highlights, in a way that is highly relevant today, the role
of information technology in the dismantling of despotic governments.
Shortwave radios, samizdat publications, and tape recordings alone did not
defeat Soviet communism. Were the system not rotten to the core, and had
brave people not exposed themselves to danger in the streets, communism
might have survived in the Soviet Union. The Voices and carbon paper, by
destroying its legitimacy with both ordinary citizens and the ruling elite,
fatally applied the Tinkerbell Principle to the Soviet Union.

The Voices and live TV broadcasts of the massacre of civilians also
dramatically increased the political costs of violence to the party; in prior
decades, the Vilnius attack would have gone unreported, and the *spetznaz*
commanders would have escaped opprobrium. But in January 1991, the
cameras in Vilnius did not blink, and the leaders were forced to scapegoat
the hapless officers. When ordered once more to murder innocent civilians,
these same commanders evidently thought, "Fool me once, shame on you;
fool me twice, shame on me."

Finally, no account of samizdat, *radizdat,* and *magnitizdat* is complete
without the story of Nikita Khrushchev's memoirs. After his October 13,
1964, ouster from power, he lived the quiet life of a pensioner, proud of
the fact that, by denouncing Stalin and liberalizing literature and politics,
he changed Soviet society for the better. On the evening of his fall from
power, he phoned his old ally Anastas Mikoyan and said,

> Could anyone have dreamed of telling Stalin that he didn't suit us anymore and suggesting he retire? Not even a wet spot would have remained where we had been standing. Now everything is different. The fear is gone, and we can speak as equals. That's my contribution.[108]

Certainly, no deposed Soviet high official before 1953 would have dictated his memoirs into a tape recorder, as Khrushchev began to do in 1966. (The former general secretary was not highly literate, and did better with dictation than with the pen.) His son Sergei then transcribed the tapes.

Like Pavel Litvinov, Nikita Khrushchev had the name recognition and self-confidence to face down the authorities. In the spring of 1968, Politburo member Andrei Kirilenko and two other high officials summoned Khrushchev to a meeting and demanded that he stop working on the memoirs. He flatly refused:

> You can take everything from me: my pension, the dacha, my apartment. That's all within your power, and it wouldn't surprise me if you did. So what—I can still make a living. I'll go to work as a metal worker—I still remember how it's done. If that doesn't work out, I'll take my knapsack and go begging. People will give me what I need. [Khrushchev then looked directly at Kirilenko.] But no one would give you a crust of bread. You'd starve.[109]

What Khrushchev didn't have to say was that if the ailing seventy-four-year-old—the man best remembered in his native land for blowing the lid off Stalin's prisons—had returned to the metal factory or gone begging on the streets, all of Russia would have instantly heard about it from the Voices.

The process of publishing his memoirs was in many ways reminiscent of other tales of dissident publication. As Solzhenitsyn had done with *The Gulag Archipelago*, Sergei Khrushchev had a trusted typist complete the transcription of *Khrushchev Remembers* under KGB surveillance. For safety, he had three transcripts typed, and he also duplicated multiple copies of the tapes. His care paid off, for when the KGB demanded the originals of both the transcript and the tape, he could hand them over at little ultimate cost; another set was smuggled abroad, probably by the mysterious agent provocateur Victor Louis, and a third was hidden somewhere in the Soviet Union. (Louis himself also made multiple carbons.)[110]

In 1970, the American publishing company Little, Brown printed the first of two volumes of *Khrushchev Remembers*. The Russians published a retranslation of the American version for party use only, even though the public had long since heard extensive excerpts from the Voices. Although the Soviets branded the book a fraud, no one believed them, and voice print analysis eventually authenticated the tapes. While historians have largely dismissed the old leader's remembrances as inaccurate, the story of how *Khrushchev Remembers* was written and then published demonstrates that by 1970, dissident methods had permeated to the highest levels of the Soviet Union.

Between roughly 1965 and 1991, the simplest of copying technologies, carbon paper, had combined with a colossal error of central planning —the production of shortwave radios—to allow the Winston Smiths of the communist world to bypass their rulers' monopoly on information. In a way that George Orwell could not have foreseen, they helped end the *Nineteen Eighty-Four* nightmare that had long oppressed eastern Europe.

The effects of these technologies would not always be uniformly positive; for example, cassette tapes and players, far more compact and easily transportable than the reel-to-reel Soviet tape systems, would play a central role in replacing the dictatorship of the shah with that of the mullahs in Iran in 1979.

In the years following, ever more powerful electronic copying and communication technologies would allow ordinary people to create and transmit text, audio, and still and moving images millions of times faster than did their dissident forefathers in the Soviet Union and eastern Europe. This current story is unfolding at warp speed.

9

THE ARGUS

If you doubt that the Internet has fundamentally altered the balance of power between the rulers and the ruled, just ask Trent Lott, the former majority leader of the United States Senate. On Thursday, December 5, 2002, Lott uttered this lulu at Strom Thurmond's hundredth-birthday party:

> I want to say this about my state: When Strom Thurmond ran for president [in 1948], we voted for him. We're proud of it. And if the rest of the country had followed our lead, we wouldn't have had all these problems over all these years, either.[1]

Parsing Lott's tribute didn't require a doctorate in political science: the nation would have been better off electing a hard-core segregationist president in 1948. The press, though well represented at the festivities, curiously failed to report Lott's words in any detail. It wasn't as if Lott had inaudibly mumbled his tribute or that the proceedings had rendered the reporters comatose; according to one attendee, Lott's remarks elicited "an audible gasp and stunned silence."[2] Rather, the press, perhaps having been co-opted by the hosts, or out of simple social decorum, elected to focus instead on the Marilyn Monroe impersonator who sang an appropriately breathy "Happy Birthday, Mr. President Pro Tempore" and planted a fat kiss on the centenarian's forehead.

To be fair, the media did not completely ignore Lott's testimonial: ABC briefly mentioned it in a newscast—at 4:30 AM. The *Washington Post* buried a small article about it in its back pages, and Gwen Ifill, the wickedly funny African-American host of PBS's *Washington Week,* dedicated the show's occasional "What were they thinking?" feature to the Lott quote.

The twenty-four-hour news cycle turned, and the story disappeared from the mainstream media. Then, something unusual happened;

the incident got taken up by bloggers, most prominently Duncan Black (Atrios.blogspot.com), Joshua Marshall (Talkingpointsmemo.com), and Glenn Reynolds (Instapundit.com), all of whom were outraged by Lott's remarks. Critically, Ed Sebesta, who maintained a database of Confederate nostalgia buffs, pointed out to the bloggers that Lott had a long history of praising southern racism to Confederate enthusiasts. The nation at large was about to find this out.

An online firestorm developed that forced the mainstream press to revisit Lott's remarks. The senator issued an apology, which only fanned the flames; on December 12, President Bush castigated the majority leader in front of a black audience, and on December 20, Lott quit the leadership post.[3]

Interestingly, the senator had made a nearly identical speech in 1980 to a southern audience, which, although well reported in the local press, did not get national coverage. What had changed? By 2002, anyone who wanted to become a columnist or journalist could go online and do so. Yes, the members of this "New Press" had, on average, less training, experience, access, and ability than their traditional, professional colleagues. ("Bloggers in pajamas," sniffed mainstream reporters.) Yet as *l'affaire* Lott illustrated, the aggregate instincts and efforts of these "amateurs" could put their mainstream colleagues to shame. It would not be the last time this would happen. Black, Marshall, Reynolds, and Sebesta were nothing more and nothing less than the digital age's direct descendants of Cobbett, Hone, Paine, and Carlile—commentators whose newly acquired access to mass communication technology allowed them to bypass the traditional channels of power and influence.

At its most basic level, the Internet functions as a duplicating machine that allows each user to easily copy documents, images, sound files, and video (and, even more easily, the hyperlinks to them), and to send them to others. This increased personal empowerment is part of the larger story of personal copying and communications technologies discussed in Chapter 8. The photocopier, whose history goes back a century, supplies a superb perspective on the Internet revolution.

A photograph of a document or drawing is essentially a duplicate, albeit an expensive one. In 1911, Eastman Kodak introduced a device that transferred a negative—that is, a white-on-black document image—directly onto photographic paper without intervening film: the famous, and massive,

Photostat machine. (If a normal black-on-white image was required, the first copy was itself then copied.)

Although the Photostat automatically performed the complicated imaging and developing processes internally, it required running water and electricity—no small thing in the early twentieth century—and could easily gobble up an entire room.[4] The device inhaled enormous quantities of expensive photographic paper and chemicals and spat out thick, foul-smelling duplicates whose curled edges made them the devil to file. It fell to a single-minded patent attorney, Chester Carlson, to devise a photographic process that used plain paper. Carlson's invention would revolutionize the business world and, a decade later, find itself at the center of a titanic struggle between the United States government and the press.

Carlson was born in 1906 in Seattle, the descendant of four immigrant Swedish grandparents and the son of a brilliant but ne're-do-well father whose various business failures endowed Chester's childhood with Dickensian poverty, intense loneliness, and prodigious self-reliance.

When he was four, his father, lured by stories of fertile land and plentiful, cheap labor, took the family to rural Mexico. When fending off scorpions, snakes, and bandits did not consume the family, rescuing cows and chickens from the thick, viscous mud that surrounded their farmhouse did. After they had returned to the United States, Chester's chronically ill mother worked as a housekeeper for a physician who took pity on the family and put them up in a tiny single back room.

The family next moved to the rural town of Crestline in southern California, where young Chester for the first time reveled in the company of his peers. The next Christmas, the dam project that employed most of the town's men closed, and Carlson found himself once again nearly alone, with only his teacher for company: "Sometimes I'd look inside, and there was the teacher at her desk, her chin in her hand, staring at the wall."[5]

Carlson somehow made it through a local college and then Caltech, just in time for the Great Depression. Upon graduation he worked briefly as an engineer at Bell Labs before the downturn vaporized his position. He next found employment as a clerk at a patent law firm; in order to advance his career, he obtained a night school law degree.

Although he prospered as a patent attorney, inventing stirred his heart. From an early age, he had been entranced by printing and copying

apparatus, and his harsh, solitary childhood had imparted to him a profound independence of thought and action. In those days a patent attorney
spent many hours, and even days, waiting for bulky, expensive document
copies; surely, he thought, there had to be a simpler way of printing them
on plain paper.

Had Marconi not transmitted wireless signals over great distances,
someone else would soon have done so; the same was also true of paper
manufacture, the printing press and all of its subsequent refinements, and
nearly all of the other communications advances discussed between these
covers. All of these inventions, wonderful as they were, depended on
well-established physical principles and evolved from similar preexisting
technologies. By contrast, the process that Carlson developed represented
such a radical departure from previous duplicating and copying methods
and rested on such arcane scientific principles that had he not spent the
greater part of his adult life pursuing photocopying, it might never have
seen light of day.

At some point, he came across a report by a Hungarian physicist,
Paul Selenyi, who had used an ion beam to lay down a pattern of electrical charges on a rotating drum. An expensive, cumbersome ion beam was
out of the question for office use, but Carlson's scientific training had also
made him aware of Albert Einstein's photoelectric effect, whereby light
rays induce an electrical charge in certain substances.

Selenyi had not thought to use light, but that was close enough for
Carlson, who realized that he just might be able to apply Einstein's photoelectric discovery to produce the same effect with a camera lens, and
then convert the drum's electrical pattern into an ink image on plain paper.
Over the next quarter century, starting in primitive home laboratories and
progressing to ever better-equipped, better-staffed, and better-funded facilities, he did just that. Eventually, he produced a working device for
the Haloid Company, whose primary business was photographic paper.
Haloid changed its name in 1958 to Haloid Xerox, and in 1961, to Xerox.

In 1959, the company produced its first practicable model, the 914,
which took the business world by storm. Contemporary accounts of the
914's introduction exude an almost millennial flavor: the machine transformed copying, previously a laborious, repugnant activity, into a pleasant
task accomplished with the push of a button.

The 914 had just one drawback: its overuse by office workers hypnotized by its capabilities. As put by author David Owen, "Invention was the mother of necessity." In other words, the new machines seemed to create their own demand out of thin air: they ejected blackboards from conference rooms and replaced them with stacks of copied notes and drawings. The venerable routing slip, attached to an original document, which in one form or another had meandered from desk to desk for centuries, disappeared in favor of mass-copied memos. Five years before the 914's invention, the old photographic machines turned out just twenty million pages annually worldwide; five years after it, Carlson's devices cranked out nearly ten billion copies per year. Almost instantly, the 914 consigned an entire generation of office mainstays—Kodak's Verifax and 3M's Thermofax photocopiers—to landfills.

Ironically, tiny Haloid/Xerox initially found no partners for this business venture; in the absence of support from a larger company, the project became a risky, bet-the-company gamble, and its unaided success vaulted it into the front rank of global commerce. Mighty IBM, for example, turned Haloid down because the computer giant did not see a big enough market for the product. Had IBM's forward vision been more acute, the verb "xerox" would not today enrich the English language and inflate Scrabble scores.

The story of Carlson's invention was unusual for another reason; it ended happily for the inventor, as the 914's royalty of one-sixteenth cent per page made him wealthy beyond counting. The money did not greatly affect his lifestyle. On European trips, his wife had to prevent him from buying third-class train tickets, and he gave almost all of his fortune away before he died in 1968.[6]

Only one other photographic copying technique survived the Xerox machine more or less intact: microfilm. Almost as soon as Louis Daguerre demonstrated his camera and pictures in 1839 to the French Academy of Sciences, inventors realized that vast amounts of information could be photographically miniaturized onto a tiny amount of film. Reginald Fessenden, the radio engineer encountered a few chapters ago, calculated that the technique could fit 150 million words onto a one-inch film square. By 1935, Eastman Kodak had perfected the now familiar sixteen- and thirty-five-millimeter rolls still used in libraries and archives today. Microfilm,

as we saw in Chapter 8, also became the medium of choice for smuggling
military secrets and seditious literature across borders.

    The Soviet Union, unsurprisingly, considered Carlson's invention
useful but dangerous, and so restricted its use to the planning elite. The
Russian version of the Xerox, the Era machine, was available only at state
facilities. All copies were logged, and misuse often resulted in jail time;
few but the bravest Russians commandeered these devices for nighttime
samizdat work.[7] Only in Poland, with its advanced dissident technology
and infrastructure, did photocopying play a significant role in the downfall
of communism. Rather, it would be in the West that the Xerox machine
proved most subversive.

Even at Harvard, few had seen the likes of Daniel Ellsberg. The son of
Jewish converts to Christian Science, he graduated third in the class of
1952 with a summa cum-laude degree in economics.[8] His senior thesis
was published in the prestigious *American Economic Review* and so impressed two giants in the field, Wassily Leontief and Carl Kaysen, that
they offered him a junior fellowship at the school. Harvard reserved these
three-year appointments, whose only formal obligation was attendance
at a posh weekly dinner party, for those too brilliant to be confined to a
run-of-the-mill doctoral program. The university almost never gave them
to newly minted graduates.

    Initially, Ellsberg refused the fellowship and instead went to Eng-
land for graduate work at Cambridge, followed by a successful stint as a
Marine Corps lieutenant; disappointed at not serving in combat during his
initial enlistment, he re-upped for an extra year in the vain hope that the
Suez crisis of 1956 would draw in American forces. Over the next dozen
years, he bounced among the RAND Corporation, where he applied his
theoretical expertise to nuclear deterrence; the State and Defense departments; and Harvard, where he earned a PhD. His dissertation described
the "Ellsberg paradox," which became a game theory staple.

    In 1965, the State Department sent him to Vietnam, where he found
himself under the command of Paul Vann, the risk-loving officer whom
New York Times reporter Neil Sheehan would later make famous in *A
Bright and Shining Lie*. Always a true believer, Ellsberg fashioned himself
into a fierce Vietnam hawk. Over the next two years, he sought out the

combat experience he had missed in the peacetime marines and regularly accompanied army patrols, often in the point position, the most likely to draw enemy fire. It did not please the local American officers to have an ex-marine with no combat experience tagging along in the rice paddies; it pleased them even less when he launched into lectures on the finer points of infantry tactics.

Ellsberg's experience in the military and political quagmires of the Vietnam conflict convinced him that the war was unwinnable. He was not the only American official who reached that conclusion: so did many in the Defense Department, starting with Secretary McNamara, who ordered a task force, under the direction of a subordinate, Leslie Gelb, to turn out a detailed examination of the war.

By 1969, the task force, which Ellsberg was peripherally involved in, completed its job; its report ran to forty-seven volumes—seven thousand pages. The published report, *The Office of the Secretary of Defense Vietnam Task Force Study,* would later become popularly known as the Pentagon Papers. It documented, often in painful detail, the brutality, lies, failures, and deceits of American policy in Indochina under four presidents. McNamara, wracked with guilt over the war, intended the project for future historians. By that point, Ellsberg had moved back to RAND's headquarters in Santa Monica; locked in his black four-drawer top-secret safe rested one of the few copies of the explosive report. (Since the standard RAND file cabinet was gray, a black one was a highly visible status symbol.)

He decided to blow the lid off the top-secret report. As he analyzed the task,

> [The Papers] would have to be copied. I couldn't do that at RAND or at a copy shop. Maybe it was possible to lease a machine. I got out of bed and picked up the phone in my living room and called a close friend, my former RAND colleague Tony Russo. I said there was something I would like to discuss with him. I'd be over shortly.[9]

Ellsberg asked if Russo could get hold of a Xerox machine. Indeed he could; Russo's girlfriend Lynda Sinay owned an advertising company that leased one, and she agreed to let Ellsberg use it after hours. On the evening of October 1, 1969, after most RAND employees had gone home, Ellsberg opened his black safe, filled his briefcase with the highest-priority sections, and headed out the front door. The RAND guards paid him no attention.

Sinay had leased a 914—by today's standards, cumbersome and slow. Even with the help of Sinay and Russo, copying just a single brief-case load of documents took all night. Beyond the logistic difficulties of clandestinely copying the documents, he also exposed his friends to prosecution. He involved his thirteen-year-old son Robert in the copying, and at one point, even his ten-year-old daughter Mary. Prosecutors would indict Russo with him, while Sinay sweated out her status as an unindicted coconspirator.

Ellsberg sent his first batch of copies to Senator Fulbright, who, although initially enthusiastic about making them public, soon demurred because of their top-secret classification. The same sequence of events played out with Senator George McGovern. Their refusal dealt a serious blow to Ellsberg's hope of avoiding questioning, because the Constitution shields members of the Senate from interrogation on subjects discussed in the chamber; therefore Ellsberg could have remained anonymous.

Their refusals forced Ellsberg to go to the press. In March 1971, he brazenly walked into a copy shop in Harvard Square and ran off more photocopies on a high-speed machine for Neil Sheehan at *The New York Times*.[10] After three months of researching, cross-checking, legal advice, and agonizing, the *Times* published the Pentagon Papers, piece by piece. The *Washington Post* and fifteen other publications followed. Although the government initially obtained injunctions against the newspapers, two weeks later the U.S. Supreme Court vacated the rulings, and in 1973, a federal court dismissed all charges against Russo and Ellsberg.[11]

For a half century after the 914's appearance in 1959, xerographic copiers constituted a halfway point in the empowerment of individuals by modern personal communications technology; for the first time, ordinary people could copy thousands of pages of written material. As explained in the introduction, because W. E. B. Du Bois did not have duplicating equipment, hundreds of thousands of black Americans suffered a form of slavery for decades after the government suppressed his explosive report on the subject; because Daniel Ellsberg *did* have duplicating equipment, he hastened the end of the Vietnam conflict. Were that not enough, Ellsberg also set into motion the events that would force the resignation of Richard Nixon. The president, upset at the release of the Pentagon Papers, authorized the burglary of the office of Dr. Lewis Fielding, Ellsberg's psychiatrist. This episode, so-called "Watergate West," provided not only the legal grounds for dismissing Ellsberg's prosecution but also a key clue that traced responsibility for the original Watergate break-in by E. Howard Hunt and Gordon Liddy back to the Oval Office.[12]

Yet copying the Pentagon Papers was anything but easy, and their public dissemination still depended upon broadcast stations and printing presses, operated by a privileged few, who themselves would soon face the full wrath of the government. Twenty-one months separated Ellsberg's first trip to Lynda Sinay's office from *The New York Times'* publication of the Pentagon Papers. During that interim, Ellsberg spent many thousands of dollars—real money in those days—worked long days and nights, and exposed both himself and others to legal peril in order to make copies that he could then not immediately disseminate. Over the next few decades, dramatic advances in digital technology would erase these barriers.

Around the time that Harvard awarded Ellsberg his PhD, a computer scientist at MIT, J. C. R. Licklider, suggested the possibility of a globally linked "Intergalactic Computer Network." The Defense Department, intrigued at the prospect of a decentralized communications system that might survive a nuclear conflict, appointed Licklider the first director of computer research at its Advanced Research Projects Agency (known at various times as either ARPA or DARPA). There, he and his successors brought his concept to fruition with the ARPANET, the Internet's forefather.

Prior to the Internet, all mid-twentieth-century electronic communications technologies shared an essential drawback: their linkages were "circuit switched," meaning that the two terminals of any connection were linked by a single, and usually temporary, channel. In that era, the pathway between two telephones typically proceeded through multiple relays; that pathway could conduct, even with the most advanced encoding technology, only a handful of calls at a time. ARPA's scientists realized that a network of any size, let alone a worldwide one, could not function in this manner; for example, an integral network of just one hundred computers requires 4,950 separate direct connections among them.[13]

In order to get around this limitation, Licklider and his colleagues devised a "packet switching" technology that broke messages and data into multiple pieces, individually labeled them, and sent them on their way along different paths to their final destination, where they were put tidily back together.

The old circuit-switching method can be thought of as a child's tin-can-and-string telephone, able to link only two terminals with a single, dedicated connection; packet switching can be imagined as a disjointed moving company that sends the drawers and body of a bedroom dresser on separate vehicles taking different routes to its ultimate destination, where the dresser is reassembled.

By the late 1960s, researchers had made packet switching a reality, and in 1969 a team at UCLA fired up the ARPANET's first active site, or "node." Before that year ended, ARPA scientists added three more nodes, and in 1972, the first e-mail traveled over the new network. By the early 1980s, ARPANET connected most of the world's major research facilities. This new network, variously called the "information superhighway" or "infobahn," began to excite the popular imagination, but it was still far from being a mass-market tool.[14]

This soon changed. Just as Gutenberg wasn't trained as a printer and the young Thomas Edison knew nothing about sound reproduction or lighting, Tim Berners-Lee, a computer scientist at CERN, the huge European high-energy physics research center, wasn't a networking specialist. In 1990, he had a more immediate problem: connecting the facility's myriad computers.

CERN straddles the French/Swiss border and is home to thousands of scientists and staff. The facility also hosts an even larger number of visiting academics who spend days, weeks, or months running their experiments on CERN's massive particle accelerator. Most of them brought along their own computers, which in the 1980s constituted a diverse collection of mainframe machines and, increasingly, the newfangled small personal computers popping up in offices and homes. Earlier, in 1989, Berners-Lee wrote a now famous proposal that asked, "How will we ever keep track of such a large project?"[15] To a computer scientist like Berners-Lee, the answer was obvious: to somehow link up all these computers, with their variegated hardware and operating systems, so that information on one system was available to all the others.

Berners-Lee conceived of a "Web browser," a software program that employed links within documents—so-called hypertext—to retrieve files from distant systems. It turned out that an English company, Owl Ltd., had created a program named Guide that linked documents in this manner, but only within a single computer; it could not retrieve pages from other computers. A similar program, HyperCard, which had been invented in 1987 and subsequently bundled into Macintosh computers, had caught the eye of Berners-Lee's colleague Robert Cailliau.[16]

In Berners-Lee's words,

> The version now commercialized by Owl looked astonishingly like what I had envisioned for a Web browser—the program that would open and display documents, and preferably let people edit them, too. All that was missing was the Internet. *They've already done the difficult bit!*[17]

Berners-Lee finished the job that Guide and Hypercard had begun by writing the now familiar Web software routines: a Hypertext Markup Language (HTML) to encode documents, the Universal Resource Identifier (URI, now URL) for addressing them, the Hypertext Transfer Protocol (HTTP) to send them on their way, and the code that drives the Web's ultimate information repositories, the servers. He credited much of his success to the sophistication and ease of use of his NeXT computer, a machine designed by Steven Jobs after Apple ousted him in 1985.

Like David Sarnoff, who had been consumed by the chicken-and-egg question—Who will buy radio music boxes if no broadcasting stations air programs, and who will build broadcasting stations if no one owns radio music boxes?—Berners-Lee was vexed by a similar concern: "Who would bother to install a [browser] if there wasn't exciting information already on the Web?"[18] To succeed, he would have to broaden his horizon beyond CERN.

In late 1991, Berners-Lee and Cailliau traveled to a hypertext software conclave in San Antonio to demonstrate their new browser. The meeting site did not have an Internet connection—in those days, almost none existed outside major research and government centers. To demonstrate their software, the two planned to call up their CERN server with a Swiss-made telephone modem and a scrounged dial-up account. One small problem remained: their modem, a European-standard 220-volt device, could not use American 110-volt current, so they had to disassemble it and solder in a connection to a voltage transformer.

The demonstration succeeded beyond their wildest dreams; when they returned to the conference two years later, almost all of the exhibits were Web-related.[19] In 1993, Mosaic, the first browser that could be easily installed and used by non-geeks, appeared, followed by Netscape Navigator in 1994 and Internet Explorer in 1995; by the end of that year, Berners-Lee's creation connected sixteen million users worldwide, or 0.4 percent of the earth's population; by mid-2011, it connected 2.1 billion people, or 30 percent.[20]

Although by 1999 increasing numbers of Americans had Internet access, it still remained largely a one-way medium. Posting information online was in many ways more difficult than submitting a document to a commercial printing company. First, the user converted the text or word processor document into Hypertext Markup Language (HTML). Next, although HTML had been designed to produce screen-ready pages, most users found that they needed to adjust the document code to get a more acceptable and professional appearance. (Documents written on early versions of Microsoft Word, the most commonly used word processor, yielded a particularly unattractive HTML appearance.)

Most challenging of all, the user had to upload the final HTML document and associated files to a Web site—assuming he or she had access to one—with a finicky File Transfer Protocol (FTP) program onto an even more finicky server. This sequence was, with some perseverance, doable, and with trial and error, it soon became routine, but before 1999, only a small percentage of ordinary people were motivated enough to surmount its hurdles.

In that year, a young man named Evan Williams conquered these difficulties. Like Berners-Lee, he harbored no grand ambition to alter the nature and tempo of human communication; he just wanted to make a living.

A mediocre student who grew up on a farm, Williams dropped out of the University of Nebraska in the mid-1990s and hitched his wagon to an Internet boom that soon went bust. His luck did not change:

> I had no business running a company at that time because I hadn't worked at a real company. I didn't know how to deal with people, I lacked focus, and I had no discipline. I'd start new projects without finishing old ones, and I didn't keep track of money. I lost a lot of it,

including what my father had invested, and I ended up owing the I.R.S. because I hadn't paid payroll taxes. I made a lot of employees mad.[21]

In the late 1990s, he cofounded Pyra Labs, which produced project management software. As part of that effort, the company created an internal software tool for quickly uploading short documents that he called "Web logs," first onto the company's internal Web site, and then onto the Internet. Williams called the tool Blogger, and it quickly became more popular than the company's original products, so he created another company, Blogger.com, to market the new software.[22]

Before Blogger, services such as Usenet and Geocities allowed contributors to post articles, but they never caught on among the general population. This may have been for aesthetic and technical reasons, or simply because at that time such a relatively small percent of the population was connected that Usenet and Geocities could not achieve "critical mass," or because of slow dial-up speeds available to most users at the time.[23]

Just as Gutenberg's triumph depended on cheap paper, advanced metallurgy, and word spacing, Blogger could not have succeeded without Berners-Lee's browser and inexpensive, always-on broadband. By 2003, when Williams sold Blogger to Google, the time was ripe for his venture. The browser, Blogger, and broadband, combined with the Web giant's resources, made uploading as easy as typing the text and pushing the send key; within minutes any grandparent or elementary school student could create and post a professional-looking page.

Almost by accident, Williams had completed the job begun by Johannes Gutenberg five-and-a-half centuries before. At a stroke, everyone was a reporter, a news photographer, a columnist, and a publisher, able to turn out a nearly infinite number of copies at a price indistinguishable from zero. Even more crucially, Blogger allowed people to connect and cooperate in ways never before possible.

The ocean of data that is the Internet flows both ways; "Googling" makes it possible to access knowledge about almost any subject and makes the bibliographic universe instantaneously available. Someone with even a modicum of research skills and access to an academic, government, or nonprofit database can plumb almost any topic to astonishing depth without, well, getting out of his or her pajamas.

The new technology also made experts much more accessible to the public. While the Web did not make Stephen Pinker, Jared Diamond, or Stephen Hawking more likely to answer casual inquiries about psychology, evolutionary biology, or astrophysics, almost anyone who needs help from a less well-known authority now has a reasonable probability of getting it. Several years ago, in the course of writing *A Splendid Exchange*, I delved into subjects as varied as the course of the Black Death in Asia and the history of refrigeration technology. I found, to my delight, that a polite e-mail to the world experts in these areas (there aren't many) usually elicited a helpful and encouraging reply.

If Blogger was all Evan Williams had invented, he would have been well enough remembered, but he was just getting started. The 2003 buyout of Blogger made him a Google employee, and this did not suit him. In 2004, he cofounded Odeo, a podcasting company. Because of competition from Apple's iTunes, his new company did not flourish, but once again, he and his colleagues at Odeo struck serendipitous gold with another incidental internal tool: Twitter.

It's easy to make fun of this 140-character medium. No one wishes Britney Spears' self-absorbed, fractured syntax on his worst enemy, let alone what movie the occupant of the neighboring cubicle saw last night. (Or even, for that matter, this one from Evan Williams: "Having home-made Japanese dinner on the patio on an unusually moderate SF evening. Lovely.")[24]

But on July 23, 2011, hundreds of millions of people around the world, particularly in China, badly wanted to know precisely what happened when a lightning-induced high-speed train collision in Zhejiang Province tossed passenger cars off a viaduct and killed dozens.

China's government certainly did not want the public to find out. It acted vigorously to contain the looming public relations disaster for the country's new bullet train system, the prestigious centerpiece of its national development plans and, until the accident, a potential major source of export revenue. An initial government press release read, "China's high-speed train is advanced and qualified. We have confidence in it." Governmental officials directed the press to focus on the human tragedy, and to stay away from the cause: "Do not question. Do not elaborate. Do not associate."[25]

Alas, China's Twitter-like service, Sina Weibo, which has over three hundred million users, shredded the government spin. Just minutes after the accident, a survivor tweeted for help, and the message got forwarded 112,000 times in a matter of hours. The nation's newspapers could no longer ignore the collision's subtext without looking foolish. Corruption, cost overruns, and inattention to safety standards had plagued the train system for years. Lamented one propaganda official, "New media triumphed over traditional media. Private media beat public media."[26]

Evan Williams had done it again: not only was everyone a publisher and a reporter, but from that moment on, the increasing ubiquity of camera-equipped smart phones relentlessly lowered toward zero the probability that any newsworthy event would go untweeted, unphotographed, or unrecorded. Twitter had become the modern Argus—all-seeing, all-knowing, unblinking, and ever-present. When a 5.8-magnitude earthquake struck northern Virginia on August 23, 2011, tweets sent from near the temblor's epicenter arrived in New York City *before* its shock waves.[27]

Across the globe, in liberal democracies and even in the world's most repressive states, the new high-access, two-way media provides citizens with a faster, and at times even more accurate, picture of both public and private events than ever before. Despite the obvious distortions and inaccuracies of much material uploaded to the Web, in the middle and long term it sifts and winnows information reasonably well.

Before the printing press, very few titles got published: the Bible, indulgences, the ancient classics, calendars, and so forth; *scriptoria* did not need to employ acquisitions editors. After Gutenberg, the range of available titles expanded into areas that appealed to the elite, and to the newly literate masses: novels, minor classics, and, of course, erotica. As the supply of available literature swelled, large, established publishers filtered and vetted what they printed.

The Web has similarly exploded outward the range of what is published, and again the same cries of how a new medium has debased standards ring: when any person can publish, anything, no matter how awful, will be published. And yet the Web is highly self-corrective, as its signature tool, Google, demonstrates.

Google's origins nicely explain how the Web sifts and winnows. The company emerged from the doctoral dissertation of one of its founders,

Larry Page, a Stanford computer science graduate student. He settled on a bibliometric analysis of the Internet—that is, the pattern of how pages were linked through hypertext.

In the mid-1990s, when Page came to Stanford, the Internet already contained a vast amount of useful information; the problem was finding it. Consequently, some of the hottest dot-coms were search engine companies, which went public in dizzying succession: Lycos, Magellan, HotBot, and Excite, among many others. (The failure of nearly all of the 1990s dot-coms was similar, in more ways than one, to the post-Gutenberg glut of poorly capitalized printing shops, particularly in Venice.)

More often than not, search results from these sites hid relevant Web pages under a vast heap of useless ones; this author recalls having to sift through links to recipes, porn sites, and product reviews to find useful returns for the term "portfolio theory." Most famously, perhaps, entering the name of one of the early search engines, Inktomi, into its own site yielded no results.[28]

Page's first step, following forward the progress of Web citations, was trivial: he simply inspected the links in each page. The reverse process, determining what pages linked back *to* a given page, was anything but easy. Page devised an algorithm for tracing these backward links, which he nicknamed BackRub.

Once that was accomplished, an even greater difficulty arose: not all links are created equal. A link from a Web page that itself was cited by a large number of other Web pages—say a seminal paper by an established expert—carries considerably more weight than one from an elementary school civics report. So Page devised another algorithm (named PageRank, after himself, of course) to compute a page's importance.

It soon became apparent to Page and his collaborator, Sergey Brin, that they were chasing a rapidly accelerating greyhound. The Web already had about ten million pages, with perhaps one hundred million links among them, and both pages and links were at that point growing twentyfold per year.

To their delight, Page and Brin found that their algorithms accurately identified the most authoritative and relevant pages on the Web. Work by highly regarded academic, government, and industry sources, for instance, reliably outranked the pages of fifth-graders and cranks, something that the Web's first search engines, such as AltaVista and Excite, notoriously did not do.

Page and Brin had caught their greyhound, and it dragged them forward at a fearsome pace. Because of the Web's explosive growth, BackRub grew to consume nearly half of the bandwidth of Stanford University, one of the world's most connected institutions. It was time for Page and Brin either to abandon the project or to deliver it from its academic womb into the wide world of commerce. The two could not have chosen a better environment to do the latter, for nearly all of Stanford's computer science faculty had at some point either founded a company or at least advised a start-up. The rest, as they say, is history.

The average reader of this book probably uses Google several times per day with the expectation that, in the overwhelming majority of cases, the company's search algorithm will float the best, most informative hits to the top of the list (just below the highlighted advertisements that generate the company's massive earnings), and sink the nutcases, preadolescent blogs, and virus-infested Russian sites to the bottom.[29]

The pedophilia scandal that has enveloped the Catholic Church over the past decade provides a perfect example of the Web's efficiency. Tragically, priests have habitually abused children sexually almost since the birth of the Church, though, in fairness, many accusations may have been politically motivated.[30]

In 1871, the hierarchy excommunicated an Australian nun, Mary MacKillop, for reporting the sexual abuse of children by Father Ambrose Keating. (She later became the only Australian saint.) In 1947, a Catholic cleric, Gerald Fitzgerald, founded the Congregation of the Servants of the Paraclete, a hostel in rural New Mexico dedicated to his brethren who had fallen on hard times or strayed from the straight and narrow. As a matter of course, the hostel received significant numbers of priests caught sexually abusing children. Fitzgerald soon realized that his pedophiles were incurable, and he recommended to the hierarchy that they be expelled from the priesthood. For decades, the Vatican routinely ignored Fitzgerald's reports, and his concerns languished both inside and outside the Church.[31]

Throughout the 1980s and 1990s, local U.S. papers occasionally broke stories about sexually predatory clergymen, but these reports failed to achieve critical mass with a national audience. In 1992, prosecutors accused a Catholic priest, James Porter, of abusing scores of children in and around Boston, a story the *Boston Globe* covered extensively. The local bishop responsible for Porter, Bernard Law, failed to act, and actually took to the pulpit and called for divine retribution against the *Globe*. The story did not reach the nation's consciousness, in spite of the fact that the *Globe* ran more than fifty articles on the subject.

Fast-forward ten years: in 2002, the *Globe* ran a nearly identical story about another sexually errant local priest, John Geoghan, whose crimes spanned decades. This time, the public outcry was widespread and loud; local Catholics reacted to the hierarchy's inattention to the situation with a group called the Voice of the Faithful (VOTF), which spread like wildfire. Within a year, the new organization gained over thirty thousand members in a score of nations. Bernard Law, by now elevated to cardinal, decreed that they could not meet on church property, that their meetings had to be overseen by a priest, and, astonishingly, that VOTF chapters from different parishes could not communicate with each other. Catholics around the world were outraged. The Vatican could not ignore this new amalgamation of laity, and at the end of 2002, Law flew to Rome and tendered his resignation.

What had changed between the Porter and Geoghan episodes? As communications academic Clay Shirky points out, before the Web, individuals could not easily spread a story nationwide. When the Porter scandal broke in 1992, Berners-Lee had barely gotten his Web invention off the ground. Assume that a woman who read the *Boston Globe* had a cousin in San Francisco who had suffered abuse by a priest, and the Boston resident wanted to inform her San Francisco cousin about the Geoghan story. She would need to phone him or clip, copy, and mail him the newspaper story, and she would need to do the same for each and every additional person she wanted to contact.

By 2002, the Web had revolutionized the process. First, the *Globe* was now truly global, as it had not been a decade earlier. Former altar boys the world over could read the story. Second, instead of clipping, copying, or calling, the reader could almost instantly forward the piece's Web page to dozens of friends or, with subsequent generations of forwards, thousands or millions of other people. In 1992, the transmission chain for a news story was limited to local readers who could forward only a few copies at a time. In 2002, several cycles of e-mail forwards could reach a significant fraction of the population of an entire nation or, in extraordinary circumstances, of the entire globe.[32]

To be sure, the Web did not render the old mainstream media obsolete, for many readers still preferred these traditional outlets, but it did force the newspapers and networks, however grudgingly, to realize that they could not completely control what gets reported, and to whom and where it gets reported. The superiority of the new media in disseminating information, compared with the limited scope of the old media, was well expressed by the late journalist William Safire:

> For years I used to drive up Massachusetts Avenue past the vice president's house and would notice a lonely, determined guy across the street holding a sign claiming he'd been sodomized by a priest. Must be a nut, I figured—and thereby ignored a clue to the biggest religious scandal of the century.[33]

The dramatic arrival of WikiLeaks highlights the nature and power of this New Press. The first massive WikiLeaks "dump" of United States government documents regarding Afghanistan, in mid-2010, included 75,000 items; later that year, WikiLeaks published 400,000 State Department documents. Few conventional news organizations can muster the manpower to digest that volume of information, but tens of thousands of interested Web surfers, most contributing just a few hours of effort, did.

Newspapers did publish the most important of these documents; critically, they have learned how to partner with the Internet browsing public, "the people formerly known as the audience," in the words of NYU journalism professor Jay Rosen.[34]

The Duke Cunningham scandal provided one of the first demonstrations of this new public analytical capacity, as well as its symbiosis with the older mainstream media. For years, the California congressman and famous Vietnam naval aviation ace had taken bribes from a defense contractor, Mitchell Wade. The largest transaction involved the sale of Cunningham's Del Mar Heights home to Wade's company at a grossly inflated price. In 2005, a team of reporters at the *San Diego Union-Tribune* led by Marcus Stern broke the story. In their book, *The Wrong Stuff,* they noted, "In another era, the story might have gone unnoticed outside [Cunningham's] home county." But in 2005, it went viral. Bloggers, including the aforementioned Joshua Marshall of Talkingpointsmemo.com, brought the episode to national attention:

> All over the country, people used the Internet to search out and pore over relevant campaign finance reports and property records. The

electronic pack would dig out other lawmakers who had benefited from Wade's campaign contributions. Realtors, real estate appraisers, and even Cunningham's neighbors began emailing their own assessments of the Del Mar Heights house sale to Stern and other San Diego reporters.[35]

The most astute news organizations took note of the benefits that this new online investigative partnership with the public offered. One that most definitely did not was London's *Telegraph*. In 2009 it broke the story of pervasive, systematic fraudulent expense deductions by members of Parliament (MPs): renovations to boyfriends' apartments, chocolate Santas, and, in the most memorable case, a £1,645 Queen Anne dollhouse for a duck pond on the property of Sir Peter Viggers, a Conservative MP. (Adding insult to injury, the ducks reportedly disliked the toy cottage.)

Parliament had supplied the *Telegraph* with two million documents. The disclosure of so much data may well have been intentional; the MPs perhaps thought that the massive data release would buy them precious time during which the scandal could die down or readers might lose interest. After all, what news organization had the resources to crawl through such a mountain of credit card slips, hotel bills, and expense claims forms?

The MPs had probably correctly judged the situation with regard to the old-line media such as the *Telegraph*, but they badly miscalculated the capability of that paper's Web-savvy competitors. The *Telegraph*'s initial coverage had badly scooped its crosstown rival, the *Guardian*, which then responded by providing its audience with links to a second release of about seven hundred thousand documents. The *Guardian* invented on the fly and almost out of whole cloth an entire investigative technique, called "computational journalism." Using sophisticated database software, the paper's staff scanned and cataloged all seven hundred thousand documents and uploaded them to its Web site for examination by its online audience.

The *Guardian* encouraged its readers to "Investigate your MP's expenses." The paper directed its audience to document index pages for each legislator, complete with mug shots, and instructed them to rate each document on a four-step scale ranging from "not interesting" to "investigate this!" Over 29,000 readers responded, and within days they had buzzed through the massive pile of chits, expense reports, and credit card slips. When the smoke had cleared, six cabinet ministers, thirteen additional MPs, and five peers resigned or did not stand for reelection. Ultimately, six of these miscreants were sentenced to prison terms averaging fifteen months.

The paper had executed a clever human-wave attack on a seemingly insurmountable wall of data. Fortune favors the prepared; for a decade prior to the MP expenses scandal, the *Guardian* ran one of the world's most sophisticated online media operations and had won three consecutive Webbies, the award given by the International Academy of Digital Arts and Sciences to the best Internet news site. The paper also occupied the front ranks of the government's Open Data Initiative.[36] While many of the changes wrought by the communications advances detailed in these pages, and the reactions to them, mirrored those from previous eras, here was something truly new under the sun: near-universal access to oceans of material and data.

The episodes involving Lott, Roman Catholic pedophilia, Cunningham, and MP expenses demonstrate three things about the New Press. First, the greater reach of the Internet dictates that more than a few of its members will be able to hold their own against the old, mainstream press with regard to control of information. Second, this corps of writers or bloggers resides, in general, far from places like Washington, D.C., and London, traditional centers of power, and is thus unencumbered by the constraints and social customs in these places: in Arianna Huffington's words, "truly free of the dependence on access, and the need to play nice with the powers that be."[37] Last, but not least, members of this new corps can connect the dots and communicate with one another in ways never before possible. Here, indeed, was Hayek's point about widely distributed knowledge suddenly writ large on the Internet: for the first time in history, someone in possession of a unique piece of knowledge can communicate it to the whole world via any combination of three routes: blog it directly, via other bloggers, or use the mainstream traditional media.

As put by Eric Schurenberg, a former editor at Time Inc.,

> We all thought we were uniquely qualified to deliver the news because we were trained writers and had access to all the important sources. But what we really had was a printing press, and no one else did. With the arrival of the Internet, we found that lots of other people

could write, too, and our readers found they didn't need us to connect with our sources.[38]

Those who decry the slow-motion demise of traditional newspapers often cite the resources and bravery of *The New York Times* during the Pentagon Papers episode. They ask if any of today's weakened, conglomerate-owned papers would be up to the task. This argument entirely misses the point, for, as previously mentioned, the Internet and social media have largely taken over the essential historical role of the newspapers: the widespread dissemination of information. In the Internet era, Daniel Ellsberg wouldn't have needed *The New York Times*.

Today's Ellsbergs can now copy even the longest documents in seconds, store them in a fingernail-size flash drive (or on a rewritable CD labeled as a Lady Gaga knockoff, as did WikiLeaker Private Bradley Manning), propel them across the planet at the speed of light by the thousands, and upload them to servers to be viewed by millions. *The New York Times* can still be part of the process, but is no longer its director.

The Web filters and sifts information to a degree not possible with the old array of newspapers and TV networks, which, because of the small number of boots these media place on the ground, simply cannot give all stories the attention and analysis they need. Yes, the Web regularly disseminates spurious and incorrect information, but increasingly used and respected sites such as FactCheck.org gradually eliminate it as well, or at least convert its true believers into targets of general ridicule, such as those who believe that the moon landings were staged or that the CIA engineered the 9/11 attacks.

Mainstream journalists know that bloggers will instantaneously fact-check their pieces, and the more honest reporters will admit that this has made them more careful. The best newspapers benefit from the Web's fire hose of information and opinion, and particularly from the analytical power distributed among its myriad online participants. The mainstream media, to be sure, still play an important role in the news process, but they have long since lost the ability to say with a straight face, like Walter Cronkite, "That's the way it is."

But isn't the Web an echo chamber of wingnuts and anarchists, full of innuendo, rumor, and incivility? Hasn't it shortened our children's attention spans, truncated their literacy skills, and vaporized their analytical abilities? Hasn't it utterly destroyed, or at least devalued, the hallowed profession of journalism, whose practitioners in an earlier golden age compulsively double-sourced, carefully weighed all available opinions, disregarded personal views, and delivered only the purest of balanced and densely informative copy?

A generation or two ago, the ability of Orson Welles to deceive the nation, or even that of Franklin Roosevelt to dominate the airwaves, sparked similar concerns. Further, if such worries don't remind you of Plato's dislike of poetry and the other imitative arts, of the calumny hurled at vernacular Bibles by the Catholic Church, and of the monk Filippo de Strata's prediction that the octavos of Ovid cranked out by the "brothel of the printing presses" would make young women wanton, then you have not been paying attention. The criticisms you are hearing are simply the age-old howls of communications elites facing the imminent loss of status and income.

Another argument made against the Web is that it has "rewired our brains" and robbed us of our ability to focus, concentrate, and think deeply. The most prominent proponent of this view, Nicholas Carr, wrote a famous piece in the *Atlantic Monthly*—"Is Google Making Us Stupid?"—as well as a book-length offering, *The Shallows.*

His evidence centers on his own anecdotal observations and laboratory experiments that examine how Internet exposure affects performance on measurements of memory and concentration, and how eye movement patterns involved in reading Web pages are different from those involved in reading a printed page. Carr also leans heavily on work showing that extended hours of Web surfing change patterns of brain metabolism observed on specially designed MRI scans.[39]

His observations would not surprise any brain researcher; the human nervous system is highly "plastic" and able to rearrange its patterns of activity and even its synapses—the actual connections among brain cells. Blindness, for example, redeploys some of the rear areas of the cerebral hemispheres that normally serve vision to the perception of touch and sound, which develop greater importance in the sightless.[40]

Brain tissue is precious, and reassigning some of it to one activity makes it unavailable for other tasks. Does the Web rewire your brain? You bet; so does *everything* you actively do or passively experience. Literacy is possibly the most potent cerebral rewirer of all; for five thousand years, humans have been reassigning brain areas formerly needed for survival in the natural environment to the processing of printed abstractions. Some of this commandeered real estate has almost certainly been grabbed, in its turn, by the increasing role of computers and the Internet in everyday postindustrial life. *Plus ça change.*

Carr also focuses on laboratory experiments demonstrating that Internet use decreases concentration on the initial task at hand.[41] One study that especially impressed him found that subjects learned material less well when they had to click through large numbers of hyperlinks.[42]

Well, yes. A doctorate in neuroscience is not needed to understand that we retain information better if all of it is presented on a single page or screen, as opposed to being chased through a hypertext maze. Real life, on the other hand, is rarely kind enough to supply us with all we need to know about something in one document, and those skilled at following informational threads through different sources will succeed more often than those who expect to be spoon-fed information conveniently packaged between a pair of cardboard covers.

The complexity of everyday life raises a broader point, which is that Web or no Web, human beings are endlessly distractible. On October 21, 2009, a Northwest Airline crew en route to Minneapolis got a little too engrossed in their laptops and overflew their destination by 150 miles.[43] For non-pilots, the message is equally clear: if you need to concentrate deeply on a given physical or cognitive task—say, driving a car or legislating, you shouldn't be playing solitaire or surfing ESPN, as some state representatives were recently caught doing.

From a longer perspective, over the centuries and millennia, technology has endowed humanity with an ever-increasing stream of information as well as the tools to process it. Any technology that accelerates the flow of information carries with it the power to distract and to disrupt. Should we eschew personal computers because they can divert airline pilots, cell phones because they can fluster automobile drivers, and the Web because it supposedly addles nearly all of us?

Carr's thesis almost automatically formulates its own counterargument: life in the developed world increasingly demands non-rote, nonlinear thought. Shouldn't learning to navigate hypertext skillfully enhance the ability to make rapid connections? Shouldn't such abilities encourage

Figure 9-1. The Great Distractor: Connecticut legislators failing to pay attention to business.

the sort of nonlinear creative processing demanded by the modern work environment, and make us smarter, more productive, and ultimately more autonomous and fulfilled?

As recently as sixty years ago, high school students spent long hours memorizing vast tracts of literature, from Virgil to Shakespeare to Byron to Longfellow's "Paul Revere's Ride." Similarly, in today's traditional Muslim societies, primary education focuses—sometimes exclusively— on commitment of the Koran to memory. Yes, something was surely lost when the educational process left such memorization behind for calculus, linguistics, evolutionary psychology, and computer science. Yet this shift liberated our neurons from rote learning, and much more was gained in terms of intellectual ability, individual well-being, and societal good. And, as always, both the old and the new styles of education rewired brains in their own ways.

Pop neuroscience—whether pro-Web or anti-Web—aside, scant aggregate-level educational or macroeconomic data support Carr's hypothesis. In fact, if the citizens of Web-saturated developed nations are losing reading comprehension, then workers' productivity would plunge; this simply hasn't happened. Verbal standardized test scores should be declining. Once again, no; over the past thirty years, verbal SAT performance has remained stable. If students are losing the ability to concentrate, then math scores should decrease as well. No again; over the same period, the average math SAT score has increased by twenty-four points.[44] If the Web really is making Americans stupid, then shouldn't citizens of more densely wired nations, such as Estonia, Finland, and Korea, be hit even harder? The question answers itself.

Such concerns recall earlier worries about the inability of laypeople to interpret properly vernacular scripture and the degradation of morals brought about by the printing press. Had Mr. Carr been around in 1470, he no doubt would have been concerned that the flood of frivolous books pouring from the new mechanical presses interfered with the intense concentration needed to hand-copy and illuminate Bibles.

Besides this debate on the effects of prolonged use of the Web on the brain and beyond its unsettling effects on the mainstream media, particularly the newspapers, the Web has clearly empowered ordinary people in free and open societies. Few can deny that it has also done so in undemocratic societies.

On December 17, 2010, a young vegetable seller named Mohammed Bouazizi, who had been shaken down and beaten up by police in the sleepy central Tunisian town of Sidi Bouzid, walked to a local government building, soaked himself with paint thinner, lit a match, and set himself, and the entire nation, aflame. Four weeks later, the nation's grotesquely corrupt leader, Zine El Abidine Ben Ali, fled the country; similar uprisings soon toppled leaders in Egypt, Libya, and Yemen, and threatened to do so in Bahrain.

The Internet played a vital role at every step of Ben Ali's fall. Ten months before his ouster, WikiLeaks released its massive cache of secret U.S. diplomatic cables. Many of the documents described in great detail the corrupt business dealings, palatial mansions, and overseas buying sprees of what American diplomats referred to as "The Family," the Mafia-style coterie of relatives and cronies surrounding Ben Ali. The State Department cables riveted Tunisians, and when Bouazizi struck his match three weeks later, the tinder was dry indeed.[45]

By that point, the Qatar-based network Al Jazeera had warmly embraced the digital age, and so provided the most influential coverage of the unfolding events in Tunisia. As luck would have it, just a month before Bouazizi's tragic death, its staff had undergone intense training in social media. Al Jazeera obtained a cell phone video of a protest led by Mohammed Bouazizi's mother; its subsequent broadcast provided many in the Arab world, including Tunisians, with their first news of the evolving events. While it would be disingenuous to point to a single cell phone camera as the spark that ignited the Arab Spring, it speaks volumes that just three months earlier, another protester had immolated himself in a different town, but this event had not been filmed, and so gained no traction.[46]

Like the *Guardian*, Al Jazeera understands the full potential of the Internet and of social media. Over the years, it has established a network of reliable volunteers around the Arab world that replaced the old-style permanent local news bureaus, and it has even largely eliminated the need to fly out correspondents to cover breaking events.[47]

Inside Tunisia, a shadowy dissident organization, Takriz, had gained vital online skills as its members hacked into Tunisia's expensive Internet service providers. The group allied itself with "Ultras," violent soccer fans in both Tunisia and Egypt whose informal organizational style and grievances against the regime proved useful to the pro-democracy activists.[48] Takriz also forged online alliances with labor leaders, particularly in the mining town at Gafsa. It also found Facebook invaluable, especially in spreading the shocking images of Bouazizi's immolation and gruesome final days.

Almost as soon as Ben Ali had abandoned Tunisia, Egyptians rose up en masse. At nearly every step, both Web-based news sources and social media tools, chiefly Facebook, helped assemble the crowds at Tahrir Square that eventually would end the decades-long rule of Hosni Mubarak.

As in Tunisia, Egyptian activists found their links with organized labor invaluable. When textile workers in the Nile delta mill town of Mahalla planned a strike for April 6, 2008, this caught the attention of Ahmed Maher, an unemployed, tech-savvy twenty-seven-year-old civil engineer. Maher decided to organize a demonstration in Cairo in support of the strike in Mahalla; he tried everything he could think of: blogs, leaflets, and Internet forums. Nothing, though, seemed to work as well as Facebook, which attracted three thousand new followers per day.[49]

The Cairo demonstration not only drew thousands of protesters but also occasioned Maher's arrest and beating, and a graphic threat of rape. After his release, he and his colleagues boned up on nonviolent civil disobedience and organized themselves as the April 6 Movement, after the day of the Mahalla strike. Critically, they contacted Optor, a youth movement founded by Serbian dissidents, who had helped overthrow Slobodan Milošević, and the Egyptians sent a member to Belgrade for training. He returned with two tools. The first was a computer game called "A Force More Powerful," which allows dissidents to simulate different anti-regime strategies.[50] The second was a copy of *From Dictatorship to Democracy*, a 1993 monograph by an American academic, Gene Sharp: a step-by-step playbook for dismantling totalitarian regimes that over the years has drawn wrath from sources as varied as Myanmar's government and Hugo Chávez.[51]

On June 6, 2010, police in Alexandria beat to death a young Egyptian man, Khaled Said, probably for filming them as they divided up some illegal drugs. Soon a Facebook page called "We are all Khaled Said" appeared; it featured photos and videos of Said in happier days as well as of his mangled corpse.[52] The page attracted nearly half a million members and so caught the attention of the April 6 Movement, one of whose members connected anonymously with the site's mysterious creator, who communicated only through Google's instant messaging service. Between the hard-won street smarts of the April 6 Movement and the on-the-fly innovation and savvy mass-market draw of the Facebook site "We are all Khaled Said," the dissidents swiftly and deftly assembled several different crowds from outlying mosques that converged on Tahrir Square on January 25, 2011.[53]

Although the creator of the Facebook page, a Google executive named Wael Ghonim, had managed to remain anonymous to the site's readers and to the demonstrators he had helped organize, the police identified him and arrested him on January 27. When the authorities finally released Ghonim on February 7, he revealed his role in "We are all Khalid Said" and found himself the recipient of a tumultuous welcome in Tahrir Square.[54]

In both Tunisia and Egypt—and this is also true of every other Middle East regime challenged by substantive protest—the authorities at some point shut off Internet service. This measure usually backfires, as it angers the uncommitted populace and draws people to public spaces, away from the blogs and Facebook pages on their monitors. At the time that the

Egyptian government threw the off switch, a communications professor at the University of North Carolina, Mohammed el-Nawawy, described with remarkable prescience how the shutdown would fail: "The government has made a big mistake taking away the option at people's fingertips. They're taking their frustrations to the streets."[55] Just as the Soviet Union could not shield its population from radio stations broadcasting from West Berlin and Washington, Arab governments cannot lightly cut off Web feeds from Qatar and London.

The digital infrastructure of the Arab Spring uprisings cannot help inspiring optimism about the prospects for democratic progress in the developing world, and the stories of Trent Lott, Duke Cunningham, Catholic priests' sex abuse, and WikiLeaks, among many, many others, augur well for the survival of open political institutions in the West.

It is even fair to ask if the Rwandan genocide could have occurred today. Recall the heartbreaking words of Nick Hughes, the cameraman who caught some of the few actual clips of the killing: "If only there had been more such images."

Now, there will be: as this is being written, Rwanda has 2.4 million cell phone subscribers out of a population of 11.4 million; that number will only increase, as will the number of Rwandan phones equipped with cameras.[56] The hope for the new two-way digital media is that they will provide more images, and, accordingly, fewer atrocities not only in Africa, but in the rest of the world as well; since genocide requires secrecy, we might even reasonably hope that Twitter has made it less frequent and more localized.

Admittedly, in the past exciting new communications technologies have lulled otherwise dispassionate observers into gullible optimism; the telegraph, contrary to the expectations of many, did not usher in world peace; neither did radio, despite the millennialist predictions of its boosters. As put by Paul Krugman:

> In 1979 everyone knew that it was a Malthusian world, that the energy crisis was just the beginning of a global struggle for ever-scarcer resources. In 1989 everyone knew that the big story was the struggle for the key manufacturing sectors, and that the winners would be those countries with coherent top-down industrial policies, whose companies weren't subject to the short-term pressures of financial

markets. And in 1999 everybody knows that it's a global knowledge
economy, where only those countries that tear down their walls, and
open themselves to the winds of electronic commerce, will succeed.
I wonder what everybody will know in 2009?[57]

In 2009, and certainly in 2012, "everyone knows" that the Internet so em-
powers ordinary citizens that it is only a matter of time before the world
is free of despots, and democracy reigns everywhere and forever. Tragically, this is unlikely in nations dominated by conservative, traditional,
religiously dominated cultures.

An appropriate amount of "cyberpessimism" about the prospects for
democracy in the developing world is in order for at least two reasons.
First, in those nations where troops obey orders to fire on demonstrators
or where leaders are willing to starve their people into submission, as in
Syria and North Korea, monarchs and despots will not fall. As long as
Bashar al-Assad can train artillery fire on his populace, and as long as the
North Korean leadership can keep its people so deprived of sustenance
that they lack the strength to revolt, and as long as these leaders can retain
the support of external allies like Russia and China, they will remain in
power. Tweets, blogs, and Facebook pages do not effect revolutions all by
themselves; the people who read them do—people who must take to the
streets and suffer casualties.

Nor is that all; soldiers must at some point decide to stop killing their
fellow citizens. It is at this nexus of dissidents, soldiers, and their leaders
that the Internet exerts its real, but by no means miraculous, effect: to
increase the cost of killing and repression.

This dynamic was already evident in the more primitive communications milieu of the Soviet Union's last years. As we saw in Chapter 8, in
late August 1991, *spetznaz* commanders, who had already been savaged
by the revelations of Latvian TV cameras, the Voices, and their own leaders, decided not to attack Boris Yeltsin and his supporters at the Russian
White House barricades. Two decades later, the Internet and social media
have further increased the cost of repression to those who undertake it.
As the Arab Spring has already demonstrated, the number of despots who
will be willing to pay that price has decreased, and so has the number of
soldiers and police prepared to obey a despot's orders. Still, as the civil
war in Syria shows, neither has that number reached zero.

Just as the Catholic Church over time co-opted the printing press to its needs, so too have repressive regimes adapted the Internet and social media to theirs. In particular, Iran has demonstrated how technologically adept despots can turn the Web's connective ability to their own advantage. That nation's repressive government has applied the usual sorts of filtering techniques and temporary slowdowns/shutdowns used by despotic regimes, similar to China's "Great Firewall." The Iranians routinely threaten expatriate bloggers by email, and they intimidate, interrogate, and jail these bloggers' relatives back home. Immigration officials regularly require returnees to log into their Facebook accounts.[58] When anti-regime Green Movement demonstrations roiled Iran in late 2009, the government uploaded photos of demonstrations with participants' faces circled in red—digital-age wanted posters. A pro-regime cleric duly appeared on television and ordered religious Iranians to report the demonstrators' identities to a dedicated hotline or Web site.[59]

In 2009, Western observers were stunned to learn that the Iranians had also deployed "deep-packet inspection," a leading-edge data analytical tool that sifts through traffic for subversive key words and phrases. Almost all Iranian Internet traffic passes through a single node in Tehran. Its equipment—and the snooping software—were thoughtfully provided by the democratic West in the form of a Nokia-Siemens joint venture, whose spokesman tartly observed, "If you sell networks, you also, intrinsically, sell the capability to intercept any communication that runs over them."[60]

The good news is that for the first time in history, ordinary people now have access to similar advanced technologies. A kaleidoscopic global cat-and-mouse cyberbattle is being fought on an ever more level playing field between the oppressed and their oppressors, and the latter's job descriptions keep getting harder.

Even so, the reasons for pessimism over the prospects for democracy in the developing world go far deeper than the online balance of power between rulers and ruled. The unavoidable fact is that, generally speaking, vigorous and stable democratic institutions do not thrive in poor nations with traditional cultures.

Why is this? An observation by Laureano Lopez Rodo, one of Francisco Franco's economic officials in the 1950s and 1960s, supplies the essential clue. At that time, Spain stood alone among western Europe's major nations as a dictatorship; Lopez Rodo famously stated that the country would be ready for democracy only after per capita income reached $2,000 per year. Democracy did come to Spain in 1975, when per capita GDP reached $2,446.[61] It did not hurt, of course, that Franco died in that year, but even so Spanish democracy just squeaked by in the rocky years that followed, a period that included the 1981 armed takeover of the Congress of Deputies; had the dictator met his end in an earlier, less wealthy era, the democratic transition probably would have failed.

Why is an average annual income of $2,000 (in 1965 currency, roughly $14,000 today) democracy's magic number? Abraham Maslow's "hierarchy of needs" provides the answer. In 1943, Maslow, a psychology professor at Brandeis University, published "A Theory of Human Motivation," a paper in which he proposed a model of psychological behavior and drives.[62] Imagine that someone has forced a thick plastic bag over your head and obstructed your airflow; all other urges and desires, including hunger, thirst, or even a strong desire to empty your bladder, will instantly disappear, and you will focus completely on removing the bag.

Only after you resume breathing do you attend to your hunger, thirst, and bladder, and only after these basic physiologic needs have been met will you attack the next rung up on Maslow's pyramid, your safety needs: a roof over your head and personal security.

Next comes the third rung: the love of family and friends and a sense of community; after those have been attained, humans seek the fourth rung: the respect of others for one's integrity, strength of character, and intellectual and physical ability.

Maslow postulated that after a person has secured the first four levels—physiological needs, safety, love, and respect—he or she seeks "self-actualization," a poorly defined state of inner personal satisfaction with one's creativity, talent, and moral role in the larger world.

In recent decades, sociologists and psychologists have criticized Maslow's pyramid as oversimplified and have doubted its relevance to the real world, yet at the international level, it has stood up tolerably well to empirical study.[63] Moreover, it provides a powerful way of understanding exactly how nations transition to democracy, and, implicitly, of understanding the limits of communications technology in that transition.

Where do democratic ideals "sit" on Maslow's pyramid? Certainly not on the first two levels: people who are hungry, lack adequate shelter, and fear for the safety of their families and themselves place political freedom far down on their list of priorities. Democracy exists on the upper rungs of Maslow's pyramid—roughly speaking, only in societies that have adequately, fed, housed, and protected their citizens; hence, Lopez Rodo's $2,000 per year.

Many observers have made the link between democracy and prosperity. The political scientist Seymour Martin Lipset, in a famous 1959 paper, explicitly drew the connection and backed it up with what was, for the era, fairly sophisticated statistical analysis. He concluded, "The more well-to-do a nation, the greater the chances that it will sustain democracy."[64] But did democracy result in prosperity, did prosperity encourage democracy, or was there some other factor that resulted in both? Lipset suspected, but could not prove, that wealth itself was the causative factor.

Recent data strongly confirm his hunch. Beginning in 1981, a consortium of social scientists, the World Values Survey (WVS), began to measure a very wide range of beliefs and attitudes around the globe. Typical of their work are the efforts of two pioneering researchers, Ronald Inglehart and Christian Welzel, who have analyzed and sorted nations according to two sociological measures. The first one of these is the "survival versus self expression" (S/SE) score—roughly, how far up Maslow's pyramid a nation's population has ascended. The second, the "traditional versus secular-rational" (T/SR) score, is a measure of how tolerant and socially liberal a society is—particularly regarding religion and respect for authority.

Table 9-1

Typical S/SE Questions (Positive Responses Lower Score):

I think that economic and physical security are more important than self-expression and quality of life

I would not sign a petition.

You have to be very careful about trusting people

I am not very happy.

Typical T/SR Questions (Positive Responses Lower Score):

God is very important in my life.

It is more important for a child to learn obedience and religious faith than independence and determination.

I favor more respect for authority.

I have a strong sense of national pride.

This type of analysis groups nations according to religion and culture, as seen in Figure 9-2.

Note how the most democratic nations cluster in the upper right part of the plot—that is, the nations with the highest S/SE and T/SR scores. The most surprising data point is the United States, which looks much more like a Latin American nation than one from the Western developed world: it is high up on Maslow's pyramid, but as socially and religiously conservative as, say, Iraq or Indonesia.

Because the WVS database now extends back three decades, researchers can examine in detail the sequence of changes that have led to democracy. The key factors seem to be economic growth and the modernization of both the workplace and education that attend it. Inglehart and Welzel have conclusively shown that prior increases in per capita GDP, improvements in education, and the growth of knowledge professions predict future increases in the S/SE score, which in turn predict a transition to democracy. This is no surprise; after all, the wealthier a person becomes, and the more that independent thought becomes an educational goal and a job requirement, and the higher he or she moves up Maslow's pyramid, the less he or she is willing to tolerate a despotic government.

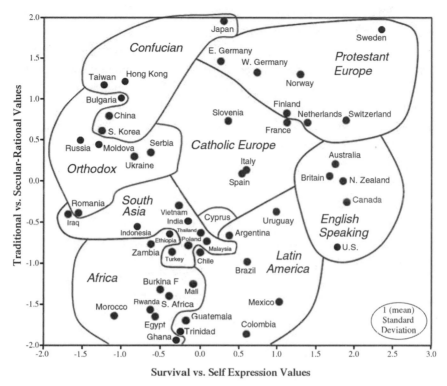

Figure 9-2. Global sociology and economics revealed. The x-axis represents the S/SE scale—roughly, how far up Maslow's hierarchy of needs a nation has ascended. The y-axis represents the T/SR score, with traditional, religiously oriented societies at the bottom and secular societies at the top. As one moves from the lower left corner to the upper right corner, per capita GDP increases.

To schematically summarize:

$$\frac{\text{Economic}}{\text{Growth}} + \text{Modernization} \rightarrow \frac{\text{Individual}}{\text{Empowerment}} \rightarrow \text{Democracy}$$

This is intuitively appealing: citizens who lead a grim, subsistence life focus on meeting their basic physical needs. Higher goals, such as individual freedom and democratic development, will take a back seat until people become wealthier and physically more secure. Only at that point will people begin to challenge corrupt institutions and despotic rulers. This process can take decades, even generations, and can be further delayed by brutal and determined despots, as occurred in the Soviet empire for nearly half a century after World War II.[65]

As powerful as the Web, Google, and Facebook are, they cannot bring democracy to poor, traditional, religiously dominated societies that live in the benighted lower left corner of Figure 9-2, such as Iraq, Egypt, and Ethiopia. The impoverished, and thus disempowered, citizens of such nations are consumed far more by immediate needs for food, shelter, and safety than with political freedom. Moreover, their cultures emphasize rule of religion over rule of law.

The historical narratives and data described in this chapter paint a coherent picture of the effects of the new digital media on individual empowerment and the prospects for democratic development.

Clearly, the Web and social media have greatly empowered citizens all around the world. In despotic states, leaders can no longer easily suppress, imprison, torture, and slaughter their people free from the gaze of the outside world; their corruption can no longer be hidden; and citizens can organize and resist with enormously powerful communications tools. Yes, the Internet has also given despots the power to spy on and suppress their citizens, but on balance, the ground has shifted in favor of the latter. Before 1995, the foes of dictators brought a communications knife to a gunfight. Now, both sides have guns.

Just as samizdat and shortwave radios were not solely responsible for the fall of communism, tweets and blogs alone cannot bring down despotic regimes. People must test their resolve in the streets; police and soldiers must stop firing; ruling elites must become demoralized and, in some cases, decide to switch sides.

Before 2011, many observers doubted the ability of the new social media to effect these sorts of changes. The most prominent of the doubters, Evgeny Morozov, particularly emphasized the surveillance and repressive capabilities offered by the Web. He saved his most scathing remarks for social media enthusiasts who believed that "tweets + young Iranians holding mobile phones = a Twitter Revolution."[66] Morozov has thus far been right about Iran, but otherwise his timing could not have been worse. He published his opus on the subject, *The Net Delusion*, in early 2011, at almost exactly the instant that social-media-powered dissidents began to topple repressive Arab regimes like so many dominoes.

The good news, then, is that digital media have empowered citizens everywhere to resist rotten regimes. The bad news is that most despotic leaders generally rule poor, socially conservative, traditional societies, a soil in which democracy does not sprout. Tragically, as the United States demonstrated in Afghanistan and Iraq, gunpoint regime change and ballot box deployment in materially impoverished traditional cultures are a surefire recipe for disaster.

The prosperity/democracy connection also explains the happier outcomes in eastern Europe. The old Communist bloc contained several relatively prosperous, socially advanced nations—Poland, Czechoslovakia, Hungary, and the Baltic republics—which now have relatively smoothly running democracies. To be sure, these nations' relative wealth and social advancement did not help them much when the Soviet army rolled over them during World War II, in 1956, and in 1968. It took until 1989–1991, by which time the Soviets had lost the will to oppress, for eastern Europe's secular, nontraditional social environments and modestly advanced economies to translate into democracy. On the opposite side of the post-Soviet ledger, all of the new Muslim central Asian republics such as Uzbekistan, Tajikistan, and Kazakhstan—the most traditional and poorest in this cohort—are more or less one-party dictatorships.

Elsewhere in the Muslim world, it is no accident that the nations with the healthiest economies—Turkey, Malaysia, and Indonesia—have the most robust democracies.

Intriguingly, all three nations also use the Latin alphabet, which enables easier literacy than does Arabic script. Admittedly, it's difficult to discern the importance of Latin script in these three countries. Kemal Atatürk, modern Turkey's founder, certainly thought that the conversion of the old Arabic-derived Ottoman script to a Latin one, which he pushed through with single-minded determination, would greatly benefit the new nation. In colonial Indonesia and Malaya, on the other hand, the analogous switch was driven, respectively, by the Dutch and British authorities, who had no clear agenda beyond maintaining colonial control.[67]

Evolving events in Egypt and Libya suggest an even more alarming scenario than that in what was formerly Soviet central Asia: societies that are technologically empowered enough to depose despotic and corrupt leaders yet are too poor and too dominated by traditional cultures to establish functioning democracies. This unhappy state of affairs may sustain a chronic, chaotic state of continuous revolution and counterrevolution, a situation already endemic in much of sub-Saharan Africa.

Perhaps the most critical geopolitical question faced by today's world is what the connection between wealth and democracy says about China, a Web-connected, rapidly modernizing, economically burgeoning, and increasingly powerful nation. The Central Intelligence Agency estimates its 2011 per capita GDP at $8,400 per year; this figure is growing at about an 8 percent annual clip.[68] The WVS gives China a low-to-middling S/SE score and a fairly high T/SR score, which suggest cautious optimism about the probability of an eastern European–style jump to a stable, democratic status. The world should hold its collective breath and wish China's economy the best, since that will to a large degree determine the empowerment of its populace and thus its prospects for democratization, and ultimately, the planet's overall geopolitical stability.

Prayers should also be said for the ability of China's democratic forces to exploit successfully the twenty-first century's advanced communications technologies, and so continue the grand historical process that began with the appearance of the proto-Semitic script nearly five millennia ago in the Sinai Desert.

As this first phonemic writing system evolved into Phoenician, Hebrew, Aramaic, and finally the ancient world's most easily mastered writing system—Greek, with its vowels—it empowered an ever broader segment of the Western world's population. As Greek script evolved into the Latin alphabet used in most of the West today, and as both became mechanized by the Gutenberg revolution, that empowerment advanced.

Information technology did not change much between 1500 and the 1840s, when the telegraph and the high-speed press debuted. The slow-moving empowerment of ordinary people suffered a setback in the nineteenth and twentieth centuries with the advent of the penny newspapers, radio, and television—expensive, complex media that could be controlled by only a few hands. Fortunately, the new digital media have once again dramatically moved the empowerment needle back toward ordinary citizens.

For the first time, a significant fraction of the world's citizens can be in instant communication with one another and send words, pictures, and videos across the planet. The coming decades will see, in China and elsewhere, the political, social, and cultural fallout from this explosion in human communication. Most of these changes should be as positive as they will be unpredictable. One thing, though, is certain: The medium is not merely the message, but the very page on which human history is written.

NOTES

Introduction

1. George Orwell, *Nineteen Eighty-Four* (New York: Alfred A. Knopf, 1987), 34.

2. For a précis of the author's novelistic intentions, see Bernard Crick, *George Orwell, a Life* (New York: Atlantic Monthly Press, 1980), 392–399. For the origins of the title, see Peter Davison, *George Orwell* (New York: Saint Martin's Press, 1996), 133–139.

3. Sonia Orwell and Ian Angus, Eds., *The Collected Essays, Journalism and Letters of George Orwell* (New York: Harcourt, Brace and World, 1968), I:380–381.

4. For an excellent summary of the Stasi's surveillance operations, see John O. Koehler, *Stasi* (Boulder, CO: Westview Press, 1999), 141–148; and David Childs and Richard Popplewell, *The Stasi* (New York: NYU Press, 1996), 82–94.

5. Data from Angus Maddison data file, http://www.ggdc.net/maddison/Historical_Statistics/horizontal-file_09-2008.xls; in 1950, the population of the world's communist nations totaled 834 million out of a world population of 2.526 billion.

6. "*Freedom in the World* Country Ratings," http://www.freedomhouse.org/uploads/fiw09/CompHistData/CountryStatus&RatingsOverview1973-2009.pdf, accessed 3/1/09.

7. See Barbara Wejnert, "Diffusion, Development, and Democracy, 1800–1999," *American Sociological Review* 70:1 (February 2005): 58. Wejnert also provides a more granular assessment of the extent of democracy in individual nations using various political and institutional indicators, which shows the same phenomenon. See also the extensive Polity IV data set from the Center for Systemic Peace, available at http://www.systemicpeace.org/.

8. Walter Wriston, the far-seeing chairman of Citibank, most clearly made this point when he observed, "Instead of validating Orwell's vision of Big Brother watching the citizen, [new communications technology] enables the citizen to watch Big Brother." Walter Wriston, "Bits, Bytes, and Diplomacy," *Foreign Affairs* 76:5 (September–October 1997): 172.

9. Donald Grove Barnes, *A History of the English Corn Laws* (New York: Augustus M. Kelly, 1961), 254.

10. V. Gordon Childe, *Man Makes Himself* (New York: New American Library, 1983), 141.

11. For a more complete discussion of the relationship between early literacy and the rise of a powerful scribal elite, see Harold A. Innis, *Empire and Communications* (Lanham, MD: Rowman and Littlefield, 2007), 33–45, quote 33.

12. Jack Goody, *The Power of the Written Tradition* (Washington, DC: Smithsonian Institution Press, 2000), 156.

13. Ibid.

14. Amos Paul Kennedy, Jr., *Once You Learn To Read, You Will Be Forever Free: Frederick Douglass* (Akron, AL: Kennedy Prints, 2007).

15. Claude Lévi-Strauss, *Tristes Tropiques,* John Weightman and Doreen Weightman, Trans. (New York: Atheneum, 1974), 299.

16. Martin Sprengling, *The Alphabet* (Chicago: University of Chicago Press, 1931), 48–50.

17. William H. McNeill, *The Rise of the West* (Chicago: University of Chicago Press, 1963), 147.

18. The Greeks were probably not the first peoples to signify vowels in their writing. In the ninth century BC, for example, scribes in Ugarit in Phoenicia, who had to deal with the various scripts and languages of their trading partners, began to experiment with vowel symbols. See A. Demsky, "The Biblical Period," in Martin Jan Mulder, Ed., *Mirka* (Maastricht: Van Gorcum, 1988), 4.

19. It is impossible to even closely approximate the number of black men who fell victim to what Douglas Blackmon has labeled "neoslavery"; he estimates that nearly a million worked under slave-like conditions on sharecropped farms, and hundreds of thousands more on chain gangs, in large-scale industrial facilities, and on outright slave farms. See Douglas A. Blackmon, *Slavery by Another Name* (New York: Doubleday, 2008), 9, 10, 258.

20. Ibid., 270–275.

21. Daniel Boorstin, *The Republic of Technology* (New York: Harper and Row, 1978), 1–35.

22. For an excellent overview of this debate, see Langdon Winner, "Do Artifacts Have Politics?" *Daedalus* 109:1 (Winter 1980): 121–136; and Winner, "Cyberlibertarian Myths and the Prospects for Community," http://www.rpi.edu/~winner/cyberlib2.html, accessed 4/23/11.

Chapter 1
Origins

1. Denise Schmandt-Besserat, *Before Writing* (Austin: University of Texas Press, 1992), I:1.

2. Herodotus, *The Histories* (Baltimore: Penguin Books, 1954), 227.

3. Herodotus, 224–227.

4. For a more formal treatment of the five abstractive technologies, see Don Ihde, *The Philosophy of Technology* (New York: Paragon House, 1993), 55–60.

5. For an excellent summary of this topic, see James R. Flynn, *What Is Intelligence?* (Cambridge: Cambridge University Press, 2007).

6. Schmandt-Besserat, I:158–160, I:184–186.

7. See, for example, Alexander Marshack, "Lunar Notation in Upper Paleolithic Remains," *Science* 146:3645 (November 6, 1964): 543–745; Francesco D'Errico, "Paleolithic Lunar Calendars: Wishful Thinking?" *Current Anthropology* 30:1 (February 1989): 117–118; and Alexander Marshack and Francesco D'Errico, "On Wishful Thinking and 'Lunar Calendars,'" *Current Anthropology* 30:4 (August–October 1989): 491–500.

8. Denise Schmandt-Besserat, personal communication.

9. Carleton S. Coon, *Cave Explorations in Iran* 1949 (Philadelphia: University Museum, University of Pennsylvania, 1951), 75.

10. Schmandt-Besserat, *Before Writing,* 192.

11. Denise Schmandt-Besserat, personal communication.

12. Stephen J. Lieberman, "Of Clay Pebbles, Hollow Clay Balls, and Writing: A Sumerian View," *American Journal of Archaeology* 84:3 (July 1980): 152. Even before Schmandt-Besserat recognized the tokens as counting devices, two researchers, Leo Oppenheim and Pierre Amiet, realized that the envelopes also served this purpose. See Leo Oppenheim, *Ancient Mesopotamia* (Chicago: University of Chicago Press, 1977), 239–242; and Pierre Amiet, "Il y a 5000 ans les Elamites inventaient l'écriture," *Archeologia* 12 (1966): 20–22. (The modern equivalent of this is the "poor man's copyright": a manuscript mailed in a tightly sealed envelope by the writer to himself or herself by certified mail, which, when opened, can provide undisputed evidence of authorship.)

13. Schmandt-Besserat, "The Envelopes That Bear the First Writing," *Technology and Culture* 21:3 (July, 1980): 384–385.

14. For a detailed criticism of the token hypothesis, see Paul Zimansky, review of *Before Writing in Journal of Field Archaeology* 20:4 (Winter 1993): 513–517.

15. William Warburton, *The Divine Legation of Moses Demonstrated,* 10th ed. (London: Printed for Thomas Tegg, 1846), II:173–178.

16. Austen Henry Layard, *Nineveh and its Remains* (New York: Frederick A. Praeger, 1970), 215.

17. Theya Molleson and Dawn Hodgson, "Human Remains from Woolley's Excavations at Ur," *Iraq* 65 (2003): 91–129; Alexandra Irving and Janet Ambers, "Hidden Treasure from the Royal Cemetery at Ur: Technology Sheds New Light on the Ancient Near East," *Near Eastern Archaeology* 65:3 (September 2002): 206–213; and H. R. Hall, "The Excavations at Ur," *The British Museum Quarterly* 4:2 (September 1929): 57–59. How the retainers died is open to question; Woolley thought they had been buried alive, but recent evidence points to a more violent end. See Aubrey Baadsgaard et al., "Human sacrifice and intentional corpse preservation in the Royal Cemetery of Ur," *Antiquity* 85:327 (March 1, 2011): 27–42.

18. Quoted in Lesley Adkins, *Empires of the Plain* (New York: St. Martin's Press, 2003), 77.

19. Ibid., 74–79.

20. George Rawlinson, *A Memoir of Major-General Sir Henry Creswicke Rawlinson* (London: Longmans, Green, 1898), 59.

21. Adkins, 78–80.

22. See Rawlinson, 57–59, 65–66, 307–333.

23. Piotr Michalowski, "Mesopotamian Cuneiform," in Peter T. Daniels and William Bright, Eds. *The World's Writing Systems* (New York: Oxford University Press, 1996), 33–34. See also Jean-Jacques Glassner, *The Invention of Cuneiform* (Baltimore: Johns Hopkins University Press, 2003), 29–31, particularly for a detailed discussion of the precise dating of the first evidence of writing at the Uruk site, which the author puts at about 3350 BC.

24. Hans J. Nissen, *The Early History of the Ancient Near East* (Chicago: University of Chicago Press, 1990), 71–72.

25. Marc Van De Mieroop, *The Ancient Mesopotamian City* (Oxford: Clarendon Press, 1997), 9.

26. Denise Schmandt-Besserat, personal communication.

27. Henri-Jean Martin, *The History and Power of Writing,* Lydia G. Cochrane, Trans. (Chicago: University of Chicago Press, 1988), 45.

28. Oppenheim, 239–242.

29. Hans J. Nissen et al., *Archaic Bookkeeping* (Chicago: University of Chicago Press, 1993), 118.

30. I. J. Gelb, *A Study of Writing* (Chicago: University of Chicago, 1963), 67, n279.

31. Geoffrey Sampson, *Writing Systems* (Palo Alto: Stanford University Press, 1990), 78.

32. E. B. Zechmeister et al., "Growth of a Functionally Important Lexicon," *Journal of Reading Behavior* 27:2 (1995): 201–212. With its five vowels and twenty-one consonants, the English alphabet, for example, contains five vowel-only, 105 each of the consonant-vowel and vowel-consonant type—for example, *la* and *al,* respectively—and 2,205 of the consonant-vowel-consonant type—for example, *pal.*

33. Robert K. Ritner, "Egyptian Writing," in Peter T. Daniels and William Bright, Eds. *The World's Writing Systems* (New York: Oxford University Press, 1996), 73.

34. Wolfgang Schenkel, "The Structure of Hieroglyphic Script," *Royal Anthropological Institute of Great Britain and Ireland* 15 (August 1976): 4–7.

35. R. I. M. Dunbar, "Coevolution of neocortical size, group size and language in humans," *Behavioral and Brain Sciences* 16:4 (1993): 681–735. Dunbar's core data focused on group size as a function of the absolute and relative size of the neocortex—roughly, the "thinking" part of the brain. However, he did specifically state that "there is a cognitive limit to the number of individuals with whom any one person can maintain stable relationships, that this limit is a direct function of relative neocortex size, and that this in turn limits group size."

36. Glassner, 213.

37. David Brion Davis, *Inhuman Bondage* (Oxford: Oxford University Press, 2006), 29.

38. Thorkild Jacobsen, "Democracy in Ancient Mesopotamia," *Journal of Near Eastern Studies* 2:3 (July 1943): 159–172. For the poem fragment detailing the story of Gilgamesh, Kish, and the council of elders, the probability of his historical

existence, and the dating of his rule, see Samuel Noah Kramer and Thorkild Jacobsen, "Gilgamesh and Agga," *American Journal of Archaeology* 53:1 (January–March, 1949): 1–18. Not all scholars accept Jacobsen's analysis; for a balanced criticism of his "ancient bicameral hypothesis," see Gonzalo Rubio, "Sumerian Literature" in Carl S. Ehrlich, *From an Antique Land* (New York: Rowman and Littlefield, 2009), 33–34.

39. Glassner, 212.

40. Ian Young, personal communication.

41. Aage Westenholz, "The Old Akkadian Empire in Contemporary Opinion," in Mogens Trolle Larsen, *Mesopotamia, Volume 7* (Copenhagen: Akademisk Forlag, 1979), 112.

42. Ibid., 107–115.

43. J. Finkelstein, "The Laws of Ur-Nammu," in J. Pritchard, Ed., *The Ancient Near East Supplementary Texts and Pictures Relating to the Old Testament* (Princeton: Princeton University Press, 1969), 88.

44. Van De Mieroop, 149–156.

45. Nissen, 51–54, 70.

46. Benjamin Foster, *Umma in the Sargonic Period* (Hamden, CT: Archon Press, 1982), 25, 46–50.

47. Gelb, 222.

48. See Samuel Noah Kramer, "Schooldays: A Sumerian Composition Relating to the Education of a Scribe," *Journal of the American Oriental Society* 69:4 (October–December 1949): 199–215.

Chapter 2
The ABCs of Democracy

1. Margaret S. Drower, *Flinders Petrie* (London: Victor Gollancz, 1985), 3–8.

2. Ibid., 8–33.

3. Ibid., 289–292.

4. W. M. Flinders Petrie, *Researches in Sinai* (New York: E.P. Dutton and Company, 1906), 129–132.

5. W. M. Flinders Petrie, *The Formation of the Alphabet* (London, Macmillan and Co. and Bernard Quaritch, 1912); see especially 19.

6. The later Arabic script, along with a large number of its extinct relatives, probably derived from a common Sabaean ancestor in western Arabia, which almost certainly was related to the Phoenician alphabet.

7. That philologists know the alphabetical order of ancient alphabets might seem strange. It is not; one of the most common archaeological artifacts is the so-called "abecedary," the complete alphabet listing universally used for pedagogical purposes in both the ancient and modern worlds.

8. Alan H. Gardiner, "The Egyptian Origin of the Semitic Alphabet," *Journal of Egyptian Archaeology* 3:1 (January 1916): 1–16, and "Once Again, the Proto-Sinaitic Inscriptions," *Journal of Egyptian Archaeology* 48 (December 1962): 45–48.

9. Drower, 424.

10. Joseph Naveh, *Early History of the Alphabet* (Jerusalem: Magnes Press, 1982), 25–27. See also William F. Albright, *The Proto-Sinaitic Inscriptions and Their Decipherment* (Cambridge, MA: Harvard University Press, 1966), 10–12; William F. Albright, "The Inscription from Gezer at the School in Jerusalem," *Bulletin of the American Schools of Oriental Research* 58 (April 1935): 28–29; and David Diringer, "The Palestinian Inscriptions and the Origin of the Alphabet," *Journal of the American Oriental Society* 63:1 (March 1943): 24–30; John Coleman Darnell et al., "Two Early Alphabetic Inscriptions from the Wadi el-Hôl: New Evidence for the Origin of the Alphabet from the Western Desert of Egypt," *Annual of the American Schools of Oriental Research* 50 (2005): 64–124.

11. See, for example, Exodus 24:4 and 34:28.

12. To get a flavor of this controversy, see Israel Finkelstein, "State Formation in Israel and Judah: A Contrast in Trajectory," *Near Eastern Archaeology* 62:1 (March 1999): 35–52; William G. Dever, "Excavating the Hebrew Bible, or Burying It Again?" *Bulletin of the American Schools of Oriental Research* 322 (May 2001): 67–77; and Israel Finkelstein and Neil Asher Silberman, "'The Bible Unearthed': A Rejoinder," *Bulletin of the American Schools of Oriental Research* 327 (August 2002): 63–73.

13. Mel Gibson's film *The Passion of the Christ* evinced recent interest in Jesus's language. The movie has Jesus and his Jewish followers speaking Aramaic, while the Romans speak Latin. In actuality, few eastern Romans spoke Latin as their first language; most spoke Greek, which had also been the administrative language of the Seleucids who had ruled Palestine for hundreds of years following the Alexandrian conquest. For this reason alone, it seems highly likely that Jesus spoke some Greek, since numerous New Testament passages have him speaking to Roman officials without need of an interpreter; in addition, Matthew was a tax collector, and thus had to be fluent in Greek. Ian Young, in "Aramaic, and Mel Gibson's T*he Passion of the Christ,*" unpublished, quoted with kind permission of the author. Also note, from Acts 21:37, when Paul asks permission to speak to his Roman captor, the latter asks, in surprise, "Do you speak Greek?"

14. William J. Bernstein, *A Splendid Exchange* (New York: Grove/Atlantic Press, 2008), 55–57.

15. Genesis 24:4, 29:21; Deuteronomy 26:5. See also Philip K. Hitti, *History of Syria* (New York: Macmillan, 1951), 164; Raymond A. Bowman, "Arabians, Aramaic, and the Bible," *Journal of Near Eastern Studies* 7:2 (April 1948): 66–70.

16. Jeremiah 36:10.

17. This formulation is referred to as the "Milman Parry thesis." For a superb treatment of the oral origins of the Bible, see Susan Niditch, *Oral World and Written Word* (Louisville: Westminster John Knox Press, 1996). For a more general treatment, see Adam Parry, Ed., *The Making of Homeric Verse: The Collected Papers of Milman Parry* (Oxford: Oxford University Press, 1987); and Walter J. Ong, *Orality and Literacy* (London: Routledge, 1988).

18. William M. Schniedewind, *How the Bible Became a Book* (Cambridge: Cambridge University Press, 2004), 101–102. See also Schniedewind "Sociolinguistic

Reflections of the Letter of a 'Literate' Soldier (Lachish 3)," *Zeitschrift für Althebraistic* 13:2 (2000): 157–167.

19. Quote from Saul Levin, "The 'Qeri' as the Primary Text of the Hebrew Bible," *General Linguistics* 35 (1997): 185. See also Paul J. Achtemeier, "Omne verbum sonat: The New Testament and the Oral Environment of Late Western Antiquity," *Journal of Biblical Literature* 109:1 (Spring 1990): 9–13. See also Niditch; and Ong, 118–121.

20. David McLain Carr, *Writing on the Tablet of the Heart* (Oxford: Oxford University Press, 2005), 116.

21. Benedikt Otzen, "Israel Under the Assyrians," in Mogens Trolle Larsen, Ed., *Mesopotamia Volume 7* (Copenhagen: Akademisk Forlag, 1979), 251–261; Van Den Mieroop, 51; and John Bright, *A History of Israel* (Philadelphia: Westminster Press, 1972), 329–368.

22. Whether or not the return saved the Jewish religion and culture will never be known for certain. Many Jews remained in Judah even after the devastation and ethnic cleansing visited on them by Nebuchadnezzar, but this was also probably true of some members of the ten tribes of the northern state, which had fallen into obscurity.

23. For a superb discussion of the "kinetics" of assimilation in the ancient world, see Van Den Mieroop, 112–115.

24. Georges Roux, *Ancient Iraq* (New York: Penguin Books, 1966), 250.

25. Martin, 55.

26. II Kings 18:17–35.

27. Bowman, 73–74.

28. E. Kautzsch and Charles R. Brown, "The Aramaic Language," *Hebraica* 1:2 (October 1884): 100. Before the exile, the Jews employed a script more closely resembling Phoenician, and probably derived from the proto-Semitic script found at Serabit el-Khadim. Paleographers most commonly refer to it as "old Hebrew"; this archaic script is closely related to the modern so-called Samaritan script used in modern Israel and the occupied West Bank, primarily for liturgical purposes by a group claiming descent from the ten tribes.

29. I Kings 9:26–28, King James Version; and Herodotus, *The Histories* (Baltimore: Penguin, 1968), 225.

30. For a more detailed survey of this debate, see Gelb, 176–191; Joseph Naveh, "The Greek Alphabet: New Evidence," *Biblical Archaeologist* 43:1 (Winter 1980): 22–25; Rhys Carpenter, "The Antiquity of the Greek Alphabet," *American Journal of Archaeology* 37:1 (January–March 1933): 8–29, and "The Greek Alphabet Again," *American Journal of Archaeology* 42:1 (January–March 1938): 58–69. An earlier, and now discredited, hypothesis has the Greek alphabet transmitted overland by Aramaean traders in southeast Asia Minor; see Raymond A. Bowman, "Aramaeans, Aramaic, and the Bible," *Journal of Near Eastern Studies* 7:2 (April 1948): 65–90.

31. Amos Oz, *A Tale of Love and Darkness,* Nicholas de Lange, Trans. (New York: Harcourt, 2004), 42–43.

32. Innis, *Empire and Communications,* 85.

33. For a discussion of the depth of oral memory, see Jan Vansina, *Oral Tradition of History* (Madison: University of Wisconsin Press, 1985), 1–15, 117, 168.

34. On the rudimentary dialogue differentiation in the Homeric epics, see Jennifer Wise, *Dionysus Writes* (Ithaca, NY: Cornell University Press, 1998): 28–29.

35. Ibid., 171.

36. Alfred Bates Lord, *The Singer of Tales* (Cambridge MA: Harvard University Press, 2000): and Adam Parry, *The Making of Homeric Verse: The Collected Papers of Milman Parry* (New York: Oxford University Press, 1987).

37. See, for example, C. J. Fuller, "Orality, Literacy, and Memorization: Priestly Education in Contemporary South India," *Modern Asian Studies* 35:1 (February 2001): 2–3; and Glenn D. Deckert, "Sociocultural Barriers to the Reading Habit: The Case of Iran," *Journal of Reading* 25:8 (May 1982): 746–747.

38. Martin, 84.

39. William V. Harris, *Ancient Literacy* (Cambridge MA: Harvard University Press, 1989), 9–11. The most frequently quoted citation referring to schooling in classical Greece, Herodutus's passing mention of 119 schoolchildren killed by a roof collapse in Chios around 496 BC, without any mention of the curriculum (Herodotus, 6.27), is symptomatic of the scarcity of historical evidence on the extent of literacy or of its teaching.

40. For those who have not been to a professional sporting event in recent years, enthusiastic crowds frequently sing the Village People hit of a few decades ago, "YMCA," while miming those four letters with their arms.

41. For the known text fragments, see John Maxwell Edmonds, *Fragments of Attic Comedy* (Leiden: E. J. Brill, 1957), I:177–181. For a detailed interpretation, see Jesper Svenbro, "The 'Interior' Voice: On the Invention of Silent Reading," in John J. Winkler and Froma I. Zeitlin, Eds., *Nothing to Do with Dionysos?* (Princeton: Princeton University Press, 1990), 381–383.

42. Aristophanes, *Frogs,* http://www.bartleby.com/8/9/3.html, accessed June 29, 2012.

43. Arthur Pikard-Cambridge, *The Dramatic Festivals of Athens* (Oxford: Clarendon Press, 1968), 190–191.

44. R. K. Sinclair, *Democracy and Participation in Athens* (Cambridge: Cambridge University Press, 1991), 46, 112–113.

45. For a sampling of this controversy, see Harris, *Ancient Literacy,* 3–115; and Eric A. Havelock, *Preface to Plato* (New York: Grosset and Dunlap, 1967), 40–41.

46. Rosalind Thomas, *Literacy and Orality in Ancient Greece* (Cambridge: Cambridge University Press, 1992), 82.

47. Robert J. Lenardon, *The Saga of Themistocles* (London: Thames and Hudson, 1978), 27–30.

48. Herodotus, 334–338; Aristotle, *The Athenian Constitution* XIV–XXII. See also Sara Forsdyke, *Exile, Ostracism, and Democracy* (Princeton: Princeton University Press, 2005), 107–133.

49. Lenardon, 31–35.

50. Forsdyke, 170–173.

51. Plutarch, *Aristides* VII: 6, from *Plutarch's Lives,* Bernadotte Perrin, Trans., (London: William Heinemann Ltd., 1964), 233–235.

52. Oscar Broneer, "Excavations on the North Slope of the Acropolis, 1937," *Hesperia* 7:2 (1938): 228–243.

53. Eugene Vanderpool, *Ostracism at Athens* (Cincinnati, OH: University of Cincinnati Press, 1970), 12. The author probably describes ostraca from the same find as Broneer.

54. Aristotle, *The Athenian Constitution,* 65–68, http://classics.mit.edu/Aristotle/athenian_const.3.3.html, accessed June 28, 2012.

55. Aristophanes, *Wasps,* 105, http://www.pereus.tufts.edu/hopper/text?doc =Aristoph.&20wasps%20106&lang=original, accessed June 28, 2012.

56. See J. E. Atkinson, "Curbing the Comedians: Cleon versus Aristophanes and Syracosius' Decree," *Classical Quarterly,* New Series 42:1 (1992): 56–64.

57. Sinclair, 19–21.

58. Aristotle, *The Athenian Constitution,* 50.

59. Sinclair, 68–70, 137, 152; and Aristotle, *The Athenian Constitution,* 49–69.

60. Plutarch, *Themistocles,* II, 3, III 1–2.

61. Whether or not Themistocles actually served as archon in 493–492 is far from settled. To get a sense of the controversy over this issue, see Erich S. Gruen, "Stesimbrotus on Miltiades and Themistocles," *California Studies in Classical Antiquity* 3 (1970): 91–98; and Alden A. Mosshammer, "Themistocles' Archonship in the Chronographic Tradition," *Hermes* 103:2 (1975): 222–234. See also Herodotus, 457.

62. Translation from Lenardon, 69–70. For a description and a superb photograph of the original inscription, see Michael H. Jameson, "A Decree of Themistokles from Troizen," *Hesperia* 29:2 (April–June, 1960): 198–223. The inscription is almost certainly not the original, or even contemporary with it; rather, it appears to have been made about two centuries later. For a discussion of its authenticity and its points of agreement with and disagreement from other historical sources, particularly Herodotus, see Charles W. Fornara, "The Value of the Themistocles Decree," *The American Historical Review* 73:2 (December 1967): 425–433; and Mikael Johansson, "The Inscription from Troizen: A Decree of Themistocles?" *Zeitschrift für Papyrologie und Epigraphik* 137 (2001): 69–92.

63. Herodotus, 541.

64. Ibid.; also see Plutarch, *Themistocles,* XXI–XXXII.

65. John Adams, Charles Francis Adams, *The Works of John Adams* (Boston: Little, Brown, and Company, 1865), IV:490.

66. Ibid., 148–151.

67. Typically, Adams criticizes Solon's reforms in the following terms: "He put all power into hands the least capable of properly using it [the *thētes*]; and, accordingly, these, by uniting, altered the constitution at their pleasure, and brought the ruin of the nation" (Adams, IV:479). For a critical and detailed review of modern opinion of Athenian democracy, see Jennifer T. Roberts, *Athens on Trial* (Princeton: Princeton University Press, 1994).

68. Paul Cartledge, "Literacy in the Spartan Oligarchy," *The Journal of Hellenic Studies* 98 (1978): 25–37. For the institution of krypteia, see J. B. Bury, *A History of Greece* (New York: Modern Library, 1937), 124.

69. Harris, *Ancient Literacy,* 116.

70. Luciano Canfora, *The Vanished Library,* Trans. Martin Ryle (Berkeley: University of California Press, 1990), 11–99; and Roger Bagnall, "Library of Dreams," *Proceedings of the American Philosophical Society* 146:4 (December 2002), 348–362.

71. Bagnall, 359.

72. Canfora, 37.

73. Ibid., 24.

74. Ibid., 46.

75. John Willis Clark, *The Care of Books* (Cambridge: Cambridge University Press, 1901), 8; Edwyn Robert Bevan, *The House of Seleucus* (London: Edward Arnold, 1902), I:200; and Innis, *Empire and Communications,* 115.

76. The huge ovine requirements of parchment documents have recently acquired the reputation of urban myth, but are factual; the Souvigny Bible, which contains 392 large-format leaves, required two hundred sheepskins. See Martin, 51.

Chapter 3
Twelve Tablets, Seven Hills, and a Few Early Christians

1. William V. Harris, *Ancient Literacy,* 206.

2. Anonymous, "Papers of Dr. James McHenry on the Federal Convention of 1787," *The American Historical Review* 11:3 (April 1906), 618. The referenced quotes are reconstructed from Dr. McHenry's somewhat fragmentary notes.

3. Sydney Homer and Richard Sylla, *A History of Interest Rates,* 4th ed. (New York: John Wiley & Sons, 2005), 40–41, 56.

4. Recent behavioral research demonstrates that humans tend to grossly underestimate the fiscal damage that can be done by debt that compounds at high rates; see, for example, W. A. Wagenaar and H. Timmers, "Extrapolation of exponential time series is not enhanced by having more data points," *Perception and Psychophysics* 24:2 (1978): 182–184.

5. Hans Julius Wolff, *Roman Law* (Norman: University of Oklahoma Press, 1951), 54–59.

6. The Greek-to-Etruscan-to-Latin sequence, though representing the consensus of modern philologists, is not universally accepted; others have postulated the direct adoption of Greek script by the Romans. See Naveh, *Early History of the Alphabet,* 186; Arthur E. Gordon, "On the Origins of the Latin Alphabet: Modern Views," *California Studies in Classical Antiquity* 2 (1969): 157–170; and Rhys Carpenter, "The Alphabet in Italy," *American Journal of Archaeology* 49:4 (October–December 1945): 452–464. Carpenter points out that the early runic alphabets of northern Europe bear a striking resemblance to Etruscan, which may have been imparted to them through trade contacts.

7. For a detailed discussion of the political considerations surrounding the Twelve Tablets, see Walter Eder, "The Political Significance of the Codification of Law in Archaic Societies: An Unconventional Hypothesis," in Kurt A. Raaflaub, Ed., *Social Struggles in Archaic Rome* (Berkeley: University of California Press, 1986), 262–300.

8. Harriet I. Flower, *Roman Republics* (Princeton: Princeton University Press, 2010), 38–39.

9. William V. Harris, *Ancient Literacy,* 249.

10. Keith R. Bradley, *Slavery and Rebellion in the Roman World, 140 BC–70 BC* (Bloomington: Indiana University Press, 1989), 19.

11. For a discussion of the relevant entries in Plutarch, Livy, and Polybius, see N. G. L. Hammond, *Epirus* (Oxford: Clarendon Press, 1967), 635.

12. Strabo, *Geography* 14.5.2. See also W. A. Laidlaw, *A History of Delos* (Oxford: Basil Blackwell, 1933), 266–267.

13. Adrienne Mayor, *The Poison King* (Princeton: Princeton University Press, 2010), 13–22.

14. William V. Harris, "On War and Greed in the Second Century BC," *The American Historical Review* 76:5 (December 1971): 1372. This act was most famously said to have been meted out to Crassus's already dead body by victorious Parthian soldiers; its metaphorical nature seems to possess a certain universality, since the Incas also applied it to the Spanish official Vincente de Valverde in 1541.

15. For a rough idea of slave imports into Rome, see Frank Tenney, *An Economic Survey of Ancient Rome* (Paterson, NJ: Pageant Books, 1959), I:187–188.

16. See, for example, Mary L. Gordon, "The Nationality of Slaves under the Early Roman Empire," *The Journal of Roman Studies* 14 (1924): 93–111.

17. The terms for many modern machines were initially associated with the humans who operated them: thus, in the late nineteen century business executives frequently attempted to seduce their typewriters.

18. Flower, 38–41.

19. Suetonius, *The Lives of the Twelve Caesars: D. Octavius Caesar Augustus* 76, http://perseus.uchicago.edu/perseus-cgi/citequery3.pl?dbname=PerseusLatin Texts&getid=1&query=Suet.%20Aug.76, accessed 6/28/12.

20. *The Letters of Pliny the Younger,* III.5, http://ancienthistory.about.com/ library/bl/bl_text_plinyltrs3.htm, accessed 9/23/20.

21. William C. McDermott "M. Cicero and M. Tiro," *Historia: Zeitschrift für Alte Geschicte* 21:2 (Second Quarter, 1972): 271–272.

22. See, for example, John M. Lenhart, "The Origin of the Invention of Printing: Its Background," *Catholic Historical Review* 25:3 (October 1939): 303; and Felix Reichmann, "The Book Trade at the Time of the Roman Empire," *Library Quarterly* 8:1 (January 1938): 62–63.

23. Romans also recognized another class of library worker, *librarioli,* who performed janitorial tasks, and of whom literacy was presumably not required; see George F. Houston, "The Slave and Freedman Personnel of Public Libraries in Ancient Rome," *Transactions of the American Philological Association,* 132 (2002): 139–176.

24. Martin, 58–59.

25. Harris, *Ancient Literacy,* 257.

26. John Eastburn Boswell, "Expositio and Oblatio: The Abandonment of Children in the Ancient and Medieval Family," *American Historical Review* 89:1 (February 1984): 10–33; and William V. Harris, "Towards a Study of the Ancient Slave Trade," *Memoirs of the American Academy in Rome* 36 (1980): 123.

27. Petronius, *Satyricon* LXXV, http://www.gutenberg.org/files/5225/5225-h/5225-h.htm, accessed 9/30/10.

28. Clarence A. Forbes, "The Education and Training of Slaves in Antiquity," *Transactions and Proceedings of the American Philological Association* 86 (1955): 334–342, quote, 341.

29. *Vegetius: Epitome of Military Science,* N. P. Milner, Trans. (Liverpool: Liverpool University Press, 1996), 51–52.

30. Harris, *Ancient Literacy,* 253–255.

31. See especially the table of contents in Robert O. Fink, *Roman Military Records on Papyrus* (Cleveland: Case Western University Press, 1971), ix–xiii.

32. "In Memoriam, Harold Idris Bell," 1879–1967, *The Journal of Roman Studies* 57:1/2 (1967): xiii.

33. Robin Birley, *On Hadrian's Wall* (London: Thames and Hudson, 1977), 132.

34. Professor Alan K. Bowman, personal communication.

35. Alan K. Bowman, *Life and Letters on the Roman Frontier* (London: British Museum Press, 1994), 127.

36. Alan Bowman and David Thomas, *The Vindolanda Writing Tablets* (London: British Museum Press, 1994), 29–30.

37. Ibid., 24, 42–49.

38. Baron de Montesquieu, *Reflections on the Causes of the Rise and Fall of the Roman Empire* (London: Printed for W. Innys in Pater-noster Row, C. Davis against Gray's-Inn Gate, Holborn, R. Manby on Ludgate-Hill, and H. S. Cox in Pater-noster Row, 1753), 147.

39. In spite of a rapidly increasing population, U.S. House membership has been limited to 435. (In 1959 the number temporarily increased to 437 after the admission of Alaska and Hawaii.)

40. Fergus Millar, *The Crowd in Rome in the Late Republic* (Ann Arbor: University of Michigan Press, 1998), 13–20.

41. C. Nicolet, *The World of the Citizen in Republican Rome,* P. S. Falla, Trans. (Los Angeles: University of California Press, 1980), 137.

42. George Willis Botsford, *The Roman Assemblies from their Origin to the End of the Republic* (New York: Macmillan Company, 1909), 262–263.

43. Flower, 45.

44. Edward E. Best, "Literacy and Roman Voting," *Historia: Zeitschrift für Alte Geschicte* 23:4 (Fourth Quarter 1978): 428–438. See also Flower, 72–75.

45. Jürgen von Urgern-Sternberg, "The Crisis of the Republic," in Harriet Flower, Trans. and Ed., *The Cambridge Companion to the Roman Republic* (Cambridge: Cambridge University Press, 2004), 90.

46. Flower, *Roman Republics,* 5, 39, 87–88.

47. Millar, 197–225. Confusingly, *ambitus* could also mean the crime of political corruption, usually through bribery.

48. Made famous by *Peter Pan*: you can fly only if you believe you can.

49. Flower, *The Roman Republics,* 101.

50. A. W. Lintott, *Violence in Republican Rome* (Oxford: Clarendon Press, 1968), 74.

51. Flower, *The Roman Republics,* 86–87.

52. Ibid., 82–85.

53. Montesquieu, 146.

54. Sallust, *The Jurgurthine War* 65:4–5 (London: Penguin Books, 2007), 102.

55. Flower, *The Roman Republics,* 159.

56. Christopher S. Mackay, *Ancient Rome* (Cambridge: Cambridge University Press, 2004), 103 126.

57. Von Ungern-Sternberg, 98–100. See also Flower, *The Roman Republics,* 93.

58. Caesar's famous cry "Et tu, Brute?" was pure Shakespearean invention; according to Plutarch, he speaks (in Latin) to the first assailant, Casca, whom he has successfully stymied: "Accursed Casca, what does thou?" Casca then implores his nearby brother, in Greek, "Brother, help," and they initiate the stab fest. Plutarch, *The Life of Julius Caesar,* 66.

59. Recall that Coptic's similarity to demotic allowed Jean-François Champollion to decipher the Rosetta Stone. Today, the term "Coptic" carries multiple connotations, including the above-described alphabet, the last incarnation of the Egyptian language before it was replaced by Arabic, the indigenous Egyptian Christians, and, finally, their religion itself.

60. Keith Hopkins, "Conquest by book," in J. H. Humphrey, Ed., "Literacy in the Roman World," *Journal of Roman Archaeology Supplementary Series* 3 (1991): 144–148.

61. Ibid., 148.

62. Ibid., 86.

63. Stephen J. Davis, *The Early Coptic Papacy* (Cairo: American University Press in Cairo, 2004), 28–30.

64. H. I. Bell, "Evidences of Christianity in Egypt during the Roman Period," *The Harvard Theological Review* 37:3 (July 1944), 185–208.

65. Davis, 1–42. See also Jill Kamil, *Coptic Egypt* (Cairo: American University Press in Cairo, 1987), 39. Coptics revere two kinds of believers: martyrs, who suffer imprisonment, torture, and death; and "confessors" such as Melitius, who suffer only the first two.

66. See, for example, Davis, 22; also, Stephen J. Davis, personal communication.

67. Bart D. Ehrman, *Lost Christianities* (Oxford: Oxford University Press, 2003), 51–53.

68. Ibid., 113–127.

Chapter 4
Before Gutenberg

1. Letter to Vratislaus, king of Bohemia, quoted in Margaret Deanesly, *The Lollard Bible* (Cambridge: University Press, 1920), 24.

2. The solido was a four-gram gold coin, equivalent to the English pound, Venetian ducat, or French livre. According to Gregory King, the average skilled English farmer or craftsman earned about £10 per year. See Paul Slack, "Measuring the national wealth in seventeenth-century England," *Economic History Review* 57:4 (November 2004): 607–635. For an online tabular summary of King's data, see http://www.york.ac.uk/depts/maths/histstat/king.htm.

3. George Haven Putnam, *Books and Their Makers During the Middle Ages* (New York: Hillary House Publishers, 1897), quote, 39; 40; 43–44.

4. Paul Saenger, *Space Between Words* (Stanford, CA: Stanford University Press, 1997), 5–12, 26.

5. William G. T. Shedd Ed., *Confessions of Augustine* (Andover, MA: Warren F. Draper, pub, 1860), 119–120.

6. Extensively described ibid., 81–242.

7. Saenger, 249–250, 258–276. The "Saenger hypothesis," that the advent of spaced script precipitated an explosion of literary activity and social change, though well accepted by paleographers and linguists, is not without its critics. See, for example, Michael Richter, untitled review, *American Historical Review* 106:2 (April 2001): 627–628; and Mark Aronoff, untitled review, *Language in Society* 31:4 (September 2002): 624–628.

8. Paul F. Grendler, "The Universities of the Renaissance and Reformation," *Renaissance Quarterly,* 57:1 (Spring 2004): 5–6.

9. Andrew Pettegree, *The Book in the Renaissance* (New Haven, CT: Yale University Press, 2010), 6–9.

10. Tsien Tsuen-Hsuin, *Paper and Paper Making* (Science and Civilisation in China V. 1, Joseph Needham, Ed.) (Cambridge: Cambridge University Press, 1985), 24–25.

11. Dard Hunter, *Papermaking* (New York: Dover Publications, 1978), 49–50.

12. Tsien, 1–2, 42–43. Another oft-repeated morsel of paper mythology has its technology transferred to the Muslim world with the capture of paper-maker Chinese prisoners after their defeat at the Battle of Talas in AD 751 in central Asia. This seems unlikely: first, because paper had been used in central Asia for decades before the Battle of Talas; and second, because the Muslims, like the later Europeans, made their paper from rags, rather than from plants, as did the southern Chinese. This author, alas, pleads guilty to perpetuating the Talas chestnut; see William J. Bernstein, *A Splendid Exchange* (New York: Grove Atlantic Press, 2008), 74–75.

13. Jonathan M. Bloom, *Paper Before Print* (New Haven, CT: Yale University Press, 2001), 8.

14. See Bernstein, *A Splendid Exchange,* 77–109.

15. Bloom, 40–81.

16. Ibid., 80.

17. Innis, *Empire and Communications,* 138.

18. Martin, 208–209.

19. Lucien Febvre and Henri-Jean Martin, *The Coming of the Book,* David Gerard, Trans. (London: Verso, 1997), 30, 34.

20. Matthew 19:24.

21. Matthew 28:19–20.

22. Gabriel Audisio, *The Waldensian Dissent* (Cambridge: Cambridge University Press, 1999), 7–15.

23. Ibid., 23.

24. Ibid., 31, anecdotally quoted.

25. Ibid., 148.

26. Alexander Patschovsky, "The Literacy of Waldensianism from Valdes to c. 1400," in Peter Biller and Anne Hudson, Eds., *Heresy and Literacy* (Cambridge: Cambridge University Press, 1994), 131.

27. Gabriel Audisio, "Were the Waldensians more literate than their contemporaries (after 1460–1560)?" in Biller and Hudson.

28. Estimates of Wycliffe's birth range from the early 1320s to slightly after 1330; see K. B. McFarlane, *John Wycliffe* (London: English Universities Press, 1953), 3.

29. Ibid., 23.

30. K. B. McFarlane, *Wycliffe and English Non-Conformity* (Harmondsworth, England: Penguin Books, 1972), 72–73, quote 41.

31. Ibid. 72–79.

32. Henry Hart Milman, *History of Latin Christianity* (London: John Murray, 1867), 184–198.

33. Richard Rex, *The Lollards* (New York: Palgrave, 2002), 54.

34. Margaret Deanesly, *The Lollard Bible* (Cambridge: Cambridge University Press, 1920), 2–3.

35. Margaret Deanesly, *The Significance of the Lollard Bible* (London: Athlone Press, 1951), 3–23.

36. For a detailed description of Purvey's authorship and later career, see ibid., 255–257 and 283–284.

37. Ibid., 268–297. For the full text of the Twelve Conclusions, see H. S. Cronin, "The Twelve Conclusions of the Lollards," *The English Historical Review* 22:86 (April 1907): 292–304. The archbishop's prohibition of Bible translation was not absolute, but can be interpreted as allowing translations approved by the Church. See, for example, H. Wheeler Robinson, Ed., *The Bible in its Ancient and English Versions* (Oxford: Clarendon Press, 1940), 142–143.

38. McFarlane, *Wycliffe and English Non-Conformity,* 144–165; for more detail on the Oldcastle episode, see W. T. Waugh, "Sir John Oldcastle," *The English Historical Review* 20:79 (July 1905): 434–456; and W. T. Waugh, "Sir John Oldcastle (Continued)," *The English Historical Review* 20:80 (October 1905): 637–658.

39. Rev. John Foxe, *Book of Martyrs* (Hartford, CT: Edwin Hunt, 1845), 194–195.

40. See, for example, Deansely, *The Lollard Bible,* 20.

41. For a detailed analysis of the connection between the English and Czech reform movements, see R. R. Betts, "English and Cˇzech Influences on the Hussite Movement," T*ransactions of the Royal Historical Society,* Fourth Series, 21 (1939): 71–102; and Anne Hudson, "From Oxford to Prague: The Writings of John Wyclif and His English Followers in Bohemia," *Slavonic and East European Review* 75:4 (October 1997): 642–657.

42. František Šmahel, "Literacy and Heresy in Hussite Bohemia," in Biller and Hudson, 243.

43. Matthew Spinka, *John Hus* (Princeton: Princeton University Press, 1968), 12–18.

44. Ibid., 29.

45. Ibid., 51, 59.

46. Šmahel, 244.

47. Spinka, 109–117, quote 114.

48. Ibid., 219–290, 296–297.

49. David Crystal and Hilary Crystal, *Words on Words* (London: Penguin Books, 2000), 123.

50. Audisio, 78–85.

51. Anne Hudson, "'Laicus litteratus': the paradox of Lollardry," in Biller and Hudson, 234.

52. Ibid., 231.

53. Audisio, 79–81.

54. For a discussion of the ultimate assimilation of the Waldensian, Lollard, and Hussite identities into Protestantism, see ibid., 190–191; for the slaughter of Waldensians as "Protestants" during the religious wars, see ibid., 192–202.

Chapter 5
Punch and Counterpunch

1. Victor Hugo, *Notre-Dame de Paris* (New York: A Wessels Company, 1902), I:206.

2. From Johannes Janssen, *History of the German people at the close of the Middle Ages,* M. A. Mitchell and A. M. Christie, Trans., 1896, quoted in A. Uhlendorf, "The Invention of Printing and Its Spread til 1470: With Special Reference to Social and Economic Factors," *The Library Quarterly* 2:3 (July 1932), 180.

3. Bloom, 203–213.

4. J. U. Nef, "Mining and Metallurgy in Medieval Civilization," in M. Postan and E. E. Rich, Eds., *The Cambridge Economic History of Europe* (Cambridge: Cambridge University Press, 1952), II: 429–492.

5. Theodore L. De Vinne, *The Invention of Printing* (London: Trübner, 1877), 50. For example, in Cicero's *The Nature of the Gods* II:37, "He who believes this may as well believe that if a great quantity of the one-and-twenty letters, composed

either of gold or any other matter, were thrown upon the ground, they would fall into such order as legibly to form the Annals of Ennius. I doubt whether fortune could make a single verse of them."

6. The Chinese did not use metal type until a few decades after Gutenberg, and when they did finally adopt it, they settled on bronze, which was difficult to cast, a problem greatly magnified by the tens of thousands of characters necessary in their language. In the eighteenth century royal printers cast one set of 250,000 sorts to make just 66 copies of a 5,020-volume encyclopedia; they then melted the sorts into coins. See Tsien, 211–216.

7. Febvre and Martin, 73–74.

8. Pow-Key Sohn, "Early Korean Printing," *Journal of the American Oriental Society* 79:2 (April–June 1959): 96–103.

9. De Vinne 53–54, quote 54.

10. Febvre and Martin, 50.

11. Harry Carter, *Fournier on Typefounding* (London: Fleuron Books, 1930), 21.

12. Fred Smeijers, *Counterpunch* (London: Hyphen Press, 1996), 74–127.

13. De Vinne, 54–61, quote 60.

14. Michael Clapham, "Printing," in Charles Singer et al., Eds., *A History of Technology* (London: Oxford University Press, 1957), III:386.

15. For a good summary of what Gutenberg may or may not have accomplished, see Febvre and Martin, 51–54.

16. Ibid., 54–58.

17. Frederick G. Kilgour, *The Evolution of the Book* (Oxford: Oxford University Press, 1998), 85–86. Since none of Gutenberg's original equipment has been located, the composition of his first type is speculative. Historian Stephan Füssel estimates the original alloy as 83 percent lead, 9 percent tin, 6 percent antimony, and 1 percent each iron and copper. See Stephan Füssel, *Gutenberg and the Impact of Printing* (Aldershot, UK: Ashgate, 2005), 16.

18. Each folio had four sides, requiring about $2,750 \times 4 = 11,000$ pieces of type. Gutenberg's operation ran six presses, requiring 66,000 pieces; to allow the margin of safety for the statistical variation in pages, about 100,000 would have been required. Füssel estimates that two years, or 330 working days, were required to produce the 230,760 passes through the press. 330 days $\times$ 8 hours per day $\times$ 3,600 seconds per hour ~ 9,500,000 seconds, which calculates out to $9,500,000/230,760 = 41$ seconds per pass. Since there were six presses running, each would have taken 246 seconds, or 4 minutes per pass per press, or 15 imprints per hour per press, not far from the historical estimate of 12 impressions per hour. See Füssel, 20; Clapham, 387–390.

19. Febvre and Martin, 77–78.

20. There seems to be some dispute about whether the items were admission badges or mirrors, or whether they were manufactured in 1438 or 1439 for the pilgrimage. See Pettegree, 22; and Füssel, 12–13.

21. See Pettegree, 26–32, for the financing and pricing of the Bibles; and Uhlendorf, 190–199 for the later careers of Gutenberg and Schoeffer. Gutenberg was allowed to keep the older, larger punches, called by scholars "B36" because Bibles

printed with the associated type contained thirty-six lines per page; the newer, smaller punches, kept by Schoeffer, are referred to as "B42" because they could yield forty-two lines per page. It is generally considered that the "B42" Bibles were the first produced. Pettegree estimates that 180 of these were produced, of which 52 are extant, while Uhlendorf agrees with a lower estimate: 25 vellum and 120 paper.

22. Elizabeth Eisenstein, *The Printing Press as an Agent of Change* (Cambridge: Cambridge University Press, 1979), 46; and Frances and Joseph Gies, *Cathedral, Forge, and Waterwheel* (New York, HarperCollins, 1994), 245.

23. Füssel, 21–23.

24. This German-language site requires a small bit of navigation that may confuse English-language users. Click on the "Die Göttinger Gutenberg-Bibel" link on the left. This will bring up the http://www.gutenbergdigital.de/gudi/dframes/index.htm page. On this page's drop-down menu on the top left, click on the book of the Bible you wish to examine. Then click on the tiny icons *under* the page images you wish to view.

25. Füssel, 111–112.

26. Febvre and Martin, 167.

27. Filippo de Strata, *Polemic Against Printing, Shelagh Grier,* Trans. (Birmingham, UK: Hayloft Press, 1986), unpaged.

28. Febvre and Martin, 81.

29. Pettegree, 36–58.

30. Jean-François Gilmont, "Printing at the dawn of the sixteenth century," in Jean-François Gilmont, Ed., and Karin Maag, Trans., *The Reformation and the Book* (Aldershot, UK: Ashgate, 1998), 34–35.

31. Füssel, 7–8.

32. Maria Grossman, "Wittenberg Printing, Early Sixteenth Century," *Sixteenth Century Essays and Studies* 1 (January 1970): 53–74. See also Febvre and Martin, 249, 268.

33. Martin Brecht, *Martin Luther* (Minneapolis: Fortress Press, 1993), 179–180.

34. Füssel, 166.

35. Grendler, 14–17, quote 17.

36. Gilmont, 24–25, both quotes from 25.

37. Ibid.,18–19.

38. Ibid., 36.

39. Ibid., 52.

40. Febvre and Martin, 289, 294–295. Number of German-speakers extrapolated from the populations of Germany, Austria, and Switzerland from Maddison data file, www.ggdc.net/maddison/Historical_Statistics/horizontal-file_02-2010.xls, accessed 1/12/11.

41. Füssel, 173–174.

42. Gilmont, 90.

43. Ibid., 33 (figure 2.1) and 43 (figure 2.2).

44. Quoted in Mark U. Edwards, Jr., *Printing, Propaganda, and Martin Luther* (Berkeley: University of California Press, 1994), 15.

45. Eisenstein, 371.

46. Febvre and Martin, 291.

47. Eisenstein, 373.

48. Ibid., 310–316.

49. Ibid., 14–16.

50. Ibid., 450.

51. David Daniell, *William Tyndale* (New Haven, CT: Yale University Press, 1994), 1–75.

52. Foxe, 259.

53. Ibid.

54. Daniell, 76–86.

55. While there is no record of Tyndale's having direct contact with the German colony in London before he left London in the spring of 1524, a year later one member of the London colony, Hans Collenbecke, carried some money for him to Hamburg.

56. Daniell, 100–106.

57. Ibid., 108–110.

58. Ibid., 155–195; and Foxe, 215–220.

59. J. F. Mozley, *William Tyndale* (New York: Macmillan Company, 1937), 147–148.

60. William Tyndale, *Doctrinal Theses and Introductions to Different Portions of the Holy Scriptures,* Henry Walker, Ed. (Cambridge: Cambridge University Press, 1849), 148–149.

61. For a more complete list of common English phrases deriving from the Old and New Testaments, see http://www.phrases.org.uk/meanings/181700.html.

62. Daniell, 312.

63. Ibid., 250–280.

64. Ibid., 362–384. See also Foxe, 262–264; and Mozley, 294–341. For speculation about John Stokesley's role as the person ultimately responsible for Phillip's betrayal of Tyndale, see Mozley, 300.

65. John Nielson and Royal Skousen, "How Much of the King James Bible Is William Tyndale's?" *Reformation* 3 (1998): 49–74.

66. "No Tyndale, no Shakespeare" is ascribed to Professor David Daniell. For example, see Daniell, "No Tyndale, No Shakespeare," Kirtling Lecture, 2005, *The Tyndale Society Journal,* 29 (2005): 8–22. Curiously, however, his authoritative biography of Tyndale contains not this phrase, but rather "Without Erasmus, No Shakespeare." See Daniell, *William Tyndale,* 42, 45.

Chapter 6
The Captive Press

1. Edward Gaylord Bourne, "The Naming of America," *American Historical Review* 10:1 (October 1904): 41–51.

2. Howard M. Solomon, *Public Welfare, Science, and Propaganda in the Seventeenth Century* (Princeton: Princeton University Press, 1977), 60–99.

3. Ibid., 100–122.

4. Ibid., 123–161, quote 139.

5. Edward A. Bloom, "Paper Wars for a Free Press," *Modern Language Review* 56:4 (October 1961): 482.

6. Guy A. Aldred, *Richard Carlile Agitator* (Glasgow: Strickland Press, 1941), 27.

7. Bloom, 492–493.

8. A. Aspinall, *Politics and the Press* (New York: Harper and Row, 1974), 69–182.

9. Thomas C. Leonard, *The Power of the Press* (Oxford: Oxford University Press, 1987), 14.

10. Ibid., 35. See also Warren Chappel and Robert Bringhurst, *A Short History of the Printed Word* (Port Roberts, WA: Hartley and Marks, 1999), 176–181.

11. Quoted epithet from Samuel K. Padover, *Jefferson* (New York: Mentor, 1970), 27.

12. Richard Ingrams, *The Life Adventures of William Cobbett* (London: Harper Collins, 2005), 1–18.

13. Ibid., 19–43.

14. Ibid., 62–65. The court subsequently convicted an Irish judge, Robert Johnson, of supplying the *Register* with several letters under the pseudonym "Juverna" concerning the affair. He too avoided jail, but was forced to resign. Upon his resignation he received a £1,200 annual pension.

15. Ibid., 93.

16. Ibid., 103–137.

17. Frederick Wm. Hackwood, *William Hone* (New York: Augustus M. Kelly, 1970), 113.

18. Ibid., 125–126.

19. Ibid., 132–158. See also William H. Wickwar, *Struggle for the Freedom of the Press* (London: George Allen and Unwin, 1928), 59.

20. The name of the debacle was taken from a poignant remark of a young veteran of Waterloo, John Lees. Mortally wounded, Lees remarked that at least on the Belgian battlefield, it had been man-to-man; what happened that day on Saint Peter's Field was "murder, pure and simple." See Joyce Marlow, *The Peterloo Massacre* (London: Panther, 1971), 16.

21. Aldred, 53.

22. Ibid., 62–84.

23. Sir Joseph Arnould, *Memoir of Thomas, First Lord Denman* (London: Longmans, Green, and Co., 1873), I:366.

24. Ibid., 85–115, quote 100.

25. Hackwood, 224–268.

26. Aspinall, 383.

27. Wickwar, 310–311.

28. Tom Standage, *The Victorian Internet* (New York: Walker Publishing, 1998).

29. See in particular Geoffrey Wilson, *The Old Telegraphs* (London: Philliomore, 1976). For mention of carrier pigeons in the ancient world, see J. T. Richmond, "Spies in Ancient Greece," *Greece and Rome* 45:1 (April 1998): 12.

30. Bernstein, *The Birth of Plenty* (New York: McGraw-Hill, 2004), 166–172.

31. A. E. Musson, "Printing in the Industrial Revolution," *Economic History Review,* New Series, 10:3 (1958): 411–426, quote 416.

32. Harold A. Innis, *The Bias of Communication* (Toronto: University of Toronto Press, 2003), 173; and Innis, *Empire and Communications,* 184.

33. Richard A. Schwarzlose, *The Nation's Newsbrokers* (Evanston, IL: Northwestern University Press, 1989), I:6–8.

34. Ibid., I:5.

35. Leonard, 54.

36. Ibid., 56.

37. Michael Schudson, *Discovering the News* (New York: Basic Books, 1978), 12–17.

38. Quoted in Schwarzlose, I:1.

39. Leonard, 64, 67, 68.

40. Charles McGrath, "And They All Died Happily Ever After," *The New York Times,* July 2, 2006.

41. Schudson, 17–22.

42. Standage, 1–2.

43. T. K. Derry and Trevor I. Williams, *A Short History of Technology* (New York: Dover Publications, 1993), 609–610.

44. Standage, 58–60.

45. John S. Gordon, *A Thread Across the Ocean* (New York: Walker, 2002), 133.

46. Charles F. Briggs and Augustus Maverick, *The Story of the Telegraph and a History of the Great Atlantic Cable* (New York: Rudd and Carleton, 1858), 22.

47. Standage, 60–62.

48. Economic historian Gregory Clark estimates the average English daily wage in the latter half of the nineteenth century at about twenty to twenty-five pence, where twelve pence = one shilling. See Clark, "Farm Wages and Living Standards in the Industrial Revolution: England, 1670–1850," http://www.econ.ucdavis.edu/faculty/gclark/papers/farm_wages_&_living_standards.pdf, accessed 11/6/10.

49. For a fascinating contemporary view of the debate over telegraph economics and politics, see William M. Springer, "The Telegraph Monopoly," *The North American Review* 132:293 (April 1881): 369–382; an essay by the president of Western Union, Norvin Green, "The Government and the Telegraph," *The North American Review* 137:234 (November 1883): 422–434; a reply by Hubbard, "Government Control of the Telegraph," *The North American Review* 137:325 (December 1883): 521–535; and a modern overview, Alexander James Field, "The Magnetic Telegraph, Price and Quality Data," *The Journal of Economic History* 52:2 (June 1992): 401–413.

50. Quoted in Schwarzlose, I:164.

51. Charles H. Levermore, "The Rise of Metropolitan Journalism, 1800–1840," *The American Historical Review* 6:3 (April 1901): 457–458.

52. Schudson, 21.

53. Leonard, 71.

54. W. A. Swanberg, *Pulitzer* (New York: Charles Scribner's Sons, 1967), 4–70. See also Leonard, 170–178, quote 178.

55. W. A. Swanberg, *Citizen Hearst* (New York: Charles Scribner's Sons, 1961), 3–7.

56. David Nasaw, *The Chief* (Boston: Houghton Mifflin, 2001), 3–63.

57. Ibid., 72.

58. Ibid., 73.

59. Ibid., 78.

60. Schudson, 61–62.

61. John Tebel, *The Life and Good Times of William Randolph Hearst* (New York: E. P. Dutton, 1952), 179–191.

62. Ian Mugridge, *The View from Xanadu* (Montreal: McGill-Queen's University Press, 1995), 17.

63. Ibid., 440–449. See also H. Wayne Morgan, *America's Road to Empire* (New York: John Wiley and Sons, 1965), 14.

64. Mugridge, 8.

65. For an excellent primer on the preeminence of the U.S. president in American foreign policy, see Bernard C. Cohen, "The Relationship Between Public Opinion and Foreign Policy Maker," in Melvin Small, Ed., *Public Opinion and Historians* (Detroit: Wayne State University Press, 1970), 65–80.

66. For the entire text of Root's speech, see *Speech of Hon. Elihu Root, Secretary of State at Utica New York, November 1, 1906* (Washington, NY: C. F. Sudwarth, Printer, 1906), quote 34.

67. Ibid., 37–38.

68. Oswald Garrison Villard, *Some Newspapers and Newspaper-Men* (New York: Alfred A. Knopf, 1923), 23.

69. Philip C. Jessup, *Elihu Root* (New York: Dodd, Mead and Company, 1938), 113–123.

70. Mugridge, 144–146.

71. Walter Lippmann, "Two Revolutions in the American Press," *The Yale Review* XX:3 (March 1931): 433–441.

72. Ibid., 437.

73. Ibid., 438.

74. "The Foxification of News," *Economist,* July 9, 2011.

75. Oron J. Hale, *The Captive Press in the Third Reich* (Princeton: Princeton University Press, 1964), 3.

76. Adolf Hitler, *Mein Kampf,* Ralph Manheim, Trans. (Boston: Houghton Mifflin Company, 1999), 240–242.

77. Michael Burleigh, *The Third Reich* (New York: Hill and Wang, 2000), 208.

Chapter 7
With a Machete in One Hand and a Radio in the Other

1. Arthur Koestler, *Janus* (New York: Random House, 1978), 15.
2. Daniel J. Czitrom, *Media and the American Mind* (Chapel Hill: University of North Carolina Press, 1982), 86.
3. Carl J. Friedrich and Evelyn Sternberg, "Congress and the Control of Radio-Broadcasting. I," *American Political Science Review* 37:5 (October 1943): 802.
4. In 1676, the Danish astronomer Ole Rømer estimated the speed of light at approximately 220,000 km/sec, about 26 percent too low; in 1849 Hippolyte Fizeau, using terrestrial techniques, estimated it at 313,000 km/sec, about 4 percent too high. Subsequent refinements in experimental technique converged on a value of 299,792.458 km/sec.
5. Hugh G. J. Aitken, *Syntony and Spark* (New York: John Wiley and Sons, 1976), 31–65. For more detailed accounts of early radio technology and its physics, see Oliver Lodge, *Signalling through space without wires,* 3rd ed. (London: "The Electrician" Printing and Publishing Company, no date); and Sungook Hong, *Wireless* (Cambridge, MA: MIT Press, 2001).
6. William Crookes, "Some Possibilities of Electricity," *Fortnightly Review,* 102 (February 1, 1892): 174.
7. The essential element of tuning is the coupling of a capacitor and inductor— the so-called *L-C* circuit—whose frequency is calculated as $f = \dfrac{1}{2\pi\sqrt{LC}}$, where L is the inductance in henries and C is capacitance in farads. Lodge's 1897 patent was the first to incorporate a mechanism for tuning both receiver and transmitter by varying the inductance of the circuit—L in the above equation. For the detailed story of Lodge's accomplishments, see Aitken, 80–178.
8. Lodge, 51.
9. Degna Marconi, *My Father, Marconi* (Toronto: Guernica Editions, 2001), 6–7; and Giancarlo Masini, *Marconi* (New York: Marsilio Publishers, 1995), 22–25.
10. Lewis Coe, *Wireless Radio* (Jefferson, NC: McFarland and Company, 1996), 4–5.
11. Masini, 18–19. For possible variants on the rifle-shot story, see 19–20.
12. Aitken, 210.
13. Tom Lewis, *Empire of the Air* (New York: Edward Burlingame Books, 1991), 37, 40.
14. Aitken, 179–237.
15. Confusingly, de Forest did not capitalize the "de" except in the names of his companies.
16. Lewis, 41–43, 50–51.
17. Ibid., 326–327, 343. The superheterodyne principle involves converting a high-frequency radio signal, often far into the megahertz range, into a low-frequency one by combining the high-frequency one with an internally produced one of a nearby frequency. For example, for receiving a signal of 1 MHz, the superheterodyne circuit

would combine it with one of 900 kHz, to yield a "beat frequency" that is the difference between the two—100 kHz—which is then amplified thousands of times and converted to an audio signal.

18. Ibid., 51–73.

19. Kenneth Bilby, *The General* (New York: Harper and Row, 1986), 11–19, quote 19.

20. Controversy surrounds the exact role played by Sarnoff in reporting the disaster. His foremost biographer, Eugene Lyons, credited him with picking up the first survivor reports and so being catapulted to fame. For a more balanced account, see Bilby, 30–34. See also Greg Daugherty, "They Missed the Boat," *Smithsonian* (March 2012), 38.

21. Gleason Leonard Archer, *History of radio to 1926* (New York: American Historical Society, 1938), 112.

22. Bilby, 45.

23. Susan J. Douglas, *Listening In* (New York: Times Books, 1999), 59–60.

24. Lewis, 141–148.

25. Robert J. Brown, *Manipulating the Ether* (Jefferson NC: McFarland and Company, 1998), 1–5.

26. Schmeling's history following his 1938 defeat should not escape notice: reviled in the United States because of his German nationality and shunned in his homeland because of his defeat, he risked his life by saving two Jewish boys during *Kristallnacht,* which occurred just three months after the Louis fight, and served as a paratrooper in the war. In later life he befriended Louis, whose funeral he paid for. Schmeling died in 2005, just short of age 100.

27. *The Nation* CXXXV:3511 (October 19, 1932): 341.

28. Hadley Cantril and Gordon W. Allport, *The Psychology of Radio* (New York: Harper and Brothers, 1971), 3–18.

29. Ibid., 211.

30. Ibid., 203.

31. Ibid., 8.

32. The text and audio of this address are available at http://millercenter.org/scripps/archive/speeches/detail/3298.

33. Susan Estabrook Kennedy, *The Banking Crisis of 1933* (Lexington: University Press of Kentucky, 1973), 181.

34. James Wooten, Dasher: *The Roots and Rising of Jimmy Carter* (New York: Summit Books, 1978), 17.

35. Brown, 75–78, quote 78.

36. For a brilliant, in-depth description of Roosevelt's radio technique and politics, see Brown, 9–32.

37. For a view of the process of the rewriting of H. G. Wells' original novel, see Howard Koch, *As Time Goes By* (New York: Harcourt Brace Jovanovich, 1979), 1–9.

38. Brown, 236.

39. Hadley Cantril, *The Invasion from Mars* (New York: Harper Torchbooks, 1960), 47–149.

40. Brown, 223.

41. Cantril, *The Invasion from Mars,* xii.

42. Ibid., 3.

43. Ernest K. Bramsted, *Goebbels and National Socialist Propaganda* (East Lansing: Michigan State University Press, 1965), 3.

44. Ibid., 29.

45. Horst J. P. Bergmeier and Rainer E. Lotz, *Hitler's Airwaves* (New Haven, CT: Yale University Press, 1997), 6.

46. Ibid., 8. See also Brown, 13.

47. Ibid., 75.

48. "German Volksempfängers," http://home.snafu.de/wumpus/volks.htm, accessed 12/9/12.

49. Michael Nelson, *War of the Black Heavens* (Syracuse, NY: Syracuse University Press, 1997), preceding three quotes, 7–8.

50. César Saerchinger, "Radio as a Political Instrument," *Foreign Affairs* 16:2 (January 1938): 249.

51. Ibid., 250–251, quote 251.

52. Bramsted, 121, 150.

53. Saerchinger, 252–257, quote 257.

54. Philip Gourevich, *We wish to inform you that tomorrow we will be killed with our families* (New York: Picador, 1998), 54–57.

55. Gerald Caplan, "Rwanda: Walking the Road to Genocide," in Allan Thompson, Ed., *The Media and the Rwanda Genocide* (London: Pluto Press, 2007), 20–25, 37. For a detailed analysis of who shot down the presidential aircraft, see Gérard Prunier, *The Rwandan Crisis* (New York: Columbia University Press, 1995), 213–229. Briefly, the case for Hutu, as opposed to Tutsi or foreign, responsibility seems overwhelming, most particularly that the missiles were fired from an area under Hutu control, and also the very close temporal association between the crash and the start of the genocide. The military response of the Tutsi-led RPF army, which the Hutus blamed for the crash, by contrast, did not occur until days after the shoot-down.

56. Gourevich, 85–88.

57. Darryl Li, "Echoes of Violence: Considerations on Radio and Genocide in Rwanda," Thompson, 90.

58. Alison Des Forges, "Call to Genocide: Radio in Rwanda, 1994," Thompson, 44–45, 48–50.

59. Roméo Dallaire, "The Media Dichotomy," Thompson, 12.

60. For a superb description of the horrific "post-genocide" events in eastern Zaire after 1994—essentially a pan-African world war in which both Tutsis and Hutus were slaughtered, and which the West got snookered into perceiving as a humanitarian crisis, not as genocide—see Gourevich, 256–341.

61. Dallaire, 17, 18.

62. Caplan, 25. See also Gourevich, 104–105, 168. Regarding Annan's refusal to allow UN personnel to testify before the Belgian senate inquiry, see "Belgian Senate, Session of 1997–1998, December 6, 1997," http://www.senate.be/english/rwanda.html, accessed 11/5/10.

63. Lindsey Hilsum, "Reporting Rwanda: The Media and Aid Agencies," and Nick Hughes, "Exhibit 467: Genocide Through a Camera Lens," Thompson, 172, 231–233.

64. Dallaire, 14.

65. Hughes, 231, 234.

66. Jean-Pierre Chrétien, "RTLM Propaganda: the Democratic Alibi," in Thompson, 58–59; and Mary Kimani, "RTLM: the Medium That Became a Tool for Mass Murder," Thompson, 117.

67. Hannah Arendt, *Eichmann in Jerusalem* (New York: Penguin Books, 2006); Laurence Rees, *Auschwitz: A New History* (New York: Public Affairs, 2005); Philip G. Zimbardo, *The Lucifer Effect* (New York: Random House, 2008).

68. Primo Levi, *The Drowned and the Saved,* Raymond Rosenthal, Trans., (New York: Summit Books, 1988), 199.

Chpater 8
The Comrades Who Couldn't Broadcast Straight

1. Aleksandr Solzhenitsyn, *Invisible Allies* (Washington, DC: Counterpoint, 1995), 73.

2. Anthony T. Salvia, "Poland's Walesa Addresses RFE/RL Conference," *Shortwaves,* November 1989, 1, quoted in Michael Nelson, *War of the Black Heavens* (Syracuse, NY: Syracuse University Press, 1997), 159–160.

3. Nigel Hawkes et al., *The Worst Accident in the World* (London: Pan Books, 1986), 5–6.

4. Ellen Mickiewicz, *Split Signals* (Oxford: Oxford University Press, 1988), 61.

5. Ibid., 1–14, 97–131, 167–193. See also Michael Dobbs, *Down with Big Brother* (New York: Alfred A. Knopf, 1997), 154–162.

6. "Truth is in the Air," *Economist,* June 6, 1987.

7. Julia Lotman, personal communication.

8. Ivan Szelenyi and Balazs Szelenyi, "Why Socialism Failed: Toward a Theory of System Breakdown—Causes of Disintegration of East European State Socialism," *Theory and Society* 23:2 (April 1994), 223.

9. Dobbs, 129–139, 179–182, 336–341, 396–406.

10. Wilson P. Dizard, *Inventing Public Diplomacy* (Boulder CO: Lynne Rienner Publishers, 2004), 211.

11. Robert Smith, "Is Democracy Still on the Dial?" *The New York Times,* March 3, 2001.

12. Nelson, xiv–xv.

13. F. A. Hayek, "The Use of Knowledge in Society," *American Economic Review* 35:4 (September 1945): 519–530. This brilliant essay is available online at http://www.econlib.org/library/Essays/hykKnw1.html.

14. Ibid., 519.

15. Ibid., 526.

16. Daniel P. Moynihan, "Introduction—The American Experiment," *The Public Interest* 41 (Fall 1975): 4–8.

17. Julia Lotman, personal communication.

18. Victoria Fineberg, personal communication.

19. Scott Shane, *Dismantling Utopia* (Chicago: Ivan R. Dee, 1994), 75–84.

20. Ibid., 3–4.

21. Norbert Wiener, *Cybernetics,* 2nd ed., (Cambridge, MA: MIT Press, 1965).

22. Norbert Wiener, *The Human Use of Human Beings* (New York: Da Capo Press, 1988), 121–122.

23. Slava Gerovich, "'Russian Scandals': Soviet Readings of American Cybernetics in the Early Years of the Cold War," *Russian Review* 60:4 (October 2001): 545–568.

24. Ibid., 561.

25. It is a commonplace that Stalin himself led the attack on cybernetics (see, for example, Shane, 62). There is little evidence, however, of his actual involvement. By contrast, he directly supervised the anti-Darwinian campaign of Trofim Lysenko, whose drafts he personally edited. See Gerovich. See also David Holloway, "Innovation in Science—The Case of Cybernetics in the Soviet Union," *Science Studies* 4:4 (October 1974), 299–337.

26. James H. Billington, *The Icon and the Axe* (New York: Alfred A. Knopf, 1966), 217–221.

27. Ibid., 51.

28. Robert W. Thurston, *Life and Terror in Stalin's Russia 1934–1941* (New Haven, CT: Yale University Press, 1966), 195–196.

29. William Taubman, *The View from Lenin Hills* (New York: Coward-McCann, 1967), 1–14.

30. Silvio Bedini, *Thomas Jefferson and His Copying Machines* (Charlottesville: University Press of Virginia, 1984), 3.

31. W. J. Barrow, "Permanence in Book Papers," Science 129:3356 (April 24, 1959): 1075–2084; Nancy E. Gwinn, "The Fragility of Paper: Can Our Historical Record Be Saved?" *The Public Historian* 13:3 (Summer 1991): 33–53; and "W. J. Barrow," *Bulletin of the American Group. International Institute for Conservation of Historic and Artistic Works* 8:1 (October 1967): 5. The novelist Nicholson Baker has famously taken up a crusade against many of the preservationist techniques pioneered by Barrow: see Nicholson Baker, *Double Fold* (New York: Random House, 2001). For an incisive and balanced analysis of Baker's thesis, see John A. Church, "William J. Barrow: A Remembrance and Appreciation," *The American Archivist* 68:1 (Spring–Summer 2005): 152–160.

32. Robert A. Harris's Statement at the Film Preservation Study, http://www.widescreenmuseum.com/rah.htm, accessed 4/18/12.

33. Barbara Rhodes and William Wells Streeter, *Before Photocopying* (New Castle, DE: Oak Knoll Press, 1999), 8–10; and W. B. Proudfoot, *The Origin of Stencil Duplicating* (London: Hutchinson of London, 1972), 21–23.

34. David Owen, *Copies in Seconds* (New York: Simon and Schuster, 2004), 21–23.35. Proudfoot, 34–98.

36. Owen, 37–39; Streeter and Rhodes, 18–19; Proudfoot, 24–26, 32–34.

37. Gordon Johnston, "What is the history of samizdat?" *Social History* 24:2 (May 1999): 122.

38. H. Gordon Skilling, *Samizdat and an Independent Society in Central and Eastern Europe* (Columbus: Ohio University Press, 1989), 3–4.

39. Aleksandr Solzhenitsyn, *The Oak and the Calf* (New York: Harper and Row, 1980), 2–3.

40. Ludmilla Alexeyeva and Paul Goldberg, *The Thaw Generation* (Boston: Little, Brown and Company, 1990), 97–98.

41. Vladimir Bukovsky, *To Build a Castle* (New York: Viking Press, 1977), 141.

42. Julius Telesin, "Inside 'Samizdat,'" *Encounter* 40:2 (February 1973): 25–33.

43. Ibid., 26.

44. Ibid., 27.

45. Ibid., 30.

46. Ibid.

47. Ibid.

48. J. M. Feldbrugge, *Samizdat and Political Dissent in the Soviet Union* (Leyden: A.W. Sijthoff, 1975), 15–19.

49. Skilling, 4–37, quote 12–13.

50. Michael Meerson-Aksenov, "Introductory," in Michael Meerson-Aksenov and Boris Shragin, Eds., *The Political, Social and Religious Thought of Russian "Samizdat"—An Anthology* (Belmont, MA: Nordland Publishing, 1977), 37–38.

51. Feldbrugge, 15–19. Telesin, 32, provides a variant of the *War and Peace* vignette, in which it is the mother of a schoolboy who retypes the manuscript. Also Julia Lotman, personal communication.

52. Ann Komaromi, "The Material Existence of Soviet Samizdat," *Slavic Review* 63:3 (Autumn, 2004): 606–609. See also Gordon Johnson, "What is the history of Samizdat?" *Social History* 24:2 (May 1999): 129–130.

53. For an excellent review of how the Soviet literary establishment lost its battle with samizdat, see D. Pospielovsky, "From *Gosizdat to Samizdat and Tamizdat,*" *Canadian Slavonic Papers* XX:1 (March 1978): 44–62.

54. Aryeh L. Unger, *The Totalitarian Party* (London: Cambridge University Press, 1974), 105–150.

55. Anton Lotman, personal communication.

56. Maury Lisann, *Broadcasting to the Soviet Union* (New York: Praeger Publishers, 1975), 4–5. See also Nelson, 19, 30.

57. Lisann, 12.

58. Jan Nowak, *Courier from Warsaw* (Detroit, MI: Wayne State University Press, 1982).

59. Alan Andrew Michie, *Voices Through the Iron Curtain* (New York: Dodd, Mead, 1963), 191.

60. Nelson, 69–82, quote 81.

61. Ibid., 128. See also Cord Meyer, *Facing Reality* (New York: Harper and Row, 1980), 134–135.

62. Ibid., 151. Ironically, during the McCarthy-era witch hunts, the VOA was investigated for supposed sabotage of its broadcasting technology and programming, which was accused of not being "hard hitting" enough. Had VOA knuckled under to the pressure to harden its edge, this would almost certainly have eroded its credibility. See Nelson, 36.

63. For a comprehensive summary of these data, see Nelson, 114–172.

64. This applied only to broadcasts in Russian and Eastern European languages; the Soviets did not, usually, jam English-language programming. Victoria Fineberg, personal communication.

65. Nelson, 21–22, 98.

66. Julia Lotman, personal communication.

67. Nelson, 4, 92–93, quote 92, 135.

68. Anton and Julia Lotman, personal communication. Also see Lisann, 2–82.

69. Stephen White, "The Effectiveness of Political Propaganda in the U.S.S.R.," *Soviet Studies* 32:3 (July 1980): 323–348. See also Lisann, 82–89; and Unger, 151–166.

70. Frida Abramovna Vigdorova, "Trial of a Young Poet," *Encounter* 23:3 (September 1964): 84–85.

71. Grigori Svirski, *A History of Post-War Soviet Writing* (Ann Arbor: Ardis Publishing, 1981), 236–237.

72. Richard Lourie, *Letters to the Future* (Ithaca: Cornell University Press, 1975), 9–37.

73. On Alexander Ginzburg's role in the transcripts (discussed below), see Lourie, 202–203.

74. Alexeyeva and Goldberg, 128–136. For the estimate of Russian listenership of foreign radio, see Lisann, 155.

75. Alexeyeva and Goldberg, 139.

76. William McLaughlin, "West European CPs' Reaction to Moscow Trial," Radio Free Europe Research, http://www.osaarchivum.org/files/holdings/300/8/3/text/63-2-289.shtml, accessed 1/2/12.

77. Max Hayward, *On Trial* (New York: Harper and Row, 1966), 1–35; for the transcript itself, see 37–198.

78. "Soviet Union: Crackdown on Dissent," *Time,* December 18, 1972.

79. Bukovsky, 32.

80. Andrei Amalrik, *Notes of a Revolutionary* (New York: Alfred A. Knopf, 1982), 191–192.

81. John Lewis Gaddis, *We Now Know* (Oxford: Clarendon Press, 1997), 23–24.

82. Joshua Rubenstein, *Soviet Dissidents* (Boston: Beacon Press, 1980), 66–67.

83. Alexeyeva and Goldberg, 1963–1964.

84. Feldbrugge, 1–2.

85. Alexeyeva and Goldberg, 181–182.

86. Ibid., 3–10. See also Aleksandr Solzhenitsyn, *Invisible Allies* (Washington, DC: Counterpoint, 1995), 13–15.

87. Solzhenitsyn, *Invisible Allies,* 72.

88. Ibid., 124, 173.

89. For the saga of Solzhenitsyn's tradecraft, see his *Invisible Allies,* especially 65–88 for Elizaveta Voronyanskaya and 142–166 for Natalya Stolyarova.

90. Nelson, 149, 167.

91. Gene Sosin, "Magnitizat: Uncensored Songs of Dissent," in Rudolf L. Tökés, Ed., *Dissent in the U.S.S.R..* (Baltimore: Johns Hopkins University Press, 1975), 277.

92. J. Martin Daughtry, "Sonic Samizdat": Situating Unofficial Recording in the Post-Stalinist Soviet Union," *Poetics Today* 30:1 (Spring 2009): 34–35.

93. Alexander Galich, *Songs and Poems,* Gerald Stanton Smith, Trans. (Ann Arbor, MI: Ardis Publishers, 1983), 172–175. See also Daughtry, 28–40.

94. Galich, 72–74. An audio of "Red Triangle" can be found at http://www.youtube.com/watch?v=ic6JDNxrNLU, and a large compendium of Galich's songs at http://www.bard.ru/cgi-bin/lists.cgi?name=%D0%93%D0%B0%D0%BB%D0%B8%D1%87_%D0%90.

95. Sosin, 308–309.

96. For a discussion of *magnitizat*'s political effect, see Daughtry, 51–54. The journalist in question was an exchange program house guest two decades ago. I remember his story well, and I can only beg his forgiveness for forgetting his name.

97. John Tusa, "Salvation on Shortwave," Times (London), December 11, 1991.

98. Lech Walesa, *A Way of Hope* (New York: Henry Holt and Company, 1987), 216.

99. Ibid., 230.

100. William H. Mahoney, *The History of the Czech Republic and Slovakia* (Santa Barbara, CA: Greenwood, Press, 2011), 223–225; and H. Gordon Skilling, *Charter 77 and Human Rights in Czechoslovakia* (London: George Allen and Unwin, 1981), 3–38.

101. Nelson, 161–162.

102. Wiener, *The Human Use of Human Beings,* 127.

103. Bill Keller, "Russians Say Western Radio Instigated Baltic Protests," *The New York Times,* August 25, 1987.

104. Nelson, 170–171.

105. Ibid., 182–190.

106. Victoria E. Bonnell and Gregory Friedin, "Televorot: The Role of Television in Russia's August 1991 Coup," *Slavic Review* 52:4 (Winter 1993): 810–838.

107. Mikhail Gorbachev, *The August Coup* (New York: HarperCollins Publishers, 1991), 26–29.

108. William Taubman, *Khrushchev* (New York: W.W. Norton, 2003), 13.

109. Sergei Khrushchev, *Khrushchev on Khrushchev* (Boston: Little, Brown and Company, 1990), 247.

110. Sergei Khrushchev, personal communication. Also see Sergei Khrushchev, 233–321.

Chapter 9
The Argus

1. Thomas B. Edsall and Brian Faler, "Lott Remarks on Thurmond Echoed 1980 Words," *Washington Post,* December 11, 2002.

2. Joe Trippi, *The Revolution Will Not Be Televised* (New York: HarperCollins e-books, 2008), 25–26.

3. Ibid. and Clay Shirky, *Here Comes Everybody* (New York: Penguin, 2008), 61–66. For a detailed and nuanced accounting of the blogosphere's role in the Lott episode, see Esther Scott, "'Big Media' Meets the 'Bloggers,'" http://www.hks.harvard.edu/presspol/publications/case_studies/1731_0_scott.pdf, accessed 9/28/11.

4. Barbara J. Streeter and William W. Rhodes, *Before Photocopying* (New Castle, DE: Oak Knoll Press, 1990), 132–134, 159–160.

5. Owen, 49–55, quote 55.

6. Owen, 72–283, quote 241. The technical details and development of the xerographic technique are too complex to be recounted here in any detail. Before the 914, Haloid had produced two earlier products—the Model D and the Copyflo—that, because they were far more difficult to operate and less reliable, and had far more limited capacity than the 914, did not sell well. For those who are interested in the story of xerography, *Copies in Seconds* cannot be recommended highly enough.

7. Julia Lotman, personal communication.

8. Neil Sheehan, *A Bright and Shining Lie* (New York: Vintage Books, 1989), 590.

9. Daniel Ellsberg, *Secrets* (New York: Viking, 2002), 290.

10. Ibid., 295–309, 330–334, 356–375.

11. After Ellsberg had photocopied and published the papers, he offered moral outrage over the war's brutal conduct and the lies surrounding it as his rationale for making the documents public. This straightforward explanation may have been more than a little self-serving, for Ellsberg's professional and personal behavior often varied between theatrical and vain. But whatever his true reasons, the Pentagon Papers could not have be published without the 914 photocopier. From Ellsberg's perspective, the Eisenhower, Kennedy, Johnson, and Nixon administrations had committed murder and lied to the world about it. This opinion compelled him to make the Pentagon Papers public. Ellsberg's principal biographer, Tom Wells, does not contradict this explanation, but makes a strong case, based on extensive interviews, that Ellsberg was at least equally angry that his counsel was ignored in the corridors of power, particularly by Henry Kissinger, who had graduated two years ahead of him at Harvard and whom

Ellsberg viewed as his intellectual inferior. Wells strongly implies that had Ellsberg's career gone better, he might not have leaked the papers. For a perspective on this question see Ellsberg; and Tom Wells, *Wild Man* (New York: Palgrave, 2001), especially 312–313 on Ellsberg's rivalry with Kissinger.

12. Carl Bernstein and Bob Woodward, *All the President's Men* (New York: Simon and Schuster, 1974), 307–315.

13. The number of discrete connections among n nodes is $n(n-1)/2$; in this case, 100 times 99 divided by 2. While the number of connections could be reduced with a central switching device, an individual terminal/user could still not simultaneously communicate with or—most important—search the content of, all of the others. Doing so is the essential feature of the Internet.

14. Barry Lerner et al., "A Brief History of the Internet," http://www.isoc.org/internet/history/brief.shtml, accessed 11/18/11.

15. Tim Berners-Lee, "Information Management: A Proposal," http://www.w3.org/History/1989/proposal.html, accessed 11/19/11.

16. James Gillies and Robert Cailliau, *How the Web Was Born* (Oxford: Oxford University Press, 2000), 213; and Karl Pfleger, personal communication.

17. Tim Berners-Lee, *Weaving the Web* (San Francisco: HarperSanFrancisco, 1999), 7–27, quote 26–27.

18. Ibid., 30.

19. Ibid., 30–51.

20. "Internet Growth Statistics," http://www.internetworldstats.com/emarketing.htm, accessed 11/20/11.

21. Evan Williams, "For Twitter C.E.O., Well-Orchestrated Accidents," *The New York Times,* March 8, 2009.

22. Kate Greene, "What Is He Doing?" *Technology Review* (November–December 2007), 44–51.

23. Todd Satterson and Karl Pfleger, personal communication.

24. Greene, 46.

25. Sharon LaFraniere, "China Finds More Bodies, and a Survivor, in Trains' Wreckage," *The New York Times,* July 25, 2011.

26. Ibid.

27. Martha T. Moore, "Rare earthquake shakes and shocks Eastern Seaboard," *USA Today,* http://www.usatoday.com/news/nation/story/2011-08-23/Rare-earthquake-shakes-and-shocks-Eastern-Seaboard/50114870/1, accessed 11/30/11.

28. See, for example, "The Evolution of Search Engine Technology—Early Technology, Early Problems," http://careers.stateuniversity.com/pages/100000932/Evolution-Search-Engine-Technology-Early-Progress-Early-Problems.html, accessed 4/24/12.

29. John Battelle, *The Search* (New York: Penguin, 2005), 65–81.

30. For an accusatory perspective on medieval priestly pedophilia, see Peter Damian and Pierre J. Payer, *The Book of Gomorrah* (Waterloo, Ontario: Wilfrid Laurier University Press, 1982); for an exculpatory one, see Mark D. Jordan, *The Silence of Sodom* (Chicago: University of Chicago Press, 2000).

31. His letters to the hierarchy can be found at http://www.bishop-accountability.org/news2009/03_04/fitzgerald.pdf.

32. Shirky, 143–151.

33. William Safire, "What Else Are We Missing," *The New York Times,* June 6, 2002.

34. "The people formerly known as the audience; Social media," *Economist,* July 9, 2011, 10.

35. Marcus Stern et al., *The Wrong Stuff* (New York: Public Affairs, 2007), 231–232.

36. Cinque Hicks, "Easy: The Guardian's Crowdsource Game," *Newsgames* (October 21, 2009), http://newsgames.gatech.edu/blog/2009/10/easy-the-guardians-crowd-source-game.html, accessed 12/10/11. See also Michael Anderson, "Four Crowdsourcing Lessons from the Guardian's (Spectacular) Expenses-Scandal Experiment," *Nieman Journalism Lab,* http://www.niemanlab.org/2009/06/four-crowdsourcing-lessons-from-the-guardians-spectacular-expenses-scandal-experiment, accessed 12/9/12; and Anna Daniel, "The *Guardian* Reportage of the UK MP Expenses Scandal: A Case Study of Computational Journalism," http://www.eprints.qut.edu.au/38701/2/38701 pdf, accessed 12/10/11.

37. Arianna Huffington, http://ariannaonline.huffingtonpost.com/columns/printer_friendly.php?id=44, accessed 9/28/11.

38. Eric Schurenberg, e-mail communication.

39. Nicholas Carr, "Is Google Making Us Stupid?" *Atlantic Monthly* 302:1 (July–August 2008): 56–63; also, Nicholas Carr, *The Shallows* (New York: W.W. Norton, 2010), 115–120.

40. Amir Amedi et al., "The Occipital Cortex in the Blind: Lessons About Plasticity and Vision," *Current Directions in Psychological Science* 14:6 (December 2005): 306–311; and I. Huang et al., "Monitoring Music Processing of Harmonic Chords using fMRI: Comparison between Professional Musicians and Amateurs," *Proc. Intl. Soc. Mag. Reson. Med.,* 11 (2003): 187.

41. Carr, *The Shallows,* 128–129.

42. Erping Zhu, "Hypermedia Interface Design: The Effects of Number of Links and Granularity of Nodes," *Journal of Educational Multimedia and Hypermedia* 8:3 (1999): 331–358.

43. B. N. Sullivan, "Northwest pilots who overflew destination settle with FAA over license revocation" http://aircrewbuzz.com/2009/10/northwest-pilots-lose-situational.html and http://aircrewbuzz.com/2009/10/northwest-pilots-who-overflew.html, accessed 12/11/11.

44. "Background on the SAT Takers in the Class of 2010," http://professionals.collegeboard.com/data-reports-research/sat/cb-seniors-2010/tables#, accessed 12/12/11.

45. Richard Spencer, "Tunisia riots: neighbours will be watching Tunisia nervously," *The Telegraph,* January 12, 2011; and Elizabeth Dickinson, "The First WikiLeaks Revolution?" *Foreign Policy,* January 13, 2011.

46. Peter Beaumont, "The truth about Twitter, Facebook and the uprisings in the Arab world," *Guardian* (February 24, 2011), http://www.guardian.co.uk/world/2011/feb/25/twitter-facebook-uprisings-arab-libya, accessed 12/20/11.

47. "The people formerly known as the audience; Social Media," 10.

48. John Pollock, "How Egyptian and Tunisian Youth Hacked the Arab Spring," *Technology Review* (September/October 2011): http://www.technologyreview.com/web/38379/, accessed 12/20/11.

49. Ibid.

50. Ibid.

51. Sheryl Gay Stolberg, "Shy U.S. Intellectual Created Playbook Used in a Revolution," *The New York Times* (February 16, 2011). Sharp's book, *From Dictatorship to Democracy* (East Boston, MA: Albert Einstein Institution, 2010), can be downloaded at http://www.aeinstein.org/organizations/org/FDTD.pdf.

52. "Wael Ghonim," *The New York Times* (December 18, 2011); and Heba Afify, "Officers Get 7 Years for Killing That Helped Inspire Egypt's Revolt," *The New York Times* (October 21, 2011).

53. For perhaps the most concise and salient description of how the April 6 Movement and the "We are all Khaled Said" Facebook page assembled the Tahrir crowds, see David D. Kirkpatrick, "Wired and Shrewd, Young Egyptians Guide Revolt," *The New York Times* (February 9, 2011), http://www.nytimes.com/2011/02/10/world/middleeast/10youth.html?ref=waelghonim&pagew6anted=all#, accessed 12/18/11.

54. David D. Kirkpatrick and Jennifer Preston, "Google Executive Who Was Jailed Said He Was Part of Facebook Campaign in Egypt," *The New York Times* (February 7, 2011), http://www.nytimes.com/2011/02/08/world/middleeast/08google.html?_r=1&scp=1&sq=Google%20Executive%20Who%20Was%20Jailed%20%20preston&st=cse, and Martin Fletcher, "Crowds Salute the Facebook dreamer who inspired nation," *The Times* (London) (February 7, 2011), both accessed 12/18/11.

55. Matt Richtel, "Egypt Cuts Off Most Internet and Cell Service," *The New York Times* (January 28, 2011), http://www.nytimes.com/2011/01/29/technology/internet/29cutoff.html, accessed 12/18/11.

56. CIA World Factbook, https://www.cia.gov/library/publications/the-world-factbook/geos/rw.html, accessed 5/6/11.

57. Paul Krugman, "Understanding Globalization," *Washington Monthly* 31:6 (June 1999).

58. Farnaz Fassihi, "Iranian Crackdown Goes Global," *The Wall Street Journal,* December 3, 2009.

59. Iason Athanasiadis, "Iran uses Internet as tool against protesters," *Christian Science Monitor,* January 4, 2010.

60. Christopher Rhoads and Loretta Chao, "Iran's Web Spying Aided By Western Technology," *Wall Street Journal,* June 22, 2009.

61. Francis Fukuyama, *The End of History and the Last Man* (New York: Simon and Schuster, 2006), 110.

62. Abraham Maslow, "A Theory of Human Motivation," *Psychological Review* 50 (1943): 370–396.

63. For a good summary of criticism of the pyramid and empirical analysis at the cross-national level, see Michael R. Hagerty, "Testing Maslow's Hierarchy of Needs: National Quality-of-Life Across Time," *Social Indicators Research* 46:3 (March, 1999), 249–271.

64. Seymour Martin Lipset, "Some Social Requisites of Democracy: Economic Development and Political Legitimacy," *The American Political Science Review* 53:1 (March 1959): 69–105, quote 75.

65. For a general survey of this area, see Ronald Inglehart and Christian Welzel, "How Development Leads to Democracy," *Foreign Affairs* 88:2 (March–April 2009): 33–48; and Inglehart and Welzel, *Modernization, Cultural Change, and Democracy* (Cambridge: Cambridge University Press, 2005). For an overview of their primary research, see Inglehart and Welzel, "Changing Mass Priorities: The Link Between Modernization and Democracy," *Perspectives on Politics* 8:2 (June 2010): 551–567; and Inglehart and Welzel, "The theory of human development: A cross-cultural analysis," *European Journal of Political Research* 41 (2003): 341–379.

66. Evgeny Morozov, *The Net Delusion* (New York: Public Affairs, 2011), quote 267.

67. For Atatürk's Latinization drive, see Geoffrey Lewis, *The Turkish Language Reform* (Oxford: Oxford University Press, 2002): 30–56. For the murkier transition to Latin script in Indonesia and Malaysia, see James Sneddon, *The Indonesian Language* (Sydney, Australia: UNSW Press, 2003), 13–14 and 91–97.

68. Central Intelligence Agency, "The World Factbook: China," https://www.cia.gov/library/publications/the-world-factbook/geos/ch.html, accessed March 10, 2012.

BIBLIOGRAPHY

Achtemeier, Paul J., "Omne verbum sonat: The New Testament and the Oral Environment of Late Western Antiquity," *Journal of Biblical Literature* 109:1 (Spring 1990): 9–13.

Adams, John, and Charles Francis Adams, *The Works of John Adams* (Boston: Little, Brown, and Company, 1865).

Adkins, Lesley, *Empires of the Plain* (New York: St. Martin's Press, 2003).

Afify, Heba "Officers Get 7 Years for Killing That Helped Inspire Egypt's Revolt," *The New York Times* (October 21, 2011).

Aitken, Hugh G. J., *Syntony and Spark* (New York: John Wiley and Sons, 1976).

Albright, William F., "The Inscription from Gezer at the School in Jerusalem," *Bulletin of the American Schools of Oriental Research* 58 (April 1935): 28–29.

Albright, William F., *The Proto-Sinaitic Inscriptions and their Decipherment* (Cambridge, MA: Harvard University Press, 1966).

Aldred, Guy A., *Richard Carlile Agitator* (Glasgow: Strickland Press, 1941).

Alexeyeva, Ludmilla, and Paul Goldberg, *The Thaw Generation* (Boston: Little, Brown and Company, 1990).

Amalrik, Andrei, *Notes of a Revolutionary* (New York: Alfred A. Knopf, 1982).

Amedi, Amir, et al., "The Occipital Cortex in the Blind: Lessons About Plasticity and Vision," *Current Directions in Psychological Science* 14:6 (December 2005): 306–311.

Amiet, Pierre, "Il y a 5000 ans les Elamites inventaient l'écriture," *Archeologia* 12 (1966): 20–22.

Anderson, Michael, "Four crowdsourcing lessons from the Guardian's (spectacular) expenses-scandal experiment," *Nieman Journalism Lab,* http://www.nieman-lab.org/2009/06/four-crowdsourcing-lessons-from-the-guardians-spectacular-expenses-scandal-experiment/, accessed 12/9/12.

Anonymous, "Papers of Dr. James McHenry on the Federal Convention of 1787," *The American Historical Review* 11:3 (April 1906), 618.

Archer, Gleason Leonard, *History of radio to 1926* (New York: American Historical Society, 1938).

Arendt, Hannah, *Eichmann in Jerusalem* (New York: Penguin Books, 2006).

Aristophanes, *Frogs,* http://classics.mit.edu/Aristophanes/frogs.html, accessed 6/1/10.

Aristophanes, *Wasps,* http://classics.mit.edu/Aristophanes/wasps.html, accessed 6/1/10.

Aristotle, *The Athenian Constitution* http://classics.mit.edu/Aristotle/athenian_const. html, accessed 7/23/10.

Arnould, Sir Joseph, *Memoir of Thomas, First Lord Denman* (London: Longmans, Green, and Co., 1873).

Aronoff, Mark, untitled review, *Language in Society* 31:4 (September 2002): 624–628.

Aspinall, A., *Politics and the Press* (New York: Harper and Rowe, 1974).

Athanasiadis, Iason, "Iran uses Internet as tool against protesters," *Christian Science Monitor,* January 4, 2010.

Atkinson, J. E., "Curbing the Comedians: Cleon versus Aristophanes and Syracosius' Decree," *Classical Quarterly,* New Series 42:1 (1992): 56–64.

Audisio, Gabriel, *The Waldensian Dissent* (Cambridge: Cambridge University Press, 1999).

Baadsgaard, Aubrey, et al., "Human sacrifice and intentional corpse preservation in the Royal Cemetery of Ur," *Antiquity* 85:327 (March 1, 2011): 27–42.

"Background on the SAT Takers in the Class of 2010," http://professionals.collegeboard. com/data-reports-research/sat/cb-seniors-2010/tables#, accessed 12/12/11.

Bagnall, Roger, "Library of Dreams," *Proceedings of the American Philosophical Society* 146:4 (December 2002), 348–362.

Baker, Nicholson, *Double Fold* (New York: Random House, 2001).

Barnes, Donald Grove, *A History of the English Corn Laws* (New York: Augustus M. Kelly, 1961).

Barrow, W. J., "Permanence in Book Papers," *Science* 129:3356 (April 24, 1959): 1075–2084.

"W. J. Barrow," *Bulletin of the American Group. International Institute for Conservation of Historic and Artistic Works* 8:1 (October 1967): 5.

Battelle, John, *The Search* (New York: Penguin, 2005).

Beaumont, Peter, "The truth about Twitter, Facebook and the uprisings in the Arab world," *The Guardian* (February 24, 2011), http://www.guardian.co.uk/world/2011/ feb/25/twitter-facebook-uprisings-arab-libya, accessed 12/20/11.

Bedini, Silvio, *Thomas Jefferson and His Copying Machines* (Charlottesville: University Press of Virginia, 1984).

"Belgian Senate, Session of 1997–1998, December 6, 1997," http://www.senate.be/ english/rwanda.html, accessed 11/5/10.

Bell, H. I., "Evidences of Christianity in Egypt during the Roman Period," *The Harvard Theological Review* (July 1944), 185–208.

"In memoriam, Harold Idris Bell," 1879–1967, *The Journal of Roman Studies* 57:1/2 (1967): xiii.

Bergmeier, Horst J. P., and Rainer E. Lotz, *Hitler's Airwaves* (New Haven, CT: Yale University Press, 1997).

Berners-Lee, Tim, "Information Management: A Proposal," http://www.w3.org/ History/1989/proposal.html, accessed 11/19/11.

Berners-Lee, Tim, *Weaving the Web* (San Francisco: HarperSanFrancisco, 1999).

Bernstein, Carl, and Bob Woodward, *All the President's Men* (New York: Simon and Schuster, 1974).

Bernstein, William J., *A Splendid Exchange* (New York: Grove/Atlantic Press, 2008).

Bernstein, William J., *The Birth of Plenty* (New York: McGraw-Hill, 2004).

Best, Edward E., "Literacy and Roman Voting," *Historia: Zeitschrift für Alte Geschicte* 23:4 (Fourth Quarter 1978): 428–438.

Betts, R. R., "English and Čzech Influences on the Hussite Movement," *Transactions of the Royal Historical Society*, Fourth Series, 21 (1939): 71–102.

Bevan, Edwyn Robert, *The House of Seleucus* (London: Edward Arnold, 1902).

Bilby, Kenneth, *The General* (New York: Harper and Row, 1986).

Biller, Peter, and Anne Hudson, Eds., *Heresy and Literacy* (Cambridge: Cambridge University Press, 1994).

Billington, James H., *The Icon and the Axe* (New York: Alfred A. Knopf, 1966).

Birley, Robin, *On Hadrian's Wall* (London: Thames and Hudson, 1977).

Blackmon, Douglas A., *Slavery by Another Name* (New York: Doubleday, 2008).

Bloom, Edward A. "Paper Wars for a Free Press," *Modern Language Review* 56:4 (October 1961): 482.

Bloom, Jonathan M., *Paper Before Print* (New Haven, CT: Yale University Press, 2001).

Bonnell, Victoria E., and Gregory Friedin, "Televorot: The Role of Television in Russia's August 1991 Coup," *Slavic Review* 52:4 (Winter 1993): 810–838.

Boorstin, Daniel, *The Republic of Technology* (New York: Harper and Row, 1978).

Boswell, John Eastburn, "Expositio and Oblatio: The Abandonment of Children in the Ancient and Medieval Family," *The American Historical Review* 89:1 (February 1984): 10–33.

Botsford, George Willis, *The Roman Assemblies from their Origin to the End of the Republic* (New York: Macmillan Company, 1909).

Bourne, Edward Gaylord, "The Naming of America," *The American Historical Review* 10:1 (October 1904), 41–51.

Bowman, Alan, and David Thomas, *The Vindolanda Writing Tablets* (London: British Museum Press, 1994).

Bowman, Alan K., *Life and Letters on the Roman Frontier* (London: British Museum Press, 1994).

Bowman, Raymond A., "Arabians, Aramaic, and the Bible," *Journal of Near Eastern Studies* 7:2 (April 1948): 66–70.

Bowman, Raymond A., "Aramaeans, Aramaic, and the Bible," *Journal of Near Eastern Studies* 7:2 (April 1948): 65–90.

Bradley, Keith R., *Slavery and Rebellion in the Roman World, 140 BC–70 BC* (Bloomington: Indiana University Press, 1989).

Bramsted, Ernest K., *Goebbels and National Socialist Propaganda* (East Lansing: Michigan State University Press, 1965).

Brecht, Martin, *Martin Luther* (Minneapolis: Fortress Press, 1993).

Briggs, Charles F., and Augustus Maverick, *The Story of the Telegraph and a History of the Great Atlantic Cable* (New York: Rudd and Carleton, 1858).

Bright, John, *A History of Israel* (Philadelphia: Westminster Press, 1972).

Broneer, Oscar, "Excavations on the North Slope of the Acropolis, 1937," *Hesperia* 7:2 (1938): 228–243.

Brown, Robert J., *Manipulating the Ether* (Jefferson NC: McFarland and Company, 1998).

Bukovsky, Vladimir, *To Build a Castle* (New York: The Viking Press, 1977).

Burleigh, Michael, *The Third Reich* (New York: Hill and Wang, 2000).

Bury, J. B., *A History of Greece* (New York: Modern Library, 1937).

Canfora, Luciano, *The Vanished Library*, Trans. Martin Ryle (Berkeley: University of California Press, 1990).

Cantril, Hadley, *The Invasion from Mars* (New York: Harper Torchbooks, 1960).

Cantril, Hadley, and Gordon W. Allport, *The Psychology of Radio* (New York: Harper and Brothers, 1971).

Caplan, Gerald, "Rwanda: Walking the Road to Genocide," in Allan Thompson, Ed., *The Media and the Rwanda Genocide* (London: Pluto Press, 2007).

Carpenter, Rhys, "The Alphabet in Italy," *American Journal of Archaeology* 49:4 (October–December 1945): 452–464.

Carpenter, Rhys, "The Antiquity of the Greek Alphabet," *American Journal of Archaeology* 37:1 (January–March 1933): 8–29.

Carpenter, Rhys, "The Greek Alphabet Again," *American Journal of Archaeology* 42:1 (January–March 1938): 58–69.

Carr, David McLain, *Writing on the Tablet of the Heart* (Oxford: Oxford University Press, 2005).

Carr, Nicholas, "Is Google Making Us Stupid?" *Atlantic Monthly* 302:1 (July–August 2008): 56–63.

Carr, Nicholas, *The Shallows* (New York: W.W. Norton, 2010).

Carter, Harry, *Fournier on Typefounding* (London: Fleuron Books, 1930).

Cartledge, Paul, "Literacy in the Spartan Oligarchy," *The Journal of Hellenic Studies* 98 (1978): 25–37.

Central Intelligence Agency, "The World Factbook: China," https://www.cia.gov/library/publications/the-world-factbook/geos/ch.html, accessed 3/10/12.

Chappell, Warren, and Robert Bringhurst, *A Short History of the Printed Word* (Port Roberts, WA: Hartley and Marks, 1999).

Childe, V. Gordon, *Man Makes Himself* (New York: New American Library, 1983).

Childs, David, and Richard Popplewell, *The Stasi* (New York: NYU Press, 1996).

Chrétien, Jean-Pierre, "RTLM Propaganda: the Democratic Alibi," in Thompson.

Church, John A., "William J. Barrow: A Remembrance and Appreciation," *The American Archivist* 68:1 (Spring–Summer 2005): 152–160.

Cicero, *The Nature of the Gods,* http://thriceholy.net/Texts/Cicero2.html, accessed 10/31/10.

Clapham, Michael, "Printing," in Charles Singer et al., Eds., *A History of Technology* (London: Oxford University Press, 1957).

Clark, Gregory, "Farm Wages and Living Standards in the Industrial Revolution: England, 1670–1850," http://www.econ.ucdavis.edu/faculty/gclark/papers/farm_wages_and_living_standards.pdf, accessed 11/6/10.

Clark, John Willis, *The Care of Books* (Cambridge: Cambridge University Press, 1901).

Coe, Lewis, *Wireless Radio* (Jefferson, NC: McFarland and Company, 1996).

Coon, Carleton S., *Cave Explorations in Iran 1949* (Philadelphia: University Museum, University of Pennsylvania, 1951).

Crick, Bernard, *George Orwell, a Life* (New York: Atlantic Monthly Press, 1980).

Cronin, H.S., "The Twelve Conclusions of the Lollards," *The English Historical Review* 22:86 (April 1907): 292–304.

Crookes, William, "Some Possibilities of Electricity," *Fortnightly Review,* 102 (February 1, 1892): 174.

Crystal, David, and Hilary Crystal, *Words on Words* (London: Penguin Books, 2000).

Czitrom, Daniel J., *Media and the American Mind* (Chapel Hill: University of North Carolina Press, 1982).

Dallaire, Roméo, "The Media Dichotomy," in Thompson.

Damian, Peter, and Pierre J. Payer, *The Book of Gomorrah* (Waterloo, Ontario: Wilfrid Laurier University Press, 1982).

Daniel, Anna, "The *Guardian* Reportage of the UK MP Expenses Scandal: A Case Study of Computational Journalism," http://www.eprints.qut.edu.au/38701/2/38701.pdf, accessed 12/10/11.

Daniell, David, "No Tyndale, No Shakespeare," Kirtling Lecture, 2005, *Tyndale Society Journal,* 29 (2005) 8-22.

Daniell, David, *William Tyndale* (New Haven, CT: Yale University Press, 1994).

Darnell, John Coleman et al., "Two Early Alphabetic Inscriptions from the Wadi el-Hôl: New Evidence for the Origin of the Alphabet from the Western Desert of Egypt," *Annual of the American Schools of Oriental Research* 50 (2005): 64–124.

Daugherty, Greg "They Missed the Boat," *Smithsonian* (March 2012), 38.

Daughtry, J. Martin, "Sonic Samizdat": Situating Unofficial Recording in the Post-Stalinist Soviet Union," *Poetics Today* 30:1 (Spring 2009): 34–35.

Davis, David Brion, *Inhuman Bondage* (Oxford: Oxford University Press, 2006).

Davis, Stephen J., *The Early Coptic Papacy* (Cairo: American University Press in Cairo, 2004).

Davison, Peter, *George Orwell* (New York: Saint Martin's Press, 1996).

Deanesly, Margaret, *The Lollard Bible* (Cambridge: University Press, 1920).

Deanesly, Margaret, *The Significance of the Lollard Bible* (London: Athlone Press, 1951).

Deckert, Glenn D., "Sociocultural Barriers to the Reading Habit: The Case of Iran," *Journal of Reading* 25:8 (May 1982): 746–747.

Demsky, A., "The Biblical Period," in Martin Jan Mulder, Ed., *Mirka* (Maastricht: Van Gorcum, 1998).

D'Errico, Francesco, "Paleolithic Lunar Calendars: Wishful Thinking?" *Current Anthropology* 30:1 (February 1989): 117–118.

Derry, T. K., and Trevor I. Williams, *A Short History of Technology* (New York: Dover Publications, 1993).

Des Forges, Alison, "Call to Genocide: Radio in Rwanda, 1994," in Thompson.

Dever, William G., "Excavating the Hebrew Bible, or Burying it Again?" *Bulletin of the American Schools of Oriental Research* 322 (May 2001): 67–77.

De Vinne, Theodore L., *The Invention of Printing* (London: Trübner, 1877).

Dickinson, Elizabeth, "The First WikiLeaks Revolution?" *Foreign Policy,* January 13, 2011.

Diringer, David, "The Palestinian Inscriptions and the Origin of the Alphabet," *Journal of the American Oriental Society* 63:1 (March 1943): 24–30.

Dizard, Wilson P., *Inventing Public Diplomacy* (Boulder, CO: Lynne Rienner Publishers, 2004).

Dobbs, Michael, *Down with Big Brother* (New York: Alfred A. Knopf, 1997).

Douglas, Susan J., *Listening In* (New York: Times Books, 1999).

Drower, Margaret S., *Flinders Petrie* (London: Victor Gollancz, 1985).

Dunbar, R. I. M., "Coevolution of neocortical size, group size and language in humans," *Behavioral and Brain Sciences* 16:4 (1993): 681–735.

Eder, Walter, "The Political Significance of the Codification of Law in Archaic Societies: An Unconventional Hypothesis," in *Social Struggles in Archaic Rome*, Kurt A. Raaflaub, Ed. (Berkeley: University of California Press, 1986).

Edmonds, John Maxwell, *Fragments of Attic Comedy* (Leiden: E. J. Brill, 1957), I:177–181.

Edsall, Thomas B., and Brian Faler, "Lott Remarks on Thurmond Echoed 1980 Words," *Washington Post,* December 11, 2002.

Edwards, Mark U. Jr., *Printing, Propaganda, and Martin Luther* (Berkeley: University of California Press, 1994).

Ehrman, Bart D., *Lost Christianities* (Oxford: Oxford University Press, 2003).

Eisenstein, Elizabeth, *The Printing Press as an Agent of Change* (Cambridge: Cambridge University Press, 1979).

Ellsberg, Daniel, *Secrets* (New York: Viking, 2002).

Fassihi, Farnaz, "Iranian Crackdown Goes Global," *The Wall Street Journal,* December 3, 2009.

Febvre, Lucien, and Henri-Jean Martin, *The Coming of the Book,* David Gerard, Trans. (London: Verso, 1997).

Feldbrugge, J. M., *Samizdat and Political Dissent in the Soviet Union* (Leyden: A. W. Sijthoff, 1975).

Field, Alexander James, "The Magnetic Telegraph, Price and Quality Data," *The Journal of Economic History* 52:2 (June 1992): 401–413.

Fink, Robert O., *Roman Military Records on Papyrus* (Cleveland: Case Western University Press, 1971), ix–xiii.

Finkelstein, Israel, "State Formation in Israel and Judah: A Contrast in Trajectory," *Near Eastern Archaeology* 62:1 (March 1999): 35–52.

Finkelstein, Israel, and Neil Asher Silberman, "'The Bible Unearthed': A Rejoinder," *Bulletin of the American Schools of Oriental Research* 327 (August 2002): 63–73.

Finkelstein, J.,"The Laws of Ur-Nammu," in J. Pritchard, Ed., *The Ancient Near East Supplementary Texts and Pictures Relating to the Old Testament* (Princeton: Princeton University Press, 1969).

Fletcher, Martin, "Crowds salute the Facebook dreamer who inspired nation," *The Times* (London) (February 7, 2011).

Flower, Harriet I., *Roman Republics* (Princeton: Princeton University Press, 2010).

Flynn, James R., *What Is Intelligence?* (Cambridge: Cambridge University Press, 2007).

Forbes, Clarence A., "The Education and Training of Slaves in Antiquity," *Transactions of the Proceedings of the American Philosophical Association* 86 (1955): 334–342.

Fornara, Charles W., "The Value of the Themistocles Decree," *The American Historical Review* 73:2 (December 1967): 425–433.

Forsdyke, Sara, *Exile, Ostracism, and Democracy* (Princeton: Princeton University Press, 2005).

Foster, Benjamin, *Umma in the Sargonic Period* (Hamden, CT: Archon Press, 1982).

Foxe, Rev. John, *Book of Martyrs* (Hartford, CT: Edwin Hunt, 1845).

Freedom House, "*Freedom in the World* Country Ratings," http://www.freedomhouse.org/uploads/fiw09/CompHistData/CountryStatusandRatingsOverview1973-2009.pdf, accessed 3/1/09.

Friedrich, Carl J., and Evelyn Sternberg, "Congress and the Control of Radio-Broadcasting. I," *American Political Science Review* 37:5 (October 1943).

Fukuyama, Francis, *The End of History and the Last Man* (New York: Simon and Schuster, 2006).

Fuller, C. J., "Orality, Literacy, and Memorization: Priestly Education in Contemporary South India," *Modern Asian Studies* 35:1 (February 2001): 2–3.

Füssel, Stephan, *Gutenberg and the Impact of Printing* (Aldershot, UK: Ashgate, 2005).

Gaddis, John Lewis, *We Now Know* (Oxford: Clarendon Press, 1997).

Galich, Alexander, *Songs and Poems,* Gerald Stanton Smith, Trans. (Ann Arbor: Ardis Publishers, 1983).

Gardiner, Alan H., "Once Again, the Proto-Sinaitic Inscriptions," *Journal of Egyptian Archaeology* 48 (December 1962): 45–48.

Gardiner, Alan H., "The Egyptian Origin of the Semitic Alphabet," *Journal of Egyptian Archaeology* 3:1 (January 1916): 1–16.

Gelb, I. J., *A Study of Writing* (Chicago: University of Chicago, 1963).

"German Volksempfangers," http://home.snafu.de/wumpus/volks.htm, accessed 12/9/12.

Gerovich, Slava, "'Russian Scandals': Soviet Readings of American Cybernetics in the Early Years of the Cold War," *Russian Review* 60:4 (October 2001): 545–568.

Gies, Frances and Joseph Gies, *Cathedral, Forge, and Waterwheel* (New York, HarperCollins, 1994).

Gilmont, Jean-François, "Printing at the dawn of the sixteenth century," in Gilmont and Maag.

Gilmont, Ed., Karin Maag, Trans., *The Reformation and the Book* (Aldershot, UK: Ashgate, 1998).

Gillies, James, and Robert Cailliau, *How the Web was born* (Oxford: Oxford University Press, 2000).

Glassner, Jean-Jaques, *The Invention of Cuneiform* (Baltimore: Johns Hopkins University Press, 2003).

Goody, Jack, *The Power of the Written Tradition* (Washington, DC: Smithsonian Institution Press, 2000).

Gorbachev, Mikhail, *The August Coup* (New York: HarperCollins Publishers, 1991).

Gordon, Arthur E., "On the Origins of the Latin Alphabet: Modern Views," *California Studies in Classical Antiquity* 2 (1969): 157–170.

Gordon, John S., *A Thread Across the Ocean* (New York: Walker, 2002).

Gordon, Mary L., "The Nationality of Slaves under the Early Roman Empire," *The Journal of Roman Studies* 14 (1924): 93–111.

Gourevich, Philip, *We wish to inform you that tomorrow we will be killed with our families* (New York: Picador, 1998).

Green, Norvin, "The Government and the Telegraph," *The North American Review* 137:234 (November 1883): 422–434.

Greene, Kate, "What is He Doing?" *Technology Review* (November–December 2007), 44–51.

Grendler, Paul F., "The Universities of the Renaissance and Reformation," *Renaissance Quarterly*, 57:1 (Spring 2004): 5–6.

Grossman, Maria, "Wittenberg Printing, Early Sixteenth Century," *Sixteenth Century Essays and Studies* 1 (January 1970): 53–74.

Gruen, Erich S., "Stesimbrotus on Miltiades and Themistocles," *California Studies in Classical Antiquity* 3 (1970): 91–98.

Gwinn, Nancy E., "The Fragility of Paper: Can Our Historical Record Be Saved?" *The Public Historian* 13:3 (Summer 1991): 33–53.

Hackwood, Frederick Wm., *William Hone* (New York: Augustus M. Kelly, 1970).

Hagerty, Michael R., "Testing Maslow's Hierarchy of Needs: National Quality-of-Life Across Time," *Social Indicators Research* 46:3 (March 1999): 249–271.

Hale, J., *The Captive Press in the Third Reich* (Princeton: Princeton University Press, 1964).

Hall, H. R., "The Excavations at Ur," *The British Museum Quarterly* 4:2 (September 1929): 57–59.

Hammond, N. G. L., *Epirus* (Oxford: Clarendon Press, 1967).

Robert A. Harris' Statement at the Film Preservation Study, http://www.widescreen-museum.com/rah.htm, accessed 4/18/12.

Harris, William V., *Ancient Literacy* (Cambridge, MA: Harvard University Press, 1989).

Harris, William V., "On War and Greed in the Second Century BC," *The American Historical Review* 76:5 (December 1971): 1372.

Harris, William V., "Towards a Study of the Ancient Slave Trade," *Memoirs of the American Academy in Rome* 36 (1980): 123.

Havelock, Eric A., *Preface to Plato* (New York: Grosset and Dunlap, 1967).

Hawkes, Nigel, et al., *The Worst Accident in the World* (London: Pan Books, 1986).

Hayek, F. A., "The Use of Knowledge in Society," *American Economic Review* 35:4 (September 1945): 519–530.

Hayward, Max, *On Trial* (New York: Harper and Row, 1966).

Herodotus, *The Histories* (Baltimore: Penguin Books, 1954).

Hicks, Cinque, "Easy: The Guardian's Crowdsource Game," *Newsgames* (October 21, 2009), http://newsgames.gatech.edu/blog/2009/10/easy-the-guardians-crowdsource-game.html, accessed 12/10/11.

Hilsum, Lindsey, "Reporting Rwanda: The Media and Aid Agencies," in Thompson.

Hitler, Adolf, *Mein Kampf*, Ralph Manheim, Trans. (Boston: Houghton Mifflin, 1999).

Hitti, Philip K., *History of Syria* (New York: Macmillan, 1951).

Holloway, David, "Innovation in Science—The Case of Cybernetics in the Soviet Union," *Science Studies* 4:4 (October 1974): 299–337.

Homer, Sydney, and Richard Sylla, *A History of Interest Rates*, 4th ed. (New York: John Wiley and Sons, 2005).

Hong, Sungook, *Wireless* (Cambridge, MA: MIT Press, 2001).

Hopkins, Keith, "Conquest by book," in J. H. Humphrey Ed., "Literacy in the Roman World," *Journal of Roman Archaeology* Supplementary Series 3 (1991): 144–148.

Houston, George F., "The Slave and Freedman Personnel of Public Libraries in Ancient Rome," *Transactions of the American Philological Association*, 132 (2002): 139–176.

Huang, I., et al., "Monitoring Music Processing of Harmonic Chords using fMRI: Comparison between Professional Musicians and Amateurs," *Proc. Intl. Soc. Mag. Reson. Med.,* 11 (2003): 187.

Hubbard, Gardiner G., "Government Control of the Telegraph," *The North American Review* 137:325 (December 1883): 521–535.

Hudson, Anne, "From Oxford to Prague: The Writings of John Wyclif and His English Followers in Bohemia," *Slavonic and East European Review* 75:4 (October 1997): 642–657.

Hudson, Anne, "'Laicus litteratus': the paradox of Lollardry," in Biller and Hudson.

Huffington, Ariana, http://ariannaonline.huffingtonpost.com/columns/printer_friendly.php?id=44, accessed 9/28/11.

Hughes, Nick, "Exhibit 467: Genocide Through a Camera Lens," in Thompson.

Hugo, Victor, *Notre-Dame de Paris* (New York: A Wessels Company, 1902).

Hunter, Dard, *Papermaking* (New York: Dover Publications, 1978).

Ihde, Don, *The Philosophy of Technology* (New York: Paragon House, 1993).

Inglehart, Ronald, and Christian Welzel, "Changing Mass Priorities: The Link Between Modernization and Democracy," *Perspectives on Politics* 8:2 (June 2010): 551–567.

Inglehart, Ronald, and Christian Welzel, "How Development Leads to Democracy," *Foreign Affairs* 88:2 (March–April 2009): 33–48.

Inglehart, Ronald, and Christian Welzel, *Modernization, Cultural Change, and Democracy* (Cambridge: Cambridge University Press, 2005).

Inglehart, Ronald, and Christian Welzel, "The theory of human development: A cross-cultural analysis," *European Journal of Political Research* 41 (2003): 341–379.

Ingrams, Richard, *The Life Adventures of William Cobbett* (London: HarperCollins, 2005).

Innis, Harold A., *Empire and Communications* (Lanham, MD: Rowman and Littlefield Publishers Inc., 2007).

Innis, Harold A., *The Bias of Communication* (Toronto: University of Toronto Press, 2003).

"Internet Growth Statistics," http://www.internetworldstats.com/emarketing.htm, accessed 11/20/11.

Irving, Alexandra and Janet Ambers, "Hidden Treasure from the Royal Cemetery at Ur: Technology Sheds New Light on the Ancient Near East," *Near Eastern Archaeology* 65:3 (September 2002): 206–213.

Jacobsen, Thorkild, "Democracy in Ancient Mesopotamia," *Journal of Near Eastern Studies* 2:3 (July 1943): 159–172.

Jameson, Michael H., "A Decree of Themistokles from Troizen," *Hesperia* 29:2 (April–June 1960): 198–223.

Jessup, Philip C., *Elihu Root* (New York: Dodd, Mead and Company, 1938).

Johansson, Mikael, "The Inscription from Troizen: A Decree of Themistocles?" *Zeitschrift für Papyrologie und Epigraphik* 137 (2001): 69–92.

Johnston, Gordon, "What is the history of samizdat?" *Social History* 24:2 (May 1999): 115–133.

Jordan, Mark D., *The Silence of Sodom* (Chicago: University of Chicago Press, 2000).

Kamil, Jill, *Coptic Egypt* (Cairo: American University Press in Cairo, 1987).

Kautzsch, E., and Charles R. Brown, "The Aramaic Language," *Hebraica* 1:2 (October 1884): 100.

Keller, Bill, "Russians Say Western Radio Instigated Baltic Protests," *The New York Times,* August 25, 1987.

Kennedy, Amos Paul Jr., *Once You Learn To Read, You Will Be Forever Free: Frederick Douglass* (Akron, AL: Kennedy Prints, 2007).

Kennedy, Susan Estabrook, *The Banking Crisis of 1933* (Lexington: University Press of Kentucky, 1973).

Khrushchev, Sergei, *Khrushchev on Khrushchev* (Boston: Little, Brown and Company, 1990).

Kilgour, Frederick G., *The Evolution of the Book* (Oxford: Oxford University Press, 1998).

Kimani, Mary, "RTLM: the Medium that Became a Tool for Mass Murder," in Thompson.

Kirkpatrick, David D., "Wired and Shrewd, Young Egyptians Guide Revolt," *The New York Times* (February 9, 2011).

Kirkpatrick, David D., and Jennifer Preston, "Google Executive Who Was Jailed Said He Was Part of Facebook Campaign in Egypt," *The New York Times* (February 7, 2011).

Koch, Howard, *As Time Goes By* (New York: Harcourt Brace Jovanovich, 1979).

Koehler, John O., *Stasi* (Boulder, CO: Westview Press, 1999).

Koestler, Arthur, *Janus* (New York: Random House, 1978).

Komaromi, Ann, "The Material Existence of Soviet Samizdat," *Slavic Review* 63:3 (Autumn 2004): 606–609.

Kramer, Samuel Noah, "Schooldays: A Sumerian Composition Relating to the Education of a Scribe," *Journal of the American Oriental Society* 69:4 (October–December 1949): 199–215.

Kramer, Samuel Noah, and Thorkild Jacobsen, "Gilgamesh and Agga," *American Journal of Archaeology* 53:1 (January–March, 1949): 1–18.

Krugman, Paul, "Understanding Globalization," *Washington Monthly* 31:6 (June 1999).

LaFraniere, Sharon, "China Finds More Bodies, and a Survivor, in Trains' Wreckage," *The New York Times,* July 25, 2011.

Laidlaw, W. A., *A History of Delos* (Oxford: Basil Blackwell, 1933).

Layard, Austen Henry, *Nineveh and its Remains* (New York: Frederick A. Praeger, 1970).

Lenardon, Robert J., *The Saga of Themistocles* (London: Thames and Hudson, 1978).

Lenhart, John M., "The Origin of the Invention of Printing: Its Background," *The Catholic Historical Review* 25:3 (October 1939): 303.

Leonard, Thomas C., *The Power of the Press* (Oxford: Oxford University Press, 1987).

Lerner, Barry, et al., "A Brief History of the Internet," http://www.isoc.org/internet/history/brief.shtml, accessed 11/18/11.

Levermore, Charles H. "The Rise of Metropolitan Journalism, 1800–1840" *The American Historical Review* 6:3 (April 1901): 457–458.

Levin, Saul, "The 'Qeri' as the Primary Text of the Hebrew Bible," *General Linguistics* 35 (1997): 185–223.

Lévi-Strauss, Claude, *Tristes Tropiques,* John Weightman and Doreen Weightman, Trans. (New York: Atheneum, 1974).

Levi, Primo, *The Drowned and the Saved*, Raymond Rosenthal, Trans. (New York: Summit Books, 1988).

Lewis, Geoffrey, *The Turkish Language Reform* (Oxford: Oxford University Press, 2002): 30–56.

Lewis, Tom, *Empire of the Air* (New York: Edward Burlingame Books, 1991).

Li, Darryl, "Echoes of Violence: Considerations on Radio and Genocide in Rwanda," in Thompson.

Lieberman, Stephen J., "Of Clay Pebbles, Hollow Clay Balls, and Writing: A Sumerian View," *American Journal of Archaeology* 84:3 (July 1980): 152.

Lintott, A. W., *Violence in Republican Rome* (Oxford: Clarendon Press, 1968).

Lippmann, Walter, "Two Revolutions in the American Press," *The Yale Review* XX:3 (March 1931): 433–441.

Lipset, Seymour Martin, "Some Social Requisites of Democracy: Economic Development and Political Legitimacy," *The American Political Science Review* 53:1 (March 1959): 69–105.

Lisann, Maury, *Broadcasting to the Soviet Union* (New York: Praeger Publishers, 1975).

Lodge, Oliver, *Signaling through space without wires* 3rd ed. (London: "The Electrician" Printing and Publishing Company, no date).

Lord, Alfred Bates, *The Singer of Tales* (Cambridge, MA: Harvard University Press, 2000).

Lourie, Richard, *Letters to the Future* (Ithaca: Cornell University Press, 1975).

Mackay, Christopher S., *Ancient Rome* (Cambridge: Cambridge University Press, 2004).

Maddison, Angus, data file, http://www.ggdc.net/maddison/Historical_Statistics/horizontal-file_09-2008.xls, accessed 3/1/09.

Mahoney, William H., *The History of the Czech Republic and Slovakia* (Santa Barbara, CA: Greenwood, Press, 2011).

Marconi, Degna, *My Father, Marconi* (Toronto: Guernica Editions, 2001).

Marlow, Joyce, *The Peterloo Massacre* (London: Panther, 1971).

Marshack, Alexander, "Lunar Notation in Upper Paleolithic Remains," *Science* 146:3645 (November 6, 1964): 543–745.

Marshack, Alexander, and Francesco D'Errico, "On Wishful Thinking and 'Lunar Calendars,'" *Current Anthropology* 30:4 (August–October 1989): 491–500.

Martin, Henri-Jean *The History and Power of Writing*, Lydia G. Cochrane, Trans. (Chicago: University of Chicago Press, 1988).

Masini, Giancarlo, *Marconi* (New York: Marsilio Publishers, 1995).

Maslow, Abraham, "A Theory of Human Motivation," *Psychological Review* 50 (1943): 370–396.

Mayor, Adrienne, *The Poison King* (Princeton: Princeton University Press, 2010).

McDermott, William C., "M. Cicero and M. Tiro," *Historia: Zeitschrift für Alte Geschicte* 21:2 (Second Quarter 1972): 271–271.

McFarlane, K. B., *John Wycliffe* (London: English Universities Press, 1953).

McFarlane, K. B., *Wycliffe and English Non-Conformity* (Harmondsworth, England: Penguin Books, 1972).

McGrath, Charles, "And They All Died Happily Ever After," *The New York Times,* July 2, 2006.

McLaughlin, William, "West European CPs' Reaction to Moscow Trial," Radio Free Europe Research, http://www.osaarchivum.org/files/holdings/300/8/3/text/63-2-289.shtml, accessed 1/2/12.

McNeill, William H., *The Rise of the West* (Chicago: University of Chicago Press, 1963).

Meerson-Aksenov, Michael, "Introductory," in Michael Meerson-Aksenov and Boris Shragin, Eds., *The Political, Social and Religious Thought of Russian "Samizdat" —An Anthology* (Belmont, MA: Nordland Publishing, 1977).

Meyer, Cord, *Facing Reality* (New York: Harper and Row, 1980).

Michalowski, Piotr, "Mesopotamian Cuneiform," in Peter T. Daniels and William Bright, *The World's Writing Systems* (New York: Oxford University Press, 1996).

Michie, Alan Andrew, *Voices Through the Iron Curtain* (New York: Dodd, Mead, 1963).

Mickiewicz, Ellen, *Split Signals* (Oxford: Oxford University Press, 1988).

Millar, Fergus, *The Crowd in Rome in the Late Republic* (Ann Arbor: University of Michigan Press, 1998).

Milman, Henry Hart, *History of Latin Christianity* (London: John Murray, 1867).

Milner, N. P., Trans., *Vegetius: Epitome of Military Science* (Liverpool: Liverpool University Press, 1996), 51–52.

Molleson, Theya, and Dawn Hodgson, "Human Remains from Woolley's Excavations at Ur," *Iraq* 65 (2003): 91–129.

Moore, Martha T., "Rare earthquake shakes and shocks Eastern Seabord," *USA Today,* http://www.usatoday.com/news/nation/story/2011-08-23/Rare-earthquake-shakes-and-shocks-Eastern-Seaboard/50114870/1, accessed 11/30/11.

Montesquieu, Baron de, *Reflections on the Causes of the Rise and Fall of the Roman Empire* (London: Printed for W. Innys in Pater-noster Row, C. Davis against Gray's-Inn Gate, Holborn, R. Manby on Ludgate-Hill, and H. S. Cox in Pater-noster Row, 1753).

Morgan, H. Wayne, *America's Road to Empire* (New York: John Wiley and Sons, 1965).

Morozov, Evgeny, *The Net Delusion* (New York: Public Affairs, 2011).

Mosshammer, Alden A., "Themistocles' Archonship in the Chronographic Tradition," *Hermes* 103:2 (1975): 222–234.

Moynihan, Daniel P., "Introduction—The American Experiment," *The Public Interest* 41 (Fall 1975): 4–8.

Mozley, J. F., *William Tyndale* (New York: Macmillan Company, 1937).

Mugridge, Ian, *The View from Xanadu* (Montreal: McGill-Queen's University Press, 1995).

Musson, A. E., "Printing in the Industrial Revolution," *The Economic History Review*, New Series, 10:3 (1958): 411–426.

Nasaw, David, *The Chief* (Boston: Houghton Mifflin, 2001).

Naveh, Joseph, *Early History of the Alphabet* (Jerusalem: Magnes Press, 1982).

Naveh, Joseph, "The Greek Alphabet: New Evidence," *Biblical Archaeologist* 43:1 (Winter 1980): 22–25.

Nef, J. U., "Mining and Metallurgy in Medieval Civilization," in M. Postan and E. E. Rich, Eds., *The Cambridge Economic History of Europe* (Cambridge: Cambridge University Press, 1952).

Nelson, Michael, *War of the Black Heavens* (Syracuse, NY: Syracuse University Press, 1997).

Nicolet, C., *The World of the Citizen in Republican Rome,* P. S. Falla, Trans. (Los Angeles: University of California Press, 1980).

Niditch, Susan, *Oral World and Written Word* (Louisville: Westminster John Knox Press, 1996).

Nielson, John, and Royal Skousen, "How Much of the King James Bible Is William Tyndale's?" *Reformation* 3 (1998): 49–74.

Nissen, Hans J., *Archaic Bookkeeping* (Chicago: University of Chicago Press, 1993).

Nissen, Hans J., *The Early History of the Ancient Near East* (Chicago: University of Chicago Press, 1990).

Nowak, Jan, *Courier from Warsaw* (Detroit, MI: Wayne State University Press, 1982).

Ong, Walter T., *Orality and Literacy* (London, Routledge, 1988).

Oppenheim, Leo, *Ancient Mesopotamia* (Chicago: University of Chicago Press, 1977).

Orwell, George, *Nineteen Eighty-Four* (New York: Alfred A. Knopf, 1987).

Orwell, Sonia, and Ian Angus, Eds., *The Collected Essays, Journalism and Letters of George Orwell* (New York: Harcourt, Brace and World, 1968).

Otzen, Benedikt, "Israel Under the Assyrians," in Mogens Trolle Larsen, Ed., *Meso-potamia* Volume 7 (Copenhagen: Akademisk Forlag, 1979).

Owen, David, *Copies in Seconds* (New York: Simon and Schuster, 2004).

Oz, Amos, *A Tale of Love and Darkness*, Nicholas de Lange, Trans. (New York: Harcourt, 2004).

Padover, Samuel K., *Jefferson* (New York: Mentor, 1970).

Parry, Adam, Ed., *The Making of Homeric Verse: The Collected Papers of Milman Parry* (Oxford: Oxford University Press, 1987).

Patschovsky, Alexander. "The Literacy of Waldensianism from Valdes to c. 1400," in Biller and Hudson.

Petrie, W. M. Flinders, *Researches in Sinai* (New York: E.P. Dutton and Company, 1906).

Petrie, W. M. Flinders, *The Formation of the Alphabet* (London, Macmillan and Co. and Bernard Quaritch, 1912).

Petronius, *Satyricon*, LXXV, http://www.gutenberg.org/files/5225/5225-h/5225-h.htm, accessed 9/30/10.

Pettegree, Andrew, *The Book in the Renaissance* (New Haven, CT: Yale University Press, 2010).

Pikard-Cambridge, Arthur, *The Dramatic Festivals of Athens* (Oxford: Clarendon Press, 1968).

Pliny the Younger, *The Letters of Pliny the Younger,* http://ancienthistory.about.com/library/bl/bl_text_plinyltrs3.htm, accessed 9/23/10.

Plutarch, *Aristides,* Vllib, from *Plutarch's Lives,* Bernadotte Perrin, Trans. (London: William Heinemann Ltd., 1964).

Plutarch, *The Life of Julius Caesar,* http://penelope.uchicago.edu/Thayer/E/Roman/Texts/Plutarch/Lives/Caesar*.html, accessed 10/14/10.

Plutarch, *Themistocles,* http://penelope.uchicago.edu/Thayer/E/Roman/Texts/Plutarch/Lives/Themistocles*.html, accessed 8/14/10.

Pollock, John, "How Egyptian and Tunisian youth Hacked the Arab Spring," *Technology Review* (September/October 2011): http://www.technologyreview.com/web/38379/, accessed 12/20/11.

Pospielovsky, D., "From *Gosizdat* to *Samizdat* and *Tamizdat*," *Canadian Slavonic Papers* XX:1 (March 1978): 44–62.

Proudfoot, W. B., *The Origin of Stencil Duplicating* (London: Hutchinson of London, 1972).

Prunier, Gérard, *The Rwandan Crisis* (New York: Columbia University Press, 1995).

Putnam, George Haven, *Books and Their Makers During the Middle Ages* (New York: Hillary House Publishers, 1897).

Rawlinson, George, *A Memoir of Major-General Sir Henry Creswicke Rawlinson* (London: Longmans, Green, 1898).

Rees, Laurence, *Auschwitz: A New History* (New York: Public Affairs, 2005).

Reichmann, Felix, "The Book Trade at the Time of the Roman Empire," *Library Quarterly* 8:1 (January 1938): 62–63.

Rex, Richard, *The Lollards* (New York: Palgrave, 2002).

Rhoads, Christopher, and Loretta Chao, "Iran's Web Spying Aided By Western Technology," *The Wall Street Journal,* June 22, 2009.

Rhodes, Barbara, and William Wells Streeter, *Before Photocopying* (New Castle, DE: Oak Knoll Press, 1999).

Richmond, J. T., "Spies in Ancient Greece," *Greece and Rome* 45:1 (April 1998): 12.

Richtel, Matt, "Egypt Cuts Off Most Internet and Cell Service," *The New York Times* (January 28, 2011).

Richter, Michael, untitled review, *American Historical Review* 106:2 (April 2001): 627–628.

Ritner, Robert K., "Egyptian Writing," in Peter T. Daniels and William Bright, Eds., *The World's Writing Systems* (New York: Oxford University Press, 1996).

Roberts, Jennifer T., *Athens on Trial* (Princeton: Princeton University Press, 1994).

Robinson, H. Wheeler, Ed., *The Bible in its Ancient and English Versions* (Oxford: Clarendon Press, 1940).

Roux, Georges, *Ancient Iraq* (New York: Penguin Books, 1966).

Rubenstein, Joshua, *Soviet Dissidents* (Boston: Beacon Press, 1980).

Rubio, Gonzalo, "Sumerian Literature" in Carl S. Ehrlich, *From an Antique Land* (New York: Rowman and Littlefield, 2009).

Sacnger, Paul, *Space Between Words* (Stanford, CA: Stanford University Press, 1997).

Saerchinger, César, "Radio as a Political Instrument," *Foreign Affairs* 16:2 (January 1938): 244–259.

Safire, William, "What Else Are We Missing," *The New York Times,* June 6, 2002.

Sallust, *The Jugurthine War* 65:4–5 (London: Penguin Books, 2007).

Salvia, Anthony T., "Poland's Walesa Addresses RFE/RL Conference," *Shortwaves,* November 1989.

Sampson, Geoffrey, *Writing Systems* (Palo Alto: Stanford University Press, 1990).

Schenkel, Wolfgang, "The Structure of Hieroglyphic Script," *Royal Anthropological Institute of Great Britain and Ireland* 15 (August 1976): 4–7.

Schmandt-Besserat, Denise, *Before Writing* (Austin: University of Texas Press, 1992).

Schmandt-Besserat, Denise, "The Envelopes That Bear the First Writing," *Technology and Culture* 21:3 (July 1980): 384–385.

Schniedewind, William M., *How the Bible Became a Book* (Cambridge: Cambridge University Press, 2004).

Schniedewind, William M., "Sociolinguistic Reflections of the Letter of a 'Literate' Soldier," (Lachish 3), *Zeitschrift für Althebraistic* 13:2 (2000): 157–167.

Schudson, Michael, *Discovering the News* (New York: Basic Books, 1978).

Schwarzlose, Richard A., *The Nation's Newsbrokers* (Evanston, IL: Northwestern University Press, 1989).

Scott, Esther, "'Big Media' Meets the 'Bloggers,'" http://www.hks.harvard.edu/press-pol/publications/case_studies/1731_0_scott.pdf, accessed 9/28/11.

Shane, Scott, *Dismantling Utopia* (Chicago: Ivan R. Dee, 1994).

Sharp, Gene, *From Dictatorship to Democracy* (East Boston, MA: Albert Einstein Institution, 2010).

Shedd, William G. T., Ed, *Confessions of Augustine* (Andover MA: Warren F. Draper, pub., 1860).

Sheehan, Neil, *A Bright and Shining Lie* (New York: Vintage Books, 1989).

Shirky, Clay, *Here Comes Everybody* (New York: Penguin, 2008).

Sinclair, R. K., *Democracy and Participation at Athens* (Cambridge: Cambridge University Press, 1988).

Skilling, H. Gordon, *Charter 77 and Human Rights in Czechoslovakia* (London: George Allen and Unwin, 1981).

Skilling, H. Gordon, *Samizdat and an Independent Society in Central and Eastern Europe* (Columbus: Ohio University Press, 1989).

Slack, Paul, "Measuring the national wealth in seventeenth-century England," *Economic History Review* 57:4 (November 2004): 607–635.

Šmahel, František, "Literacy and Heresy in Hussite Bohemia," in Biller and Hudson.

Small, Melvin, Ed., *Public Opinion and Historians* (Detroit: Wayne State University Press, 1970).

Smeijers, Fred, *Counterpunch* (London: Hyphen Press, 1996).

Smith, Robert, "Is Democracy Still on the Dial?" *The New York Times,* March 3, 2001.

Sneddon, James, *The Indonesian Language* (Sydney, Australia: UNSW Press, 2003).

Sohn, Pow-Key, "Early Korean Printing," *Journal of the American Oriental Society* 79:2 (April–June 1959): 96–103.

Solomon, Howard M., *Public Welfare, Science, and Propaganda in the Seventeenth Century* (Princeton: Princeton University Press, 1977).

Solzhenitsyn, Aleksandr, *Invisible Allies* (Washington, DC: Counterpoint, 1995).

Solzhenitsyn, Aleksandr, *The Oak and the Calf* (New York: Harper and Row, 1980).

Speech of Hon. Elihu Root, Secretary of State at Utica New York, November 1, 1906 (Washington, NY: C. F. Sudwarth, 1906).

Sosin, Gene, "Magnitizat: Uncensored Songs of Dissent," in Rudolf L. Tökés, Ed. *Dissent in the U.S.S.R..* (Baltimore: Johns Hopkins University Press, 1975).

"Soviet Union: Crackdown on Dissent," *Time,* December 18, 1972.

Spencer, Richard, "Tunisia riots: neighbours will be watching Tunisia nervously," *The Telegraph,* January 12, 2011.

Spinka, Matthew, *John Hus* (Princeton: Princeton University Press, 1968).

Sprengling, Martin, *The Alphabet* (Chicago: University of Chicago Press, 1931).

Springer, William M., "The Telegraph Monopoly," *The North American Review* 132:293 (April 1881): 369–382.

Standage, Tom, *The Victorian Internet* (New York: Walker Publishing, 1998).

Stern, Marcus, et al., *The Wrong Stuff* (New York: Public Affairs, 2007).

Stolberg, Sheryl Gay "Shy U.S. Intellectual Created Playbook Used in a Revolution," *The New York Times* (February 16, 2011).

Strabo, *Geography,* http://rbedrosian.com/Classic/strabo14d.htm, accessed 9/14/10.

de Strata, Filippo, *Polemic Against Printing,* Shelagh Grier, Trans. (Birmingham, UK: Hayloft Press, 1986).

Streeter, Barbara J., and William W. Rhodes, *Before Photocopying* (New Castle, DE: Oak Knoll Press, 1999).

Suetonius, *The Lives of the Twelve Caesars: D. Octavius Caesar Augustus,* http://www.gutenberg.org/files/6400/6400-h/6400-h.htm, accessed 9/16/10.

Sullivan, B. N., "Northwest pilots who overflew destination settle with FAA over license revocation," http://aircrewbuzz.com/2009/10/northwest-pilots-lose-situational, accessed 12/11/11. html and http://aircrewbuzz.com/2009/10/northwest-pilots-who-overflew.html.

Svenbro, Jesper, "The 'Interior' Voice: On the Invention of Silent Reading," in John J. Winkler and Froma I. Zeitlin, Eds., *Nothing to Do with Dionysos?* (Princeton: Princeton University Press, 1990).

Svirski, Grigori, *A History of Post-War Soviet Writing* (Ann Arbor: Ardis Publishing, 1981).

Swanberg, W. A., *Citizen Hearst* (New York: Charles Scribner's Sons, 1961).

Swanberg, W. A., *Pulitzer* (New York: Charles Scribner's Sons, 1967).

Szelenyi, Ivan, and Balazs Szelenyi, "Why Socialism Failed: Toward a Theory of System Breakdown—Causes of Disintegration of East European State Socialism," *Theory and Society* 23:2 (April 1994): 223.

Taubman, William, *Khrushchev* (New York: W.W. Norton, 2003).

Taubman, William, *The View from Lenin Hills* (New York: Coward-McCann, 1967).

Tebel, John, *The Life and Good Times of William Randolph Hearst* (New York: E.P. Dutton, 1952).

Telesin, Julius, "Inside 'Samizdat,'" *Encounter* 40:2 (February 1973): 25–33.

Tenney, Frank, *An Economic Survey of Ancient Rome* (Paterson, NJ: Pageant Books, 1959).

"The Evolution of Search Engine Technology—Early Technology, Early Problems," http://careers.stateuniversity.com/pages/100000932/Evolution-Search-Engine-Technology-Early-Progress-Early-Problems.html, accessed 4/24/12.

"The Foxification of news," *Economist,* July 9, 2011.

The Nation CXXXV:3511 (October 19, 1932): 341.

"The people formerly known as the audience; Social Media," *Economist,* July 9, 2011.

Thomas, Rosalind, *Literacy and Orality in Ancient Greece* (Cambridge: Cambridge University Press, 1992).

Thompson, Allan, Ed., *The Media and the Rwanda Genocide* (London: Pluto Press, 2007).

Thurston, Robert W., *Life and Terror in Stalin's Russia 1934–1941* (New Haven, CT: Yale University Press, 1966).

Trippi, Joe, *The Revolution Will Not Be Televised* (New York: HarperCollins e-books, 2008).

"Truth is in the Air," *Economist* June 6, 1987.

Tsien, Tsuen-Hsuin, *Paper and Paper Making* (*Science and Civilisation in China* V:1, Joseph Needham, Ed.) (Cambridge: Cambridge University Press, 1985).

Tusa, John, "Salvation on shortwave," *Times* (London), December 11, 1991.

Tyndale, William, *Doctrinal Theses and Introductions to Different Portions of the Holy Scriptures,* Henry Walker Ed. (Cambridge: Cambridge University Press, 1849).

Uhlendorf, A., "The Invention of Printing and Its Spread til 1470: With Special Reference to Social and Economic Factors," *The Library Quarterly* 2:3 (July 1932): 180.

Unger, Aryeh L., *The Totalitarian Party* (London: Cambridge University Press, 1974),

Van De Mieroop, Marc, *The Ancient Mesopotamian City* (Oxford: Clarendon Press, 1997).

Vanderpool, Eugene, *Ostracism at Athens* (Cincinnati, OH: University of Cincinnati Press, 1970).

Vansina, Jan, *Oral Tradition of History* (Madison, WI: University of Wisconsin Press, 1985).

Vigdorova, Frida Abramovna, "Trial of a Young Poet," *Encounter* 23:3 (September 1964): 84–85.

Villard, Oswald Garrison, *Some Newspapers and Newspaper-Men* (New York: Alfred A. Knopf, 1923).

von Urgern-Sternberg, Jürgen, "The Crisis of the Republic," in Harriet Flower, Trans. and Ed., *The Cambridge Companion to the Roman Republic* (Cambridge: Cambridge University Press, 2004).

Wagenaar, W. A., and H. Timmers, "Extrapolation of exponential time series is not enhanced by having more data points," *Perception and Psychophysics* 24:2 (1978): 182–184.

Walesa, Lech, *A Way of Hope* (New York: Henry Holt and Company, 1987).

Warburton, William, *The Divine Legation of Moses Demonstrated*, 10th ed. (London: Printed for Thomas Tegg, 1846).

Waugh, W. T., "Sir John Oldcastle," *The English Historical Review* 20:79 (July 1905): 434–456.

Waugh, W. T., "Sir John Oldcastle (Continued)," *The English Historical Review* 20:80 (October 1905): 637–658.

Wejnert, Barbara "Diffusion, Development, and Democracy, 1800–1999," *American Sociological Review* 70:1 (February 2005): 58.

Wells, Tom, *Wild Man* (New York: Palgrave, 2001).

Westenholz, Aage, "The Old Akkadian Empire in Contemporary Opinion," in Mogens Trolle Larsen, *Mesopotamia Volume 7* (Copenhagen: Akademisk Forlag, 1979).

White, Stephen, "The Effectiveness of Political Propaganda in the U.S.S.R.," *Soviet Studies* 32:3 (July 1980): 323–348.

Wickwar, William H., *Struggle for the Freedom of the Press* (London: George Allen and Unwin, 1928).

Wiener, Norbert, *Cybernetics* 2nd ed. (Cambridge, MA: MIT Press, 1965).

Wiener, Norbert, *The Human Use of Human Beings* (New York: Da Capo Press, 1988).

Williams, Evan, "For Twitter C.E.O., Well-Orchestrated Accidents," *The New York Times*, March 8, 2009.

Wilson, Geoffrey, *The Old Telegraphs* (London: Philliomore, 1976).

Winner, Langdon, "Cyberlibertarian Myths and the Prospects for Community," http://www.rpi.edu/~winner/cyberlib2.html, accessed 4/23/11.

Winner, Langdon, "Do Artifacts Have Politics?" *Daedalus* 109:1 (Winter 1980): 121–136.

Wise, Jennifer, *Dionysus Writes* (Ithaca, NY: Cornell University Press, 1998).

Wooten, James, *Dasher: The Roots and Rising of Jimmy Carter* (New York: Summit Books, 1978).

Wolff, Hans Julius, *Roman Law* (Norman: University of Oklahoma Press, 1951).

Wriston, Walter, "Bits, Bytes, and Diplomacy," *Foreign Affairs* 76:5 (September–October 1997): 172.

Zechmeister, E. B., et al., "Growth of a Functionally Important Lexicon," *Journal of Reading Behavior* 27:2 (1995): 201–212.

Zhu, Erping, "Hypermedia Interface Design: The Effects of Number of Links and Granularity of Nodes," *Journal of Educational Multimedia and Hypermedia* 8:3 (1999): 331–358.

Zimansky, Paul, Review of *Before Writing* in *Journal of Field Archaeology* 20:4 (Winter 1993): 513–517.

Zimbardo, Philip G., *The Lucifer Effect* (New York: Random House, 2008).

ACKNOWLEDGMENTS

Anyone who undertakes the survey of so wide a subject as the history and impact of communications technology must of necessity rely on the knowledge and generosity of others, since no author can bring to the table the requisite expertise in so many different fields.

The following people provided much-needed reference guidance in these respective areas: Stephen Bales, ancient Greek literacy; Amira Bennison, medieval Arab translators; Robert Biggs, Sumerian script and translations; Douglas Blackmon, the history of post–Civil War neoslavery; Jonathan Bloom, early paper technology; Alan K. Bowman, the Vindolanda excavations; Euan Cameron, the writing materials of the Waldensians; David Carr, literacy in ancient Judah; Jonathan Clements and Jason Zweig, modern press history; Stephen Davis, Coptic script and history; Peter Downie, radio broadcast history; Bart Ehrman, Gnostic history; Robert Englund, Sumerian accounting; Victoria Feinberg, Soviet communications technology; Harriet Flower, the Roman republic; William V. Harris, ancient literacy in general; Charles Hedrick, Greek archaeology; Sergei Khrushchev, the copying and publication of his father's memoirs; Tom Leonard, penny newspapers; Monty Marshall, data on world democratic development; Victor Matthews, literacy in remote antiquity; Nelson Minnich, the Waldensians; Jennifer Roberts, Athenian politics; Gonzalo Rubio, Sumerian literature and grammar; Royal Skousen, statistical analysis of the King James Bible; Paul Saenger, origins of word spacing; William Schniedewind, literacy and Judean politics; William Uphaus, medieval printing; and John Wolff, Roger Paget, Brett McCabe, Joe Errington, and Jeff Barlow, the alphabetization of the Malay and Indonesian languages.

I particularly pushed the limits of charitable help with many individuals. Roger Burt, as he also did with *A Splendid Exchange,* shared his deep knowledge of deep mining and its effects on printing technology. Jean Clipperton and Ron Inglehart plumbed the depths of the Interuniversity Consortium for Political and Social Research database to produce illustrations. Anne Hudson and Mark Gregory Pegg sorted out for me the writing materials used by the Waldensians. Anton and Julia Lotman shared their radio listening experiences in the former Soviet Union and reviewed much of the book's later material. The late William H. McNeill generously offered his thoughts on the book's central topic, the relationship between communication technology and political structure. I had many helpful conversations with Ronald Mertens about the interplay of digital communications devices and neurophysiology. Karl Pflegler and Todd Satterson guided me through the finer details of early Internet history. Denise Schmandt-Besserat prevented me from embarrassing myself about preliterate recording systems, provided illustrations, and reviewed what turned out to be the first two chapters. Brad Schmidt, Eric Schurenberg, and Marcus Stern provided their perspectives on the changes wrought by digital media on traditional journalism. Last, and certainly not least, Ian Young corrected my many mistaken impressions about ancient literacy, particularly in Judea, and reviewed relevant material.

Morgan Entrekin at Grove/Atlantic Press supplied expert editorial and marketing advice, as also did Wesley Neff. Robert Richardson produced the book's handome maps and many of its illustrations, Lewis O'Brien supplied imaging and permission assistance, and Molly Blalock-Koral assisted with my bibliographic needs. My editor, Jamison Stoltz, proved expert in the handling and care of both manuscript and author throughout the editorial and production process, and provided a layer of polish and structure that I could hardly have achieved on my own.

Finally, my wife, Jane Gigler, as she always does, helped me convert the jagged and disorganized chapter rough drafts I sent her way into prose that I could send to my publisher without blushing and tolerated with amusement and grace a husband who could charitably be called distracted and self-absorbed. No author could ask for a better companion.

ILLUSTRATION CREDITS

Page 4: Figure I-1. Percent of Nations Considered Democracies. Graph by author. Source Data: Jean Clipperton and Ronald Inglehart.

Page 4: Figure I-2. Percent of Nations Considered Despotic: Graph by author. Source Data: Jean Clipperton and Ronald Inglehart.

Page 18: Figure 1-1. The first long-lasting notation systems were likely notched bones, like this specimen from the Ksar Akil site in Lebanon, ca. 15,000–12,000 BC. Source: Peabody Museum, Harvard University, collection of Professor Alexander Marshack, from Denise Schmandt-Besserat, *Before Writing,* (Austin: University of Texas Press, 1992), I:159.

Page 20: Figure 1-2. Simple tokens, representing measures of grain. Courtesy of Denise Schmandt-Besserat.

Page 21: Figure 1-3. An ancient legal contract? Envelope containing one large cone, three small cones, and three disks; note the impressions of each on the face of the envelope. Courtesy of Denise Schmandt-Besserat.

Page 27: Figure 1-4. Ancient Mesopotamia; greatest extent of Sargonic Empire, ca. 2300 BC. © 2012, William J. Bernstein. Original graphics by Robert C. Richardson and Lewis W. O'Brien, OBrienEditorial@verizon.net.

Page 29: Figure 1-5. The evolution of cuneiform symbols from 3000 BC (left) to 600 BC (right). See text for detailed description. Source: Samuel Noah Kramer, *History Begins at Sumer,* (New York: Doubleday, 1959), and Margaret S. Drower, *Flinders Petrie,* (London: Victor Gollancz, 1985). Republication permission kindly granted by Richenda Kramer and Judy Kramer Gueive.

Page 30: Figure 1-6. The top row shows an early pointed stylus, and the sharp, narrow stroke it left in clay, which was prone to cracking. The Sumerians accordingly developed a round stylus for numerical notation (middle row), and a wedge-shaped one. © 2012, William J. Bernstein. Original graphics by Robert C. Richardson and Lewis W. O'Brien, OBrienEditorial@verizon.net.

Page 32: Figure 1-7. Egyptian single-phoneme (monoconsonantal) symbols. These would eventually give rise to the first Western alphabets. © 2012, William J. Bernstein. Original graphics by Robert C. Richardson and Lewis W. O'Brien, OBrienEditorial@verizon.net.

Page 33: Figure 1-8. Early Hieratic top, corresponding hieroglyphic below. (Ca. 1900 BC). Source: Alan H. Gardiner, *Egyptian Grammar,* 3ed Ed., Published upon behalf of the Griffith Institute, Ashmolean Museum, Oxford, by Oxford University Press © 1957. Copyright of Griffith Institute, University of Oxford, Gardiner, A., Egyptian Grammar (2012).

Page 33: Figure 1-9. Demotic above, corresponding hieroglyphic below. (Ca. 200 BC). Source: Alan H. Gardiner, *Egyptian Grammar,* 3rd Ed., Published upon behalf of the Griffith Institute, Ashmolean Museum, Oxford, by Oxford University Press © 1957. Copyright of Griffith Institute, University of Oxford, Gardiner, A., Egyptian Grammar (2012).

Page 34: Figure 1-10. These three symbols sound out the Egyptian word "Jmn," the god Amun. The left symbol stood for the uniconsonantal "j"; the top right symbol, the biconsonantal "mn"; and the bottom right symbol, the uniconsonantal "n." © 2012, William J. Bernstein. Original graphics by Robert C. Richardson and Lewis W. O'Brien, OBrienEditorial@verizon.net.

Page 45: Figure 2-1. The ancient Levant, ca 800 BC, before the destruction of Israel, Judah, and the Aramaean states. © 2012, William J. Bernstein. Original graphics by Robert C. Richardson and Lewis W. O'Brien, OBrienEditorial@verizon.net.

Page 47: Figure 2-2. Early proto-Semitic letters, ca. 1400 BC. *Top:* Serabit Tablet. *Bottom:* Proto-Semitic Alphabet. Source, Top: William Foxwell Albright, *The Proto-Sinaitic Inscriptions and their Decipherment,* (Cambridge MA: Harvard University Press, 1966). Source, Bottom: © 2012, William J. Bernstein. Original graphics by Robert C. Richardson and Lewis W. O'Brien, OBrienEditorial @verizon.net.

Page 56: Figure 2-3. The evolutionary tree of the Western alphabets. © 2012, William J. Bernstein. Original graphics by Robert C. Richardson and Lewis W. O'Brien, OBrienEditorial@verizon.net.

Page 68: Figure 2-4. Bronze jury ballots; the hollow stemmed ballot on the far left signifies a vote for the plaintiff; the solid stemmed ones, a vote for the defendant. Source: Originally posted to Flickr as Athenian Secret Ballot, by Sharon Mollerus, http://www.flickr.com/people/clairity/. Reprinted with permission.

Page 71: Figure 2-5. Ancient Greece in the classical period (ca. 500 BC). © 2012, William J. Bernstein. Original graphics by Robert C. Richardson and Lewis W. O'Brien, OBrienEditorial@verizon.net.

Page 94: Figure 3-1. The growth of the Republic, 400 BC–218 BC. © 2012, William J. Bernstein. Original graphics by Robert C. Richardson and Lewis W. O'Brien, OBrienEditorial@verizon.net.

Page 94: Figure 3-2. The growth of the Republic, 218 BC–44 BC. © 2012, William J. Bernstein. Original graphics by Robert C. Richardson and Lewis W. O'Brien, OBrienEditorial@verizon.net.

Page 112: Figure 4-1. Separating words with interpuncts. Source: "Picture of a long latin text carved on a stone wall" © Maxiphoto 09-26-11, "Latin Words" Stock photo File #: 17873151, http://www.istockphoto.com. ©iStockphoto.com/Maxiphoto

Page 115: Figure 4-2. Livy's *History of Rome,* written in *scriptura continua.* Source: Livy, *The History of Rome,* 1880.

Page 143: Figure 5-1. Appearance of print from poorly cast type. Source: Theodore L. De Vinne, *The Invention of Printing* (London: Trübner, 1877), 52, and reworked by Robert C. Richardson and Lewis W. O'Brien, OBrienEditorial@verizon.net.

Page 145: Figure 5-2. Capital H and its counter. © 2012, William J. Bernstein.

Original graphics by Robert C. Richardson and Lewis W. O'Brien, OBrienEditorial@
verizon.net.

Page 145: Figure 5-3. From left to right, blank punch face, counterpunch, unfinished punch face after counterpunch strike, and finished punch face after filing away of
outside edges. Final capital H after *The Invention of Printing* (London: Trübner, 1877),
55, and reworked by Robert C. Richardson and Lewis W. O'Brien, OBrienEditorial@
verizon.net. Other 3 images, © 2012, William J. Bernstein. Original graphics by Robert
C. Richardson and Lewis W. O'Brien, OBrienEditorial@verizon.net.

Page 147: Figure 5-4. Copper matrix for capital H, before it has been cut down
to size to fit in mould. Source: Theodore L. DeVinne, *The Invention of Printing* (London: Trübner, 1877), 55.

Page 147: Figure 5-5. Type mould. For clarity, a finished type for capital H has
been placed in the location where the copper matrix shown above, after cutting down
to size, would go. Source: Theodore L. DeVinne, *The Invention of Printing* (London:
Trübner, 1877), 57.

Page 149: Figure 5-6. Dangerous work: type caster, ca. 1683. Note the crucible
in the right hand, type mould in left. Source: Theodore L. DeVinne, *The Invention of
Printing* (London: Trübner, 1877), 59.

Page 157: Figure 5-7. Gutenberg and his successors strove to produce a print
appearance indistinguishable from written manuscripts. Jenson's remarkably modern
appearing Roman font, ca. 1470, changed that paradigm to fonts that were easy to read.

Page 159: Figure 5-8. Johannes Rhau-Grunenberg, Luther's first printer. That
both he and Luther had been sent to Wittenberg in 1508 by their superior, Johann von
Staupitz, may not have been a coincidence. Source: Reprinted with permission from
Jean-François Gilmont, Ed., and Karin Maag, Trans., The Reformation and the Book
(Aldershot, UK: Ashgate, 1998).

Page 164: Figure 5-9. The "lamb, chalice and flag," and "Luther Rose" served
as Luther's symbols of authenticity, assuring readers that a book or pamphlet had been
printed under his supervision. Source: Reprinted with permission from Jean-François
Gilmont, Ed., and Karin Maag, Trans., The Reformation and the Book (Aldershot,
UK: Ashgate, 1998).

Page 223: Figure 7-1. Schematic drawing of Hertz' apparatus. © 2012, William
J. Bernstein. Original graphics by Robert C. Richardson and Lewis W. O'Brien,
OBrienEditorial@verizon.net.

Page 230: Figure 7-2. Detail from de Forest's 1907 patent application for the
audion. [F] represents the filament and [b] the plate, whose basic design he "borrowed"
from a scientific publication by John Fleming, an employee of Thomas Edison. the
"grid" [a] between the two was probably de Forest's idea; his bulb manufacturer,
Henry McCandless, suggested bending the grid into its zig-zag shape. Source: U.S.
Patent Office.

Page 275: Figure 8-1. *"I won the Nobel Prize for Literature. What was your
crime?"* Bill Mauldin did not win a Nobel for this 1958 cartoon, but it did earn him
a Pulitzer the next year. Source: St. Louis Dispatch, October 30, 1958. Copyright by
Bill Mauldin (1958). Courtesy of Bill Mauldin Estate LLC.

Page 325: Figure 9-1. The Great Distractor: Connecticut legislators failing to pay attention to business. Source: House Minority Leader Lawrence F. Cafero Jr., R-Norwalk, far right, speaks while colleagues play solitaire on their computers as the House convenes to vote on a new budget for the fiscal year in the Capitol, in Hartford, Conn., Monday, Aug., 31, 2009. (AP Photo/Jessica Hill).

Page 335: Figure 9-2. Global sociology and economics revealed. The x-axis represents the S/SE scale-roughly, how far up Maslow's hierarchy of needs a nation has ascended. The y-axis represents the T/SR score, with traditional, religiously oriented societies at the bottom and secular societies at the top. As one moves from the lower left corner to the upper right corner, per capita GDP increases. Courtesy of Ronald Inglehart.

INDEX

A NOTE ON THE AUTHOR

William J. Bernstein is a historian and financial theorist whose books include *The Birth of Plenty*, *The Four Pillars of Investing* and, most recently, *A Splendid Exchange*, which was an *Economist* 'Book of the Year' and was shortlisted for the *Financial Times*/Goldman Sachs Business Book of the Year Award, 2008. He lives in the United States.